English Poetry Since 1940

Longman Literature in English Series

**General Editors: David Carroll and Michael Wheeler
Lancaster University**

For a complete list of titles see pages xii and xiii

English Poetry
Since 1940

Neil Corcoran

Longman

London and New York

Longman Group UK Limited,
Longman House, Burnt Mill,
Harlow, Essex CM20 2JE, England
and Associated Companies throughout the world.

Published in the United States of America
by Longman Publishing, New York

First published 1993

British Library Cataloguing-in-Publication Data
A catalogue record for this book is
available from the British Library

ISBN 0 582 00323 7 CSD
ISBN 0 582 00322 9 PPR

Library of Congress Cataloging-in-Publication Data
Corcoran, Neil.
  English poetry since 1940 / Neil Corcoran.
  p.   cm – (Longman literature in English series)
  Includes bibliographical references and index.
  ISBN 0-582-00323-7 (CSD). – ISBN 0-582-00322-9 (PPR)
  1. English poetry – 20th century – History and criticism.
I. Title. II. Series.
PR601.C58 1993
821'.91409–dc20   92-28298
                                                        CIP

Set by 7L in 9½/11pt Bembo
Produced by Longman Singapore Publishers (Pte) Ltd
Printed in Singapore

Contents

Acknowledgements

We are grateful to the following for permission to reproduce poems:

Carcanet Press Ltd for 'The Priory of St Saviour, Glendalough' by Donald Davie from *Collected Poems 1950–1970* & 'Snail on the Doorstep' by Christopher Middleton from *Selected Writings*; Faber and Faber Ltd for 'Glasgow Schoolboys, Running Backwards' from *Barbarians* by Douglas Dunn, 'Young Women in Rollers' from *Terry Street* by Douglas Dunn, 'Newscast' from *Fifty Poems* by Ian Hamilton, 'Dockery and Son' & 'The Importance of Elsewhere' from *The Whitsun Weddings* by Philip Larkin & 'The Wiper' from *The Collected Poems of Louis McNeice* by Louis McNeice; N. Graham for 'Listen. Put on Morning' by W.S. Graham from *Collected Poems 1942–1977* (Faber and Faber Ltd, 1979), © The Estate of W.S. Graham; the author, Pamela Holmes for 'War Baby', copyright Pamela Holmes; the author, Michael Longley for 'The Linen Workers' from *Poems 1963–1983* (The Gallery Press, 1985); James MacGibbon & New Directions Publishing Corporation for an extract from 'Scorpion' by Stevie Smith from *The Collected Poems of Stevie Smith* (Penguin 20th Century Classics, 1985); Macmillan London Ltd for 'The Combat' by R.S. Thomas from *Later Poems* (1983); Martin Secker and Warburg Ltd, part of Reed International Books, for 'Great Britain' from *Ukele Music* by Peter Reading (1985); the author's agent for 'Open Secrets' & 'Princess Elizabeth' from *Dangerous Play: Poems 1974–1984* by Andrew Motion (Penguin Books Ltd, 1985); Oxford University Press for extracts from 'Canoe' & 'How to Kill' by Keith Douglas from *The Complete Poems* edited by Desmond Graham (1978), 'It is Writing' by Roy Fisher from *Poems 1955–1987* (1988), an extract from 'Courtyards in Delft' from *The Hunt by Night* by Derek Mahon (1982), an extract from 'A Disused Shed in Co. Wicklow' by Derek Mahon from *Poems 1962–1978* (1979), extracts from 'Where the Animals Go' & 'From Men of Letters' by Anne Stevenson from *Selected Poems* (1989), extracts from 'Against Extremity' & 'Oppositions' by Charles Tomlinson from *Collected Poems* (1985) & 'The White Hair' by Hugo Williams from *Selected Poems* (1989); Oxford University Press, New York, for 'Of Commerce and

Society' by Geoffrey Hill from *Collected Poems* (1985); Penguin Books Ltd & Oxford University Press, New York, for an extract from 'Two Formal Elegies' by Geoffrey Hill from *Collected Poems* (1985), copyright © Geoffrey Hill, 1959 & 'Hymn XVII "Offa's Journey to Rome"' from 'Mercian Hymns' by Geoffrey Hill from *Collected Poems* (1985), copyright © Geoffrey Hill, 1971; the author, J.H. Prynne for an extract from 'The Holy City' & an extract from 'Moon Poem' from *The White Stones* by J.H. Prynne (1969), as reprinted in *Poems* (Agneau 2, an imprint of Allardyce, Barnett, Publishers, 1982), © J.H. Prynne 1969, 1982; Random Century Group Ltd for 'Houses By Day' by Carol Rumens from *Selected Poems* (Chatto and Windus Ltd, 1987); the author, Denise Riley for 'The Savage' & 'The Cloud Rose'; the author's agent for 'A Refusal to Mourn' & 'In my Craft or Sullen Art' by Dylan Thomas from *The Poems* (J. Dent and Sons Ltd); Gwydion Thomas for 'A Peasant' by R.S. Thomas from *Selected Poems* (Grafton Books, 1973).

We have been unable to trace the copyright holder of 'Smoke' by Medbh McGuckian from *Single Ladies* (Interim Publishing Co Ltd, Canada) and would appreciate any information that would enable us to do so.

Editors' Preface

The multi-volume Longman Literature in English Series provides students of literature with a critical introduction to the major genres in their historical and cultural context. Each volume gives a coherent account of a clearly defined area, and the series, when complete, will offer a practical and comprehensive guide to literature written in English from Anglo-Saxon times to the present. The aim of the series as a whole is to show that the most valuable and stimulating approach to the study of literature is that based upon an awareness of the relations between literary forms and their historical contexts. Thus the areas covered by most of the separate volumes are defined by period and genre. Each volume offers new and informed ways of reading literary works, and provides guidance for further reading in an extensive reference section.

In recent years, the nature of English studies has been questioned in a number of increasingly radical ways. The very terms employed to define a series of this kind – period, genre, history, context, canon – have become the focus of extensive critical debate, which has necessarily influenced in varying degrees the successive volumes published since 1985. But however fierce the debate, it rages around the traditional terms and concepts.

As well as studies on all periods of English and American literature, the series includes books on criticism and literary theory, and on the intellectual and cultural context. A comprehensive series of this kind must of course include other literatures written in English, and therefore a group of volumes deals with Irish and Scottish literature, and the literatures of India, Africa, the Caribbean, Australia and Canada. The forty-seven volumes of the series cover the following areas: Pre-Renaissance English Literature, English Poetry, English Drama, English Fiction, English Prose, Criticism and Literary Theory, Intellectual and Cultural Context, American Literature, Other Literatures in English.

David Carroll
Michael Wheeler

Longman Literature in English Series

General Editors: David Carroll and Michael Wheeler
Lancaster University

Pre-Renaissance English Literature

★ English Literature before Chaucer *Michael Swanton*
English Literature in the Age of Chaucer
★ English Medieval Romance *W. R. J. Barron*

English Poetry

★ English Poetry of the Sixteenth Century *Gary Waller*
★ English Poetry of the Seventeenth Century *George Parfitt (Second Edition)*
English Poetry of the Eighteenth Century, 1700–1789
★ English Poetry of the Romantic Period, 1789–1830 *J. R. Watson (Second Edition)*
★ English Poetry of the Victorian Period, 1830–1890 *Bernard Richards*
English Poetry of the Early Modern Period, 1890–1940
★ English Poetry since 1940 *Neil Corcoran*

English Drama

English Drama before Shakespeare
★ English Drama: Shakespeare to the Restoration, 1590–1660 *Alexander Leggatt*
★ English Drama: Restoration and Eighteenth Century, 1660–1789 *Richard W. Bevis*
English Drama: Romantic and Victorian, 1789–1890
English Drama of the Early Modern Period, 1890–1940
English Drama since 1940

English Fiction

★ English Fiction of the Eighteenth Century, 1700–1789 *Clive T. Probyn*
★ English Fiction of the Romantic Period, 1789–1830 *Gary Kelly*
★ English Fiction of the Victorian Period, 1830–1890 *Michael Wheeler*
★ English Fiction of the Early Modern Period, 1890–1940 *Douglas Hewitt*
English Fiction since 1940

English Prose

★ English Prose of the Seventeenth Century, 1590–1700 *Roger Pooley*
  English Prose of the Eighteenth Century
  English Prose of the Nineteenth Century

Criticism and Literary Theory

Criticism and Literary Theory from Sidney to Johnson
Criticism and Literary Theory from Wordsworth to Arnold
Criticism and Literary Theory from 1890 to the Present

The Intellectual and Cultural Context

  The Sixteenth Century
★ The Seventeenth Century, 1603–1700 *Graham Parry*
★ The Eighteenth Century, 1700–1789 *James Sambrook*
  The Romantic Period, 1789–1830
  The Victorian Period, 1830–1890
  The Twentieth Century: 1890 to the Present

American Literature

  American Literature before 1880
★ American Poetry of the Twentieth Century *Richard Gray*
★ American Drama of the Twentieth Century *Gerald M. Berkowitz*
★ American Fiction 1865–1940 *Brian Lee*
★ American Fiction since 1940 *Tony Hilfer*
★ Twentieth-Century America *Douglas Tallack*

Other Literatures

  Irish Literature since 1800
  Scottish Literature since 1700
  Australian Literature
★ Indian Literature in English *William Walsh*
  African Literature in English: East and West
  Southern African Literature in English
  Caribbean Literature in English
★ Canadian Literature in English *W. J. Keith*

★ *Already published*

Author's Preface

'Poetry is the poem, or a part of it; nothing else, and nowhere else,' says Geoffrey Grigson in his 'poet's notebook', *The Private Art*;[1] and this chastening formalism has its place in what follows in this book, where I attempt to discuss a large number of modern and contemporary poems in the belief that, formally constructed as poems, they are not to be mistaken for any other kind of discourse. Yet, attempting to plot these numerous poems into a narrative, what follows does consider 'poetry' as more than 'the poem'. Poetry has an apprehensible and describable public history, making its way in a world of publishers, reviewers, little magazines and journals, anthologies, book societies, public funding, and examination syllabuses. Tracing a history of poetry in this period, I attempt, in my introductory sections to each part of the book, the historicist task of recovering the context of its primary reception, with something of the ambition recommended by one of the most profound contemporary theorists of literary history, Hans Robert Jauss, when he speaks of the necessity of establishing the 'horizon of expectation' which forms the boundary of all new literary work.[2]

It seemed most fruitful to do this on a decade-by-decade basis (until the final section, where the decade of the 1980s was still in train as I wrote), since this kind of division is manifestly not only the creation of subsequent criticism but, since at least the 1890s, a presumption among creators too, who characteristically perceive themselves as belonging to generational decades. Despite the resistance of some contemporary literary theory to the search for origins, it still seems to me that one of the crucial ways of understanding bodies of work by individual poets is by recognising the circumstances and impulses of their beginnings. Naming points of origin, however, is only one function of the individual parts of the book: the diachronic historicism of the introductory sections is complemented by a synchronic consideration of individual careers and groupings of poets in what follows in each section. The aim is to provide both a situating of poets in the originating moment of their work and a general overview of the course of their progression or development.

I have also, therefore, attempted to chart what might be called a 'horizon of recognition', by referring frequently to what poets of the period have said about one another and by emphasising the degree to which poems are intertextually interdependent. If art derives from art, however, it does so in often circuitous and oblique forms; and I hope that in what follows I maintain an awareness of the ways in which an anxiety of influence may produce misreadings or misrecognitions, and of the moves and strategies of a poet's criticism which make it frequently, and illuminatingly, an element of self-construction and self-recognition. You don't have to be a fully paid-up member of the Harold Bloom Promotions Board theory of poetry, with its radically anti-historicist bias, to believe nevertheless that the history of poetry must be in part a history of poets reading, responding to and, it may well be, rewriting one another in an endless process of admiration, modification, appropriation and contestation.

These contexts of reception and recognition are, then, major strands of the narrative into which I am plotting my texts; but there is also, of course, the narrative of public history itself, that narrative of official date and event. Much modern historiography has manifested a sceptical awareness of the way fact is inseparable from interpretation;[3] and anyone who wishes to talk about the way poetry contains history should be at least as anxiously sceptical about both of those categories. In what follows I elaborate some public and large interconnections (such as Eliot's wartime patriotism in 'Little Gidding', Heaney's responses to Northern Ireland after 1968, and the indictment of Thatcherism encoded or explicitated in some of the 'new narrative' poetry of the 1980s) and propose some more private or concealed ones (in Stevie Smith's 'The Face', for instance, in Dylan Thomas's 'A Refusal to Mourn', and in what I define as Philip Larkin's 'post-imperial pastorals'), aware that, as Pierre Macherey has put it, texts often say what they do not say.[4] Good poems are always both symptomatic and exemplary: if they enable us to test the conditions of the historical influences or events which produced them, they also offer paradigms of how the inchoate in a culture may be made to cohere, ratifyingly, in language and form. Bound by their historical moment, they are also our access to their moment.

The 'moment' covered by the whole period of this book is one in which the idea of an 'English' poetry is itself the matter of profound scrutiny and debate. At various points in the book I examine persistent ideas of 'Englishness' in a period in which Britain lost its empire and most of its colonies, and I also focus on different perceptions of the English language among native English writers. But this history of 'English' poetry since 1940 also concerns itself with writing which is not nationally English: with the Anglo-Welsh David Jones, Dylan Thomas and R.S. Thomas; with the Scots Edwin Muir and W.S. Graham (I exclude treatment of Scottish writers who spent their writing lives mainly in Scotland, simply on the pragmatic grounds that they will be

part of a separate book in this series); with the contemporary poets of
Northern Ireland, who will undoubtedly also figure in the Irish volume
in the series but whose presence is vital to a history of 'English' poetry
in the period; and (though admittedly very skimpily) with the work of
Westindian-British writers.

In much of this writing the focus is, it might be said, on ideas of
'not-being-English' while using the English language, with all of the
post-colonial antagonism and stress which that situation supplies for a
number of these writers. 'English' poetry in this book therefore means
poetry written in English in these islands. Jauss tells us that the aim of
the literary histories of the nineteenth century was 'to represent in the
history of literary works the idea of national individuality on its way to
itself'. [5] Much of the poetry in English covered by this book represents a
questioning of or search for different national identities within the
English language, or a coming to terms among English writers
themselves with a national individuality newly and differently defining
itself in relation to a vastly altering historical circumstance and political
status. The history contained in this book is one not of 'individuality'
but diversity, not of singularity but plurality. 'For literary purposes,'
Marilyn Butler has recently reminded us, 'the British Isles have always
been what the Australian poet Les Murray recently termed them in the
present day, "the Anglo-Celtic archipelago". As a social institution,
literature models an intricate, diverse, stressful community, not a bland
monolith'. [6]

Having reached this point, these prefatory remarks may as well
conclude with a register of incapacity. However much I insist on the
diversity and plurality of my own narrative here, it is *my* narrative: the
narrative, that is to say, of a white, middle-class, male academic. There
are elements within this narrative which it seems appropriate to me to
gesture towards, but which it would be presumptuous of me to attempt
to recount in any detail. One of them is the story of Westindian-British
poetry, to which I nod my recognition in Part Five, assuming that this
important but still relatively new tale is as yet better told elsewhere.
Another, it may seem to some readers, is the story of women's poetry in
the period. I deal, in the 'Since 1970' section, with some of the impacts
of post-1960s feminism; and, apart from the work of Stevie Smith which
I discuss earlier (and some women's war poetry), this seems to me the
finest women's writing of the time. Future feminist accounts, however,
will undoubtedly offer different views of some other still relatively
invisible women's writing between 1940 and 1970. If this work has
remained relatively invisible (or inaudible) to me, then that is of course a
measure of the way this historian and literary critic is constrained by his
own horizons of expectation and recognition. Undoubtedly, he will be
judged accordingly; but not, I hope, for any failure to realise that there
is more than one tale to tell.

For help of various kinds I am grateful to Lawrence Aspden of Sheffield University Library; Peter Banks; John Haffenden; Colin Raw; Martha Smart of the Poetry Book Society; Cornelia Turpin; several generations of students on the Sheffield University MA in 'Poetry in Our Time', with whom I have discussed many of the matters raised here, to my own enjoyment and profit; and the Research Fund of Sheffield University for a number of useful grants.

Neil Corcoran
Sheffield, January 1992

Notes

1. Geoffrey Grigson, *The Private Art: A Poetry Notebook* (London: Allison and Busby, 1982), p. 1.

2. See Hans Robert Jauss, *Toward an Aesthetic of Reception* (Brighton: The Harvester Press, 1982).

3. See, in particular, Hayden White, *Metahistory: The Historical Imagination in Nineteenth Century Europe* (Baltimore: Johns Hopkins University Press, 1973).

4. See Pierre Macherey, *A Theory of Literary Production* (London: Routledge and Kegan Paul, 1978).

5. *Toward an Aesthetic of Reception*, p. 3.

6. Marilyn Butler, 'Repossessing the Past: The Case for an Open Literary History', in Marjorie Levinson *et al.* (eds), *Rethinking Historicism: Critical Readings in Romantic History* (Oxford: Basil Blackwell, 1989), p. 69.

For David and Thomas, with love

Part One
(Dis)continuities and (Dis)placements After Modernism

Introduction

The history of poetry since 1940 is in large part the history of reactions to the high Modernist moment of writing in English from the turn of the century up to the end of the 1930s. At various points in this study I describe some of the ways in which the assumptions of Modernism maintain a persistence in later poetry; some of the reactions against it; some of the varying subsequent accommodations made with it; and some of the results of the recognition that it has, now, a definite literary and cultural past whose genealogy and heritage can be, at least approximately, classified and clarified. I also suggest that the term 'postmodern' may be invested with real content and taxonomic usefulness, and propose that the neglected term 'neo-Modern' be newly applied. In this preliminary section I want to consider the later work of those poets who continued to publish well into the period and whose work influentially focuses some crucial points in this debate. I omit any account of two such poets: Robert Graves, whose large lyric output persisted deep into the period and whose prose work *The White Goddess* (1947) has been, as I suggest elsewhere, variously influential, but the continuities of whose lengthy career are such as not to demand any separate treatment of his later work in a history of this kind; and of William Empson who, although influential on poetry of the English 1950s in some of the ways I describe in Part Three, ceased to publish poetry after his volume *The Gathering Storm* in 1940.

Chapter 1
Eliot or Auden

T.S. Eliot, addressing an audience in his home town of St Louis, Missouri on the subject of 'American Literature and the American Language' in 1953, made a wry comparison of himself and W.H. Auden. 'I do not know,' he said, 'whether Auden is to be considered as an English or as an American poet: his career has been useful to me with an answer to the same question when asked about myself for I can say: "whichever Auden is, I suppose I must be the other"'.[1] The point of comparison here is that of national identity: Eliot, born an American, had taken British citizenship in 1927, the year in which he was baptised into the Church of England, and was to progress to an Order of Merit and a grave in Westminster Abbey; Auden, Yorkshire public schoolboy and Oxford graduate, had notoriously left England for America in 1939, a move coinciding with such an alteration in the nature of his poetry that numerous critics think reflexly of two virtually opposed phases of the career, and his earlier work has been posthumously edited as *The English Auden*.

If Eliot and Auden are 'other' in their later national identities and affiliations, they are opposed in much else too. By 1953, when he made these remarks, Eliot had already long since assumed his late poetic near-silence, interrupted only by those poetic dramas which gave him a strangely metamorphosed later career in London's West End. Auden, on the other hand, maintained an extremely fertile later career, producing a vast number of poems of great formal and metrical variety. Both Eliot's later silence (which is in some ways programmed by or inscribed in his final poem *Four Quartets*) and Auden's later volubility may also be regarded as opposed modes of withdrawal from an earlier commitment to some of the principles, presumptions and structures of Modernism. In the *Quartets* Eliot brings Modernist free verse and Mallarméan symbolism to their ultimate pitch in English writing, even in the act of chastising their inadequacy; Auden in his later work wilfully insists on a discursive model of pre-Modernist, even Augustan formal and technical civility, accompanied by a startlingly mechanistic theory of poetry as 'contraption' (only in the bath is he tempted to 'retreat from rhyme and reason into some mallarmesque / syllabic fog', he tells us in the sequence 'Thanksgiving for a Habitat'). Where Eliot cites and attempts the Mallarméan effort to 'purify the dialect of the tribe', Auden revels in the impurities of lexical variety, arcana and neologism, and reverses all symbolist principle by revising himself in public, attempting to make his earlier work proteanly coincident with his later beliefs, regarding poetry as an element of honest behaviour. In their withdrawals from Modernism, Eliot develops a poetic of lack, Auden one of plenitude; Eliot is a metaphysician, Auden a moralist. In these antithetical reactions, Eliot and Auden, figures of large and unpredictable influence, provide opposed models for other poets of the period; and their opposition may in some ways be read as a tension within individual poets and within the larger history of the period itself.

Eliot's *Four Quartets* is a poem in which the symbolism of his earlier work is disciplined and placed by alternative and oppositional discourses. Prominent among these is an altogether less private and hermetic mode desired as appropriate to a poet addressing a nation in a time of war. Apart from the earliest poem in the sequence, 'Burnt Norton' (1935), the *Quartets* were composed and published during the early years of the war, and their local imagery, metaphor and allusion frequently concern the circumstances of the time. Beyond this, however, the whole poem holds up the idea of an England worth defending. It celebrates specific places whose near-anonymity is newly named with resonant familial, personal or historical association; it offers a vision in 'Little Gidding' of the capital city enduring the German air-raids of 1940; it proposes an idea of a national identity and solidarity developed as an alternative to a faction-torn history of civil war. England in the *Quartets* is also the location of a lovingly evoked rural antiquity whose cultural persistences are incarnate in the liturgy and architecture of the Anglican Church. The patriotic figuring of this England has all the hallmarks of some of the quasi-propagandist work of the time, such as the Powell and Pressburger film *A Canterbury Tale* (1944) for instance, which includes imagery of urban devastation and rural and agricultural continuity, and climaxes in one of the greatest shrines of English Anglicanism, Canterbury Cathedral (the location of the first performances of Eliot's play *Murder in the Cathedral*, 1935, leftover fragments of which initiated 'Burnt Norton'). *Four Quartets* both is part of and helped establish and define the Christian literary revival of the war and post-war period (in the work of Dorothy Sayers, Charles Williams and C.S. Lewis, among others).

This quasi-propagandist inspiration in the poem was clearly visible to its earliest critic, Eliot's friend John Hayward, when he said, prior to the publication of 'Little Gidding', that it is 'the kind of work that consolidates one's faith in the continuity of thought and sensibility when heaven is falling and earth's foundations fail'.[2] It is, therefore, virtually the opposite of what *The Waste Land* had been widely taken to be: evidence for the 'collapse of a civilisation'; and the *Quartets* may be read as Eliot's construction of a valuable continuity as an adequate response to the 'humiliation' he felt in September 1938 (the time of Munich), according to an uncharacteristically personal passage from his book *The Idea of a Christian Society* (1939). This humiliation, he says there, 'seemed to demand an act of personal contrition, of humility, repentance and amendment':

> We could not match conviction with conviction, we had no ideas
> with which we could either meet or oppose the ideas opposed to
> us. Was our society, which had always been so assured of its
> superiority and rectitude, so confident of its unexamined
> premisses, assembled around anything more permanent than a
> congeries of banks, insurance companies and industries, and had it
> any beliefs more essential than a belief in compound interest and
> the maintenance of dividends?[3]

The note of personal penitence combined with public responsibility is very much the dual note sounded by *Four Quartets* itself: the 'idea of a Christian society' is to be founded in the individual soul as well as in the public realm, and the 'idea' in relation to both is, for Eliot, expressed by the finest, and most ascetic, traditions of the Anglican Church, which are to be discovered above all in the writings of seventeenth-century divines: which is why, in 'Little Gidding', 'while the light fails / On a winter's afternoon, in a secluded chapel / History is now and England'.

One of the major aims and ends of the poem is therefore a religious or metaphysical idea of the English *patria* formulated in time of war by this American poet who had, in 1928, declared his 'general point of view . . . classicist in literature, royalist in politics, and anglo-catholic in religion'.[4] The poem's evocations of England, meditating the history of a sensibility out of the associations, affiliations and affections of specific English places, are made all the sharper by the fact that this American-born poet is consciously seeking a new identity, and declaring an older ancestry, as an English Anglican and a British citizen; the one quartet with a partly American setting, and an American placename title, 'The Dry Salvages', places this intention in some relief. The megalopolitan and European-cosmopolitan genesis of high Modernism could hardly have undergone a stranger metamorphosis: the deracination of a waste land is supplanted by the chthonic rootedness that is now and England, beginning and end, 'nourishing the corn'. The poem's patriotism is therefore the enemy of Eliot's early symbolist manner: it insists on acknowledgements and recognitions, on decorums of public tact and accountability, which the *symboliste* hermeticisms, fragmentations and obliquities of *The Waste Land*, and of *The Hollow Men* and *Ash-Wednesday*, were, it might be thought, almost designed to avoid. The symbolist and the discursive therefore jostle each other in the poem in an anxious and self-chastising or self-corrective mobility. The characteristic movement of the *Quartets* is a wavering oscillation between modes; of *The Waste Land* it is the absolute authoritative fiat of judgemental Modernist assurance: 'Time present and time past / Are both *perhaps* present in time future', but 'April *is* the cruelest month'. *Four Quartets* becomes thereby a poem in which the high Modernist moment of writing in English apologises for and reduces itself: 'That was a way of putting it, not very satisfactory: / A periphrastic study in a worn-out poetical fashion'; 'You say I am repeating / Something I have said before. I shall say it again. / Shall I say it again?'; and, in 'East Coker', with an allusion to his own earlier work of a kind not untypical of the *Quartets*, in this case the opening of 'Gerontion':

> So here I am, in the middle way, having had twenty years –
> Twenty years largely wasted, the years of *l'entre deux guerres* –
> Trying to learn to use words, and every attempt
> Is a wholly new start, and a different kind of failure
> Because one has only learnt to get the better of words
> For the thing one no longer has to say, or the way in which
> One is no longer disposed to say it.

The sharp regretfulness of that is slightly undermined by its oscillation between 'I' and 'one' as personal pronouns, between an apparently genuinely confessional Eliot and an Eliot rather primly observing some of the dictates of his essay 'Tradition and the Individual Talent'. The self-corrective modes and styles of the *Quartets* sometimes have this unsettling tendency to lurch and lapse between tones, as Eliot reaches for a form that will both contain his own distresses and establish relationship with a realm of public discourse. When the impersonal personal pronoun 'one' starts repeating itself in these lines Eliot is not far from the lecturer's or preacher's tone; and the portentous or pontifical is never altogether out of earshot in the final three *Quartets*. The tone of 'The Dry Salvages' is so odd indeed that it has prompted a notorious essay from Donald Davie (following a hint from Hugh Kenner) suggesting that the entire quartet is a parody;[5] and it is the element guyed by Henry Reed in his well-known 'Chard Whitlow'. At the very least, Eliot's withdrawal from Modernist obliquity and 'invisibility' leads to an uneasy alternation between the Mallarméan-symbolist and the Arnoldian-discursive in the *Quartets*. The occasional pomposity to which this gives rise makes the poem, for many readers, less completely realised and satisfying than Eliot's earlier work.

Four Quartets is, nevertheless, alert to its own deficiencies, inscribing them as elements of the constantly revised 'attempts' of writing ('For us there is only the trying') and saving itself from dogmatic assertiveness by the quality of its own painful misgiving. It is, in the end, that strangest of all poetic kinds, the poem which seeks to replace aesthetic delight with ascetic purgation; and it is peculiarly appropriate that it should have ended Eliot's poetic career twenty years before his actual death. In Eliot, the fate of the modern in its symbolist mode is to be subsumed by a contrite Christian apologetics. The poem's numerous paradoxes hinge on this central one: that this poetry is a poetry which insists that 'the poetry does not matter'. In its self-cancelling audacity it manifests, it may be, an exhaustion with style which is itself a new but, in the Eliot *oeuvre*, a terminal style; and its truest note is that of a melancholy serenity which bids farewell to its symbolist origins and sources, to that poetic of luminous intensity, pleading a recourse to other personal, familial, national and religious pieties and fidelities:

> Not the intense moment
> Isolated, with no before and after,
> But a lifetime burning in every moment
> And not the lifetime of one man only
> But of old stones that cannot be deciphered.

Along with the various ascetic renunciations of his last poem, Eliot dramatises, in what is frequently considered its finest episode, an acknowledgement of the natural term of any poetic and the insufficiency of all styles. In the passage from 'Little Gidding' on the 'familiar compound ghost' the ghost is, along with other subliminal figures, partly Mallarmé and partly Yeats. In the almost explicitly wartime setting (London in the early morning after an air-raid) the poetic ghost offers counsel in the necessary surrender of one's own work to an unimaginably different future:

> And he: 'I am not eager to rehearse
>   My thought and theory which you have forgotten.
>   These things have served their purpose: let them be.
> So with your own, and pray they be forgiven
>   By others, as I pray you to forgive
>   Both bad and good. Last season's fruit is eaten
> And the fullfed beast shall kick the empty pail.
>   For last year's words belong to last year's language
>   And next year's words await another voice.

The note of summation and valediction struck throughout the *Quartets* is at its most insistent, chastened and vulnerable here, where Eliot ventriloquises, on behalf of a composite figure of the symbolist poet, an instruction in the end of that poetic, in the necessity of being resigned to the fact that all thought and theory outlives its time. In the essay from *To Criticize the Critic* which I cited above it is clear that Eliot himself regarded Auden as one of the most significant bearers of 'next year's words'; and, if Eliot is witnessed in the *Quartets*, and in this very passage, subsuming the act of poetry in the act of prayer, much discussion of Auden's later work has also focused on an ideological conversion: from early Communist sympathies to Christianity.

Unlike Eliot's, Auden's Christianity is resolutely unmystical, discovering and articulating itself during the course of inquiries into forms of human behaviour in specific historical and socio-political circumstance. It is, it might be said, not a mystical but virtually a material, certainly an incarnational Christianity; and it aspires not to an Eliotic silence but to an all-inclusive, argumentative volubility. The ideological move in the later Auden from his Communist-affiliated poetry of the 1930s to an American Christianity, and his accompanying tonal and technical moves from a glamorously secretive and coded poetry of the minatory and apocalyptic – a hermetic, partly Eliot-derived Modernism – to a discursively neo-Augustan poetry of alternatingly strenuous, wry, jocular, even cosy moral debate has frequently been read as a loss (some would say a fatal one) of poetic power and authority. Randall Jarrell, Auden's finest early critic, in one of his finest essays, laments the 'degeneration into abstraction', as does Philip Larkin in his well-known 'What's Become of Wystan?'; and Seamus Heaney regrets the passing of 'the element of the uncanny' from the later work.[6] There are alternatives to these dualistic views of the Auden career, notably Stan Smith's deconstruction of the traditional Auden narrative in favour of an account of 'the doubleness of the text' which offers us 'a babble of discordant jargons, contending for dominance, or slinking away in defeat from contestation'.[7]

If Smith's at times brilliant reading of Auden nevertheless makes the poet sound suspiciously more like the postmodern John Ashbery (who does owe a great deal to Auden), it is in one sense continuous with the traditional readings: it places primacy on Auden's departure for America in 1939. Smith's sense of the work's discordant babble derives explicitly from his view of Auden as an émigré; Larkin's version of the Auden falling-off is that in America he lost contact with a sustaining English vernacular, along with his primary subject matter and emotion, Europe and the fear of war. Whatever the reasons for Auden's departure, and whether it is found virtually treacherous, merely graceless, or – as Smith finds it – perfectly comprehensible and justifiable, since 'There was nothing, really, to abandon',[8] the move to America rendered Auden incapable of sustaining anything like a nationally hortatory voice. It is one of the ironies of the literary history of the period that it is the Eliot of the *Quartets* who develops that rhetorical mode, a tone at one stroke denied to the émigré Auden, and develops it in the service of an intense and gloomy conservatism diametrically opposed to the buoyant radicalism of the young Auden's exhortations in a poem such as 'Spain'. In Eliot the idea of the English *patria* has its rightist, nationalistic bias and, in any Marxian analysis, its mystificatory element, transmuting class and regional faction into a utopian dream of solidarity and common purpose: if the parties of the English Civil War are 'united in the strife which divided them', then so, by implication, are the parties of the wartime coalition government. Auden's departure for America, on the other hand, is read by Smith as a further phase in his radicalism: 'For any decent radical in the thirties, England was not a *patria* to be proud of but a burden of betrayal, shame and perfidy presided over by that "Beethameer, Beethameer, bully of Britain" lampooned in *The Orators*, a composite newspaper proprietor made up of the Lords Beaverbrook and Rothermere and by a venal and hypocritical elite based in the Home Counties'.[9] The England Auden left was an England not of chthonic pieties but of capitalist collusions and collaborations, appeasing European Fascism.

Not living in England, however, Auden lacked further rights on both the diagnostic and the hortatory; and the later work is the result of an adjustment to, and an accommodation with, the fact that his first and astonishingly successful and influential poetic mode had become unusable. His early political Modernism, employing very English geographical and mental landscapes and chastising its audience into action, is replaced by a civil poetry of international citizenship, in which the living of a good life in a social *urbs* is prelude to, and a figure for, the redeemed life in the city of God. Significantly, just as Eliot makes Yeats the focus of his own poetic anxiety and valediction in the *Quartets*, Auden makes him the figure of his in 'In Memory of W.B. Yeats', written in 1939, a month after Yeats's death. The poem is famous for one crucial line, but less well remembered for the context in which it situates that line. It is worth restoring the context when thinking about the kind of effort that the later Auden represents:

> Now Ireland has her madness and her weather still,
> For poetry makes nothing happen: it survives
> In the valley of its saying where executives
> Would never want to tamper; it flows south
> From ranches of isolation and the busy griefs,
> Raw towns that we believe and die in; it survives,
> A way of happening, a mouth.

That 'poetry makes nothing happen' is often taken as Auden's apologia for his post-1930s ideological re-orientation, a refusal any longer to place faith in the validity of poetry as a call to political action, and a refusal indeed to place any ultimate faith in poetry at all: 'a verbal contraption', it is not 'quite that important', as he coat-trailingly puts it in his inaugural lecture as Oxford Professor of Poetry in 1956.[10] Yet this poem proposes no quietist refusal as its alternative; rather, it offers the conception of poetry as itself a mode of action: both river and mouth, it is a space in which an articulation adequate to event may occur, and it remains as definition and consolation. Furthermore, it is markedly contiguous with the quotidian social world of those 'raw towns' and their systems of affiliation and obligation, maintaining an expressive continuity with social discourses: the lush metaphoricity of 'the valley of its saying' chafes against the contemporary journalese of 'executives' who 'tamper'. When executives figure in Eliot's 'East Coker' they come solemnly robed as 'Industrial lords and petty contractors'; and they do not 'tamper', 'They all go into the dark'. Even as the objects of judicial sentence they maintain their symbolic poetic decorum; in Auden they are merely morally objectionable irritants.

Auden's later work, then, may lack the authoritative, august calm of Eliot and the authoritatively lacerating panache of his own earlier work, but it substitutes for them a more replete, if also more fumbling, variety and largesse. It offers the concept of the poet as a survivor among a detritus of manners and discourses: thumbing the technical manuals and the lexicons; exploiting the natural sciences for both their human analogues and their alienatingly corrective examples; synoptically attempting a moralising of the contemporary life; striving towards an archaeology of knowledge, from the deposits of prehistory to the scorned 'phallic triumph' of 'Moon Landing'. The moralising volubility is threaded through an increasing reliance on poetic sequences, forms or structures in which discursive conversation with a reader may be continued in alternations of relaxation and arrest: 'New Year Letter', 'The Sea and the Mirror', 'Bucolics', 'Horae Canonicae' and 'Thanksgiving for a Habitat'. In the poem 'The Cave of Making' from the latter, written in memory of Louis MacNeice, Auden offers an image for himself which is ironising yet purposefully self-defining too; and he does so in the act of defending a discursive, non-symbolist, implicitly anti-Modernist poetic:

> I should like to become, if possible,
>   a minor Atlantic Goethe,
> with his passion for weather and stones but without his silliness
>   re the Cross: at times a bore, but,
> while knowing Speech can at best, a shadow echoing
>   the silent light, bear witness
> to the Truth it is not, he wished it were, as the Francophile
>   gaggle of pure songsters
> are too vain to. We're not musicians: to stink of Poetry

is unbecoming, and never
to be dull shows lack of taste. Even a limerick
    ought to be something a man of
honor, awaiting death from cancer or a firing squad,
    could read without contempt: (at
that frontier I wouldn't dare speak to anyone
    in either a prophet's bellow
or a diplomat's whisper).

This may be read as a deliberated apologia for the later Auden
manner, called forth by an elegy for a friend in the art. The 'vanity' of
Francophile symbolism is that it disconnects poetry and truth; and for
the later Auden approximate quotidian truth serves that greater
(presumably religious) 'Truth' given its initial capital in this passage
Augustanly unafraid of capitalisation/personification. The approximations
of later Auden oppose the purity of symbolist utterance with the clutter
of the contingent, the transcendent Mallarméan Word with the
accumulation of many words and many forms. Turning against
presumptuous 'musical' chastity, they willingly risk and defend the
danger of an occasionally boring verbal incontinence. Yet the passage
insists nevertheless on the value of 'this unpopular art'. Even in its most
minor modes, this verbal contraption may provide consolation in the
face of death, where no other discourse will serve: the prophet and the
diplomat are as excluded here as is the 'executive' in the Yeats elegy.
The death-threat interestingly provokes a sudden evocation of early
Auden: the 'firing squad' has that slightly glamourising adventure-story
minatoriness of many of the Thirties poems – an impression
acknowledged, possibly, by that italicised late return to one of the central
early Auden tropes, the frontier. There are several such moments in the
later Auden where the earlier manner seems decipherable inside a more
fleshy exterior; and they are partly responsible, it may be, for the reader's
occasional feeling that the deftness of control in the later work is a
self-imposed brake on emotional or intellectual recklessness or excess.
Here, for instance, the idea of a man reading a limerick before going to
the firing squad has a potential farcicality which could easily spiral off in
the direction of the camp or the surreal.

If the reader may sometimes wish that the later Auden had allowed
himself more rein, 'The Cave of Making' is nevertheless a poem which
amply justifies the control, its serious elegiac address persisting through a
witty, even exuberant range of tones and dictions. Subverting the
generic bathos of elegy, in which the elegiser characteristically complains
for himself as well as or even instead of the elegised other, this elegy
openly confesses itself an 'egocentric monologue'; and in doing so it
sustains a civilised conversation with the reader while also testifying to
what another poem in 'Thanksgiving for a Habitat' calls 'the baffle of

being'. If, for many readers of the later Auden, the dangers of dullness and even sententiousness – Auden as supreme exemplar of the Higher Cosiness, on good terms with 'our First Dad' – are too little avoided during the course of his vastly prolific output, the risk itself is the begetter of some of his finest individual poems: of 'In Praise of Limestone', for instance, and 'The Shield of Achilles'. In the latter, in particular, written in 1952 out of post-war distress, Auden's abandonment of Modernist obliquity and hermeticism reaps one of its richest rewards. The poem's fiction has Thetis, the mother of the Greek hero Achilles, looking over the shoulder of the smith Hephaestos as he fashions her son's shield. Hoping to discover on the shield images of civility, grace and good order, the figures of a classical serene, she sees instead the waste brutalities and barbarism of modern warfare: its destroyed landscapes, its concentration camps, its refugees, its atrocities. The mother's 'dismay' as she reads the emblems fashioned for her 'man-slaying' son – soon himself to be slain – supplies a memorable figure for the sorts of brutalising and repressive political power which this poet's work opposes at its most profound level, as it aims for consolation, but self-misgivingly, all too anxiously aware of everything in 'being' that might deny us it:

> The mass and majesty of this world, all
>   That carries weight and weighs the same,
> Lay in the hands of others; they were small
>   And could not hope for help and no help came:
>   What their foes liked to do was done, their shame
> Was all the worst could wish; they lost their pride
> And died as men before their bodies died.

Such moments in the later Auden are predicated on the knowledge expressed in the preface to the long poem *The Age of Anxiety* (1947), that 'in wartime . . . everybody is reduced to the anxious status of a shady character or a displaced person'. In his finest later work there persists some element of anxiety and stress in Auden, some topographical, political, emotional or sexual displacement always threatening to fracture serenity.

The various recensions of the Auden-minatory have been deeply influential on the subsequent course of British poetry: in a line traceable most notably through Roy Fuller, Peter Porter, James Fenton and Tom Paulin we can follow its persistence. On these poets among numerous others, different kinds of Auden example have also been provocative and enabling: the technical variety; the capacious social inclusiveness; the view of poetry as a discourse that must make its way among other competing discourses, without any assumption of privileged or quasi-sacerdotal status. The anti-Modernism implicit in such examples has set one definite course for English poetry in the post-war period, and various heritages of that reaction will be discussed in the following chapters of this book. Yet the longing for the symbolist has also persisted, and occasionally as a definite indebtedness to the Eliot of the *Quartets*: notably in the Geoffrey Hill of *The Mystery of the Charity of Charles Péguy* (1983); in the Donald Davie of 'Three for Water Music' (1981) and in the Seamus Heaney of 'Station Island' (1984) which reads its encounters with the dead through Eliot's Dantean encounter in 'Little Gidding', as well as through the Dantean example itself. In the post-symbolist poetics of the post-war period the longing for the pure, uncluttered space of the symbolist modes of transcendence finds its opportunity, if also its humbling correction, permanently lodged in *Four Quartets*. The Eliot of the *Quartets* may also be thought to persist in English poetry in another way: the poem's dream of English Anglicanism, with its culmination in the church building of 'Little Gidding', further writes itself, and, it may be, demolishes itself, in a large number of subsequent English poems, from the bewildered inquisitions of Stevie Smith's 'Oh Christianity, Christianity' through the awkward agnostic reverence of Philip Larkin's 'Church Going' to the secular vision of the church-as-theatre, with its 'tall tale of the cross', in Christopher Reid's 'Magnum Opus'.

Notes

1. T.S. Eliot, *To Criticize the Critic* (London: Faber and Faber, 1965), p. 60.

2. Cited in Helen Gardner, *The Composition of 'Four Quartets'* (London: Faber and Faber, 1978), p. 22.

3. *The Idea of a Christian Society* (London: Faber and Faber, 1939), p. 64.

4. T.S. Eliot, *For Lancelot Andrewes: Essays on Style and Order* (London: Faber and Faber, 1928; 1970), p. 7.

5. See Donald Davie, 'T.S. Eliot: The End of an Era', in *The Poet in the Imaginary Museum: Essays of Two Decades*, ed. Barry Alpert (Manchester: Carcanet Press, 1977), and Hugh Kenner, *The Invisible Poet: T.S. Eliot* (London, 1960; Methuen, 1965).

6. See Randall Jarrell, 'Changes of Attitude and Rhetoric in Auden's Poetry', in *The Third Book of Criticism* (London: Faber and Faber, 1975); Philip Larkin, 'What Became of Wystan?', in *Required Writing* (London: Faber and Faber, 1983); Seamus Heaney, 'Sounding Auden', in *The Government of the Tongue* (London: Faber and Faber, 1988).

7. Stan Smith, *W.H. Auden* (Oxford: Basil Blackwell, 1985), pp. 7, 21.

8. ibid., p. 118.

9. ibid.

10. W.H. Auden, 'Making, Knowing and Judging', in *The Dyer's Hand and Other Essays* (London: Faber and Faber, 1963; 1975), p. 51.

Chapter 2
Varieties of Parable
Louis MacNeice and Edwin Muir

Although it has not been usual to consider the work of Louis MacNeice and Edwin Muir in tandem, it is nevertheless possible to claim that parallel and unpredictable developments in the later work of both supply us with further models of how some elements of Modernism were recognised, taken up and profitably developed in post-war British writing, though in forms and structures not much indebted to the explorations and experiments of the high Modernist moment. The late recognition of these developments, and the new affinities and alignments which they propose, have presented us recently with different and newly usable and sensitive readings of these always respected but not fully assimilated writers.

Louis MacNeice's work stood for a long time in the shadow of W.H. Auden's. As a member of 'Macspaunday', the group of Thirties poets which also included Spender, Auden and Day-Lewis, and co-author with Auden of *Letters from Iceland* (1937), MacNeice was almost always associated with Auden, and suffered in the association. The connection was made all the stronger, probably, since MacNeice's best-known poem, *Autumn Journal*, published in 1939, seemed conveniently to bring the Thirties to a close (and remains, in its journalistic exuberance and panache, and in its register of personal and public anxiety, the definitive literary evocation of the Munich mood). Closing the decade, it appeared also to close the finest phase of MacNeice's career. With the publication of some of his post-war volumes he did lapse too easily into verbosity, particularly in a number of lengthy sequences, including the unreadably garrulous *Autumn Sequel* about which Edna Longley, one of his best critics, has said, 'The fusion of *Autumn Journal* has become fission'.[1] By the time he died in 1963 his reputation had already entered a decline, and little assent was given to Auden's observation (in his introduction to a selection of MacNeice which he published in 1964) that 'his last three volumes contain . . . his finest work'.[2]

More recently, however, a major revaluation has been under way, inspired by those poets and critics from the North of Ireland publishing since the mid-1960s, who have recognised in MacNeice a mentor or precursor, a figure whose Anglo-Irish identity and affiliations – the crossed strain of his poetic consciousness – have proved an enabling cultural resource. Although MacNeice's Irishness has been the subject of acrimonious dispute, the embracing of him by this generation of Irish writers seems to make the case in the only way in which posterity will recognise it: the poet, after all, becomes his admirers (as Auden said in his elegy for Yeats, that Irish poet on whom MacNeice wrote an excellent critical book). Coming from a prominent Church of Ireland family; born in Belfast and brought up in his earliest years in the North of Ireland; conscious of and half-romanticising, half-mythologising an ancestral origin in the West of Ireland; educated in English prep and public schools and at Oxford; working for the BBC and recognisably part of a London-metropolitan English establishment; and weaving all of these autobiographical strands prominently into the texture of his poems: it is not hard to see how MacNeice might act as a major point of reference for a generation of Northern Irish writers preoccupied with matters of cultural identity. Michael Longley has edited an excellent selection of MacNeice. Paul Muldoon's *Faber Book of Contemporary Irish Poetry* features him prominently. Derek Mahon has written vividly of his attraction to him, and there are manifest affiliations between their respective poetries. Tom Paulin has defined the 'maritime' fluidity of MacNeice's imagination in a way that suggests an element of self-recognition: the elusive imagination is that of 'the displaced exile who is condemned to be a tourist in the land of his birth'.[3] Even Seamus Heaney, who has never written on MacNeice, alludes to him in the title of a poem in *The Haw Lantern* (1987), 'Parable Island': in his posthumously published critical book *Varieties of Parable* (1965) MacNeice refers to the 'parable islands' reached by the voyager Maelduin in an ancient Irish legend.[4]

This new context of debate brings into relief the extent of MacNeice's Irish subject matter, the range of his Irish interests and the sometimes baffled and hurt ambivalence of his responses to his native country. In the poetry published after the 1930s this relationship becomes a particularly fraught one, since Ireland's neutrality during the war seemed to MacNeice indefensibly self-interested and hypocritical. A number of poems written just before and during the war meditate on Ireland's meaning to him in the context of its indifference or even hostility to those English aspirations to which MacNeice had committed himself by returning to England from America in 1941 (a transatlantic journey which may be read as a symbolic as well as a literal opposite to that taken by Auden in 1939). In the poem actually called 'Neutrality', from *Springboard* (1944), his feelings about de Valera's Ireland are articulated with a bitter directness which recalls some of the most sharply political moments in his 1930s *oeuvre*. The poem gives a newly approbatory force to the word 'journalistic' as a critical term for MacNeice's work: he is a poet manifestly unafraid of making enemies. Provoked by the violent wartime death of a close friend, the poem makes its public political point by pleading individual human instances, addressing an Ireland which is as much an interiorised country of the heart as it is an exterior world of senate and people. The poem brings to a late fruition that worried, sceptical humanism which is, throughout, the note – sometimes baffled but here steeled into the confidence of satirical rebuke – of MacNeice's very private public address system:

> But then look eastward from your heart, there bulks
> A continent, close, dark, as archetypal sin,
> While to the west off your own shores the mackerel
> Are fat – on the flesh of your kin.

More typical of his Irish preoccupations at this time, however, are poems in which his childhood and youth are remembered in separation. 'The Closing Album', 'Carrick Revisited' and 'The Strand' are among MacNeice's finest poems, sharpening the poignancy of memory even further by a political as well as a geographical and temporal divorce. 'The Strand', for instance, written in 1945, evokes a visit by MacNeice to the West of Ireland. Walking by the sea, he becomes conscious of repeating one of the numerous visits there made by his now dead father, a figure who recurs often in MacNeice's work. The poem ends with an image of isolation and mutual mortality, father and son effaced by the processes of nature and time:

> And the mirror caught his shape which catches mine
> But then as now the floor-mop of the foam
> Blotted the bright reflections – and no sign
>
> Remains of face or feet when visitors have gone home.

Tom Paulin has noted that the word 'visitors' 'is filled with a sense of dispossession – it is the word used in the West of Ireland to describe tourists'.[5] This is well said, and it is good to have the connotations of the word explicated; but the poem also makes it clear how the MacNeiceian dispossession has its metaphysical as well as its topographical dimension. The dispossession here is the desolation of contemplating, in an elegy for your father, your own eventual absence from the world; being a visitor or tourist in Ireland is always, for MacNeice, image of and prelude to being a visitor or tourist in the world. Both the obsession with brilliant surfaces and the deep melancholia find their figure here.

MacNeice's responses to the war as a civilian in London, enduring the Blitz, themselves form the material of some excellent individual poems in the wartime volumes *Plant and Phantom* (1941) and *Springboard* (1944), in particular 'The Streets of Laredo', 'Brother Fire', and the *grand guignol* of one of his most anthologised poems, 'Prayer Before Birth'. That poem is ghosted by George Herbert's 'Sighs and Grones'; and Herbert is one of the writers eventually discussed in *Varieties of Parable*. One of the other matters highlighted by the new contexts for MacNeice's reputation, and especially by Edna Longley's criticism, is his own development later in his career of a 'parable poetry'; and this, probably his most original and arresting contribution to the poetry of the period, may well be regarded as a formal removal into another sphere or dimension, and an intensification there, of the memory-obsessed and death-oriented anxieties apparent in a poem like 'The Strand'.

Varieties of Parable is actually, as its title perhaps gives it permission to be, a rather brisk and not always very well-focused or adequately discriminating tour of writers (ranging from Spenser, Bunyan and Herbert to Beckett and Golding) in whom MacNeice discovers elements of parable, a kind in which he was permanently interested and to which he manifestly wished to add when, in 1948, he published his radio play *The Dark Tower* with the subtitle 'a radio parable play'. *Varieties of Parable* does supply one usable if capacious definition or formulation when it describes its literature as 'a kind of double-level writing, or . . . sleight-of-hand'.[6] This comprehends a variety of kinds more usually distinguished in literary criticism as, among others, ballad, folktale, allegory, fantasy and fable; and it also registers, with due obeisances to Freud, an interest in dream and in the literary representation of dream. Fragments of all of these varieties of parable constitute, in numerous later poems, the distinct MacNeicean parable. Taking his own lead, we should undoubtedly use the term more impressionistically than categorically in relation to his work; but it seems clear that it is his way of moving his later poetry into areas of the disoriented consciousness, anxious states of being in which identity itself is placed at risk, which may properly be considered a Modernist kind of dislocation.

The MacNeicean parable poem is short and often sinuously syntaxed, abandoning customary connectives in an accumulative forward movement; the effect is both taut and driven, with the sense of an anxiety or terror great enough to veer quite out of control unless held in check – just – by syntactical restraint. Some of these poems ('The Truisms', 'The Habits') are little moralising anecdotes of dread and genetic conditioning; they further advance that proto-existentialist morality developed throughout his *oeuvre* by MacNeice, a child of the rectory, in the shadow of an abandoned but (it appears) persistently attractive Christian metaphysic. In the most interesting of them, however, the fear which always supplies the underlying level of their 'double-level' writing, although it often has to do with a fear of failure, ageing and death, is never fully articulated or specified at the surface level of the poem. Indeed in some ('The Taxis', 'Charon' and 'After the Crash') the fear appears to be the grim nightmare that the consciousness will either not be able to die properly or, having died, will continue to exist in some fraught and panic-ridden posthumous state; and this fear is also – in poems written in the 1950s and early 1960s – associated with anxiety about a potential nuclear holocaust.

Cinematic perspectives, montages and dissolves have almost certainly been a telling influence on these poems. When, in 'Soap Suds', the man washing his hands is Proustianly reminded of a big house from his childhood, the present is made transparent to the past by moving the poem's syntax ('the walls of the bathroom open / To reveal a lawn where a great yellow ball rolls back through a hoop') as a camera might move on a set, and a film editor dissolve from one scene to another: the poem actually uses the word 'dissolves'. 'The Taxis' and 'Charon' have something of the quasi-surreal journey we find in early Ingmar Bergman (*Varieties of Parable* makes reference to him).[7] And 'The Wiper', reminiscent of some suspense-filled drive in Hitchcock, is a poem quite *sui generis*: one that manages an effect of excitement outside the realm of narrative, as though emotion usually dependent on chronology and sequence has been all compacted into image. The poem's final stanzas are one of the most chilling exercises in the MacNeicean minatory:

> For now we cannot remember
> Where we were when it was not
> Night, when it was not raining,
>   Before this car moved forward
> And the wiper backward and forward
> Lighting so little before us
> Of a road that, crouching forward,
>   We watch move always towards us,
>
> Which through the tiny segment
> Cleared and blurred by the wiper
> Is sucked in under the axle
>   To be spewed behind us and lost
> While we, dazzled by darkness,
> Haul the black future towards us
> Peeling the skin from our hands;
>   And yet we hold the road.

These stanzas may be thought to bring to its climax that imagery of journeying constant in these late poems, whose properties frequently include a nighmarishly metamorphosing transport system of cars, taxis, buses, boats. As an image of or emblem for persistence under duress, for the effortfulness and stress of merely keeping on, the poem's 'parable' image has its memorable force and logic. The lines also perhaps contain, in the phrase 'dazzled by darkness', a parable in miniature of MacNeice's career: the early brio and panache, the apparently effortless parade of detail and circumstance, all illuminated under the strong and steady gaze of his regard, darken in the later work into unease, uncertainty and melancholy. But they too persist in dazzling their poet with opportunity and invitation; the darkness which dazzles provides MacNeice with this late and unpredictable flowering. The final stanza of 'House on a Cliff' may be read as a self-image for this dream-haunted and history-haunted poet; but it may also focus the remarks I have been making here, since the 'house' of the poem's title may well be read as a metonym for Ireland, and what meets at the cross in this parable poem of 'cross purposes' may be a hybrid national identity and a faltering self-identity:

> Indoors ancestral curse-cum-blessing. Outdoors
> The empty bowl of heaven, the empty deep.
> Indoors a purposeful man who talks at cross
> Purposes, to himself, in a broken sleep.

MacNeice briefly considers Edwin Muir as a writer of parables in *Varieties of Parable*, but his approbation is muted: Muir, he says, was 'so consistent in his aims, which merge into a single aim, and his metaphysico-mystical writing is so unadulterated either by topical or documentary elements . . . that I find reading many of his poems on end is like walking through a gallery of abstract paintings'.[8] This is vulnerably prejudiced against abstraction, but it does suggestively evoke that element of the undifferentiated which the reader of Muir's *Collected Poems* may well feel. 'This is the Pattern, these the Archetypes', he writes in 'The Sufficient Place', and his is resolutely a poetry of the mythopoeic, breathing the rarified atmosphere of a Platonised sublime and a Jungian serene. This is all the more surprising since, as his excellent autobiography (called, neutrally, *An Autobiography*) makes plain, the biographical circumstances of his life would appear to have supplied him with more than sufficient 'topical' and 'documentary' elements to satisfy MacNeician requirements. He moved from an Orkney childhood through the Glasgow slums to a later life in pre- and post-war Germany, Austria and Czechoslovakia, becoming, *en route*, a translator of Kafka and Charles Eliot Norton Professor at Harvard University, despite suffering periodic nervous depression and collapse. Although some of these circumstances are intermittently articulated in the poems (the Scottish theme recurs, for instance), it is bizarre to see so much apparent 'raw material' in the autobiography remaining largely profitless to the poetry. An earlier version of the autobiography was published in 1940 as

The Story and the Fable; and too often in Muir's poetry the fable – the dream, the archetype, the symbol, the myth – proves unsustaining in the way MacNeice implies, and probably under the sway of an insufficiently absorbed Yeatsian example. Usually the imagery of dream and vision, much of it drawn from biblical and classical sources, fails to rise fully to the ramifying inclusiveness of Yeatsian poetic symbol and remains inertly lodged at the level of mere emblem and device, coldly frozen into a kind of heraldic stasis, too dignified and too displayed. Lacking friction and arrest, his poems can seem blandly portentous.

There is, however, a handful of post-war poems which makes MacNeice's criticism nugatory: that group of dramatic monologues which begins with 'Moses' in *The Voyage* (1946), continues through such poems as 'The Interrogation', 'The Good Town', 'Soliloquy' and 'The Absent' in *The Labyrinth* (1949) and culminates in 'The Killing', 'The Difficult Land' and 'The Horses' in *One Foot in Eden* (1956). They may be regarded as kinds of Modernist parable-poem by this translator of the century's greatest parable-maker, Franz Kafka. They articulate, in the oblique mode inherited from the rest of his work, but with an altogether new urgency, Muir's response to the devastated post-war landscape of Europe which he travelled across by car shortly after the war to take up a British Council appointment in Prague, where he witnessed the Communist coup in 1948.

The exceptionality of these parable poems may be gauged by comparing them with some of the more traditional kinds of dramatic monologue which also feature in Muir's later books. Developed from Tennyson rather than Browning, those are poems in which named heroic figures from history and myth articulate self-definitions in a way that makes them emblematic of some phase or aspect of contemporary consciousness. Odysseus, for instance, becomes a representative of communal post-war guilt when he says that 'all must bear a portion of the wrong / That is driven deep into our fathomless hearts'. It is probably not merely contemporary jadedness with such a moral that makes these lines appear a little obvious and banal: they seem to glance off their matter of scrutiny rather than to engage or confront it with any real urgency, and they have the almost laboured and pedantic solemnity of the pedagogue. The very form of the traditional monologue seems to render the emotion over-literary, to abstract it to a point where the particularity of post-war guilt becomes a too readily available moral wisdom, even a sententiousness. In the new monologues evolved in these post-war volumes, however, which take a hint, probably, from Eliot's 'Journey of the Magi' (an Eliotic cadence and syntax is also noticeable at times), this element is subdued or eradicated by the character of the speakers. They are not names ('Odysseus', 'Oedipus', 'Prometheus') but anonyms, and yet, in their isolation and moral stature, they retain something of the heroic capacity of the named figures. They tend to be observers or spectators rather than participants: in 'The Killing' the speaker has been a passer-by at Christ's crucifixion; in 'Soliloquy' (modelled on the medieval Welsh 'Boast of Taliessin', like a crucial section of David Jones's *In Parenthesis*), he has been a spectator at numerous, chronologically quite widely separate events. Their status as witnesses, combined with the poems' informing principles of historical irony, in which speakers are given prophetic gifts of foresight, creates their uncanny power. Their anonymity also tends to give them a representative authority; they come to speak on behalf of a people or a community.

In the finest of these poems this representativeness provides Muir with a means of bearing, in English poetry, the brunt of the physical and political desolation of Europe after the Second World War. It is a burden which immeasurably enlarges the whole scope and density of his later work. 'The Interrogation' is the poem most clearly spoken out of the contemporary desolation itself. Using, as many of these poems do, the representative first person plural, it picks out with a new vividness some of the characteristic signals of fraught individual experience under totalitarianism: the sense of utterly destabilising unpredictability, of the enormous significance of apparently insignificant decisions ('We could have crossed the road but hesitated, / And then came the patrol'); the 'Question on question', inquiry for inquiry's sake, of the interrogation itself; the sense of moral worlds inconceivably remote from one another in immediate physical contiguity ('And watched across the road beyond the hedge / The careless lovers in pairs go by, / Hand linked in hand, wandering another star, / So near we could shout to them'); and the persistence of lacerating and identity-destroying intrusion beyond all hitherto anticipated limits:

> We are on the very edge,
> Endurance almost done,
> And still the interrogation is going on.

Seamus Heaney observes of this poem that it 'anticipates by a couple of decades the note which would be heard [in the] influential Penguin Modern European Poets series in the late 1960s, a note as knowledgeable as it was powerless to survive with any sort of optimism in the light of what it knew': the persona of 'The Interrogation', compared to Eliot's wartime persona in 'Little Gidding', is 'more truly our representative, stunned and ineffective at the centre of a menacing pageant'.[9] In this reading Muir becomes the 'road not taken' by immediately post-war English poetry, but (implicitly) a road recovered, partly under the influence of European poetry in translation, from the later 1960s onwards and also (again, of course, implicitly) in some of Heaney's own work which, under another set of fraught political circumstances, itself employs parable modes and features more than one 'interrogation'. (There is, I think, a direct influence of Muir's 'The Horses' on Heaney's 'The Mud Vision' in *The Haw Lantern*; and he is interestingly anticipated in his assimilation of Muir by the older Ulster poet John Hewitt who, in 'The Colony', employs the Muir-like monologue-parable of a Roman centurion speaking on behalf of an Ulster unionist mentality.) It seems curious to me, however, that Heaney nevertheless regrets that, despite this poem, Muir 'did not succeed better in bringing the insular/vernacular/British imagination into more traumatic contact with' the post-war Eastern European reality.[10]

I am unsure what 'better' might mean here, since 'The Interrogation' itself inscribes just such a traumatisation; and others of these monologues also register the shock. 'Moses', the earliest of them, is the monologue of an anonymous Israelite commenting on Moses and his vision of the Promised Land; in his own dreams this spokesman is unable to envisage the future which he nevertheless, with that tragic historical irony endemic to these poems, prophetically realises awaits his people:

> We did not see, beyond, the ghetto rising,
> Toledo, Cracow, Vienna, Budapesth,
> Nor, had we seen, would we have known our people
> In the wild disguises of fantastic time,
> Packed in dense cities, wandering countless roads,
> And not a road in the world to lead them home.

And in 'The Good Town' the representative voice, speaking of the depredations befalling the place of his warmly remembered affections, offers an account of a police state as persuasive, convinced and – in its final line – as grimly, unconsolingly ironic as anything that subsequently entered English with the Modern European Poets:

> If you see a man
> Who smiles good-day or waves a lordly greeting
> Be sure he's a policeman or a spy.
> We know them by their free and candid air.

It is in lines such as these that Muir appears to justify his self-definition in the autobiography, during his period in the Glasgow slums, as 'a Displaced Person', a definition which, without the evidence of such poems, might seem self-aggrandisingly appropriative.[11] The poems suggest that he has known at least part of these realities from the inside, that he has been enabled to write an English European poetry of post-war displacement by his own experience of pre-war Scottish disablement, which he found it impossible to embody in his work in any direct way. In the personae of these monologues written towards the end of his career Muir is finally writing his own story, rather than his own fable, too. Far more than all those versions of the Fall, of expulsions from Eden, of irrecoverably lost paradises which figure throughout his work, these poems are deepened into significance by the authentic sound of an empathetic personal distress.

A similar combination of subliminal personal recall – now of the Orkney island community, with its agricultural and piscine economy, which was Muir's own birthplace – and the most terrifying of all the new subjects offered by the war, the threat of atomic holocaust, is also to be found in 'The Horses'. In this outstanding poem, however, that is not the only sustaining or invigorating conjunction. Everything seems uniquely to come together, as the form inherited from Muir's late monologues is newly startled and perturbed into poetic inevitability. The anonymous persona here has suffered an ultimate displacement, as a refugee from the lost community that was humankind before 'The seven days war that put the world to sleep'; but he also speaks, in the poem's peculiarly unsettling tenses of what we might think of as the past and present posthumous, as a representative of a new community of survivors. Unlike the isolate 'I' in those other poetic imaginings of apocalypse, Bob Dylan's 'A Hard Rain's A-Gonna Fall' and Thom Gunn's 'Misanthropos', this voice can still utter the word 'we'. An imagining of the alternative community is also the poem's point, and it will be a more than merely human community, involving a new but newly traditional relationship with the world of the animal, a 'long-lost archaic companionship' to set against 'That old bad world that swallowed its children quick'. This post-holocaustal future is projected, therefore, from a very ancient past, the past which was in its closing phase during Muir's early years on Orkney. The autobiography has a fine passage in which the horses of his childhood are imagined simultaneously terrifying and fascinating in a way that suggests an origin for the poem:

> . . . my fear was infused by a longing to go up to them and touch them and simultaneously checked by the knowledge that their hoofs were dangerous: a combination of emotions which added up to worship in the Old Testament sense. Everything about them, the steam rising from their soft, leathery nostrils, the sweat staining their hides, their ponderous, irresistible motion, the distant rolling of their eyes . . . filled me with a stationary terror and delight for which I could get no relief.[12]

The actual horses of childhood here turn into the symbolic object of religious awe; and the poem, which brings both biblical and Homeric resonances to bear on its central symbol, makes the archaic companionship which it represents a proper object of veneration. That feeling for the communities of the dispossessed and displaced which informs many of Muir's monologues is here realised in its most memorable form, and in a way proleptic of our more contemporary ecological diseases and desires. Uncharacteristically particular in its local imagery, 'The Horses' also exceptionally articulates a symbol of great power, drawing its suggestiveness from the deepest personal memory and from ancestral piety as well as from the weighty texts of epic and religion:

> Among them were some half-a-dozen colts
> Dropped in some wilderness of the broken world,
> Yet new as if they had come from their own Eden.
> Since then they have pulled our ploughs and borne our loads
> But that free servitude still can pierce our hearts.
> Our life is changed; their coming our beginning.

Notes

1. Edna Longley, *Louis MacNeice: A Study* (London: Faber and Faber, 1988), p. 114.

2. *Selected Poems of Louis MacNeice*, ed. W.H. Auden (London: Faber and Faber, 1964), p. 10.

3. Tom Paulin, *Ireland and the English Crisis* (Newcastle upon Tyne: Bloodaxe Books, 1984), p. 76.

4. Louis MacNeice, *Varieties of Parable* (Cambridge: Cambridge University Press, 1965), p. 12.

5. *Ireland and the English Crisis*, p. 78.

6. *Varieties of Parable*, p. 3.

7. ibid., p. 23.

8. ibid., pp. 124–5.

9. Heaney, *The Government of the Tongue* (London: Faber and Faber, 1988), pp. 42, 43.

10. ibid., p. 41.

11. See *An Autobiography* (London: The Hogarth Press, 1954; 1987), p. 280.

12. ibid., p. 22.

Chapter 3
A Modernism in Place
David Jones and Basil Bunting

The two poets of the period who most radically pursued the technical experiments of high Modernism are also those who have had to wait longest for adequate assimilation. In David Jones's case this was due partly to the extreme slowness of his composition and publication. After the long poem drawing on his experience in the First World War, *In Parenthesis* (1937), he worked for the rest of his life on the material which he was unwillingly led to publish in what he always considered fragmentary and unfinished form as *The Anathemata* (1952) and *The Sleeping Lord and Other Fragments* (1974); although he also produced during this period a large body of work as a visual artist. Basil Bunting published his earlier work (including *The Spoils*, 1951, and the poems eventually collected in his 'First Book of Odes') extremely obscurely, and usually abroad, until in 1966 he published in England the long poem *Briggflatts* on which his reputation is most securely based. Both Jones and Bunting also lived and worked largely outside the usual frameworks of literary production and reception. Jones suffered severe mental breakdown (partly, it is presumed, as a result of his war experience) and lived in some isolation, even reclusiveness. Despite the enthusiastic praise of other poets, including Eliot and Auden, his reputation during his lifetime remained largely a coterie one. Bunting travelled widely in Europe and America and lived in Persia during the Second World War, until he eventually returned to his native Northumberland where he lived quietly, in some poverty, until the comparative acclaim of the 1960s which brought a new American audience in its wake.

The work of both deliberately cultivates certain kinds of difference. Jones opposes to what he calls 'the bland megalopolitan light' a conception of 'locality' derived largely from his affiliations, familial and intellectual, with the culture and language of Wales. Hence his work bristles with Welsh words and historical and mythological references which render most non-Welsh readers helpless without one of his many explanatory footnotes. The alienating otherness is strategic, intended to make the reader painfully aware of the cultural, political and linguistic diversity of which the 'Great Britain' of the post-war period is in fact composed, despite the imposed uniformities of Whitehall and the metropolitan media. The poet's true function, according to Jones, is the recovery and 're-presentation', or 'anamnesis' of his own 'mythos', the foundational elements of his own place. His 'anathemata' are those 'blessed things that have taken on what is cursed and the profane things that somehow are redeemed', those known and loved objects which must be attentively transformed into 'signs' in the poet's language.[1]

Jones's private terminology here is part of a body of prose (collected most notably in *Epoch* and *Artist*, 1959) in which he moulds from heterogeneous and sometimes arcane sources a substantial, if makeshift, body of theory to underwrite his poetry and painting. Basil Bunting produced nothing similar, but his oppositional and antagonistic stance is similar to Jones's and can be measured by a note to *Briggflatts* which tells us that 'Southrons would maul the music' of many of its lines. Making its own anamnesis, Bunting's poem celebrates not only particular areas of the north of England but also the dialect of Northumberland: 'spuggies' for sparrows, 'becks' for brooks, 'saltings' for marshland, and so on. Like Jones too, Bunting recovers a history of his territory: Eric Bloodaxe, the Dark Ages king, acts as a sort of second self for the poet in the first two sections of *Briggflatts*; the sixth-century poet Aneurin (whose survivor's account of the Battle of Catraeth also supplies epigraphs for each part of Jones's *In Parenthesis*) is overheard in the poem's fourth section; and the 'plaited lines' of the seventh-century illuminated Lindisfarne Gospels, which contain a tenth-century gloss in Northumbrian-dialect Anglo-Saxon, are used as a metaphor for the text itself at one of the poem's high points.

This recovery of non-standard languages and dialects and of unacknowledged histories, with its edge of cultural and political animus – the element we might consider the most local and indigenous in Jones and Bunting – is also, paradoxically, what connects them most intimately with their major Modernist influences and precursors: Eliot and Joyce in Jones's case, Pound in Bunting's. Both Jones and Bunting began with a strong sense of how an English national culture was only one among many in the British Isles, even if a powerfully organised, constructed and propagandised one; they both entirely lack the normative points of reference of a southern English, middle-class upbringing and education (neither attended a university). It was probably this above all which urged them towards the self-exiled writers of Modernism, who had rejected singular national and cultural identity and embodied in their work a generous if necessarily personally manufactured cultural, literary and linguistic pluralism.

Joyce is, for Jones, 'the most incarnational of artists' because 'never . . . has such absorption with a microcosm been the means of showing forth the macrocosmic realities';[2] and the fifth section of *The Anathemata*, 'The Lady of the Pool', is one of the very few works to show the successful assimilation of the later Joycean manner. Bunting lived near and worked with Pound in both Paris and Rapallo in the 1920s and 1930s, and his 'On the Fly-Leaf of Pound's Cantos' refers to Pound's poem as 'the Alps': necessary, absolute and unavoidable. The third section of *Briggflatts* (which is in part a version of the Persian poet Ferdosi's account of Alexander's legendary journey up the mountains of Gog and Magog towards Israfel, the Angel of Death) may also be read as an allegory of Bunting's wrestle with Pound as the unignorable and terrifying precursor. If the *Cantos* are the Alps in the 'Fly-leaf' poem, Pound, at the centre of *Briggflatts*, may be figured as Alexander, resolutely scaling the 'glazed crag' while his retinue longs for the 'familiar games' of Macedonia; and this section of the poem resembles, in its scatology, Pound's Hell Cantos.

Both Jones and Bunting, then, inscribe a conjunction quite exceptional in the poetry of the period, though less unusual in the visual arts: their work is the site of the fullest taking into native possession of the hitherto alien or suspect forms and effects of high Modernism, and the most belated possible renovation of that Modernism by its encounter with the genuinely other. The belatedness is intrinsic to the undertaking, and it registers as a tendency in both poets (Jones more than Bunting, probably) to the mannered, pedantic and antiquarian. Nevertheless, the further making of it new has added extraordinary long poems to the language and has provided subsequent poets with models not necessarily so much of present technical use as of general hint and gesture, ways of proceeding through and beyond Modernism into a future which accommodates it with a difference. Seamus Heaney, John Montague, Christopher Middleton and Geoffrey Hill are among those who have appreciated Jones, and Thom Gunn and Donald Davie – making their own varied accommodations with American Modernism, as I suggest in Part Three – have illuminatingly defined the value they locate in Bunting: one of Davie's essays on *Briggflatts*, written in 1977, and significantly placed at the end of his prose collection *The Poet in the Imaginary Museum*, concludes that 'This is where English poetry has got to, it is what English poets must assimilate and go on from.'[3]

While I do not wish to suggest too radical a twinning of writers who are also quite distinct, I think it is therefore worthwhile to pause over what seem to me their most significant areas of correspondence and alignment. Jones's use of macaronic forms drawing especially on Welsh, and Bunting's Northumbrian dialect in *Briggflatts* and Arabic names and Persian references in *The Spoils* are the main indications of something more generally applicable too: their works heavily emphasise the materiality of the signifier. They do this with self-conscious sophistication: *The Anathemata* opens with an ambivalently artist-priest figure 'making this thing other' with a 'groping syntax' which 'already shapes'; and in the opening section of *Briggflatts* the injunction is 'Pens are too light. / Take a chisel to write.' Jones's texts place the emphasis more obviously than Bunting's, with their use of a range of technical vocabularies, their typographical adventures, and their poetic text embedded deeply in proliferating and often digressive annotation (the model for which is usually said to be the much sparser annotation of *The Waste Land*, but which may actually be the modern scholarly edition) and, in *The Anathemata*, embedded further in a considerable amount of visual material – drawings, engravings, inscriptions.

Some of Jones's annotation is concerned with matters of pronunciation, and his instruction in the preface to *The Anathemata* is that it be spoken 'with deliberation'. This materiality of the aural is even stronger in Bunting (once a music critic), who notes in *Briggflatts* that 'It looks well on the page, but never / well enough'. He elaborates in interviews an account of the music of poetry which has its woolly-mindedness but nevertheless supports his own sonorous readings of his work, and in particular his insistence on reading *Briggflatts* accompanied by a Scarlatti sonata: a feat managed quite without the pretentiousness which would accompany it in any writer with less integrity.[4] Bunting's conception of a 'shape of sounds' and Jones's of a 'shape in words' supply the basis for long, intricate works patterned not according to traditional metrics or models, but with a vigour and resource responsive to their mixed genetic constitutions.

The materiality of the signifier combines in their work with an interest in materialities of other kinds too: with signs of human habitation and culture, artefacture and expression, inscribed on landscape and in history. Primary among such signs are, for both, the architectural signs of religious practice. *The Anathemata* opens in a Roman Catholic church, where a priest is celebrating mass, and 'The Lady of the Pool' names a large number of London's churches in a way continuous with the wartime evocation of the church building in Eliot's 'Little Gidding'. Bunting's Ode 36, in the 'First Book of Odes', written in 1948, celebrates a Persian mosque in terms which, while acting as an emblem for a self-transcending artistic integrity, draw on the biblical language of St John's gospel ('a glory neither of stone / nor metal, neither of words / nor verses, but of the light / shining upon no substance; / a glory not made / for which all else was made'); and *Briggflatts* is titled after the Quaker meeting house in Northumberland in which Bunting worshipped as a child.

Their complex and heterodox versions of religious traditions are prominent in their poems. In Jones's *The Anathemata* this involves a gathering together of motifs drawn from Catholicism, reconceived as a harmony of emblems of consolation and assuagement. In the poem's opening section, 'Rite and Fore-Time', for instance, pre-history is viewed as a searching through the processes of geological development for the places where the 'New Light' penetrates. This is named from, but not dogmatically attached to, specific Christian concept, just as a Catholic funeral lament is uttered for the makers of pre-historic artistic and religious artefacts. Bunting's probably atheistic Quakerism informs his work in a necessarily less visible but none the less potent way: the imperialistic cultural rapine evoked in *The Spoils* ('Broken booty but usable / along the littoral, frittering into the south'), the savagery of modern warfare also described there, and the terrors of ancient battles inscribing the landscape of *Briggflatts* all derive their force from Bunting's residual Quaker pacifism (he was gaoled as a conscientious objector during the First World War). The poignantly vulnerable materiality of human flesh, erotically sexed but prey to the depredations of time, mortality and conquering kings, is his abiding theme: *Briggflatts* opens paradigmatically with amorous children kissing on a 'marble bed' of tomb-stones, and closes with the 'silence by silence' of a Quaker meeting house.

In so far as the concepts of traditional religious systems are kept in sight in Jones and Bunting, their work may be considered essentially elegiac, written with an awareness of the ways in which such concepts have, in the latter part of the twentieth century, lost common adherence or accessibility. In both, the elegiac note is most clearly sounded by the rhetorical questions which close their texts inconclusively. *The Sleeping Lord* sequence ends by asking:

> Does the land wait the sleeping lord
>   or is the wasted land
> that very lord who sleeps?

The final despairing question of *The Spoils* is:

> What else do we live for and take part,
> we who would share the spoils?

And *Briggflatts* culminates in a lyric coda whose final stanza asks:

> Where we are who knows
> of kings who sup
> while day fails? Who,
> swinging his axe
> to fell kings, guesses
> where we go?

It is as elegies, laments, acts of preservation and memorialisation, efforts of inquiry and willed hope for the future that all these poems have their greatest significance; they bring into British poetry capacious forms in which the Modernist encyclopaedic elegy has its final recensions.

Jones's late work, in its various fragmentary shapes, derives from a single originating impulse and a single syncretic myth of origin, continuity, succession and remembrance. It is given its most straightforward expression in the populist epigram uttered by the Lady of the Pool in *The Anathemata*: 'What's under works up'; which she glosses for the benefit of the sea-captain she is addressing:

> Though there's a deal of subsidence hereabouts even so:
>   gravels, marls, alluviums
> here all's alluvial, cap'n, and as unstable as these old annals
>   that do gravel us all. For, captain:
> even immolated kings
>   be scarce a match for the deep fluvial doings of the mother.

The myth inscribes a surety of constancy below metamorphosis, of permanent substance beneath historical or geographical accident. Origin, source and fountainhead will always rise through the deposits and accretions of time and place; and the myth is intended to rhyme geology and human psychology. If this has its intensely conservative, even reactionary elements, Jones's is also explicitly a revisionist myth of gender: those powerful masculinist kings will always be disturbed and disrupted by a deep fluvial mother, some feminine principle or agency of opposition and possible regeneration. *The Anathemata* locates ultimate value in dramatised or mythologised figures of woman: the Lady of the Pool who utters her composite, undermining historical monologue, in which she turns imperial 'Roma' on its head as erotic 'Amor'; the Welsh Guinevere, Gwenhwyfar, whose iconic appearance is the subject of a lengthy celebration in Part VII, 'Mabinog's Liturgy'; and Mary herself, who figures, with an erotic Oedipal charge, as both mother and lover of Christ in the concluding Part, 'Sherthursdaye and Venus Day'.[5]

In *The Sleeping Lord* sequence (which is the best point of entry for the reader of late David Jones), the myth is organised dramatically into eight separate poems or 'fragments'. After an initial lament or jeremiad from the artist, they fall into two distinct groups, the 'Roman' fragments ('The Wall', 'The Dream of Private Clitus', 'The Fatigue' and 'The Tribune's Visitation') and the 'Celtic' fragments ('The Tutelar of the Place', 'The Hunt' and 'The Sleeping Lord'). The Roman fragments are dramatised and spoken in character; the Celtic pieces vary formally from a lyric prayerfulness reminiscent of Eliot's *Ash-Wednesday* to the complexly digressive, even prosily convoluted, form of 'The Sleeping Lord' fragment itself. The Roman poems inter-relatedly centre on a garrison of Roman troops stationed in Palestine at the time of Christ's death, 'The Fatigue' being set on the day of the crucifixion and dealing with the soldiers detailed to execute it. The troops are of mixed

recruitment, the NCO from Rome itself, some of the men Celts from
Gaul or Britain. Jones is contradicting the known historical facts here in
order, he says in a note, to emphasise the 'unific aspect of an imperium'.
The Celtic pieces, complementing the expressed anxieties and despairs of
the Roman soldiers, intricately oppose the ideological dominance of any
unific imperium with a celebration of diversity and difference. They
oppose the Roman world-order with local cult; they oppose the
masculine will to power and death with a beneficent female alternative:

> Queen of the differentiated sites, administratrix of the
> demarcations, let our cry come unto you.
> In all times of imperium save us
>   when the
>   *mercatores* come save us
>   from the guile of the *negotiatores* save us from the
> *missi*,
>   from the agents
>   who think no shame
> by inquest to audit what is shameful to tell
>   deliver us.

The dramatisations of sections of *The Sleeping Lord* give the
underlying myth both a plot and a psychological interest of a kind not
attempted in the denser but also more static form of *The Anathemata*.
'The Wall', while it articulates its complaint against imperium, conveys
the baffled hopelessness of the soldiers compelled to administer it, aware
that they are serving only a plutocracy. 'The Dream of Private Clitus', a
dream of maternal protection and uterine longing which cuts across the
nightmare waking of endless Roman conquest, is one of the finest of
modern prose-poems, its dense and learned intertextuality carried easily
and persuasively by the dignified and subtle tenderness of its
dramatic-monologue form. 'The Fatigue' is a small masterpiece of
historical and dramatic irony, as is 'The Tribune's Visitation', in which
the eponymous tribune revealing a divided personality also reveals the
way a cultural fault line may be inscribed deep within an individual
psyche. Such poems as these are fragments tellingly extruded and
intricately crafted from a central core of great integrity and weight.

Although some similar matters of cultural lament and memorialisation
inform Bunting's work, he is a much less resolutely impersonal poet than
Jones, and the epic or bardic elements of *Briggflatts* are subsumed in its
acts of psychosexual remembrance; this may be what he meant by
subtitling the poem 'An Autobiography'. At its heart is a radiantly
intense childhood memory, a moment with exactly the quality Eliot
desired for, and felt he lacked in a draft version of 'Little Gidding': a
'sharpening   of   personal   poignancy . . . . some   acute   personal

reminiscence (never to be explicated, of course, but to give power from well below the surface)'.[6] Two children accompany a monumental mason as he journeys through the Northumbrian countryside in spring, and they are left alone together at bedtime:

> Rain rinses the road,
> the bull streams and laments.
> Sour rye porridge from the hob
> with cream and black tea,
> meat, crust and crumb.
> Her parents in bed
> the children dry their clothes.
> He has untied the tape
> of her striped flannel drawers
> before the range. Naked
> on the pricked rag mat
> his fingers comb
> thatch of his manhood's home.
>
> Gentle generous voices weave
> over bare night
> words to confirm and delight
> till bird dawn.
> Rainwater from the butt
> she fetches and flannel
> to wash him inch by inch,
> kissing the pebbles.
> Shining slowworm part of the marvel.
> The mason stirs:
> Words!
> Pens are too light.
> Take a chisel to write.

It has been said that Bunting's uniqueness derives from the conjunction in him of the Poundian and the Wordsworthian; but the sexuality of *Briggflatts*, as it is apparent there, is quite unWordsworthian. Associated with childhood, it is an aspect of innocence, even a confirmation of it, not a falling from it, as it is in the Wordsworthian tradition manifest in a poem such as 'Nutting'.

The prelapsarian sweetness of the moment is at the origin, centre and end of *Briggflatts*; and it is literally there through the cohering figure of the slowworm itself. This appears first in the poem's opening stanza, in its most simply natural aspect – the lizard identified with seasonal and cyclical process, its way paved by the spring mayflower. In the stanza quoted above, the slowworm is the penis, rising in its natural, but still (particularly to children) marvellous human process. In the poem's third section the slowworm is a definition of identity itself ('I am the slowworm'); and, in the return from dream to reality which concludes that section, an assured identity is offered as a transformation of threatening external nature: 'every bough repeated the slowworm's song'. Ultimately, after the poem's fifth and final section has asserted the persistence of memory ('Then is Now'), it is again the phallic slowworm which acts as the quite unassertive focus of that starlight which measures the continuities and lapses of time: 'light from the zenith / spun when the slowworm lay in her lap / fifty years ago'.

The slowworm is the most prominent of the several delicately handled figures and motifs which bind the five sections of *Briggflatts* together: others include the Bloodaxe material; references to music and composers (Schoenberg, Byrd, Monteverdi and Scarlatti); images of weaving; and the transformation of the 'sweet tenor bull', whose 'brag' opens the poem, into the bull which rapes Pasiphae in the novel version of that myth which offers us, in the second section, a savagely erotic trope for the process of artistic creativity, Pasiphae's 'expectant hand' guiding the bull until she has 'gloried in unlike creation'. These binding motifs give *Briggflatts* an exceptional coherence for a Modernist long poem; and they make a case for what might otherwise seem Bunting's pretentious description of these poems as 'sonatas'. This is a poem which uniquely moulds characteristic Modernist disjunctions, abruptions and dislocations into a more than merely factitious formal organisation.

This kind of structure, which combines licence and restraint, enacts what I take to be the poem's central impulse. *Briggflatts* is a poem derived from the necessity of leaving home and the constant desire to return there; and it is articulate about the ways in which the poet who would inscribe himself in language is always inscribing a final home for himself in any case, since, in writing, he is inscribing his own absence. When, in the two stanzas from the first section which I have quoted above, the penis is figured as the slowworm, its own name is erased, only to return immediately as 'pen'; but this hard act of inscription needs the sturdier mason's chisel, that implement which marks the marble tombstone with 'a name / naming none, / a man abolished'. At the end of *Briggflatts* the man is abolished in his own book, in the letters which write an 'autobiographical' inscription or epitaph:

> The sheets are gathered and bound,
> the volume indexed and shelved,
> dust on its marbled leaves.
> Lofty, an empty combe,
> silent but for bees.
> Finger tips touched and were still
> fifty years ago.

A psychoanalytical account of the poem might find a neurotic element in its fixation on childhood sexuality, its implication that no more fulfilling relationship could subsequently be discovered in life than was found then, and might therefore perceive a failure of power where the greatest poetry might be thought to be imaginatively strongest. But this is to scrutinise *Briggflatts* with the keen-sightedness demanded by poetry of a very high order indeed; which is undoubtedly the demand it makes.

In 1934 David Jones visited Jerusalem to stay with two friends: Eric Gill, who had been commissioned to make some sculptures for the Hebrew Library, and Thomas Hodgkin, who was on the staff of the Governor of Palestine, which was then British mandated territory. In an extremely interesting letter written in 1971, Jones describes this visit as the origin of not only *The Anathemata*, but of most of his later poetry. In the contrast between the Palestinians and the British troops in the narrow streets of Jerusalem – the troops with their 'heavy field-service hob-nailed boots and above all the riot shields . . . and in each right fist the half-grip of a stout baton' – Jones immediately sensed a Roman analogy.[7] The central oppositions and analogues of his own work, then, are rooted in a contemporary politics. Seamus Heaney was instinctively restoring this dimension to the work when, in his review of *The Sleeping Lord* in 1974, with the Vietnam war in mind, he wrote that the Celtic fragments represented 'the jungle's complaint to the napalm';[8] and his own poem 'The Toome Road' in *Field Work* (1979) addresses a British soldier driving behind the turret of his armoured car on a Northern Irish road as a 'charioteer'. Jones's poetry may also be fed and read back into current circumstances in Jerusalem: which is no longer, of course, in Palestine; although (making one of Jones's points exactly) the spirit of his Celtic poems would undoubtedly be understood by the government of Palestine-in-exile.

In the early 1930s, while he was living close to Pound in Rapallo, Bunting began a version of the work of the classical Persian poet Ferdosi which he had come across accidentally in an Italian translation. Wishing to continue his version beyond what was available in the translation, he taught himself classical Persian; the third section of *Briggflatts* is presumably an eventual development of this material. As a consequence of this knowledge Bunting was, in one of the oddest displacements of a very oddly displaced life, sent to Persia as an interpreter during the Second World War; he eventually became Vice-Consul in Isfahan, and afterwards *The Times* correspondent in Teheran. Out of this experience, he developed the long poem published in 1951 as *The Spoils*, which is one of the most interesting and complex poetic accounts of the imperial and colonial theme that we have in the period which has witnessed the virtual extinction of British imperial and colonial power, if not of colonial mentality.

The poem confronts an unidealised indigenous Persian culture with the despoliators of a mercantile empire and the apocalyptic ravages of desert warfare. If David Jones's Roman soldiers speak Cockney, Bunting's Persians speak Northumbrian: Asshur, in the opening section, pauses under a brothel wall to 'bait' on his journey; and the poem's persuasive depiction of Persian life and culture is developed out of a gentle empathy. The images of destruction in *The Spoils* are the imperialist's guilt and the Quaker pacifist's shame; and the poem grows beyond its own time into ours, as Persia has grown into Iran.

The effortful and exceptional conjunctions in the texts of David Jones and Basil Bunting may be regarded, then, as exemplary in their preoccupation with what continue as major elements of our own history: the break-up of empire and the heritage of colonialism; the struggle towards a different perception of what has traditionally been considered a 'centre' and a 'periphery' in British political and cultural life; and the insistence on the strength and necessity of speaking, in modern English poetry, one's own resourceful dialect. Anti-universalist in their most intimate linguistic assumptions, *The Anathemata* and *Briggflatts* are native acknowledgements of the lesson preached by Salman Rushdie when he says that 'English, no longer an English language, now grows from many roots.'[9]

Notes

1. See the preface to *The Anathemata* (London: Faber and Faber, 1952), pp. 28–9.

2. David Jones, *Epoch and Artist* (London: Faber and Faber, 1959), p. 304.

3. Donald Davie, *The Poet in the Imaginary Museum: Essay of Two Decades*, ed. Barry Alpert (Manchester: Carcanet Press, 1977), p. 292.

4. See the record *Basil Bunting Reads 'Briggflatts'* (Newcastle upon Tyne: Bloodaxe Books, 1980), no. YRIC 0001.

5. I have discussed this text at length in *The Song of Deeds: A Study of 'The Anathemata' of David Jones* (Cardiff: University of Wales Press, 1982).

6. Cited in Helen Gardner, *The Composition of 'Four Quartets'* (London: Faber and Faber, 1978), p. 24.

7. David Jones, *Dai Greatcoat: A self-portrait of David Jones in his letters*, ed. René Hague (London: Faber and Faber, 1980), pp. 56–7.

8. Seamus Heaney, 'Now and in England', *Spectator*, 6 June 1974, pp. 741–2.

9. Cited in Robert Burchfield, *The English Language* (Oxford: Oxford University Press, 1985), p. 34.

Part Two
From the Forties

Chapter 4
A New Romanticism
Apocalypse, Dylan Thomas, W.S. Graham, George Barker

When W.H. Auden and Christopher Isherwood sailed from England to America in January 1939, and did not return during the war, Cyril Connolly, editor of the significant 1940s journal *Horizon*, characterised it as 'the most important literary event since the outbreak of the Spanish war'.[1] This remark might seem, on the face of it, a typical piece of Connollyite hyperbole; but it does suggest the way the transatlantic move was read at the time as a decisive literary reorientation at the close of one decade and the opening of another. Whether Auden's removal was read as betrayal, careerism, or psycho-sexual necessity, it signalled an endpoint to the politically committed, socially engaged poetry of the English 1930s. The British Left was subsequently to suffer the shock of the Russo-German pact of August 1939, a cynical piece of mutual totalitarian agreement between Russian Communism and German Fascism which seemed to ignore everything the Spanish Civil War had been fought for; and the beginning of the war in September 1939 inevitably changed all the rules of poetic engagement.

In the later 1930s there had been, also, the setting-up of a kind of counter-movement to the Auden-political, itself avowedly leftist in inception but increasingly individualistic and withdrawn from the world of public politics. This counter-movement achieved high definition at the International Exhibition of Surrealism in London in 1936, an exhibition at which the young Dylan Thomas handed around cups of boiled string, asking 'Weak or strong?' The impact of French Surrealism on British poetry was, perhaps, neither weak nor strong, but diffused in various transformations and metamorphoses. David Gascoyne, who published *A Short Survey of Surrealism* in 1935, was its prime English exponent, but George Barker, whose first book was also published in 1935, began with a more boisterously resilient absorption of some of its practices and effects. It is, however, Dylan Thomas who offers the most significant assimilation of it in poetry in English; and it was Thomas who became the focal point for the anti-Auden disaffection.

Geoffrey Grigson's magazine *New Verse*, which was to expire before the end of the decade, published in 1937 a double issue in tribute to Auden, and it includes a piece by Dylan Thomas which usefully illuminates the disagreement and the new orientation. 'I sometimes think of Mr Auden's poetry,' writes Thomas, 'as a hygiene, a knowledge and practice, based on a brilliantly prejudiced analysis of contemporary disorders, relating to the preservation and promotion of health, a sanitary science and flushed of melancholics'.[2] Thomas is by no means merely hostile to Auden (and his own work is, indeed, in certain respects indebted to him), but the terms of this apparent approbation contain their own deflating ironies: the aesthetic of purgation, with poetry as the surgery (or lavatory) of social engineering, is made to seem an almost comically reduced one. In Thomas's own early work, of course, the 'melancholics' flood back: the body, in its most intimately glandular processes, reasserts an obdurate primacy. The Thirties Auden ego – analytic, diagnostic, judgemental (and public-school, Oxford English upper-middle-class) – is replaced by the Thomas id: dionysian, permissive, self-entranced (and non-university, Welsh lower-middle-class).

That replacement seemed a liberation to a generation of poets who, in the 1940s, developed a 'movement' out of a combination of Surrealism and early Thomas, and prosecuted it through a number of journals and anthologies. Known initially as the poetry of 'Apocalypse', but soon merging into the general movement known as the 'New Romanticism', and culminating in a theory of 'Personalism', it gave the period that character which laid it open to the mockery of the 1950s Movement poets, and it is largely what is meant by 'Forties' poetry in some of the memoirs which have defined, or mythologised, the period, such as Julian Maclaren-Ross's *Memoirs of the Forties* and Derek Stanford's *Inside the Forties*. The journals in which the 'Apocalypse' was advanced are Wrey Gardiner's *Poetry Quarterly* and Tambimuttu's *Poetry London*; and the significant stages of its existence are defined by the anthologies *The New Apocalypse* (1939), *The White Horseman* (1941) and *A New Romantic Anthology* (1945). Dylan Thomas features in only the first of these and, always sceptical, he refused to act as signatory to a manifesto in 1938. The movement is more primarily associated with Henry Treece, J.F. Hendry and Nicholas Moore; but poets subsequently as diverse as Norman MacCaig and Vernon Watkins were also connected with it. The anthologies include essays as well as poems, and they spell out a rationale clearly, if with a rather overwrought effortfulness. Referring to some of the high priests of Modernism (Joyce, Lawrence, Kafka, Freud), they define the aims of Apocalypse as a new 'organicism' to oppose 'the machine-world', a new mythical integration of the individual personality to set against the forms of public-political utopianism in the work of the Thirties poets, and a New 'Romanticism' (variously defined, but viewed as a 'dialectical development' of Surrealism) to combat the perceived classicism of Eliot and Auden.

The expression of these ideas is not very subtle but it is clear that a genuine personal and social crisis is being addressed. This is made plainest in a piece by G.S. Fraser in *The White Horseman*, written while he was in the army. His apologia for Apocalypse is that the times are bound to produce the loneliness, gloom and excess evidenced everywhere in the poetry. 'The obscurity of our poetry,' he writes, 'its air of something desperately snatched from dream or woven round a chime of words, are the results of disintegration, not in ourselves, but in society; we have not *asked* to be thrown back on our own imagination for comfort and consolation, or to exercise our function in quite this isolated way.'[3] This hardly saves itself from self-pity, it may be (and a self-pity all the more reprehensible when we realise the ways in which some combatant poetry of the war – that of Keith Douglas and Alun Lewis in particular – does so save itself), but it nevertheless suggests the kind of mass that the forces of Apocalypse were attempting to move. The poetry – fraught, emphatic and obsessive – is understandable as the response to the unbearable sensation of being intruded upon: by conscription; by German air-raids on British cities; by the anxiety and anguish of separation and bereavement.

If such crises of identity find their finest expression in the explicit war poetry of the period, the febrility and alarm apparent in the poetry of Apocalypse testify to the urgency and community of the crisis itself. This does not prevent the following lines from a poem by Hendry from typifying the movement in an apparently almost self-propelling rhetoric of extremity which quickly comes to seem self-cancelling; but it does perhaps account for the temporary attraction of the style:

> Splint for the shriven skin I foster mantrump out
> Of festered history; sprout pointed fingers
> Where an afterbirth is dung and rubble-teat.
> I am the eyeball blown world! Axis of anger!

As a response to intolerable intrusion, these lines also suggest how closely allied some of this poetry was with the 'New Romantic' movement in the plastic arts of the time. The human body growing into, or invaded by, an apocalyptic, decayed or desperately frail pastoral landscape is a common motif in paintings by John Minton, for instance, by John Craxton and by Ceri Richards (some of whose paintings are heavily interdependent with the poems of Dylan Thomas).[4] Such an imagery of hideously deformed metamorphosis is also proleptically consonant with the horrors thrown up by the all too literal apocalypse of the Allied bombing of Hiroshima on 6 August 1945. For all the wilful self-indulgence in a great deal of this work, it did in some significant ways have its finger on a pulse of the time. Rejecting the Auden model, it was also rejecting a model of rational control and enlightenment; its frenetic irrationalism and hypersensitive subjectivity are witness to the human subject victimised by a 'festered history' – dispersed, fractured and dislocated, propelled by public event into radical instability.

The New Romanticism of the 1940s, as it may be read in its more significant literary exponents, is one in which poetry removes the surgeon's gown and vests itself again in bardic robes; the 'function' (as Thomas calls it in his remarks on Auden) becomes not hygienic but quasi-religious (Christian, pagan, or permissively – even licentiously – a mixture of both). Such poets as Thomas, Barker, Vernon Watkins, Sidney Keyes, W.S. Graham, John Heath-Stubbs, the later David Gascoyne and Kathleen Raine may be included under this rubric, and Robert Graves's influential prose work *The White Goddess* (1947) is manifestly an outgrowth of the same impulses. The capacity for self-aggrandisement and arrogance implicit in the mid-twentieth-century poet's once again putting on these unironic singing robes is clear; and in several cases the bardic investiture quite fails to disguise a paucity of genuine imagination and technique, 'vision' vainly trying to do the duty of both. There are too many poems from the 1940s in which the nebulously vatic seems repellent in its myopic self-assurance or triumphalism.

The 'bardic' may also license a sentimentality about some forms of experience alternative to a despised bourgeois behaviour: childhood, for instance, and an idea of the 'Celtic'. Many of these poets were not English. There is, in some of their work and in the way it was read, a discriminating Forties regionalism or cultural nationalism of a kind also found in John Hewitt's Ulster poetry, in Norman Nicholson's poetry of Cumberland, and in the early R.S. Thomas's Wales. But there is also a tendency to play the Celtic card occasionally in both the life and the work, using its reputation for linguistic exuberance and wild behaviour as licence and excuse, and powerfully contributing to a ludicrous stereotype. Thomas the Welshman, Graham the Scot and Barker (who emphasises an Irish family background), are none of them entirely free of this vice, but they seem to me by far the most interesting of these poets; and, in the case of Graham, the origins in a 1940s manner whose prime exemplar was Dylan Thomas are transformed and transcended in a lengthy career of finely self-revising scrupulousness.

Although his reputation has failed to maintain itself with anything like the vigour and tenacity predicted for it by his most enthusiastic critics, it is not hard to understand the sources of Dylan Thomas's influence on his contemporaries. In reaction against the Audenesque, he derives an astonishingly heady brew from the assimilation, in his early adolescence, of a variety of, it would appear, conflicting influences: Auden himself, Joyce, Donne, the Jacobean dramatists, Hopkins, Blake, contemporary film and Surrealism, and – it is often claimed, but never satisfactorily demonstrated – Rimbaud and early Welsh poetic forms. To these may be added the one Welsh element which did undoubtedly remain with him, that of Nonconformist chapel preaching. The brio with which the young Thomas absorbed and transformed these sources still seems remarkable: 'The force that through the green fuse drives the flower', for instance, was written when he was only nineteen. This is particularly worth remembering since, with the publication in 1968 of Ralph Maud's *Poet in the Making: The Notebooks of Dylan Thomas* (subsequently newly edited as *Dylan Thomas: The Notebook Poems 1930–1934*), it has been known that Thomas used material written in his very early years for a great deal of the work he published up to 1941 when he sold the notebooks to an American university. The Dylan Thomas manner is derived not only from the assimilation of a number of striking (and fashionable) sources but from the application of the poetic derived there to a range of primarily adolescent preoccupations. The world of a large part of Thomas's poetry is one in which the body narcissistically delights in its own sexuality and is terrified by its own mortality – and is also nervously or guiltily delighted with its own terror. The way the world is read through, or dreamed across, the human body in this poetry surely *Bakhtin!* makes Thomas overdue for a contemporary Bakhtinian reassessment.

If the adolescent subject supplies the essential body resorted to so frequently in these poems, however, the poems themselves attempt some negotiation between that body and a more than merely solipsistic world. Thomas – as some of his Donnean and Joycean debts attest – is here drawing on some very traditional Renaissance conceptions of microcosm and macrocosm, the human body as the little world which imitates the processes of the cosmos. The largely gesturing 'I' of poem after poem in the Thomas canon identifies the poet's ego with something much less specifically individuated: with a Christ figure; with the unborn child in the womb (the 'ungotten', as one poem coins it); with a natural force or process (that 'force that through the green fuse drives the flower'); with the dead; and, often enough, with an almost inextricable combination of these.

The preoccupation with the child in the womb, in particular, suggests something essential in Dylan Thomas: his is a poetry much taken up with the fact of, and with the emotions attached to, certain forms of psychological regression. It seems entirely appropriate that such a poetry of the previous, of mother and womb, of an unrecoverable origin, should itself have depended so much on the later reworking of what was already written in early adolescence. It is as though in their networks of reiterated figure and image Thomas's poems are attempting to reticulate some area of primary cellular development, to return to an origin by opening a poetic space or field in which images may stir, congeal, combine, split off, recombine, lapse, dissolve and circulate in a process of quivering or pulsating genesis imitative of the process of bodily genesis itself. The play of imagery is all in the direction of the instinctual and sensorial: if many of these poems do not completely defeat rational analysis they certainly come close, and the disinterested contemporary critic must think that their appeal to our comprehension is the least significant appeal they make. What still compels in the best of them is a display of energy, primitive and unlocalised, but almost entirely selfish; they work by a series of coruscating implosions, the body of the poem always turning back in upon itself in the fascinations of self-delight and self-loathing. With their libidinous dictions of friction and flow, their ⌈phallic imagery of breathtaking obviousness⌉(the 'candle in the thighs'), their frequent recourse to the verbal implosions of neologism and pun, and their haughty (or complacent) adoption of that bardic neo-Romantic attitudinising which sets the solitary or solipsistic poet over against the social crowd, these poems perform an astounding self-display.

The old criticism that the display (works better line by line) than it does poem by poem still seems to me, however, a well-founded one. Thomas is markedly a poet of the extraordinarily memorable individual line or two: 'O see the poles are kissing as they cross'; 'I am the long world's gentleman, he said, / And share my bed with Capricorn and Cancer'; 'Time is the tune my ladies lend their heartbreak' (the kind of line that surely impressed itself deeply on the young John Berryman, an early whisper of Henry's voice in *The Dream Songs*). When the lines are combined into stanzas and poems they seem often merely aggregation and apposition, lacking any deeper syntactical or rhythmic impulsion. This is particularly marked in the cases where Thomas uses tight traditional forms: the sonnets of 'Altarwise by owl-light', for instance, where the leaden and unvaried rhythms testify to some inertia at the heart of the whole conception. The trouble with numerous poems is that their glamour and charm cannot disguise the fact that they are elaborate tautologies, always aspiring to the condition of the 'Prologue' to his 1952 *Collected Poems*, which rhymes its opening with its closing line, its second with its penultimate, and so on, in a shape which eats itself: the poem as self-consuming artefact.

This kind of tautologising goes hand in hand with a characteristic, and enervating, type of organisation. This is to move, inside a surreal dream or nightmare landscape, through a set of binary oppositions from the negative to the positive term: death/life; lack/plenitude; darkness/light; masturbation/sexual mutuality; the innocence of the unborn/ the too great experience of the mature; origin or genesis/ time or eternity. The movement progresses in a rising cadence, to culminate in some cryptic quasi-aphorism, often associated, though not very specifically, with a pantheistic impulse. The effect can seem like being insistently told, in some baffling way, some extremely simple things that we already know perfectly well, and in a form whose cadences and circularities are suspiciously consolatory. The Thomas visions, as a result, can appear much less than real discoveries, and they constantly run the risk of bathos. There is something deeply apt and suggestive about Thomas's writing three poems celebrating his own birthday ('Twenty-four years', 'Poem in October' and 'Poem on his Birthday'). The poem as a birthday present from the self to the self, with all that that suggests of self-approbation, seems significantly in tune with the way this consolatory cadence may appear to gift-wrap material which would do better to seem more rawly painful and unprepossessing.

The poems written after Thomas sold his adolescent notebooks, and published in *Deaths and Entrances* (1946), do mark a significant advance, however. The combination of the abandonment of his customary working methods and the dual circumstances of the war and a troubled marriage brought to his work a new vigour and transparency, particularly in the elegies written for those who died in the London air-raids. A handful of poems in this volume seem to me the poems on which Thomas's reputation will ultimately rest: 'A Refusal to Mourn the Death, by Fire, of a Child in London', 'Into her lying down head' (with its chillingly neo-Jacobean depiction of 'libidinous betrayal'), 'In my craft or sullen art' and 'Fern Hill', together with the famous poem subsequently published in the volume *In Country Sleep*, 'Do not go gentle into that good night'. Poems such as these turn the mesmerised and self-obsessed narcissism of the earlier work outwards to a recognisable external world of action, event, suffering and relationship, though without losing the neural exacerbation which is the characteristic Dylan Thomas signature. To adapt a line by Sylvia Plath, the pain Thomas wakes to in these poems is not his, or not his alone: they diffuse the glandular compulsiveness into the compunctions of lament and love.

'A Refusal to Mourn', for instance, appears to function as a further classic locus of the Thomas-pantheistic vision. The child burnt to death in an air raid remains unmourned by the poet, since her death is an incorporation back into the earth's natural processes:

> Deep with the first dead lies London's daughter,
> Robed in the long friends,
> The grains beyond age, the dark veins of her mother,
> Secret by the unmourning water
> Of the riding Thames.
> After the first death there is no other.

The poem, as a defence of the poet's refusal to mourn, again sets his ego implicitly at one with natural process, presuming to discern the truths of a cosmic nature beyond the control and reason of any individuated human nature. In his refusal to mourn, the poet is at one with the river and its 'unmourning water', in an identification deeply consonant with the whole neo-Romantic endeavour. The characteristically cryptic-epigrammatic final line may mean either that this death is at least a release from pain for the child, since this natural incorporation is a consolatory terminus for human life (unlike, say, the potential eternal terrors of Welsh Nonconformist Christianity); or it may mean that all human deaths are (in some mystical-pantheistic way) one, that we must learn to see death as part of the cycle, that the reason we are so unwilling to do so is the fault of our own (human) self-consciousness.

If these are indeed some of the implications of the poem – and they would be in line with a great deal else in Thomas – then it would not be hard to criticise them. The lack of any individuation of this death is surely deeply questionable: it moves into the realms of consolatory inevitability what should remain obdurately disturbing and even deranging. The child's death has a cause in a specific politics, which is neither natural nor inevitable and is actually one of the most appalling features of modern life: the bombardment of civilians in warfare. However, even if the poem cannot defend itself against such objections, its power undoubtedly derives from a setting of its 'refusal to mourn' in the deliberated context of a refusal to make a poem which mourns, an English 'elegy':

> I shall not murder
> The mankind of her going with a grave truth
> Nor blaspheme down the stations of the breath
> With any further
> Elegy of innocence and youth.

The refusal articulated in the pun 'grave truth' is a refusal to have one's own language appropriated to serve a particular reading of such facts; and this is a refusal in which the neo-Romantic gestures expose, subliminally, a political insistence of their own, not merely a resigned and passive refusal of involvement. William Empson persuasively makes the case that 'A Refusal to Mourn' is a disguised refusal to write wartime propaganda, a refusal to make use of the child by deploying the expected, usable rhetoric of indignation.[5] In this reading the neo-Romanticism becomes a maintenance of the poet's purity in a context of suasive and manipulative linguistic corruption: to indulge in indignation would itself remove rights of individuality from the dead child by absorbing her into propagandist purpose. The poem's insistence that nature has its rights acts as an implicit rebuke to the manipulators of the war machine: 'After the first death there is no other' is the staking of a claim on behalf of the utter, unique unavailability of individual death to any further commentary, even an 'elegy of innocence and youth', that most powerfully irresistible of poetic modes (which is often nevertheless, as

Thomas knew perfectly well, an elegy for the elegist as well as the elegised).

That these later poems invite the reader to ponder such issues of poetic tact, decorum and responsibility is a measure of their superior discrimination and scruple. This Empsonian reading of 'A Refusal to Mourn' is supported by the newly saddened and humbled tone of the poem in which Thomas once again contemplates his own place and role as poet, 'In my craft or sullen art'. The stance is still recognisably neo-Romantic and possibly derived from Yeats: the poet writes in a state of isolated abstraction, 'in the still night' while 'the moon rages'. His morose solitude, however, is corrected by the desire to write on behalf of a particular community – the erotic community of lovers – but with the self-deprecating knowledge, both helpless and resilient, that they will have no interest. The impossible gesture ironically made, and the poem's tender delicacy, suggest a newly approachable and reflective mode towards which Thomas might have moved, had he lived, well beyond the ultimately wearying incantations and runes of the earlier work:

> Not for the proud man apart
> From the raging moon I write
> On these spindrift pages
> Nor for the towering dead
> With their nightingales and psalms
> But for the lovers, their arms
> Round the griefs of the ages,
> Who pay no praise or wages
> Nor heed my craft or art.

W.S. Graham's earlier work is helplessly parasitic on Thomas. It has the same incantatory rhythms; the same small field of reiterated, unspecific imagery of plant, season, sexuality and the 'Celtic'; and the same melodramatic and portentous straining towards 'vision', towards some illuminative or revelatory ecstasy. Collisions of apparent accident and spontaneity tenuously negotiated into coherence by a fraught will to closure, these poems seem as a result not only derivative but unreadably and earnestly verbose, a prime case of that fevered neo-Romanticism whose combating gave an initial impetus and rationale to the 1950s Movement. It is all the more surprising, then, that with *The White Threshold* (1949) Graham begins to develop a manner distinctively his own which, in his three subsequent volumes, becomes arguably the finest contribution to post-war poetry by a poet who began publishing in the 1940s.

The distinguishing characteristics of the new manner may be seen compacted in the relatively brief poem 'Listen. Put On Morning' from the 1949 volume. There is, as the title alone makes clear, an interest in verbal pun and play. There is a use of the short, typically three-stressed line, with constant enjambement, together with some use of assonantal patterning and internal rhyme; the result is an alert buoyancy and tentativeness, almost at times a Mozartian gaiety and delicacy. There is, along with this, an approach to areas of subject matter ironically caught up into such apparent levity: the references are to the working-class locations and experiences of Graham's tenement childhood in Greenock, on Scotland's Clydeside, in the 1920s and '30s (the 'Black Marias' patrolling the streets; the 'suiciding principle' working on its inhabitants). The economic and cultural depredations of this background persist in Graham in a way that may make his a poetry of working-class experience less visible than, but perhaps as interesting as, that theatre of resentment and alienation (with its perverse egotistical sublime) subsequently to be performed in the work of Tony Harrison.

In 'Listen. Put On Morning' the theme which is centrally to sustain Graham's finest later work declares itself as a heartfelt response to these conditions:

> The centuries turn their locks
> And open under the hill
> Their inherited books and doors
> All gathered to distil
> Like happy berry pickers
> One voice to talk to us.
> Yes listen. It carries away
> The second and the years
> Till the heart's in a jacket of snow
> And the head's in a helmet white
> And the song sleeps to be wakened
> By the morning ear bright.
> Listen. Put on morning.
> Waken into falling light.

The 'wakening' of the poem is, that is to say, a wakening out of the world of tenements, sugar docks and Black Marias into the world of reading; the book will become the doorway to a new community of shared discourse where an enriching dialogue may be entered into, where there will be 'morning' instead of 'mourning'. The distillation of that 'one voice' may also involve recognition of how your own isolated voice may harmonise with it: as it is, indeed, self-reflexively doing in this very poem, where the imperative to 'listen' is being directed primarily from the poet to another part of himself. Which in turn implies that, in the act of writing the poem, the poet is making and remaking himself; the poem is the instantiation of metamorphosis and self-transformation, the 'script of light'. If an individualism and political quietism are implicit in this (those rather forbidding images of incarceration in snow – to recur in 'Malcolm Mooney's Land' – may blame rather than neutrally figure that tendency), there is nevertheless a politics inscribed in the urgency of the desire with which it is registered. In his long poem 'The Nightfishing' (1955) and in his later books *Malcolm Mooney's Land* (1970) and *Implements In Their Places* (1977), Graham pursues this self-reflexive dialogue in a very refined distillate of his own, carrying it frequently into an explicit preoccupation with language. In its radical sense of identity as an unstable dispersal among the letters of a text, a play of difference and dislocation, this preoccupation clearly allies Graham's poetry with Barthesian and Derridean concepts of textuality. And, indeed, Graham's way into this material was partly through the absorption of influences also at work on the French theorists. Although his early neo-Romantic view of the poet as both bardic and *maudit* appears to persist as far as 'The Thermal Stair' in *Malcolm Mooney's Land* ('The poet or painter steers his life to maim / Himself somehow for the job'), the break with the earlier manner comes through the recognition of a sturdier and more philosophically interesting kind of Modernism. 'I am fashionable enough wearing / The grave-clothes of my generous masters', he says, punningly, in 'Approaches To How They Behave'; and those masters are, pre-eminently, Joyce, Eliot and Beckett. From Joyce, especially the Joyce of *Finnegans Wake*, he takes a sense of the meaningfully directed and compacted linguistic playfulness that is contained in the pun; from Eliot, especially the later Eliot of *Four Quartets* and 'Marina', a poignant post-symbolist anxiety about the semantic and referential properties of a poem; and from Beckett a sense of how to characterise and organise interestingly a densely self-reflexive monologue, one in which the inclination to solipsism may be corrected only by the capacity of language itself to act as 'company'.

It is testimony to Graham's stature that these influences are rarely overwhelming; and this, I think, for two reasons also worth particularising. Firstly, Graham's preoccupation with language derives at least as much from the realities of his own first tongue as it does from later literary experimentation. His Greenock childhood supplies, along with a range of subject matter, a distinct language for his work: even the earlier poems are invigorated by a use of Scots vocabulary. A diction which recurs throughout his *oeuvre*, it serves to remind us at a primary textual level that his written English is never 'standard', that it is fissured by a consciousness of nationality and class in a way that makes the title of a late poem, 'What Is The Language Using Us For?', a political as well as an aesthetic question. Secondly, Graham spent most of his later life in Cornwall, among a community of artists who, beginning as figurative painters, gradually moved towards abstraction (without necessarily, in all cases, wholeheartedly or permanently embracing it). 'The Thermal Stair' is an elegy for one of them, Peter Lanyon; others, who also feature in the poems, include Roger Hilton and Bryan Winter. Their move away from figuration towards self-reflexively 'painterly' values, towards a primary concentration on the material itself and the material's behaviour, undoubtedly influenced Graham's own linguistic experiments.

The purity and single-mindedness of his central, self-reflexive theme mean that Graham may appear monotonous. The relative meagreness of his output is perhaps an implicit acknowledgement of this as a potential danger; but the published work in fact manages an intricate variety of accommodations of the theme. What compels the reader is the resourcefulness of Graham's diversions of it through insidiously pleasurable fantasies and fictions, often handled with a wit and humour, a comic zest, remarkable from the author of the earnest earlier pieces. Throughout the work, for instance, the idea of the poem as 'letter' recurs: many poems are actually named 'letters', and others are written to named dedicatees (such as his wife, Nessie Dunsmuir, and his painter friends), or are written in the vocative. This both intensifies that view (which lies at the heart of his aesthetic) of the poem as a private communication in a public arena, and also resonates with something of Hopkins's idea, in one of his 'terrible sonnets', of the poem as uttering 'cries like dead letters sent / To dearest him that lives alas! away', the inscription of a blank and desolating absence. In Hopkins it is of course God who remains absent; in Graham not only the letter's absent nominal addressee but the absent reader too is always evoked, or interpellated, by the poet's vocatives and imperatives. This reader is occasionally not merely acknowledged but fictionally characterised and located in the poems, even to the extent, in 'Implements In Their Places', of being offered a blank space and invited to 'Write an Implement in it'. Being reconstituted, in one's own absence as a reader, as fictionally or imaginatively present to the writer, is a jolt of undermining estrangement – comic, intimate but also mutually isolating – exceptional even in the reflexive and deconstructive strategies of Modernist and postmodernist writing.

If there is the self-aware anxiety of desertion in his writing, the fear that, in leaving you, your work will no longer contain the identity you recognise, there is also a pleasurable curiosity about the destination it may arrive at. Solipsism is mitigated by the sense that consciousness becomes most alive in these written exchanges between writer and reader, that the most alert self-consciousness may be created and shared within the poem's language: so that the poem is always dialogue, community, invitation and intertext, 'The longed-for, loved event, / To be by another aloneness loved', 'the continual other offer', 'an aside from the monstrous'. In the 'letter' poems the acknowledgements of friendship and love win out sustainingly over the impulses to elegy, and there is always too the delighted recognition of creativity as value: the creativity of painters in their work; of lovers in relationship; and of the poet at his labour of remaking, of metamorphic self-invention, within the space of the poem. Some of Graham's finest work discovers fictions for this last crucial complex of effort, which only in some of his very latest poems comes to seem more painfully self-lacerating than consolatory. 'The Nightfishing', a lengthy sequence, runs the theme through a partly realistic account of the voyage of a herring trawler; 'Malcolm Mooney's Land' diverts it through the diary (or 'interior' diary) of an Arctic explorer; 'Johann Joachim Quantz's Five Lessons' develops it in the Browningesque dramatic monologue of an (actual) eighteenth-century German flautist and composer giving classes to an outstanding pupil; and 'Ten Shots of Mister Simpson' explores it through an intrication of the roles of poet-as-victim-of-twentieth-century-European-history and poet-as-photographer-and-assassin.

'The Nightfishing' is Graham's most concentrated and brilliant development of that marine imagery reiterated throughout his work. Its lengthiest second section is, on one level, an extremely vivid narrative of the setting out to sea, the laying-out and hauling back in of the nets, and the return to port of a herring trawler fishing presumably (although it is never named) off the Clydeside coast. The depiction has real narrative development and tension, and is an accurate rendering, often in technical nautical vocabulary, of the isolation, excitement, fear and effortfulness of the job. The 'nightfishing' is also, however, a trawling of the darkness of the mind, of the dreamlife of the unconscious, rendered articulate and communicable in the journey made by the inscriptions on the white page below the writer's lamp. In a way that perhaps owes something to Eliot's 'The Dry Salvages' and to David Jones's *The Anathemata*, the one voyage is not a mere allegory of the other but implicatively contiguous with or parallel to it. This 'nightfishing' becomes a kind of palimpsestic metaphor, the one journey written across liberatingly by the other, as writing was, literally, Graham's own liberation from the constraints of his childhood Clydeside world:

> The weather's come round. For us it's better broken.
> Changed and shifted above us, the sky is broken
> Now into a few light patches brightly ground
> With its rough smithers and those swells lengthening
> Easy on us, outside us in a slow follow
> From stern to stem. The keel in its amorous furrow
> Goes through each word. He drowns, who but ill
> Resembled me.

The old self is put off in this writing-voyage in ways that make the poem's occasional uses of a quasi-Christian vocabulary (of 'grace' and 'innocence') understandable, if both too insistent and too unexamined, a suspiciously easy and available rhetoric. The liberation is better registered, as it is here, in an erotic diction and imagery; the sequence contains its explicit love poem (with its memorable folk-like refrain, 'O my love, keep the day / Leaned at rest, leaned at rest'), and it is worth remarking how notable a love poet Graham is.

'The Nightfishing' presses almost explicitly towards a notion of the act of writing as release, enablement, revelation, *jouissance*; and in this it acts as a paradigm of the way the theme of writing is itself written in numerous shorter poems of Graham's. Some of the later sequences, however, do place more emphasis on the hardship, uncertainty and loneliness of the activity. In 'Malcolm Mooney's Land' the act of writing is read contiguously or palimpsestically with the psychological and emotional condition of Mooney, the eponymous explorer: with, that is to say, a mind in an extreme and hallucinatory state. The poem realises its basic fiction with as much imaginative vigour and particularity as the herring expedition of 'The Nightfishing', drawing on the journals of the nineteenth-century explorer Fridjof Nansen;[6] but it too accumulates a self-reflexive density and resonance, as the increasingly desperate journey across the Arctic waste is written into a (real or imaginary) notebook constituting 'This diary of a place / Writing us both in'. In 'Johann Joachim Quantz's Five Lessons' the master–pupil relationship is more straightforwardly dramatised as a *mise-en-scène* for an exploration of ageing and inheritance in an art, for a staging of tradition in process; the proud, even arrogant Quantz – Graham's most distinctively dramatised figure – comes to an unwilling acceptance of his mortality, ceding his rights in performance to the admired but envied pupil, while wryly aware of their mutual entrapment in a system of patronage rendering both the victims of snobbery and condescension.

In his last poems, however, Graham does move towards a more threatened and terrified depiction of the writerly act, one which perhaps draws on an appalled sense of twentieth-century history newly concentrated for him by such conflicts of the 1960s and 1970s as the war in Vietnam and the situation in Northern Ireland. Poems such as the remarkable 'Clusters Travelling Out' and 'What Is The Language Using Us For?' include images of institutional incarceration (political prisons, possibly, concentration camps, or madhouses) which threaten to collapse the element of joy altogether into depictions of a sinister appropriation and victimisation. 'Ten Shots of Mister Simpson' forbiddingly and unrelentingly discovers its definition in the oppositional but also, it appears, identical personae of intrusive photographer and unwilling model and of guilty but willing assassin and frightened but stealthy, pseudonymous, moving target:

> The camera nudges him to scream
> Silently into its face.
> Silently his thought recalls
> Across the side of Zennor Hill.

He is here only recalling
Himself being pointed at
By somebody ago and even not
Understanding the language.

The art that this brings to mind is not the joyfully erotic semi-abstraction of Roger Hilton but the ghastly figuration of Francis Bacon, his silent screams from bodies in confined spaces. Yet Mister Simpson's plight is evoked not only by the language's description of his physical and mental gestures but by its own more 'abstract' properties too. His fearful incomprehension of the language of his terroriser is written across as well as into the poem by a disintegration, in the final lines, of correct English idiom and skilfully managed cadence, by the effect of a translation suddenly gone terribly awry.

This is a long way from the derivative pseudo-Apocalyptic manner with which Graham began. Yet it shares with it, perhaps, a certain preservation in the poem's final form of the improvisatory and the impulsive, no longer expressed as fecund patterns of homogeneous imagery but as more integrally organised and expressive structures of syntax and rhythm. As we might anticipate from such a self-reflexive writer, towards the end of his career he articulates his own journey from the one to the other in the wittily aphoristic punning of 'Implements In Their Places':

When I was a buoy it seemed
Craft of rare tonnage
Moored to me. Now
Occasionally a skiff
Is tied to me and tugs
At the end of its tether.

The flavour of the infatuation with Dylan Thomas among his contemporaries and juniors, and of the bardic conception of the role of the poet which it manifests, is accurately caught in what now seems a hilariously solemn and reverential remark of George Barker's. Thomas, he says in a memorial essay, 'had married the art of poetry not in a registry office or a library or a lecture room, but in a church'.[7] The true note of the neo-Romantic bohemianism of Barker himself is caught in those terms of approbation. Poetry is both sexuality and sacrament; it is a commitment to a style of life as well as a style of writing; it is anti-academic and anti-official; it takes cognisance of values attaching to a religion which, even if its official forms are lost to the modern world, still questions the automatically assumed values of that world; and it may well include an element of reactionary social snobbery: if the priest always incarnates a value lost to the registrar, then perhaps the aristocrat preserves a value lost to the contemporary bourgeois. Barker lived the life of the poet according to this conception with verve, panache and a certain elegantly autocratic hauteur. If Thomas was, as he once called himself, 'the Rimbaud of Cwmdonkin Drive', Barker has been a native Villon: the bohemian hero of the sexual and legal transgressions recorded in Elizabeth Smart's poetic novel *By Grand Central Station I Sat Down And Wept*, and surely also coded into a number of his own early poems; the cataloguer of his own sexual, social and intellectual adventures in a world of poets and artists in Italy as well as England, whose habitués include some of the minor 'characters' of the time (Robert Colquhoun, Robert MacBryde, John Minton), and the eventual sad elegist of that world; the scapegrace always in search of grace, praying an agnostic's anxious prayers, a *jongleur* before an absconded God and his absconded Mother; a Dionysus tempted by the ascesis of crucifixion.

The association with Villon, 'frank villain', is made by Barker himself in the two parts of *The True Confession of George Barker*, published in 1950 and 1964. The poem's stanza form is taken from Villon's *Le Testament*, as is its provision of the poet with a capacious structure in which to review a life of some apparent disgrace. The jauntiness of Barker's tone and the withholding of any very deep self-castigation probably owe as much to Byron as to Villon, as the casual, ironised and sceptical licentiousness catches a tone from Catullus; and the form decisively saves him from the temptations of what had become a rather too easy neo-Romantic manner. In his earlier work there is considerable surface attractiveness but the eye is hardly ever stayed or steadied by anything arresting. The attractiveness is the attractiveness of liquescence, and Barker lacks Thomas's flair for the memorable line and the pungent aphorism. As a result, even the most savage messiahs appear in this poetry with a peculiarly equable tread, unhurried by the nurturing deliquescence:

> My nine-tiered tigress in the cage of sex
> I feed with meat that you tear from my side
> Crowning your nine months with the paradox:
> The love that kisses with a homicide
> In robes of red generation resurrects.

Indeed, in his earlier as in his later work, the finest poems are often those which have the least dependence on the characteristic Barker 'vision': the much-anthologised 'To My Mother', for instance, with its larger-than-life affectionate caricaturing ('She is a procession no one can follow after / But be like a little dog following a brass band') and the remarkable 'On a Friend's Escape from Drowning off the Norfolk Coast' from *A Vision of Beasts and Gods* (1954).

The True Confession diverts the Barker-Apocalyptic into a more meditated, personal and reserved manner which can accommodate both Villonesque poignancies and Swiftian excoriations, moving limpidly between satire and elegy. Confessing himself an 'Augustinian anarchist', Barker locates moments of self-scrutiny in a way that preserves the Catholic dimension of the word 'confession': the references to Augustine (as to Pascal and Newman) are those of a man genuinely learned in a Christian-moralistic tradition. If the posture is penitential, however, the sentiment is agnostic, and the effort is, however shamefacedly, oriented at least as much towards poetic ambition as towards metaphysical assurance or moral absolution:

> Those that speak most are most dumb.
>> Who speaks for me? The poem speaks.
> I confess, Rhetorician, I'm
>> At heart one of those moral freaks
> Not satisfied that they exist
>> Until they make a noise in rime.
> But then, He's dumb most of the time,
>> My heavenly ventriloquist.

In such lines Barker's true Penelope is not Dylan Thomas, with his pantheist acceptance, but Eliot: misgiving even when making an act of faith; sceptical, withheld and suspicious even when attempting to affirm. Behind Eliot too there is Baudelaire and the notorious Eliotic view in his essay on Baudelaire that 'it is better, in a paradoxical way, to do evil than to do nothing: at least, we exist'.[8] Barker is a poet who, even if he cannot bring himself to believe in a Christian God, has no trouble believing in sin.

This may well be Barker's essential contribution: he is a poet of the neo-Romantic whose rhetoric is always fissured by a very traditional sense of original sin (his poems frequently cite Newman's 'aboriginal calamity'). Where in a large number of neo-Romantic poems the Christian imagery seems deployed more for its emotional, rhetorical or theatrical appeal, in Barker it is guiltily haunted by doctrinal demand. God's silence in *The True Confession* persists into the long poem which seems to me Barker's finest, 'Anno Domini', the title poem of a volume published in 1983. The way Barker addresses the absent God in the earlier poem ('Rhetorician' in the lines above, for instance) also persists: in 'Anno Domini' God is, variously, 'magister', 'professor', 'lord chief justice', 'dominie' and also 'mediator', 'arbiter of dreams', 'star of the sea' and even 'Leda'. The desired God is not, then, in any sense, the God of Christian orthodoxy, but an outsider God, a kind of pariah God: hermaphroditic, both judging and accommodating. Written as a form of prayer, the poem seems almost a cross between some of John Berryman's late poems (Berryman is commemorated in the volume *Dialogues, Etc.* of

1976, whose title also almost certainly alludes to Berryman's final posthumous volume, *Delusions, Etc.* of 1972) and David Jones's *The Tutelar of the Place*. The manner is both idiomatic and incantatory, vulnerable and autocratic – in, as it seems, virtually the same breath:

> – at a time of bankers
>   to exercise a little charity;
> at a time of soldiers
>   to cultivate small gardens;
> at a time of categorical imperatives
>   to guess about clouds;
> at a time of politicians
>   to trust only to children and demigods.

As these opening lines suggest, 'Anno Domini' works by a series of oppositions in which a strikingly neo-Romantic Arcadian ideal of the small, the ecologically sound, the childlike and the Barker-religious position themselves against an idea of the Modern constituted of the homogeneous, the bourgeois-capitalist, the militaristic, the debasedly secular and the mercenary or opportunistic. These oppositions are unlikely to meet with much opposition from many of Barker's readers; and they therefore run the risk of appearing self-flatteringly righteous or sentimentally unworldly. The risk is met, however, by the depth of Barker's intellectual and emotional response to the world he is castigating. If this is a poem hostile to various conceptions of the modern (or the postmodern), it is also a poem capable of alluding sympathetically to the theories of Heisenberg and Max Planck; if it opposes the behaviourist theories of B.F. Skinner, it conveys a strong sense that it has understood them in a more than merely layman's way. The poem's form, at once drifting and tensile, draws on King James cadences and early English alliterative metres; it makes room for a variety of tone and address in which the sharply satiric is matched with wit, good humour and affection, and matched too by a strongly elegiac mood in which this modern Villon begins almost to speak in the accents of *Ecclesiastes*. However, if the poet is perturbed by 'the huge masonry of / collapsing belief', this poem is no jeremiad: the house in which traditional belief is collapsing is all too anxiously, self-laceratingly and bewilderedly his own. The poem as a prayer addressed to 'the huge sybil / of your absence' restrains its urge to condemnation in gestures of self-mockery and self-doubt. The Apocalypse and neo-Romanticism of the 1940s thereby find one of their most unpredictable and satisfying later transformations at the end of 'Anno Domini' when, out of the wreckage of some imagined future catastrophe, not a Christian God but that pagan poet-god who so often seems implicitly to attend Dionysus in the neo-Romantic dream steps explicitly forward:

    The snows of yesterday have returned
to those clouds from which they will fall
    tomorrow disguised as summer and
one day the seas will part and from the fissure
    Orpheus rise up festooned
with telephone wires to teach us
    the triumph of the incommunicable.

Notes

1. Cited in Robert Hewison, *Under Siege: Literary Life in London 1939–1945* (London: Weidenfeld and Nicolson, 1977), p. 7.

2. See *New Verse*, nos. 26–7 (November 1937), p. 9.

3. J.F. Hendry and Henry Treece (eds), *The White Horseman: Prose and Verse of the New Apocalypse* (London: Routledge, 1941), p. 30.

4. See, for instance, David Mellor (ed.), *A Paradise Lost: The Neo-Romantic Imagination in Britain 1935–1955* (London: Lund Humphries, 1987).

5. William Empson, *Argufying*, ed. John Haffenden (London: The Hogarth Press, 1988), pp. 382–6.

6. For an account of Nansen's influence on the poem, see Tony Lopez's illuminating reading of it in *The Poetry of W.S Graham* (Edinburgh: Edinburgh Univesity Press, 1989).

7. See E.W. Tedlock (ed.), *Dylan Thomas: The Legend and the Poet* (London: Heinemann, 1960), p. 72.

8. T.S. Eliot, *Selected Essays* (London: Faber and Faber, 1951), p. 429.

Chapter 5
The Poetry of a Second War
Keith Douglas, Alun Lewis and Others

I have suggested above that some of the major attributes of the 1940s
Apocalyptic and New Romantic styles were shared with some of the
poetry of the period more explicitly concerned with the war itself: in
particular, the strong sense of the material body and of personal identity
being under threat of invasion or disintegration. To this extent, there is
no absolute disjunction between neo-Romanticism in poetry and the
poetry of war in the period, particularly since some of the significant
war poetry is poetry by non-combatant civilians. The connection is at its
most intense in the career of Sidney Keyes, who died as a combatant in
Tunisia in 1943, aged twenty; his neo-Romantic style culminates in
poems such as 'The Wilderness', in which the common imagistic stock
takes on a new intensity of contemporary meaning: 'Flesh is fire, frost
and fire: / Flesh is fire in this wilderness of fire / Which is our
dwelling'. Once the 'phoney war' of autumn 1939 to spring 1940 ended
with Hitler's invasion of Belgium and Holland, and particularly, of
course, when British cities became the target of German air-raids,
civilians were at least as much under threat as the armed forces, and the
whole country was under threat of invasion. The civilian mood of this
moment is caught at its highest pitch of intensity, probably, in prose by
Graham Greene, Elizabeth Bowen and Henry Green; but there is a
substantial body of interesting poetic response too.

There are, as I have already suggested, the large works which include
a reaction to the war, Eliot's *Four Quartets* and David Jones's *The
Anathëmata* (together with the American poet H.D.'s *Trilogy*), but there
is also a significant range of shorter lyrics. These include a number of
poems employing a heightened Christian symbolism, such as Edith
Sitwell's 'Still Falls The Rain' and her poem on Hiroshima, 'The
Shadow of Cain' ('And yet – who dreamt that Christ has died in vain? /
He comes again on the Sea of Blood. He comes in the terrible Rain.')
and David Gascoyne's 'Ecco Homo' and 'Miserere'. There are important
Blitz poems, as we have seen, by MacNeice and Dylan Thomas. There
is C. Day Lewis's 'Watching Post', a kind of eclogue in which the poet

crosses class and educational barriers by watching with a farmer. Together they figure the England worth preserving or 'watching' over and, indeed, Day Lewis worked during the war on a translation of Vergil's *Georgics*, those poems of the land by the poet of imperial Rome. And there are such much-anthologised poems glancingly incorporating references to the war as George Barker's 'To My Mother' ('She will not glance up at the bomber or condescend / To drop her gin and scuttle to a cellar') and R.S. Thomas's 'A Peasant', written in 1944 ('. . . he, too, is a winner of wars, / Enduring like a tree under the curious stars'). There are also the poems by women, retrieved by Catherine Reilly in her anthology *Chaos of the Night* (1984), such as Alice Coats's feminist satire about war work by women ('The newsboy and the boy who drives the plough: / Postman and milkman – all are ladies now') and the classical calm of E.J. Scovell's 'Days Drawing In' ('Sweet the grey morning and the raiders gone'); but most harrowingly the large number of elegies for lovers, husbands, brothers, sons, including the achingly sad 'War Baby' by Pamela Holmes (preceded in the anthology by two poems entitled 'Parting in April' and 'Missing, Presumed Killed'):

> He has not even seen you, he
> Who gave you your mortality;
> And you, so small, how can you guess
> His courage or his loveliness?
>
> Yet in my quiet mind I pray
> He passed you on the darkling way –
> His death, your birth, so much the same –
> And holding you, breathed once your name.

The fact that non-combatants were often as much under threat as combatants made for some difficulties for the combatant poets of the war (in addition, of course, to their difficulties as men coping with the fact that those they loved were often in more danger than they were themselves). Unlike the poets of the First World War, they had no scope for the kind of ambition which sustained Wilfred Owen: to 'educate' civilians to 'the actualities of war'. The danger of being burnt alive in a tank in the desert was equalled by the danger of being burnt alive in the streets of London or Sheffield. This simple fact, which is a fact about all modern warfare, meant that poetry in anything of the First World War manner was an impossibility, and that, consequently, it was much harder to establish a 'genre' of Second World War poetry. This may partially explain why there are so few sustained bodies of notable work by individual poets, and why single poems by particular writers seem to make the whole statement that that writer has to make, very much in the manner of the civilian poetry of the period. Roy Fuller's 'The

Middle of a War' is one such instance. Contemplating Fuller's own youthful photograph as if from the perspective of posterity after his early death, the poem has been wittily and truly said by Ian Hamilton to have a 'defeated, sardonic manner' which conveys 'the sense of being in an obvious novel written by someone hardly known and not admired, a slightly boring cycle that is "historic" and "preordained" ' – a comment applicable to a number of other combatant poems.[1] Other striking single poems include Charles Causley's 'Song of the Dying Gunner AA1', the most memorable of his numerous early ballad-metre poems; Gavin Ewart's serious *humoresque*, 'Officer's Mess' (harbinger of a career of numerous others of the kind); F.T. Prince's 'Soldiers Bathing' which, exceptionally (as Paul Fussell has shown), inherits a central motif of the poetry of the First World War;[2] and Henry Reed's outstanding sequence 'Lessons of the War', a definitive account of the way a military discourse sullies and dishonours the objects it reifies:

> The still white dwellings are like a mirage in the heat,
> And under the swaying elms a man and a woman
> Lie gently together. Which is, perhaps, only to say
> That there is a row of houses to the left of arc,
> And that under some poplars a pair of what appear to be humans
>   Appear to be loving.

The great exceptions to these intermittent wartime poems are the careers of Keith Douglas and Alun Lewis, who were both killed during the war and both of whom have suffered from under-representation in the literary histories. Douglas's poems were not collected until 1951, and he was only properly edited, by Desmond Graham, in 1978 (although Ted Hughes edited and introduced an excellent selection in 1964); and there has never been a collected edition of Alun Lewis, though there ought to be. Both are poets meriting sustained critical attention: Douglas has, to some extent, received it, notably from Ted Hughes and Geoffrey Hill, and has therefore belatedly insinuated himself into a continuity in English poetry of the period; but Lewis has been allowed to drop from proper visibility.

In a draft for an essay entitled 'Poets in this War' probably written in May 1943, Douglas explores some of the reasons why, in his view, the war has, by that stage, thrown up no genuinely significant poetry. The long period of the 'phoney war' left little to write about, particularly among poets who had already commemorated the Spanish Civil War; if there were poets at Dunkirk then 'they stayed there'; the preoccupations and manner of the younger civilian poets lead them to contemplate the war only by turning a 'delicate shoulder' to it (he cites John Heath-Stubbs's, *Wounded Thammuz*); the mechanisation and mobility of the present war offer unique practical difficulties to the writer. But the greatest obstacle is the intrinsic literary one:

> . . . hell cannot be let loose twice: it was let loose in the Great
> War and it is the same old hell now. The hardships, pain and
> boredom; the behaviour of the living and the appearance of the
> dead, were so accurately described by the poets of the Great War
> that everyday on the battlefields of the western desert . . . their
> poems are illustrated. Almost all that a modern poet on active
> service is inspired to write, would be tautological.[3]

Douglas's own effort is therefore shadowed by this unillusioned
recognition of the obstacles, this testimony to a fairly comprehensive
anxiety of influence. His own poem 'Russians', written before his war
experience, is satiric in a way clearly deriving from Owen and Sassoon;
and even two poems written during his time in the Middle East, 'The
Trumpet' and 'Gallantry', maintain the association, while the fine poem
'Desert Flowers' memorably acknowledges an indebtedness: 'Rosenberg
I only repeat what you were saying'.

   This anxiety about being drawn back into a literary past is paralleled
in Douglas by an equal and opposite anxiety about being drawn forward
into a dangerous and all too predictable future, a future which will
include one's early death in combat; from a very early stage his is a
poetry of foreboding. The unique style he achieved in his finest poems
derives from the effort both to cope with the former and to
accommodate the latter. His own formulation of his later procedures is
expressed in two letters of 10 June and 10 August 1943 in which he
rejects some criticisms made by his correspondent. The necessity of the
time, he claims, is that he write a 'réportage [sic] and extrospective (if
the word exists) poetry'; his style must 'reflect the cynicism and careful
absence of expectation (it is not quite the same as apathy) with which I
view the world':

> To be sentimental or emotional now is dangerous to oneself and
> to others. To trust anyone or to admit any hope of a better world
> is criminally foolish, as foolish as it is to stop working for it. It
> sounds silly to say work without hope, but it can be done; it's
> only a form of insurance; it doesn't mean work hopelessly.[4]

What gives Douglas's works its strength is that the programme outlined
here, while it was of course a response to the conditions in which he
found himself in the mechanised slaughter of tank warfare in the Middle
Eastern desert (and about which he wrote excellently in his prose
account *Alamein to Zem Zem*, 1946) was also, as it were, a programme
inscribed in his whole nature and system. The lack of trust (for him
perhaps consequent upon his father's desertion of the family in his

childhood); the refusal (or fear) of any direct statement of emotion; the stoic, sardonic 'absence of expectation' (how revealing his word 'careful' is, as though this absence is to be nurtured in the face of a desire for its opposite, which self-knowledge realises can lead only to disappointment): all are present too in much of his earlier work, which is astonishingly precocious. There is, in particular, 'Canoe', which could be said to be heavy with foreboding, were it not that the poem's rhythms and cadences are so light, spontaneous and effortless, with exactly that kind of approximation and tentativeness characteristic of the war poems too. Written while he was an undergraduate, the poem opens with its poet 'thinking this may be my last / summer'; and it ends with a vision of his own ghost appearing in this otherwise exactly similar scene the following summer:

> Whistle and I will hear
> and come another evening, when this boat

> travels with you alone toward Iffley:
> as you lie looking up for thunder again,
> this cool touch does not betoken rain;
> it is my spirit that kisses your mouth lightly.

These lines are themselves written 'lightly' in many senses, which is not to say that they are not also in deadly earnest; in fact it is their certainty of their own prophetic power that restrains them from all morbidity. Soliciting nothing from the reader, they are calm in their annotation of the moment of foreboding, but calm with the certainty that nothing is to be expected, that everything is to be endured – not heroically or defiantly, by the exceptional individual, just naturally and inevitably, by everyone, as a consequence merely of living in this place at this time. They are lines implicitly refusing both the pathos of Owen and the grimly embittered satire of Sassoon; but they make it altogether appropriate that Rosenberg should be the one poet of the First World War actually named in Douglas's own poems: such a poem as Rosenberg's 'Break of Day in the Trenches', with its casually quotidian sense that the soldier is merely keeping an appointment, seems close to Douglas's own calmly unsettling recognitions.

The deep self-estrangement witnessed in 'Canoe', and the poem's radical association of sexuality and death, both figure as significant subsequent preoccupations. In 'Dead Men', thinking of the lovemaking going on elsewhere, Douglas notes: 'I in another place / see the white dresses glimmer like moths': he is, of course, on the desert battlefield. His finest poems of the war derive from this sense of being in 'another place'. The 'reportage' of 'Cairo Jag' views the Alamein dead as tourists: 'a man with no head / has a packet of chocolate and a souvenir of

Tripoli'. In 'Vergissmeinnicht' the dead soldier in his 'gunpit spoil' lies next to the photograph of 'Steffi', his lover, who 'would weep to see today / how on his skin the swart flies move'. Such contiguities, in which social and moral worlds usually inconceivably remote from one another are newly aligned, seem a major feature of Douglas's modernity; but they are underwritten by that most traditional of contiguities: a consciousness of the dead skeleton inside the living body. This is expressed in its most charged form in 'The Prisoner' where, touching the face of the beloved woman, Cheng, is to discover, instantly, a death-mask:

> There was the urge
> to escape the bright flesh and emerge
> of the ambitious cruel bone.

Such an alignment of separate places in discordant and disconcerting ways and the establishment of new necessities and contiguities form the basis of Douglas's final style. Ted Hughes has notably remarked of it that it is 'a utility general-purpose style' . . that seems able to deal poetically with whatever it comes up against'; and Geoffrey Hill has discovered in it an attitude to metaphor such that it is always 'changing position slightly, seeking the most precise hold'.[5] Adaptability, mobility, speed, flexibility, subtleties of accommodation and exchange, are of its essence. It is a style evolved to bear the brunt of great pressure, and to withstand such pressure from a position of real strength, but it is a strength like that of the ballet dancers who form the subject of several of his earlier poems: a strength at the service of delicacy, fragility and grace. A ballet of limpid approximation and discovery, his style is also developed out of a reticence which is more that of the anxious child than that of the officer and gentleman (in 'Saturday Morning in Jerusalem' he actually sees himself as 'the boy lost on his first morning at school'). It is a style in which a deeply reserved and complex sensibility veers close to and pulls back from its own inwardnesses, withdrawing to a fine edge of nervousness. Some of its greatest successes come when the complexity of emotion is at its most baffled and delicate and the moment of recognition feels forward into the suppleness of exact transcription.

'How to Kill' is one such poem. It handles that most intractable subject, the soldier's duty to kill, and handles it in the most direct fashion: by recreating the moment when the soldier-poet trains his sights on his victim. It is almost as though the poem is written as opposition and antithesis to Owen's 'Strange Meeting', where the killing is removed from its actual specification and location into the mythologised Hades of an afterlife, with its consequent Vergilian pathos of mutual recognition. Douglas foregrounds the decisive moment when the trigger is pulled by printing the decision in upper case ('NOW'), and the poem moves to its conclusion by gradually withdrawing from decision into reflection:

> Death like a familiar, hears

> and look, has made a man of dust
> of a man of flesh. This sorcery
> I do. Being damned, I am amused
> to see the centre of love diffused
> and the waves of love travel into vacancy.
> How easy it is to make a ghost.

> The weightless mosquito touches
> her tiny shadow on the stone,
> and with how like, how infinite
> a lightness, man and shadow meet.
> They fuse. A shadow is a man
> when the mosquito death approaches.

These lines are unsettling in the most literal sense: they fail to settle on any single response or any single figure. The soldier-poet cries 'NOW' and a personified Death answers: so the degree of responsibility is shared if not off-loaded; it is as though the poet is acting as the mere agent of death for the enemy soldier – which, of course, he is, according to the rules of military engagement (which make him, legally, non-culpable). But this poet refuses non-culpability. Threaded through the figure of a personified Death is the metaphor of sorcery. Death is the sorcerer's familiar, doing his bidding; the 'sorcery' is the transformation of a live into a dead body; and the poet-sorcerer is of course 'damned' for such black magic. That Christian register is itself immediately undermined by the shockingly urbane 'amusement' to which its acknowledgement gives rise; but that urbanity is then the opportunity to introduce the idea that this now dead body was, like that in 'Vergissmeinnicht', loved by someone. And that prompts the more sombre, saddened and self-doubting reflection with which the penultimate stanza concludes. The final stanza seems itself almost weightless, as it moves from its literal mosquito to its resonantly metaphoric 'mosquito death'. The transition is managed with extraordinary deftness, but it is a transition suddenly and unpredictably organising and focusing the whole poem. Death now, far from being a personified abstraction (and to that extent a time-honoured and probably anachronistic poetic device) becomes a mere element of the environment. The figure reduces the complexities of responsibility, guilt, permission and justification which have hovered over the metaphors of the previous stanza to a feature of geography; the implication is that death in a war comes as naturally and inevitably as death in nature. Once you are in this place you cannot avoid either killing or being killed.

The poem does not choose among the range of implications of the figures it slips and slides between; the slippage itself is the point. 'How to Kill' manifestly does not know how it feels about how to kill; and its syntactical and metaphoric procedures imitate its confusions. It is itself a testing and probing of what might be said, a spider-like reticulation of possibilities: 'and with how like, how infinite / a lightness' puts its spider foot here, and again here, in an attempt actually to ask the question asked by the title, 'how?', and the repetitions and the assonantal move from 'like' to 'lightness' quietly insinuate a conception of the poem as a process of constantly readjusted moral perspective. In the finest of Douglas's war poems it is as though a Donnean kind of 'metaphysical' poem has been assimilated and adapted into something more plastic, fluid and transparent, providing a vehicle whose technical ingenuity acts as a moral and emotional resource.

Edna Longley has memorably characterised Keith Douglas's work as 'not skeletal poetry, but poetry with no superfluous flesh, fighting fit, the cadence of energy'.[6] Alun Lewis, the other fine talent killed in the war, may be said, rather, to possess a cadence of withdrawal. In a poetry much given to silence, darkness and isolation, Lewis names Edward Thomas rather than Isaac Rosenberg; and Thomas's ruminative melancholy is a constant shadow. If this derives from Lewis's personality, however, it also measures the difference between his war and that fought by Douglas. The cadence of Douglas's nervous energy responds to the unpredictability and danger of tank warfare in the desert. The cadence of withdrawal in Lewis, on the other hand, responds to long enforced periods of idleness in training camps in England; to the sadness of parting from a wife for service overseas (and the deep empathy for women enduring civilian warfare and bereavement which this primary absence seems to have provoked); to the despairing imperial guilt suffered by this Welsh socialist while stationed in India (learning at first hand 'the subterfuges of democracy'); and to the process of attrition and sudden cruel engagement which was the reality of jungle warfare in Burma, where Lewis died mysteriously in 1944.

Lewis is, however, manifestly fighting some of the same demons as Douglas, seeking a strategy to cope with the fact that he may well not survive. 'Acceptance seems so spiritless, protest so vain,' he wrote in a letter of 1943: 'In between the two I live'.[7] The mood induced by this position of balanced stasis is superbly caught by one of the poems in which he names Edward Thomas, 'All Day It Has Rained'. The poem clearly remembers the many poems of Thomas in which rain figures as an emotional as well as an actual weather (particularly one of Thomas's best-known poems, 'Rain' – written in 1916 – with its explicit 'love of death'). In Lewis the rain figures as a correlative for the boredom, frustration and lassitude of the soldier's life in a training camp, the endless weary monotony of a routine away from longed-for companions; and the poem is one of the most sensitive and penetrating records left of this kind of military experience during the war. But the rain also develops in implication as the poem proceeds, taking on a more than merely descriptive connotation. Itemising the soldier's talk – of girls, bombs, 'the quiet dead', the 'loud celebrities / Exhorting us to slaughter' and 'the herded refugees' – the poem deepens into an evocation of the mood or atmosphere in which such talk has its being:

> – Yet thought softly, morosely of them, and as indifferently
> As of ourselves or those whom we
> For years have loved, and will again
> Tomorrow maybe love; but now it is the rain
> Possesses us entirely, the twilight and the rain.

This almost hallucinatory indifference is Lewis's response to the imposed facts of his wartime experience, as Douglas's is the energised will to action. When the end of 'All Day It Has Rained' includes a reference to Edward Thomas, it is to remember how he 'brooded long / On death and beauty – till a bullet stopped his song': the clear implication is that Lewis's own similar melancholy brooding may have a similar end in sudden violent death.

The deepest impulsion in Lewis's work is what might, indeed, be considered the tragedy of indifference necessitated by the war for this man of deep, subtle and complex feeling. A willed indifference is his perfectly comprehensible response to such evidence of transience as is offered by the imagist stillness at the end of the ironically exquisite 'Raiders' Dawn', for instance, where, after the dawn raid:

> Blue necklace left
> On a charred chair
> Tells that Beauty
> Was startled there.

Like some of the London wartime prose of Graham Greene and Elizabeth Bowen, this poem pits the frailty of human lovers against the fury of aerial bombardment. The terror is compacted into this deftly controlled quatrain, the coloured necklace (still mutely carrying its history of sexuality and relationship) surviving the charring to ash of everything else in the lovers' bedroom, and the abstracting personification 'Beauty', combined with the devastating exactness of 'startled', supplying a steely, reserved understatement. The stanza has something of the intensity of elided emotion and narrative to be found in the best of haiku.

Against such lucid sensings of inevitability Lewis's poems seek out areas of solitude and quiet where 'the long Unseen', 'the strange Unknown', and 'the hinted land' into which Edward Thomas is imagined disappearing at the end of a poem addressed to him may be both given identity and endured. In some of his finest poems, to look into the heart of various silences is also to look proleptically into his own death; the quiet of his work is, in the end, the sign of an ultimate indifference, one in which Nature has become indifferent to him, since he has become absent from the world, invisible to it. As in 'All Day It Has Rained', these episodes in Lewis often have an almost hallucinatory or dreamlike quality. 'The dream / Emerging from the fact that folds a dream' is how the moment is evoked in the Edward Thomas poem; and the phrase may be usefully held in apposition with central moments in Lewis himself. In 'The Soldier', for instance, a mood of calm is induced by watching 'the flash and play' of finches and responding to their 'indifference' to him; in 'Karanje Village' a statue of the Indian god Vishnu is read as 'Silently and eternally simply Being, / Bidding me come alone' into a state of virtual disembodiment; in 'Water Music' the dark interior of an Indian lake is imagined singing a song of ineffable yearning, heralding the 'ending / Of the heart and its ache'; and in 'Burma Casualty', imagining the near-death of a badly wounded soldier, Lewis names the dark quiet of a foreseen death in an astonishing trope, both erotic and religious, reminding us how potent an influence the J.B. Leishman translations of Rilke (that poet much obsessed by death and transfiguration) were for many poets of this generation:

> The dark is a beautiful singing sexless angel
> Her hands so soft you scarcely feel her touch
> Gentle, eternally gentle, round your heart.
> She flatters and unsexes every man.

If 'Burma Casualty' is one side of the tragedy of indifference and necessity in Lewis, the other is less self-preoccupied. In 'All Day It Has Rained' 'those whom we / For years have loved' are prominent in the itemisations of those things to which the soldiers are now indifferent; and the pitch of quasi-mystical intensity to which the Vishnu brings Lewis in 'Karanje Village' culminates in anguished self-questioning:

> And when my sweetheart calls me shall I tell her
> That I am seeking less and less of world?
> And will she understand?

For a poet who has, occasionally, his youthfully bittersweet sentimentalities, Lewis is unafraid to face in his work this most perturbing of all potential indifferences: the fact that the enforced separations of wartime appear to cancel out the image of the beloved (possibly replacing it with some of those 'strange desires' alluded to in 'A Troopship in the Tropics'). It is perhaps the complex response to such knowledge, with its anxieties, guilts, self-doubtings and despairs, that makes Lewis such a fine poet of the moment of parting and of the sorrows of women in separation and bereavement, selflessly desiring what 'After Dunkirk' names as 'The dark imagination that would pierce / Infinite night and reach the waiting arms / And soothe the guessed-at tears'.

That 'dark imagination' is finely at work in such varied poems as 'The Departure' with its evocation of the woman's bravery at the barrier on the quay, 'Giving the world a dab of rouge and powder, / A toss of the head, a passing hatred'; the tenderly erotic 'Goodbye', with its almost cinematic interior with figures, the lovers poignantly trying to find a way to 'make an end of lying down together'; and 'Lady in Black', which allegorises, in an almost expressionist manner, the combat between Death and a mother bereaved of a son. One of the strongest of these poems, however, is 'Song (On seeing dead bodies floating off the Cape)', which transposes some apparently autobiographical elements into the monologue of the grief-stricken widow of (presumably) one of the soldiers whose bodies now lie drowned in the ocean. The poem's final stanza reads back into the bereaved woman's consciousness feelings which are also clearly Lewis's own, and compounds the self-reflexiveness and involution even further by having her, in the final line, envisage the man's disappearance from her consciousness as well as from the world:

> But oh! the drag and dullness of my Self;
> The turning seasons wither in my head;
> All this slowness, all this hardness,
> The nearness that is waiting in my bed,
> The gradual self-effacement of the dead.

The issues of gender and identity to which such poems give rise are complemented by an explicitly anti-imperialist politics in Lewis. His first poems took as material the victimisations of Welsh colliery communities; and in South Africa, India and Burma he is brought face to face with the realities of twentieth-century imperialism. Consequently, the word 'dark' undergoes a newly politicised metamorphosis in the ironically entitled 'Home Thoughts from Abroad', where a consciousness of the 'troubled continents' created by the 'blue nostalgic moods' of 'the West' fractures with revulsion whatever home thoughts may be had of an England 'Whose bridle paths all end in dark'. As in Edward Thomas himself, the private melancholy of the rural English scene is made to bear the brunt of a newly international distress. In the end for Alun Lewis the moments of quiet sought with greater and greater urgency in his final poems are sought as a means of excluding the exploitative policies of British imperialism. 'The Jungle' puts this at its finest and suggests how significant and badly neglected a poet Alun Lewis is:

> But we who dream beside this jungle pool
> Prefer the instinctive rightness of the poised
> Pied kingfisher deep darting for a fish
> To all the banal rectitude of states,
> The dew-bright diamonds on a viper's back
> To the slow poison of a meaning lost
> And the vituperations of the just.

Notes

1. Ian Hamilton, *A Poetry Chronicle: Essays and Reviews* (London: Faber and Faber, 1973), p. 59.

2 See Paul Fussell, *The Great War and Modern Memory* (New York and London: Oxford University Press, 1975), p. 307.

3. Keith Douglas, *A Prose Miscellany*, ed. Desmond Graham (Manchester: Carcanet Press, 1985), pp. 117–20.

4. ibid., pp. 121 and 127–8.

5. See Hughes's introduction to his edition of Douglas's *Selected Poems* (London: Faber and Faber, 1964) and Hill's review of this, ' "I in Another Place": Homage to Keith Douglas', *Stand*, vol. 5 no. 4 (1964–5), pp. 6–13.

6. Edna Longley, *Poetry in the Wars* (Newcastle upon Tyne: Bloodaxe Books, 1986), p. 111.

7. Cited in Alun Lewis, *Selected Poetry and Prose*, edited with a biographical introduction by Ian Hamilton (London: George Allen and Unwin, 1966), p. 53.

Chapter 6
Two Solitudes
Stevie Smith and R.S. Thomas

Becoming known as poets in the 1940s, both Stevie Smith and R.S. Thomas have affinities with some of the poetries I have discussed above. I have noted that, to some extent, Thomas's famous poem 'A Peasant' is to be regarded as a war poem, and that the foregrounded Welshness of his work has its analogues in other types of 1940s regionalism and cultural nationalism. Stevie Smith is the author of a civilian war poem of a kind, 'The Poets Are Silent', which typifies her in its spirited decidedness and in its refusal to defend its point of view ('I say that it is to the poets' merit / To be silent about the war'). And, in both, a series of attitudes to Christianity is a focus of attention, in a way manifestly part of the intellectual apparatus of the 'Forties poet'. Yet neither was ever involved in any more official grouping, nor will any general rubric suffice for them: partly for reasons of gender and of cultural and national identity. Excluded from some of the usual 1940s channels of metropolitan literary and cultural power, they are poets of lonely singularity and distinction.

One of Stevie Smith's strongest anecdotal poems is 'A Soldier Dear to Us' published in a posthumous volume, *Scorpion and Other Poems* (1971). It recalls the presence, in her suburban household during the First World War (when she was twelve), of invalided Army officers, one of whom has died, just prior to the poem's composition, as a long-delayed result of his shrapnel wounds. The poem remembers the child's interest and involvement and celebrates the soldier's fortitude:

> Coming to our house
> Were the brave ones. And I could not look at them,
> For my strong feelings, except
> Slantingly, from the hearth rug, look at them.
> Oh Basil, Basil, you had such a merry heart
> But you taught me a secret you did not perhaps mean to impart,
> That one must speak lightly, and use fair names like the ladies

> They used to call
> The Eumenides.

Smith's poems often set her – or one of her narrators, characters or voices – in the position of child, pupil or *ingénue* (*Mother, What Is Man?* is the ingenuous title of a volume she published during the war); and 'A Soldier Dear to Us' makes plain the lesson and the 'secret' which seem to me to inform all of her finest work. She is indeed a poet of 'strong feelings', particularly about loneliness, conventionality and death, but, like Emily Dickinson, she believes that if a truth is to be told about such things, it must be told 'slant'; and it will almost certainly prove to be a truth dependent on an ideal stoicism. There are not many poets who would associate speaking lightly, as Stevie Smith does here, with those voices of Greek fatalism and prophetic doom, the Eumenides: her own levity of speech, however, should never be mistaken for 'light verse'. Its style and manner is her perverse, entirely *sui generis* and inimitable way of exploring some of the darkest and most disintegrative emotions.

Speaking lightly, for Stevie Smith, is a matter of employing, in much of her work, various oral and quasi-oral forms – ballads, folk-songs, hymnodic patterns, carols – and, in other pieces, particularly those of a more extended kind, using rhythm and rhyme with a childlike, seemingly improvisatory approximation. (She did actually sing or chant her work at poetry readings with an effect Seamus Heaney has characterised as 'pitching between querulousness and keening, her quizzical presence at once inviting the audience to yield her their affection and keeping them at bay with a quick irony'.[1]) With their casual, impressionistic punctuation, the poems seem cadenzas for the human voice, clipping, darting and spurring: proceeding, it might be said, by veering. She also employs an exceptional simplicity of diction: 'The Best Beast of the Fat-Stock Show at Earls Court' may be regarded as the condition towards which much of her work aspires, being written entirely in monosyllables. An integral element of a reader's reception of her work is, also, the fact that it comes illustrated with her own nervously quick though sometimes fairly slight drawings: their complementarity opens up the scope of interpretation. Sometimes this is not much to the poems' credit, however: 'The Face', for instance, from *Mother, What Is Man?*, is a poem about 'a human face that hides / A monkey soul within', and the owner of the face is no more clearly specified. The poem's accompanying drawing, however, presents a figure walking past a shopsign reading 'Gold'. If this is a Jewish name, then the poem becomes inevitably anti-semitic, in a way no less scandalous for being so obliquely rendered. It seems particularly worth making reference to the presence of such a thing in Stevie Smith, since it has been largely ignored or elided by her critics: perhaps it is the dark underside of what Heaney discovers in her of an English 'disenchanted gentility'.[2]

Allied to these forms and shapes is the frequent use of material
derived or imitated from myth, legend, folktale and literature,
reinterpreted into radically variant narratives and crossed with fragments
of French and Latin allusion. Kings, queens, princes, princesses, angels
and maidenly *distraites* float in and out of the work in vaguely Arthurian
castles, forests, lakes, places of enchantment. As if this did not in itself
offer sufficient danger of collapsing into the terminally fey or whimsical,
the poems also contain an almost medieval bestiary: in particular, cats
and dogs roam freely throughout. But these properties are almost always
strengthened by being the vehicle for a dream of alterity. For all her
explicit rejection of any official or corporate feminist alignments ('Girls!
I will let down the side if I get a chance / And I will sell the pass for a
couple of pence'), these narratives are frequently slanted in a feminist
direction. Their notoriously wayward procedures have come to seem
almost prototypical of some subsequent feminist deconstructions of
mythical archetype and fairytale. Such poems as 'The Frog Prince',
'Voices about the Princess Anemone', 'Die Lorelei', 'Persephone',
'Phedre', 'The Last Turn of the Screw' and 'At School' play their classic
narratives into revisionist fables of anti-bourgeois hostility, of the
sceptical mistrust of marriage, of painful familial feeling (particularly
connected with mother/daughter relationships), of frustrated and
transgressive libidinous desire. Stevie Smith's Eumenides are the
querulous, garrulous, prickly and unaligned spirits of a feminism not
content with any name it might have been given at the time of writing.
And it would be wrong to underestimate their knowledge of the greatest
horrors and terrors: witness, in particular, the way the poems are often
drawn to murder and molestation.

'The Frog Prince' shapes the clearest refusal of the conventional
narrative, and does so by taking on, and taking in, the familiarity of that
narrative itself, the frog prince's own already-writtenness:

> The story is familiar
> Everybody knows it well
> But do other enchanted people feel as nervous
> As I do? The stories do not tell,
>
> Ask if they will be happier
> When the changes come
> As already they are fairly happy
> In a frog's doom?

Given the comparative valuation of the animal and human worlds in
Stevie Smith, it should not surprise anyone that an enchanted frog in her
work will prefer to remain a frog rather than to be disenchanted into a
prince. Although this poem does culminate in the frog's self-exhortation

to take on a disenchantment which may be '*heavenly*', ruefully raising the possibility that his feeling happy may itself be part of the enchantment, this is (the reader will surely feel) against his truest instincts and, possibly, against his better nature. It is with, always, something of that degree of scepticism, suspicion and self-mistrust that these poems try to tell the stories that 'the stories do not tell'. In doing so they discover, for instance, a 'Princess Anemone' narcissistically dreaming into her own 'golden reflection' in a stream: a female anemone to replace a male narcissus. Accompanied by a quasi-erotic drawing in which Anemone's naked legs are entangled in undergrowth and bend upwards and outwards in imitative alignment with the branches of a tree, the poem concludes in one of Smith's many epigrams:

> She bends her head, her hands dip in the water
> Fear is a band of gold on the King's daughter.

The completed narcissistic circle of self-reflection itself provides the serenity usually made available to the fairytale princess only by the encirclement of her finger in the prince's wedding ring, his 'band of gold'; the poem is a dream of self-desire, excluding and refusing male (and social) containment. A similar rejection of the imposed narrative figures in 'Persephone', where the daughter is unwilling to return from her underworld winter, glad to have rejected the too consuming love of Demeter, the mother: 'In this wintriness / Is my happiness'. It is a poem that harmonises disquietingly with Sylvia Plath's 'The Disquieting Muses' in *The Colossus*, that other poem of unaccommodatable anti-maternal feeling; and it is not surprising (for this among other reasons) to discover that Plath was, in her own words, 'a desperate Smith-addict'.[3]

It is possible here, as elsewhere in Stevie Smith's fables and tales, to discover some of the circumstances of her own biography in transmuted form: 'Persephone', for instance, is complemented and complicated by a poem such as 'A Dream of Nourishment', in which the mother's breast is 'withdrawn violently' from the child in a more nakedly Freudian exploration of maternal rejection ('And oh the famishment for me'). If such personae as the frog prince, Anemone, Persephone and Phedre have the authority and stability of a stoical acceptance of their plight, or even a resilient ability to turn it to profit, others of the isolated, rejected and excluded in her work are more merely desolate. Lacking companionship, and lacking solace in an Anglicanism for which they nevertheless retain a worried, uneasy, combative regard ('Oh Christianity, Christianity' is probably Smith's definitive statement of this theme), their ultimate stoicism is virtually indistinguishable from a death wish. Suicide is always a possibility, and her work throughout maintains a dialogue with death, often indeed with a personified 'Death'. Some of her most achieved poems, such as 'Come, Death', 'Dirge', 'Not Waving but Drowning' and 'Scorpion', enter this dialogue in ways that seem, in the range of their plangencies, variously medieval, Jacobean and Tennysonian. 'Scorpion', published posthumously, is among her very finest lyrics, its evocation of the desire for death as far from self-pity as is conceivable, making a wry fiction from its dire necessity. Imagining an afterlife for itself, this soul of Scorpion can still sting, retaining the vigour of a quite unspiritual petulance; but that petulance itself finally settles into the most poignant of cadences:

Sea and *grass* must be quite empty
Other souls can find somewhere *else*.

O Lord God please come
And require the soul of thy Scorpion

Scorpion so wishes to be gone.

Since he began publishing in the mid-1940s R.S. Thomas, a poet who is also a Christian priest, has had two preoccupying themes: rural Wales and his difficult relationship with the Christian God. The work consequently plots the graph of a double journey in which Thomas moves towards an identification with the desires and methods of Welsh nationalism (including, of course, a commitment to the use of the Welsh language), and in which he concurrently enters into a dialogue with a God who seems, almost always, extraordinarily remote, unaccommodating and even, on occasion, cruel and oppressive in ways that could hardly be very different were this poet-priest intent on an embittered satire on Christianity. The qualities of grim endurance, desolation and comfortlessness evident in these preoccupations – physical, cultural, political and metaphysical – are inherent too in Thomas's forms: he writes a bare, austere, chaste, sometimes (it seems) wilfully graceless poetry, simple in diction and increasingly devoid of image as it moves towards statement or assertion. 'Bone' is one of its most prominent words; and, increasingly skeletal and spare, it is a poetry ultimately generated and impelled by the purity of an engagement with idea and concept.

This seems to me true even of the best known among his earlier poems, in which imaginative figures of Welsh rural life are explored and exposed with an almost brutally empathetic rigour: such poems as 'Hireling', 'A Welsh Testament' and 'Evans'. The meditations on these solitaries – figures of both depredation and resilience – sometimes run the risk of self-parody (the Puw family of 'On the Farm', in particular, seem much too close to *Cold Comfort Farm* for comfort); but at their best they have an abrupt, ungainsayable definitiveness of scrutiny and judgement. The most famous of Thomas's figures is the hill farmer Iago

Prytherch who features in a number of the earlier poems; and the best-known poem in which he appears, 'A Peasant', to which I have already referred, suggests the relationship in Thomas between idea and image. After the first half of the poem has identified Prytherch in some of the features and gestures of his work and being, it concludes:

> There is something frightening in the vacancy of his mind.
> His clothes, sour with years of sweat
> And animal contact, shock the refined,
> But affected, sense with their stark naturalness.
> Yet this is your prototype, who, season by season
> Against siege of rain and the wind's attrition,
> Preserves his stock, an impregnable fortress
> Not to be stormed even in death's confusion.
> Remember him, then, for he, too, is a winner of wars,
> Enduring like a tree under the curious stars.

The ultimate precursors of this poem are the great Wordsworthian solitaries; but, compared to the slowly unravelled witness and revelation of such poems of Wordsworth's as 'Michael' and 'The Ruined Cottage', there is something almost busily managerial about this Thomas poem, insisting on Prytherch's representative and prototypical status in a discursive language rather than in the presentation of the figure itself; that 'something frightening', in particular, would need to be elaborated much further before it could seem other than merely appropriative, a consequence of the poet's own terror and helplessness before the object of his gaze rather than of anything demonstrably inherent in the object itself.

Thomas does not always avoid the condescension – a *de-haut-en-bas* distaste – which this suggests. In so far as this kind of poetry nevertheless impresses, it does so as a function of an argument he is sustaining with himself about the conditions of his own existence, and those of his parishioners. This is an argument which runs frequently enough to the rancorous and irascible, particularly when dealing with the treatment of the Welsh by the English and, latterly, when dealing with the fate of the Welsh language. The embitterment and embattlement, however, are virtually inevitable and endemic to the poet self-consciously taking on the fate of a subjected and marginalised people (the locution 'my people', of ambivalently sacerdotal and political connotation, is one Thomas is not unwilling to use). Thomas's is, we might say, a poetry whose language is always tormented by the necessity that it is an English, not a Welsh language; his work constitutes a Welsh anti-pastoral, unaccommodating because unaccommodated, a poetry in which the 'Celtic' maintains a defiant if abject persistence. Like the Arthurian myth of 'A Welshman to Any Tourist', it is 'the bright ore / That seams our history, / But shame has kept . . . late in bed'. Such themes of cultural and linguistic depredation are continuous with themes in the work of David Jones (Thomas has a poem commemorating him); if his work never presumes Jones's complexity or complication, it remains, nevertheless, an unignorable reminder of the realities of Welsh cultural and national difference for an English-speaking readership.

The anguish associated with such matters is itself continuous with the predominant emotions in Thomas's religious poetry, if 'religious' is at all the right name for it. Beginning with *H'm* in 1972 – whose title raises, presumably, a sceptical eyebrow – Thomas's books have become sequences or quasi-sequences of an increasingly meditative or contemplative kind. The figure of 'God' or 'the god' is often discovered only in his 'absence', and these poems have been read as latter-day explorations of the traditional mystical notion of the hidden God or *Deus absconditus*. Yet the god figure may also be almost a new version of Blake's Urizen, a cruel and depraved interferer in human affairs: he is notoriously so in 'Rough' from *Laboratories of the Spirit* (1975) in which 'God took a handful of small germs, / sowing them in the smooth flesh', a poem which would not seem at all out of place among the most anti-Christian passages of Ted Hughes's *Crow*, and an astonishingly heterodox poem for a Christian priest to publish ('after such knowledge, what religion?' the sceptical agnostic reader may well ask). There is a Calvinism in these poems which seems at times almost Manichaean in its gloom. There are some suggestions too that their *mise-en-scène* is post-holocaustal, a world reminiscent of Edwin Muir's in 'The Horses', but one in which any potential renewal is pitted against a range of forces identified – portentously, it may be – as 'the Machine'. It is just as well, perhaps, that the symbology implicit in these poems is not made any more structurally coherent: its fragmentariness allows us to read the work as the annotations of some virtually unrecoverable narrative of an interior life, often sour with a rumble of dissatisfaction and unease.

'The Combat', for instance, turns, as many of these poems do, on the paradox that God is approachable only within language but is actually beyond language in a way that makes the approach to him through language a process of endless desire and deferral:

> For the failure of language
> there is no redress. The physicists
> tell us your size, the chemists
> the ingredients of your
> thinking. But who you are
> does not appear, nor why
> on the innocent marches
> of vocabulary you should choose
> to engage us, belabouring us

with your silence. We die, we die
with the knowledge that your resistance
is endless at the frontier of the great poem.

These lines typify the later Thomas. There is the address to God which is, of its nature, prayerful, but not respectful; on the contrary, there is a strong note of recrimination at God's withholding of himself, a recrimination which can at times seem close to petulance or self-pity. There is also the ambivalent combination of irony and respect directed towards the physical sciences. Scientists are part of 'the Machine' – in that rather uninspected rejection of the modern to which Thomas is prone – but they are also admired as scrupulous and detached inquirers into source and origin (they manage to sound, here, a bit like Stephen Hawking) and, as such, their experiments become, almost, models of what a certain kind of desirable prayer might be like. There is, finally, the bareness of near-philosophical inquiry suddenly opened up by metaphor ('the innocent marches / of vocabulary' and death or the afterlife as 'the great poem'). Although this is not a mindscape many would care to inhabit, it is one revealed with integrity and scruple.

Notes

1. Seamus Heaney, *Preoccupations: Selected Prose 1968–1978* (London: Faber and Faber, 1980), p. 199.

2. ibid., p. 200.

3. Cited in Frances Spalding, *Stevie Smith: A Critical Biography* (London: Faber and Faber, 1988), p. 256.

Part Three
From the Fifties

Introduction

If the history of poetry since 1940 is, in part, a history of action and reaction, then the reaction of the early 1950s very neatly coincides with the change of decade. In the work of those poets of 'the Movement' with which the decade of the 1950s is usually primarily associated (anthologised in D.J. Enright's *Poets of the 1950s*, 1955, and Robert Conquest's *New Lines*, 1956), the neo-Romanticism of the 1940s is denigrated and opposed. The Movement has been called, by Ian Hamilton, 'the *Spectator's* PR job',[1] and it clearly owed a great deal to the skilful use of a metropolitan publicity machine in the creation of audience expectation and taste; but, as Blake Morrison has persuasively shown, it also derived, however briefly, from a genuine homogeneity of interest and feeling.[2] Since several of the Movement's poets were also literary critics (at a time famously characterised by Randall Jarrell as 'The Age of Criticism'), the documents in which its history may be most clearly read are critical essays as well as poems, and are occasionally critical essays disguised as poems. Such documents would include: Kingsley Amis's poem 'Against Romanticism'; John Wain's essay on William Empson in the final issue of *Penguin New Writing* (1950); Philip Larkin's statements in the Enright anthology, and his introductions to the 1966 edition of his first book, *The North Ship*, and to his jazz reviews, *All What Jazz* (1970); Donald Davie's poems 'Creon's Mouse', 'Remembering the Thirties' and 'Rejoinder to a Critic', his critical book *Purity of Diction in English Verse* (1952; but given an illuminating postscript on its reissue in 1967) and his essay 'Remembering the Movement' (1959).

In the introduction to *New Lines*, Conquest has some difficulty in describing exactly what it is his poets – Elizabeth Jennings, John Holloway, Philip Larkin, Thom Gunn, Kingsley Amis, D.J. Enright, Donald Davie, John Wain and Conquest himself – share in common apart from the 'negative determination to avoid bad principles'.[3] But, extrapolating from the documents above, it is clear that there are some shared principles too. The anti-neo-Romanticism is a hostility to a perceived formlessness, excess and self-indulgence, which are to be replaced by a new formal discipline (frequently a resort to traditional metres); neo-Romantic 'vision' is to be replaced by Movement scepticism or witty intellectual toughness, indebted either to Empsonian practice (Wain) or to an exemplary neo-Augustanism (Davie); what Larkin calls in his *North Ship* preface the 'Celtic fever' is to be replaced by a certain kind of Englishness; Dylan Thomas's 'Fern Hill', we might say, is to be replaced by Larkin's 'I Remember, I Remember' (with its English Midlands city Coventry as the place not where his 'roots' might be found but where, on the contrary, he 'did not invent / Blinding theologies of flowers and fruits').

The attack on neo-Romanticism is an aspect of a fundamental hostility to Modernism itself, read – as it has been frequently since – as a heritage from, not a reaction against, Romanticism. In Larkin this memorably takes the form of the replacement of the early seductive influence of the 'Celtic' Yeats with the English Hardy, and of an attack on the 'pleasantly alliterative' (and representative) Parker, Pound and Picasso for their 'irresponsible exploitations of technique in contradiction of human life as we know it'.[4] In Davie's *Purity of Diction* it takes the form of an antagonism to post-symbolist (and especially Poundian) disruptions of syntax; and, in his later, strange book *Thomas Hardy and British Poetry* (1973), of a discovery of Hardy as the presiding spirit of the previous fifty years of British poetry. The effort in Larkin's case, forwarded spectacularly in his *Oxford Book of Twentieth-Century English Verse* (1973), is to give an allegiance to a native British tradition cut across but not destroyed by Modernism. In Davie, it is to relocate a strength of 'chaste diction' and coherent, prose syntax in the solid ground of eighteenth-century rationalism: *Purity of Diction* is written explicitly to 'help some practising poet to a poetry of urbane and momentous statement'.[5] The Modernist lack of interest in, or even aggression towards an audience is thereby decisively rejected in favour of a poetry which will once again court its readers. Such a move is, it could be said, in tune with the cultural moment which saw the advance in literary influence of the recently created Arts Council of Great Britain and the establishment, in 1954, of the Poetry Book Society, both organisations committed to the encouragement of a poetry-reading public.

The product of such efforts was a poetry characteristically empiricist, wry, discursive-argumentative, emotionally restrained, much given to aphorism, marked by the use of reader-aware asides, hesitations and interjections, desiring to establishing a level-toned and civilised conversation, often of a fairly literary kind. The urbanity, civility and decorum of the typical Movement poem derive in part from the class backgrounds, education and academicism of some of these poets, as Morrison has demonstrated. The typical Movement poet shared some of the characteristics of the 'coming' class, that lower middle class newly empowered by the post-war Labour government: he (and apart from

Elizabeth Jennings they were all men) was a grammar-school scholarship boy, Oxbridge English graduate, influenced by Leavisian and American New Criticism; a redbrick university teacher of English (the world of Amis's *Lucky Jim* and Wain's *Hurry On Down*); and of a left-oriented consensus, though in effect 'apolitical' (with all that that implies of a tendency to conservatism eventually to become openly Tory in Amis, Larkin and Davie). The politics harmonises with the anti-Modernism; it sinks to virtual inertia in an attempt to be everything that a Modernist politics was not. This becomes explicit in Davie's *Purity of Diction* in a passage in which he equates Poundian syntactical disruption with Poundian Fascism: 'the development from imagism in poetry to fascism in politics is clear and unbroken,' he says, and 'to dislocate syntax in poetry is to threaten the rule of law in the civilized community'.[6] Syntax, measure and a logic of statement were, in the Movement poem, almost an act of post-war reconstruction: to build the decorous shape of the poem was to provide a defence against barbarism.

In the more explicitly political among Davie's early poems the critical axioms are given poetic concretion. 'At Dachau Yeats and Rilke died,' he writes in 'Hawkshead and Dachau in a Christmas Glass', implying that the symbolist project – heritage of English and German Romanticism – will seem intolerably presumptuous in the light of post-war knowledge. 'Creon's Mouse' recommends the virtues of a refusal of daring in what amounts to an allegory of the necessity of non-intervention:

> If too much daring brought (he thought) the war,
> When that was over nothing else would serve
> But (no one must be daring any more),
> A self-induced and stubborn loss of nerve.

The peculiarity here is that 'loss of nerve' is made to appear volitional: the paradoxical requirement is, as it were, that people nerve themselves to a loss of nerve, against an instinct for its opposite (the 'daring' which may lead to a Fascist politics). In this reversal of customary expectation, 'Creon's Mouse' is very much a poem of the post-war moment, its recommendation profoundly in tune with a recognition of Britain's imperial decline, that decline whose crucial dates bookend the 1950s: the beginnings of colonial independence in 1947 and the application for membership of the EEC in 1961. Published in Davie's *Brides of Reason* (1955), the poem, insisting that it is better not to enter at all than to suffer the indignities of withdrawal, foreshadows the political realities enforced by the Suez crisis of the following year, the terminal moment of British imperial presumption. Some of the most interesting poetry of the Movement in the 1950s may be read as inscribed with the sense – anxious, distressed, nostalgic, stoic – of a great national termination and reorientation. Blake Morrison wittily describes Larkin's 'At Grass' as 'a poem of post-imperial *tristesse*',[7] for instance, and the phrase may also differently serve for Enright's many ironic, bemused and undeceived vignettes of life as a university teacher of English Literature in some of the last British colonies. This is not at all to claim, however, that some of the work is not itself prey to the blindness of a post-imperial distress which it elsewhere provides insight into. Nostalgia; a defensive xenophobia; a boring pretence of philistinism: all are displayed in, as well as placed by this poetry.

The attitudinising associated with a 'little Englandism' in the Movement has always come under suspicion. It met with argument and hostility as soon as it was first sounded, in the shape of an anthology edited by Howard Sergeant and Dannie Abse, *Mavericks* (1957), which included work by Michael Hamburger and Jon Silkin. Hamburger has been one of the most significant translators of modern European poetry into English in the period, and a poet whose own interesting work is best represented in the sequence 'Travelling' of 1977; and Silkin has, since 1952, edited the journal *Stand* (the location of an antagonistic and radical poetry completely at odds with the premises of the Movement), and has continued to produce his own 'poetry of the committed individual' which reaches two of its finest expressions in the 'Flower Poems' sequence of 1965 and the 'Killhope Wheel' sequence of 1974.[8] Among the Movement's original practitioners some of the attitudes were also short-lived. Indeed, the prose pieces by individual contributors included in the Enright anthology are remarkably critical of the potential dangers of the manner, Amis noting its tendency to aridity and Davie remarking on its lack of ambition and adventurousness. This aboriginal unease from the participants themselves anticipates Charles Tomlinson's savage criticisms of the whole undertaking in an essay-review of *New Lines* in which he castigates the Movement for 'a singular want of vital awareness of the continuum outside themselves, of the mystery bodied over against them in the created universe, which they fail to experience with any degree of sharpness or to embody with any instress or sensuous depth'.[9] If the serene confidence in the distinction to be made between language and world displayed here sounds remote to our post-structuralist ears, its quasi-religious diction (with allusions to Hopkins and Martin Buber) clearly wishes to insist a Romantic-Modernist alternative as the proper sphere and function of poetry.

The short-lived homogeneity of the Movement may be judged by the fact that as early as 1959 Donald Davie appeared to be in full agreement with Tomlinson. In 'Remembering the Movement' he castigates its 'craven defensiveness' and describes it as writing in which 'the poet is never so surrendered to his experience, never so far gone out of himself in his response, as not to be aware of the attitudes he is taking up'.[10] But of course, according to the original Movement prescriptions, this refusal of self-surrender was precisely the point: this was to be the essential protection against neo-Romantic excess. For Davie, at least, an embattled rearguard neo-Augustanism was, by 1959, no longer a viable alternative to Modernism; and his own progress, as I suggest below, has been through an absorption of quite other, and Modernist, sources and influences. Gunn, who was in any case only peripherally associated with the Movement, has absorbed some similar (American Modernist) models and has pursued an early interest in some popular-cultural or counter-cultural forms (bike-boys, Elvis Presley, S&M) into an explicitly gay writing. Enright has maintained the anecdotal kind, but in *The Terrible Shears* (1973) puts it at the service of an account of his own working-class childhood in the 1920s which makes the essentially unflappable urbanity of his own manner seem an extraordinary instance of the pervasiveness in English mid-century writing of an educated ironic tone. The childhood described in this sequence is, for instance, more deeply reduced financially and culturally than the one more persistently advertised in the work of Tony Harrison: we learn from it what we would surely never have guessed from Enright's earlier work, that he began to write poetry as a response to his grandmother's screams as she was being forcibly taken to the workhouse. The reader is torn between admiration for the restraint with which Enright has refused to capitalise on such material (it is easy to imagine how a later generation might have mythologised this poetic origin) and unease that it was withheld for so long, with an awareness that Enright's work is newly and powerfully energised by its late surfacing.

Only in the poetry of Elizabeth Jennings and Philip Larkin (among those members of the Movement who have continued to produce significant work) do some of the Movement procedures persist. In Elizabeth Jennings, for all the grace of her delicate lyricism, this leads to a certain repetitiveness, even though a manner adopted from Movement procedures, and adopted uniquely by a woman, is made to bear the imprint of a range of distinct and exceptional experiences, including those of orthodox Roman Catholic belief and mental breakdown. Larkin is, however, the major case in post-war English poetry of a thoroughgoing resistance to Modernism; and in what follows I consider some of the implications of his challenge.

Notes

1.   Ian Hamilton, *A Poetry Chronicle: Essays and Reviews* (London: Faber and Faber, 1973), p. 129.

2.   See Blake Morrison, *The Movement: English Poetry and Fiction of the 1950s* (London: Methuen, 1986; first published 1980).

3. Robert Conquest (ed.), *New Lines: An Anthology* (London: Macmillan 1956), p. xv.

4. Philip Larkin, *Required Writing: Miscellaneous Pieces 1955–1982* (London: Faber and Faber, 1983), p. 297.

5. Donald Davie, *Purity of Diction in English Verse* (London: Routledge and Kegan Paul, 1952; 1967), p. 107.

6. ibid., p. 99.

7. *The Movement*, pp. 82–3.

8. *Poetry of the Committed Individual* (Harmondsworth: Penguin, 1973) is an anthology of poems from *Stand* edited by Silkin.

9. Charles Tomlinson, 'The Middlebrow Muse', *Essays in Criticism*, 7 (1957), p. 215.

10. Donald Davie, *The Poet in the Imaginary Museum: Essays of Two Decades* (Manchester: Carcanet Press, 1977), p. 74.

Chapter 7
A Movement Pursued
Philip Larkin

Philip Larkin is undoubtedly the most Movement of Movement poets in the sense that in him the true spirit of post-war English dispiritedness quickly reached, and subsequently maintained, its most quintessential form. Charles Tomlinson's early castigation of his 'tenderly nursed sense of defeat' and Donald Davie's characterisation, in *Thomas Hardy and British Poetry*, of 'a poetry of lowered sights and patiently diminished expectations' caustically put the negative case.[1] Their antagonism has, too, an animus deriving from the attempt to correct taste. What they are arguing with is the work of a writer who managed to establish (quite unlike Tomlinson and Davie themselves) a successful rapport with a large and wide audience. Blake Morrison's reference to a 'post-imperial *tristesse*' in Larkin might suggest that the popularity derives from an element of readerly self-recognition. The poetry's melancholy, its sense of loss, its fatalism or weary determinism are profoundly in tune with the deepest insecurities and anxieties, hesitations and fumblings of identity of an English audience suffering the withdrawal from imperial and colonial power in the aftermath of the war. The appropriately lugubrious wit of Morrison's phrase makes the personal regret and misery in Larkin vividly transparent to the political nostalgia; it brings that early poem of post-coital *tristesse*, 'Deceptions' (the poem which gave the volume *The Less Deceived* its title), into alignment with the later 'Homage to a Government', in which the 1969 Labour government's decision to pull British troops out of Aden is bitterly characterised as an irresponsible self-interest and greed. Larkin's idea of England is as deeply and intimately wounded by such post-imperial withdrawals as some of the personae of his poems are wounded by sexual impotence, incompetence, anxiety or distress.

The essential Larkin attitude may be discovered in one of its most intense forms in the desolate closing lines of 'Dockery and Son'. The poem famously recounts the visit of its persona to his old college (possibly after a funeral, since he is 'death-suited') and his return train journey north. An encounter with the college Dean brings to his attention how widely his own fortunes have differed from those of a junior contemporary (the eponymous 'Dockery') who has produced a son old enough to be a current undergraduate. Moving, as many of Larkin's finest stanzaic poems do, in and out of directly quoted speech, private meditation, reflection, moralisation and external scenic description, the poem appears to be about to conclude in saddened, self-diminishing reflection on 'how much had gone of life, / How widely from the others'. However, veering away from the mood and the thought as the syntax trails off into a characteristically droll ellipsis, the poem becomes instead the means not of self-defeat, exactly, but of a strange kind of self-defence, exclaiming of Dockery in depreciating mockery, how

> Convinced he was he should be added to!
> Why should he think adding meant increase?
> To me it was dilution. Where do these
> Innate assumptions come from? Not from what
> We think truest, or most want to do:
> Those warp tight-shut, like doors. They're more a style
> Our lives bring with them: habit for a while,
> Suddenly they harden into all we've got
>
> And how we got it; looked back on, they rear
> Like sand-clouds, thick and close, embodying
> For Dockery a son, for me nothing,
> Nothing with all a son's harsh patronage.
> Life is first boredom, then fear.
> Whether or not we use it, it goes,
> And leaves what something hidden from us chose,
> And age, and then the only end of age.

Barbara Everett has observed how Larkin sometimes 'fuses . . . outcry and anecdote'.[2] Here the apparently level-toned anecdotal reminiscence fractures unnervingly into a minatorily deterministic outcry. Instead of concluding with – what might have been predicted – a wan regretfulness, the lines become a vacuum into which the lives of both Dockery and the persona are devastatingly sucked. The real outrage of the final lines of 'Dockery and Son' is that what we might casually read as blank desolation is actually, for the persona of the poem, a kind of perverse consolation: since even if it is tendentious to claim as a universal truth that 'life is first boredom, then fear', it is indubitably the case that lives that are used, as well as lives unused (like his), culminate inexorably in an 'only end'. What the poem has earlier evoked as his 'numbness' when comparing his life and Dockery's has been thawed by an extraordinary combination of empathy and *schadenfreude*.

The word 'persona' is a more than usually difficult one to use of a

Larkin poem. While it makes it plain that the speaker of the poem is not to be naïvely identified with the historical person Philip Larkin, it tends to elide the fact that one really does not wish to separate them with any absoluteness. The anecdote, with its representations of character, speech, setting and plot, may well be thought to protect the outcry from too personal an identification; and Larkin slyly includes in his collection of critical essays, *Required Writing*, a piece on Julian Hall's novel, *The Senior Commoner*, which supplies (without, of course, saying so) a likely literary source for 'Dockery and Son'.[3] Yet the insistence on the falsity of 'innate assumptions' and the defence of the view that 'increase' might mean 'dilution' (the defence, that is, of selfishness) are entirely characteristic of the Larkin *oeuvre*. If a sufficient number of the personae in the poems manifest extremely similar attitudes and values then it must seem that, for all its elements of anecdote and theatre (even slightly self-parodistic theatre – those bicycle clips removed in 'awkward reverence' in 'Church Going', for instance), Larkin's poetry presents us with an apologia.

At its most basic the apologia has to do with a fear of and desire for death and a defence of solitude. Death is figured in 'Ambulances' as 'the solving emptiness that lies just under all we do'; and the word 'solving' punningly fuses both 'resolving' and 'dissolving'. Death provides an answer, but only in nothingness; and it effects the dissolution of an identity which we may well find burdensome. Against its inevitability various forms of personal and social ritual – work in 'Toads' and 'Toads Revisited', company in 'Reasons for Attendance' and 'Vers de Société', marriage in 'To My Wife', children in 'Dockery and Son' – seem so many pathetic attempts at self-protection. Larkin is pre-eminently a poet of the terror of ageing, of the permanence of 'extinction's alp', both in some of his most intricately architectured poems such as 'The Building', 'The Old Fools' and 'Aubade' and elsewhere in casual comment or irony. The discourse of his poems is forged in the face of a stoic but undermining certainty that death leaves 'nothing to be said'.

If there is not much in this that does not accommodate itself fairly readily to some of the traditional themes of English lyric and elegy, there is nevertheless in Larkin a chilling persistence and a refusal of succour which argue an element of almost neurotic exacerbation. The death-directed nature of his imagination is intimately, perturbingly caught up in his emotional or sexual unease and dissatisfaction. This appears at its most startling in the early poem 'On Being Twenty-Six'. Never was there an older twenty-six-year-old than this one, recognising that 'What caught alight / Quickly consumed itself in me / As I foresaw'. The deterministic force of that is ferociously impregnable, since not only is the young man prematurely aged, but has always known he will be so. It tallies completely with such Larkinisms as naming childhood a 'forgotten boredom' and agreeing, in 'Wild Oats', 'That I was too selfish, withdrawn, / And easily bored to love'. The contours of a very special sensibility may be perceived through these anecdotes and generalisations, and they become virtually explicit in 'Aubade' and 'Love Again'. In the former, 'An only life can take so long to climb / Clear of its wrong beginnings, and may never'; and in the latter the reason why 'it never worked for me' has

> Something to do with violence
> A long way back, and wrong rewards,
> And arrogant eternity.

Appearing almost on the verge of confessional declaration, but still very oblique, these lines suggest a desire to address some hidden perturbation and distress more openly than through the customary personae and anecdotes. Never published in Larkin's lifetime, and written as late as September 1979, 'Love Again' may suggest a reason why he wrote so little after *High Windows* (1974): the most urgent matter of his interior life was perhaps in the end failing to respond to the techniques of discipline, reserve, hesitation and obliquity with which his 'Movement' manner had provided him. To explicate the word 'Something' in those lines any further within the poem itself would be to collapse anecdote altogether into outcry; the poem is the stifling of a cry. Although some of his best critics – Barbara Everett, Andrew Motion – have persuasively alerted us to the persistence of a symbolist element in Larkin, a counter-movement towards self-transcendence, this is often in fact a very negative kind of transcendence, carried in images of absence and nullity: 'Such attics cleared of me! Such absences!'; 'the deep blue air, that shows / Nothing, and is nowhere, and is endless'.[4]

Denying so much of what makes life satisfactory or fulfilling for many people, and making explicit a religious denial too in such central statements of English post-Christian consciousness as 'Church Going' and 'Aubade' ('That vast moth-eaten musical brocade / Created to pretend we never die'), Larkin does nevertheless have his sources of alternative value and affirmation. One is jazz music: the excellent 'For Sidney Bechet' proposes Bechet's saxophone playing, in an entirely characteristic shrug of almost pawky self-deprecation, as a qualified affirmative ('On me your voice falls as they say love should, / Like an enormous yes'); another is a conception of English 'nature' (in such poems as 'First Sight', 'Cut Grass' and 'The Trees') in which Larkin plays the anachronistic pseudo-Georgian in a way not particularly surprising from the anthologist of the *Oxford Book of Twentieth-Century English Verse*; but a far more significant one, and a constant in his career, is what 'The Importance of Elsewhere' calls 'customs and establishments'. Thinking about Larkin's popularity and his Englishness is to think, above all, about the way the peculiarly mistrustful, unallied, 'less deceived' sensibility relates to and regards some of the rituals of English social and cultural life.

'The Importance of Elsewhere' is written remembering his time in Ireland, where loneliness and strangeness are actually enabling. (It is an irony which Larkin never makes anything of, but Tom Paulin in his poem 'Chucking it Away' in *Fivemiletown* does, that in one respect he would not have seemed all that separate in Belfast, since his surname is Irish, not English.) The contrast with England is absolute:

> Living in England has no such excuse:
> These are my customs and establishments
> It would be much more serious to refuse.
> Here no elsewhere underwrites my existence.

It is revealing that Larkin should be enabled to relax where his circumstances and context insist on difference, that he should find rebuff bracing; but the poem's actual tone is very difficult to catch. The enablement of difference − being proved 'separate' and therefore 'not unworkable' − is a desirable condition clearly impossible at home, and consequently the allegiance to English decorums and probities is a diminishment in personal freedom: one's identity is merged into a national identity, no longer 'underwritten' or authenticated by distinction. In defining an allegiance to English *mores*, the poem's closing lines perform a self-chastising, almost prissy correctiveness ('no such excuse'; 'much more serious'); they pull themselves up, or straighten themselves out, into the proper attitude. What appears here to have its element of theatre appears elsewhere in Larkin, however, to be offered much more straight. In a range of poems from 'The March Past' of 1951 to 'In times when nothing stood', his poem for the Queen's Jubilee in 1978, the 'customs and establishments' of an advertised Englishness are given their assent by this otherwise most nay-saying of post-war English poets. Such poems constitute perhaps not so much a post-imperial *tristesse* as a post-imperial pastoral.

I am thinking particularly of 'Church Going', 'The Whitsun Weddings', 'MCMXIV', 'To the Sea', 'The Explosion' and 'Show Saturday'. In all of these an acute sense of English social history (which is often also vivifyingly accurate and peculiar in Larkin's underestimated critical prose) is crossed over with, or nurtured into, a dream of thwarted potential or desired persistence. 'The March Past' (written in 1951, the year of the Festival of Britain) names the sentiment at its most unguarded when the imperialistic militarism associated with a marching band (the 'discipline' of 'music bullying aside / The credulous, prettily-coloured crowd') brings 'a blind / Astonishing remorse for things now ended'. Such feelings sleep lightly just under the surface of these poems which offer a conception of an Englishness as the repository of value and identity for this poet who could find precious little of either anywhere else. In Philip Larkin the idea of the nation is given an allegiance fundamentally at odds with the disenchanted scepticism manifest in relation to almost all other sources of potential value.

Each of these poems proposes an idea of organic English community (sometimes either vanished or under threat) in which differences of class are subsumed into, or transmuted by, an ideal of incorporation or continuity. 'MCMXIV', whose title freezes the date of the beginning of the First World War into the marmoreal stasis of a war-memorial inscription, also freezes the organic idea into a participial stasis. Lacking any main verb apart from an implied copula, the poem acts as a kind of linguistic translation of the sepia of an Edwardian photograph. Its powerfully evocative images of an immediately pre-First World War England are, it appears, designed to display the truth of its reiterated quasi-refrain, 'Never such innocence again', and they even include a notation of the way the English fields of 1914 'shadow . . . Domesday lines', making 1914 transparent to a lengthy national history. Yet these images prominently include 'The differently-dressed servants / With tiny rooms in huge houses'; and it is impossible to gauge what kind of irony, if any, may attach to the notion of 'innocence' when it is set against such instances of class privilege and underprivilege. It is obviously possible for a poem written in 1960 to favour a traditional English class hierarchy; but it is hardly to be believed that such a thing might constitute an element of 'innocence'. The poem's poignantly patriotic regret therefore seems remarkably unearned: the compulsions of nostalgia betray Larkin himself into an odd kind of historical 'innocence'.

It is also remarkable in these poems how ready Larkin is to surrender some of the most signal elements of his apologia elsewhere. Suddenly in them, for instance, unpredictably and unarguably, emotional and familial attachments (exposed to the most undermining scrutiny in much of the rest of the work) become the first premise and *sine qua non* of valued continuity and persistence. The persona still remains separate from the posited community ('Someone would know: I don't' is the paradigm, in 'Church Going', of the vaguely disingenuous Larkinian agnosticism), and this contributes a very seductive poignancy of desire and longing to the theme; but familial pieties, utterly rejected elsewhere, are now the measure, and the vehicle, of significant tradition. In 'The Whitsun Weddings' the ritual of the title (a ritual demanded by the mundane exigencies of the English taxation system) is read as an almost sacramental irruption into the forms of ordinary existence. The poem includes the response of the young unmarried girls of the wedding parties, who read the weddings as 'a religious wounding'; but if this response is to some degree ironised by others in the poem there is little doubt that the magnificent concluding lines with their imagery of the arrow-shower and their tumescent/detumescent rhythms, establish these weddings as both sexually regenerative and pentecostal, 'with all the power / That being changed can give'. Moving from an English provincial place, 'where sky and Lincolnshire and water meet' (and how remarkably that phrase makes the English shire county seem an element of nature, not of culture), to the English capital, London (named twice in the concluding stanzas), the poem's train journey offers itself as an image of redemptive continuity, reflecting back on the English landscape through which it travels a figure of its own best and most sustaining future. Contained within the train, we might almost claim, is an agnostic equivalent of the lost Anglican organicism simultaneously ironised and lamented in 'Church Going', where the 'serious' church is a place 'In whose blent air all our compulsions meet, / Are recognised and robed as destinies'.

It might be argued that this is to extrapolate a unified meaning from a poem whose complexities of anecdote and perspective make any such singularity hard to sustain interpretatively; but there can be no such doubt about 'To The Sea' and 'Show Saturday'. In the former, a contemplation of the decorums of an English seaside holiday releases an amazed and delighted recognition of continuity ('Still going on, all of it, still going on!') and an explicitation of its more than merely casual significance ('half an annual pleasure, half a rite') before the poem culminates in a moralising reflection on the present generation at its ritualised play as the channel of English continuity: 'teaching their children by a sort / Of clowning; helping the old too, as they ought'. And 'Show Saturday' – that poem in which the Larkinian capacity for exact itemisation breaks out into an almost Hopkinsian amplitude and crowdedness – concludes with what is in effect a kind of prayer:

> Let it stay hidden there like strength, below
> Sale-bills and swindling; something people do,
> Not noticing how time's rolling smithy-smoke
> Shadows much greater gestures; something they share
> That breaks ancestrally each year into
> Regenerate union. Let it always be there.

The sense of the 'ancestral' in these lines is almost Yeatsian, and their desire for a register of common purpose, their willingness to use a diction implicated in a Christian past ('regenerate'), and their liturgical tone are a long way from the agnosticism of both belief and feeling evident elsewhere in Larkin's work. It would hardly be going too far to claim that they witness to genuine religious feeling, but a feeling attached not to a metaphysical but to a social religion: the religion of an enduring Englishness.

It is surely significant, though, that the persona or person regarding and commenting, presuming the moralising or even reverential tone, is not himself part of what he observes. The word 'they' is prominent at the close of 'Show Saturday': a third person which denies that the poem's first person could ever himself be part of the reconciliation; just as in 'To the Sea' the world depicted is one which the poem's 'I' acknowledges as having once been his own, in childhood, and which is therefore, implicitly, his no longer. There is here a register not merely of loneliness but of class distinction, social and educational: it is as if the objects of the commentator's contemplation and anecdotage all merited the snobbery (sexual as well as social) wonderfully ventriloquised on behalf of the speaker of 'Lines on a Young Lady's Photograph Album', 'Not quite your class, I'd say, dear, on the whole' (wonderfully, because it runs its insinuation so knowingly along the regular iambic line, making stress and caesura the most intimately functional elements of characterful articulation). These are versions of English pastoral to which the Larkinian personae offer allegiance, but from which they are themselves socially separate; they are versions of a pastoral in which class is supposed to have no part, but in which in fact it sets the entire tone of poetic address. They are, that is to say, fantasies of an impossibly idealised community.

In 'The Explosion' this is true too, and arrestingly so. This poem about a mining disaster appears to cut itself clear of history, to articulate at its close a self-transcending image of apotheosis, as

> Wives saw men of the explosion
>
> Larger than in life they managed –
> Gold as on a coin, or walking
> Somehow from the sun towards them,
>
> One showing the eggs unbroken.

In another of Larkin's versions of domestic relationship, wives here watch husbands; and the husbands themselves have been, earlier in the poem, 'Fathers, brothers, nicknames, laughter', indulging in talking, smoking, chasing after rabbits, robbing birds' nests on their way to work. Here is 'innocence' too, prior to its apocalypse inside the 'tall gates' of the mine. But when is the poem set? Nineteenth century? Turn of the century? The 1920s? Did miners ever engage in this kind of activity on the way *to* work? Or is this a condescending donation to them of a pastoral pseudo-childhood? One which makes their sudden deaths seem more cruel (or more 'poetic', perhaps), but which in fact acts as a mystification of actual economic circumstance – an economic circumstance whose repression perhaps returns strikingly in that image of the 'coin', reminding us, despite the poem's pastoral no-time, that miners work, rather than play, for a living (the only activity they actually engage in during the poem is playful), and that this work sometimes involves their deaths, since (if the poem is set at any point in pre-war English history) no sufficient funds were spent on their safety.

'The Explosion' creates a pastoral no-time but was itself, of course, written in a very specific time: 5 January 1970, the *Collected Poems* tells us. Four years later, in 1974, the English miners under Arthur Scargill brought down Edward Heath's Conservative government, and subsequently Margaret Thatcher ousted Heath as leader of the Tory party. Is the English pastoral of 'The Explosion' not implicated in a very specific English politics too? Is it conceivable that 'The Explosion', for all its brittle beauty of image and cadence, represents English miners in a way not entirely dissimilar to the way the *kitsch* porcelain statue which Margaret Thatcher was seen admiring on British television screens after the Falklands war represents British soldiers? To ask such questions is to be reminded of Larkin's extraordinary powers of image-making and quasi-mythologising, his way of making an English historical moment appear utterly clarified and named; but it is to be alerted too to the complex ideological fractures in the apparent purity of that image, fractures which, beyond the Larkinian moment, were to widen to a point where the Larkinian pastoral would seem a much less than 'innocent' construction. 'The Explosion' meets its match, it may be, in Tony Harrison's *v.* (1985), which takes its epigraph from Arthur Scargill.

Notes

1.   Charles Tomlinson, 'The Middlebrow Muse', *Essays in Criticism*, 7 (1957), p. 214, and Donald Davie, *Thomas Hardy and British Poetry* (London: Routledge and Kegan Paul, 1973), p. 71.

2.   Barbara Everett, 'Larkin and Dockery: The Limits of the Social', in George Hartley (ed.), *Philip Larkin 1922–1985: A Tribute* (London: The Marvell Press, 1988), p. 140.

3.   See 'The Traffic in the Distance', in *Required Writing: Miscellaneous Pieces 1955–1982* (London: Faber and Faber, 1983), pp. 274–7.

4.   See Barbara Everett, *Poets in Their Time: Essays on English Poetry from Donne to Larkin* (London: Faber and Faber, 1986) and Andrew Motion, *Philip Larkin* (London and New York: Methuen, 1982).

Chapter 8
Movements
Donald Davie, Charles Tomlinson,
Thom Gunn

In Larkin the persistence in Movement attitudes is at its most provocatively obvious in his renowned hostility to 'foreign' poetry. In the critical writings of Donald Davie, Charles Tomlinson and Thom Gunn, on the other hand, there is a notable enthusiasm for it. They have all been propagandists on behalf of modern American poetry in particular. Davie's critical career has been, in part, a long, wavering, sometimes even self-contradictory struggle with the work of Ezra Pound, on whom he has written two full-length books, *Ezra Pound: Poet as Sculptor* (1965) and *Pound* (1975), in addition to a large number of articles; and he has also championed some post-Poundian poets, notably Charles Olson and Ed Dorn. Tomlinson's most significant effort has been on behalf of William Carlos Williams, whose *Selected Poems* he edited in 1976 and on whom he also compiled a critical anthology. But his interest in and personal involvement with other American poets such as Marianne Moore, Louis Zukofsky and George Oppen are recorded in his spirited short book *Some Americans: A Personal Record* (1981); he edited a special Black Mountain poetry issue of *the Review* in 1964; and that his American audience is in a certain sense possibly his primary one is attested by the fact that his first full collection, *Seeing Is Believing* (1958), was first published in New York. Thom Gunn's collection of critical essays, *The Occasions of Poetry* (1982), mixes essays on Fulke Greville, Thomas Hardy and Ben Jonson with others on such Americans as Williams, Gary Snyder and Robert Duncan.

In addition, all three have celebrated the work of Basil Bunting (that British post-Poundian), Davie most notably in an essay called 'English and American in *Briggflatts*' which discusses the whole issue of an 'Anglo-American poetry'.[1] So involved have they been in America both biographically and poetically that it seems not inappropriate to think of them, in a phrase from a poem addressed by Davie to Gunn, as 'mid-Atlantic people', although the American interest, particularly in Davie and Tomlinson, is only one element in a general feeling for other literatures. Pushkin is an extremely important figure in Davie's pantheon, as is Boris Pasternak, whom he has translated and whose influence is prominently on display in some of his work; and Tomlinson has produced a volume of translations and is also editor of the *Oxford Book of Verse in English Translation* (1980).

In his *Collected Poems 1950–1970* Donald Davie annotates his poem 'With the Grain' with a suggestive piece of critical self-analysis:

> I am not a poet by nature, only by inclination; for my mind moves most easily and happily among abstractions, it relates ideas far more readily than it relates experiences. I have little appetite, only profound admiration, for sensuous fullness and immediacy; I have not the poet's need of concreteness.[2]

The judgement is enforced by a number of poems in which he blames himself (sometimes wryly, sometimes laceratingly) for a bookish, scholarly knowledge of the world which seems to preclude any more intimately sensuous or emotional one. It is a judgement which implies many features of the poet Davie is. He is a poet-critic who debates and diagnoses within his poems as well as outside them, constructing an *oeuvre* which makes the discourse of poetry continuous with discourses often, in post-Romantic criticism, considered extraneous to it; he is a neo-classicist 'pasticheur of late-Augustan styles', turned towards rationality, interpretation and the dream of order; and he is a sometimes envious hankerer after alien kinds of gift and scope which may appear exotically ill-allied (Pound's, Boris Pasternak's, Austin Clarke's and Robert Lowell's, for instance). The strain and stress, the occasionally awkward labour of articulation in his work, are the product of these hesitations and deliberations; but they are also the register of what his best poetry always offers: the tense and effortful, but energetically alert drama of the extended mind in action.

As actors in this drama, Davie the critic and Davie the poet are exceptionally at one: even after the versified critical essays of some of his Movement poems, the debate about poetry is pursued. The Poundian interest ('obsession' would scarcely be putting it too high), and the consequent discovery of a range of other post-Poundian American poetries, therefore feature in his own poetry at a primary and foregrounded level. This is one reason for its variable quality: the lengthy 'England' in the sequence of 'Los Angeles Poems' of 1968–9, for instance, seems more a mere catch-it-all reticule for opinion than the sinuous interweavings of thinking and feeling in some of the poems from Ed Dorn's *Geography* which were probably its model; and Davie's use of documentary material sometimes manages to be even more effortful than it is in Pound's *Cantos* which presumably gave it its permission. And when, in his lengthy sequence *Six Epistles to Eva Hesse* (1970), he attempts to show how the Poundian 'variety of space, time and action' may be as readily encompassed by English octosyllabics as by Poundian free form, he in fact falls rather flat on his face, writing a very heavy light verse indeed.

But Pound and the American model nevertheless constantly provoke Davie into self-challengingly variant registers: they act as a freeing of the often too constrained and corseted decorums of his earlier volumes. The provocation is probably particularly necessary for a poet who has, manifestly, so many misgivings about the seductive appeal of poetic rhetorics: it is one of his ways of coping with a crucial misgiving in post-war poetry, expressed also, as I suggest below, in the earliest work of Geoffrey Hill. In a curiously puritan kind of accommodation, the stylistic variety of Davie's work has something almost recklessly driven about it, as though to push himself any less would be a reprehensible failure to combat the seductive and consolatory hubris involved in the poetic act. 'The sickles of poets dazzle / These eyes that were filmed from birth', the early poem 'The Hill Field' puts it; and 'The Fountain of Cyane', the first poem of his sequence *Three for Water-Music* (1981), dramatises the misgiving with a less epigrammatic but more subtle and supple acuity:

> Sky-blue, dark-blue, sea-green, cerulean dyes
> Dye into fables what we hoped were lies
> And feared were truths. A happy turn, a word,
> Says they are both, and nothing untoward.
> Coloured by rhetoric, to die of grief
> Becomes as graceful as a falling leaf;
> No chokings, retchings, not the same as dying
> Starved and worn out because you can't stop crying.

The graceful rhyming couplets are turned almost against their own decorous fidelity by the burden they must carry. That 'the truest poetry is the most feigning' is one thing, but that poetry merely decorates terror is another still; and the stumbling of the last two lines over their extra syllables is the stumbling of this poem's own historically sanctioned form against the undermining recognition the poem makes.

Limits voluntarily imposed, nerve voluntarily lost, decencies and decorums voluntarily acknowledged: if these are symptomatic of the early, Movement Davie engaged in a well-prosecuted polemic, they are also, perhaps, strategies of self-avoidance. When the poem is 'grid', not 'juice' (the terms of 'Poem as Abstract'), it is likely to remain well under authorial control. There are, nevertheless, poems in Davie's earlier books which scarily testify to the virtues of reticence. 'The Priory of St Saviour, Glendalough' in *A Winter Talent and Other Poems* (1957) is one such. The first two stanzas wryly describe a carving of 'Two birds affronted with a human head / Between their beaks' and evoke Davie's difficulties in finding the eponymous chapel. Then comes the final stanza's surprise – the surprise, to Davie, of the event, and the surprise, to the reader, of the poem:

> I burst through brambles, apprehensively
> Crossed an enormous meadow. I was there.
> Could holy ground be such a foreign place?
> I climbed the wall, and shivered. There flew out
> Two birds affronted by my human face.

A genuine poetic strength accrues when such unease is so curtly intruded on humdrum ironies. The tendency of some Movement poems to make incident and event emblematic or even quasi-allegorical is resisted here with a finely tactful judgement. The poem's flurry of panic, and its unsettling association of contemporary fright with the ancient Christianised-pagan emblem – more than 'association': identification, rather, since the poem makes Davie himself into a living, imitative emblem – are mediated chillingly through formal precision, control and delicacy. An apprehension of fundamental anxiety and disturbance has been manipulated with great care along the patient but not emollient lines of the poem's containing form.

Under the Poundian pressure, however, similar apprehensions are given a more original and more vibrantly inclusive formulation. The 'holy ground' of his own emotional life is, we might say, discovered as a 'foreign place' under the influence of this foreign writing: Pound makes Davie strange to himself in a poetically enriching *ostranenie*, and in a more risk-taking art. In the sequence 'In the Stopping Train' (1977) this is managed at its most fluidly alive and poised. Exasperation, irritation and what the title of one poem in the sequence names as 'Revulsion' form no small part of the feelings eventually on display during the lengthy course of Davie's *oeuvre*. His poems of the 1960s, in particular, notoriously manifest such emotions in relation to the England he was becoming expatriate to; and their disdain, spleen, wounded *amour propre* and grumpy reactionary sentiment make the latter half of the *Collected Poems 1950–1970* an at times gruelling exercise in disenchanted self-justification. One of the major virtues of 'In the Stopping Train' is that it self-misgivingly converts or subsumes such feelings into the far more poetically rewarding and humanly venerable emotion of self-recrimination. Something of the kind is the final Poundian emotion in the *Cantos* too, in such fragments of wearily resigned self-knowing as 'I have brought the great ball of crystal. / I cannot make it cohere' and 'J'ai eu pitié des autres. / Pas assez'. Davie almost insinuates himself into a Poundian persona of regretfulness and self-castigation in this poem, but it is a persona in which he also vividly re-invents himself. Or, as it happens, *himselves*, since the poem employs a *doppelgänger* fiction as the chastising vehicle of its painful autobiography, one in which the relationship between art and truth is again, but with a difference, at issue:

> I have got into the slow train
> again. I made the mistake
> knowing what I was doing,
> knowing who had to be punished.
>
> I know who has to be punished:
> the man going mad inside me;
> whether I am fleeing
> from him or towards him.
>
> This journey will punish the bastard:
> he'll have his flowering gardens
> to stare at through the hot window;
> words like 'laurel' won't help . . . .
>
> Jonquil is a sweet word.
> Is it a flowering bush?
> Let him helplessly wonder
> for hours if perhaps he's seen it.
>
> Has it a white and yellow
> flower, the jonquil? Has it
> a perfume? Oh his art could
> always pretend it had.

Bernard Bergonzi has written excellently about this poem and its Poundian derivations and affiliations; but when he describes it as 'a nakedly confessional poem in cold, disdainful language', he is both exaggerating its confessionalism and underestimating its dramatic subtlety.[3] 'In the Stopping Train' is a poem in which self-rebuke is enacted by the splitting of the self in two: the poem's subjective first person castigates its objective third in a way that conveys the potential duplicity of such emotion, where the capacity for self-disgust may actually be a sly self-regard. The poem's tropes of *doppelgänger* and of a self-punishing journey in a stopping train figure these uneasy and anxious emotions in artful formal ellipses and in a wary astringency of tone; the drama of mind involving debate with, and diatribe against others elsewhere in his work here contracts into a self-laceration which is personally bruising but poetically enriching. 'In the Stopping Train' is a notable poem of existential dread, a remarkable point for a poet of Davie's beginnings to have reached, but a poem only perhaps possible to one with such beginnings, maintaining control even while painfully exploring the deepest personal perturbations. As ever in Davie, an essential element of that dread is the blame for the easy consolations of his own creativity: his self-rebuke centres on the 'pretence' of his own cunningly manipulative and camouflaging art. The poem sustains at the deepest imaginative level that ultimate irony: that only in an art brought to such poised intensity can such an undermining misgiving be given its proper due. This self-excelling poem reminds us too, both in its osmotic absorption of a Poundian example and its trope of the train journey, that Davie is, pre-eminently, a poet *en route*, between cultures, unestablished in a single place, the reader of himself and of his own home through the self-exiling strangeness of an alien poetry and an alien place. In 'Advent' from *The Battered Wife and Other Poems* (1982), he perhaps offers us his truest self-image: 'Knowing himself of those / No sooner settled in / Than itching to get out'.

In the Browningesque (or Poundian) monologue 'To a Brother in the Mystery', published in the early 1960s, Davie constructs a fiction in which a medieval monastic stonemason discusses his craft with a brother worker. When he collected the poem in *Collected Poems 1950–1970*, he appended a note which explained that 'the relationship explored in the poem is in some sort that between myself and Charles Tomlinson'.[4] Tomlinson had been Davie's pupil at Cambridge, and the personal and poetic relationship between the two has always been close. 'To a Brother in the Mystery' is a generous sketch of their alliance, Davie presenting himself as desiring to emulate Tomlinson's 'fine-drawn / Severity that is tenderness', and counselling Tomlinson against absorbing too much from him: Tomlinson's genius is for an isolated compact with the material of his own art ('A sort of coldness is the core of it, / A sort of cruelty') which might sacrifice its essential nature were it to warm too readily to human sympathies:

> For the common touch,
> Though it warms, coarsens. Never care so much
> For leaves or people, but you care for stone
> A little more.

The lines are a reminder of how perspicacious a critic Davie can be in his poetry as well as in his criticism; but in characterising Tomlinson's earlier work so well, they also raise what has often been taken as the essential critical problem with it. Where Davie's work is occasionally almost fraught with its density of human contact, Tomlinson's is, in contrast, quite remarkably devoid of the sustenance of the ordinary social world. A painter as well as poet, his fundamental engagement is not with the human but with the natural world; his fundamental preoccupation is with the nature, quality and regulation of perception itself. Where Davie has his almost lurching discontinuities of form and address, as his work attempts to keep pace with the conflicts and exacerbations of his social being, Tomlinson is quite remarkably homogeneous. There are some variations: the poems of *The Way In* (1974) which deal with his working-class childhood in Stoke-on-Trent; the more politically charged poems on the French Revolution which form a short sequence in *The Shaft* (1978); and such lighter pieces as the satirical 'Mélisande' (on a 1960s flower child) in *Written on Water* (1972). Nevertheless, the essential endeavour of Tomlinson's large body of work is an almost luminously single-minded one. It is the search for a right relation between the perceiving mind and the natural world, a world whose essential objects and attributes are light, water, stone, clouds and bone.

The natural worlds evoked in his poems are those of both England (especially Gloucestershire) and America (especially New Mexico); and his forms embrace both the characteristic meditative or discursive model of a four-stress and blank-verse line derived from English sources, and the more extemporised triplet or 'triad' inherited from Carlos Williams. Both, however, are bent to the requirements of a punctilious, austere descriptive sense concerned to give the contours of the perceived world their due without self-servingly making them either part of an aesthetic or the vehicle of a personality. Tomlinson's whole enterprise as a poet is hostile to the notion of poetry as the revelation of personality: his work is among the most rigorously impersonal of the period, as genuinely impersonal as that of Robert Graves, and far more so than that of poets who more insistently claim impersonality, such as Eliot himself and Geoffrey Hill.

The objection to poetry as the vehicle of personality rises to expression several times in the work itself, most powerfully in 'Against Extremity' in *The Way of a World* (1969). The poem's manifesto-like title was impelled, no doubt, by Tomlinson's principled resistance to the assumptions of the Alvarez anthology *The New Poetry* (which I discuss in the introduction to Part Four); and it clearly has Sylvia Plath and Anne Sexton in mind as its extremist cases. Tomlinson may well be judged less than humanly sympathetic here, where actual instances are almost named: 'The time's / Spoiled children' is a remarkably unfeeling judgement if we know anything of the case histories which Plath and Sexton dragged along with them. Donald Davie's 'sort of coldness . . . sort of cruelty' criticism takes on a sharper edge, a more pejorative implication, as a result of it. When the largest claims are made for Tomlinson – and they are made, by critics such as Davie himself and Hugh Kenner – this kind of failure in empathy should be brought into the reckoning. There is something disconcertingly unalienated about Charles Tomlinson: which is to accuse him not of complacency, but of too resolute a setting of himself against the modern fall into subjectivity. This can make some of his work seem a muted susurrus of self-communion, the contented mind performing itself in a sometimes almost podial manner (particularly where he uses that impersonal personal pronoun 'one'). John Berryman (another spoiled child of the time?) gave this kind of thing its proper judgement, to my mind, in his ambiguous elegy 'So Long? Stevens' where he asked of Wallace Stevens (the earliest, formative influence on Tomlinson): 'What was it missing, then, at the man's heart / so that he does not wound? It is our kind / to wound, as well as utter / a fact of happy world'.

Nevertheless, the gracefully measured conclusion of 'Against Extremity' is a perfect statement of the principles informing Tomlinson's work:

> Against extremity, let there be
>   Such treaties as only time itself
> Can ratify, a bond and test
>   Of sequential days, and like the full
> Moon slowly given to the night,
>   A possession that is not to be possessed.

Tomlinson has spoken of the influence on him of Coleridge's conversation poems;[5] and these lines seem to take cognizance of the conclusion of 'Frost at Midnight', with its 'silent icicles, / Quietly shining to the quiet moon', an image of delicately natural reciprocity. This Coleridgean moment in 'Against Extremity' suggests that the poet who would work against extremity, against the petulance or arrogance of personality, may, by bonding himself to a continuing and self-effacing labour, eventually discover a similar gift of reciprocity in his own language and forms. The self-possession which would protect against self-regard ensures the only proper poetic possession: the knowledge that the world may be possessed by the imagination only when the imagination is undesigningly intent on its own object, unpossessively directed outwards from its own subjectivity. This will be the true 'Eden', a concept named often, and in a large variety of contexts, in Tomlinson, and in *The Way of a World* finding one of its most memorable expressions in the fine poem 'Swimming Chenango Lake', where the body 'reads the water' when it swims, 'making a where' for itself, a place delightedly but temporarily held, 'a possession to be relinquished / Willingly at each stroke'.

The prose-poem 'Oppositions', also in *The Way of a World*, is both a statement of, and itself an exercise in, the desire for such selfless reciprocity. Subtitled 'debate with Mallarmé', it takes issue with the French symbolist's deconstructive 'echo-chamber' of absence and posits a repletion of substance not merely as challenge or prejudice (like many Anglo-Saxon attitudes to French symbolist writing and deconstructive criticism), but as seriously engaged debate:

> If the skull is a memento mori, it is also a room, whose
>   contained space is wordlessly resonant with the steps that
>   might cross it, to command the vista out of its empty eyes . . .

> The mind is a hunter of forms, binding itself, in a world that
>   must decay, to present substance.

> Skull and shell, both are helmeted, both reconcile vacancy with
>   its opposite. *Abolis bibelots d'inanité sonore.* Intimate
>   presences of silent plenitude.

The word 'bind' is interestingly repeated from 'Against Extremity': the relationship between language and world is both a ligature and a contract. The skull (derived from one of Mallarmé's sonnets) and the shell are both images for the enclosure of emptiness or absence within shape and form; a potential for 'plenitude' is present prior to, but only released by words. Both skull and shell figure frequently in Tomlinson's poems (and in his graphics): their inward–outward reciprocity is clearly one that this poet would wish to stand as an emblem of his own work. And the work is given its tension and its courage by being conducted with a full awareness of what lies over against it, the absence and emptiness of death itself, the pressure of mortality inevitably attendant on the contemplation of a skull. The mind as 'a hunter of forms' is a citation of the theologian Thomas Gilby which Tomlinson has possibly derived from its prominent quotation by David Jones in his preface to *The Anathemata*:[6] it implies a quasi-religious search for the forms of plenitude in the world, and certainly Tomlinson's work often enough appears to wish to establish an agnostic's continuity with such central Christian concepts as sacrament and grace, particularly where it derives a diction from Ruskin and from Hopkins.

The adventure of this single-minded quest is one which Tomlinson has not been slow to define himself. Sometimes with an irritating condescension, he has berated much contemporary English poetry for its small-mindedness and defeatism. His American mentors have been chosen for their greater adventure, spaciousness, attack and precision in what 'The Flight' in *A Peopled Landscape* (1963) calls 'that prime vernacular / made keen / by silence'. It is the sense of a language carefully posing itself against silence that draws him, I suspect, to the Williams triad. He almost always, however, gives it a very English inflection too, by assonating and rhyming internally where Williams's overt aim was for the utter plainness of a demotic speech – 'a reply to Greek and Latin with the bare hands', as he put it in his epigraph to *Paterson*.[7] The forms as Tomlinson derives and develops them do bring a novel delicacy, tact and gracefulness into English poetry. In the fine poem 'The Farmer's Wife: at Fostons Ash', for instance, in *A Peopled*

Landscape, they do so in a way that brings Williams into a nodding acquaintance with Hardy, and also states the principle it enacts:

> Distrust
> that poet who must symbolize
>   your stair into
>   an analogue
> of what was never there.
>   Fact
>   has its proper plenitude
> that only time and tact
>   will show, renew.

These lines could be re-lineated in a way that would almost approximate to irregular rhyming couplets; and, like Carlos Williams's own 'technical experimentation', they are perhaps best regarded as experiments in typography rather than in metre. But, emphasising pause and check, and surrounding themselves with blank paperspace, the lines make typography the realisation of preoccupation. The anti-symbolist polemic (which may be more specifically anti-Eliot, since the 'stair' figures prominently in *Ash-Wednesday*) and the insistence on the fulfilments of a poetry of fact, are formed into a structure itself mistrustfully hesitant, stealthily probing forward, an imitation of the analytic. In contrast to the flaccidity and inertia of so much modern verse deriving from the Williams line, such poems of Tomlinson's reveal the strength of a full absorption by an English poet of some of the most energising elements in the Williams poetic.

Donald Davie is much given to including his fellow poets and peers in his poetry; and just as 'Brothers in the Mystery' incorporates a reckoning with Charles Tomlinson, his poem 'To Thom Gunn in Los Altos, California' brings Gunn into a defining relationship with Davie himself. This poem works, however, by direct address; and Davie's opening lines have a bravura swagger and flourish:

> Conquistador! Live dangerously, my Byron,
> In this metropolis
> Of Finistere. Drop off
> The edge repeatedly, and come
> Back to tell us!

The peculiarly imperialist address chimes with Gunn's self-description in one of his prose pieces, 'Cambridge in the Fifties', where he says that the writing of poetry was for him then 'the act of an existentialist conqueror, excited and aggressive';[8] and the word 'edge' is knowingly derived from its frequent occurrence in Gunn's poetry, with a variety of figurative as well as literal meanings; indeed, the word 'edge' (and its cognates) is as rich in implication in Thom Gunn as the words 'risk' and 'pose'. All three summon, in numerous contexts, the dangerous pitting of oneself against life's chances and choices, and the free acceptance of consequences. If in his work of the 1950s and earlier 1960s the risks are manifestly those of an existentialism derived from Sartre and Camus, and in the later 1960s and 1970s they most notably have their origin in an experimentation with hallucinogenic drugs, they are also, throughout his *oeuvre* — as Davie's affectionately provocative identification of him with the bisexual Byron suggests — the risks of homosexual orientation and behaviour.

In speaking of Thom Gunn as a 'mid-Atlantic' poet, then, it is of course important to note his own stylistic accommodation of the work of a number of American poets (in particular Williams, Robert Creeley and Robert Duncan) and to observe the remarkable transformations of his poetic character: the crucial one is usually located between Parts I and II of *My Sad Captains* (1961) and is signalled by his choosing to write subsequently in syllabics and free verse as well as in the traditional metres which led to his association with the Movement in the 1950s. His essay on Duncan in his collection of prose pieces, *The Occasions of Poetry*, also suggests, however, the other liberation brought by his American experience: 'Homosexuality in Robert Duncan's Poetry' applauds Duncan for coming out as a gay poet as early as 1944 and makes clear Gunn's own *parti-pris*. America acted for Gunn, as it did for other gay English expatriate artists (Auden, Isherwood, David Hockney), as the scene of greater permission, the location for the more adequate performance of the sexual identity which had to be muffled or repressed at home. Thom Gunn's San Francisco is repeatedly the scene of liberation: it is stepped across into as the place where stepping across ('transgressing') becomes feasible. In many critical discussions of Gunn the philosophical has tended to occlude the libidinous, and the later work is usually read as inferior to the earlier. The notoriously varied body of his work seems to me to take on coherence if he is read as, from the start, an exceptionally libidinous writer. He is not only a poet in whom the sexualised male body is the object of desire, but a poet greatly preoccupied with the ambivalent origins and trajectories of sexual fantasy, and with the kinship between sexuality and violence.

When he discusses his early work in 'Cambridge in the Fifties', Gunn makes light of those theories of 'pose' (constructed from an eclectic mixture of Donne, Stendhal and Yeats) which then helped him write; but the repetitions of the word, if not the pursuit of the project, throughout his work, incline me to take it much more seriously as a fundamental poetic source and resource. Two chronologically widely separated instances may indicate its constancy and variety. One is from the early poem 'Carnal Knowledge', where the knowledge is that 'Even in bed I pose'; and the other from 'The Missing', part of a sequence written in the later 1980s on friends of his who have died from Aids: in a complex and unsentimentally hard-edged metaphor, he imagines their absence from him as an exposure of the contours of his own statue, 'Eyes glaring from raw marble, in a pose / Languorously part-buried in the block'.[9] The word has many connotations, the most significant of which for a study of Gunn are, I think, those of narcissism, theatricality and advertisement. The human subject watches itself and performs itself in a play of styles and gestures, aware of its status as an erotically marketable commodity. 'Whether he poses or is real / No cat bothers to say', as he writes in 'Elvis Presley': authenticity, in this world of images and slogans, is unjudgeable; significance attaches only to the held gesture itself, which may be both self-assertion and self-arousal.

Presley is one of the many 'toughs' who figure in early Gunn, the bike-boys and leather-boys too casually read as metaphors by some critics. Probably the best-known of his earlier poems, 'On The Move' in *The Sense of Movement* (1957), has been most frequently taken as an existentialist credo, as it accumulates its ringingly conclusive epigram from an impressively Yeatsian stanzaic and syntactical organisation:

> A minute holds them, who have come to go:
> The self-defined, astride the created will
> They burst away; the towns they travel through
> Are home for neither bird nor holiness,
> For birds and saints complete their purposes.
> At worst, one is in motion; and at best,
> Reaching no absolute, in which to rest,
> One is always nearer by not keeping still.

'Will', pitted self-definingly against nature, is another central concept in the earlier Gunn; and here it is given a memorable embodiment in image.[10] The poem, as a result, seems in a poised attunement to its historical moment, in no merely modish way. The restlessness, dissatisfaction and self-generation, all set resolutely against traditional ideas of nature and theology, are the very impulse of dissidence in the 1950s, whether in French existentialism or in the explosion of a youth culture inventing itself as 'teenagers' and 'teddy boys'. Presley, Marlon Brando and James Dean were the major spurs to that invention, and there are, of course, famous images of all three in leathers astride motor-bikes. Gunn's subscription very punctiliously locates the poem in 'California'.

The poem's erotic charge is muted throughout but at one point almost overt: when 'their hum / Bulges to thunder held by calf and thigh', the verb seems subliminally transferrable making the boys' pants, as well as the sound of their machines, 'bulge', as in one of the cartoons of Tom of Finland. The eroticism focuses the poem's historical definition through the lens of personal desire, a desire which is partly the narcissistic desire of self-identification. It is unsurprising, after reading 'On The Move', to discover Gunn writing a range of poems in which men in leathers, and in gay leather bars, feature as the explicit objects of erotic attachment and pursuit. Associated themes and motifs of sado-masochism ('Conquistador!') reappear throughout the work, most memorably in 'The Beaters' in *The Sense of Movement* and 'An Amorous Debate' in *Jack Straw's Castle* (1976). In the latter it features as an element of an amusing flirtation, and in a skewed assimilation of the decorums of seventeenth-century pastoral; but in 'The Beaters' it figures more perturbingly as an attraction to the paraphernalia of Nazism (a 'swastika-draped bed'), in a poem which makes a case for sado-masochistic fantasy as the imposition of necessary 'limitation' on such dangerous desire, the enactment of the fantasy as a solvent for the impulse.

'The Beaters', however, also acknowledges the 'ambiguous liberty' of such a sexuality: 'it is the air / Between the raised arm and the fallen thud'. That air or space between two possibilities, two worlds or even two selves, is the air breathed by some of Gunn's most interesting work. In his earlier poems a *doppelgänger* motif frequently appears, most strikingly in the very early 'The Secret Sharer' in his first book *Fighting Terms* (1954), where he imagines calling to himself from the street below his own window. In the earliest poetry the split self may be partly that of the homosexual unable (because of internal psychological anxiety or external social pressure) to name his sexual nature. Yet when that nature is named, the motif recurs, is even intensified and mythologised; the conflict persists beyond any specific occasion or impetus, into a division of the human psyche itself. This thematising of self-division prevents Gunn from ever becoming a simple celebrant of the liberated body and spirit: even in his books of the 1960s and 1970s, where LSD and gay promiscuity figure frequently, the emotions of his work are rarely unalloyedly pleasurable.

The theme of self-division receives its most interesting expression in two sequences: 'Tom-Dobbin: centaur poems' in *Moly* (1971) and the title sequence of *Jack Straw's Castle*. The former – partly coded for a homosexual sex act – employs the centaur as a linking figure of self-division: Tom has 'mind', Dobbin can 'fuck'. Yet at a climactic point of the poem, which is also presumably the moment of orgasm, the two are indissolubly allied in a union both consolatory and terrifying in its threat to individual identity: 'there is the one / and at once it is also the other'. The sequence moves dreamily, or narcotically, through five stages until Tom and Dobbin are balanced into stable and harmonic identity, 'Selves floating in the one flesh we are of'. In 'Jack Straw's Castle' the eponymous castle is a figure for the solipsistic entrapment inside one's own skull; and the sequence alternates between third and first person, resolving into completion only with a move towards the real exterior, a translation of solipsistic dream into sexually embodied other: 'Thick sweating flesh against which I lie curled – / With dreams like this Jack's ready for the world'. The resolution does not come, however, before the dream has included, 'close as close', the bearded, taunting Charles Manson, perpetrator of the horrific Sharon Tate murders in Hollywood in 1969, and often regarded as a prime instance of the dark underside or obverse of 1960s hippy California. This experimental and approximate poem, proceeding with the feline tentativeness of movement of which Gunn is capable in both metrical and free forms, nowhere identifies the poem's hero with Manson, but in the ninth section Manson's experience is recalled 'as if it were my own'; and one might think that here Gunn's sense of the interior *doppelgänger* reaches its nadir. The preoccupation with the socially repressed other, and with sado-masochistic experience, has produced a driven and ultimate poem of the 'dangerous'.

Such confrontations with the psyche's most disintegrative elements, which suggest a conception of the poem as the therapeutic space of psychic salve and resolution, are complemented by an implicitly radical-libertarian politics, emblematised by sexual community. 'Jack Straw's Castle', as I have said, escapes its solipsism in the reality of another body: it moves into sexual ease from a depiction of what the poem's eighth section calls 'Little Ease'. In his essay on Fulke Greville, Gunn writes of Greville's use of this phrase to indicate 'the cell where one cannot stand, sit or lie', and he observes that Camus also makes use of the image in *La Chute* to evoke 'the state of a man constrained by a sense of guilt in a world where there is no god and thus where there can be no redemption for that guilt'.[11] The guilt of murder, that primal guilt, is one of the guilts exposed in 'Jack Straw's Castle', and in the light of such self-knowledge, 'ease' is hard to come by. It may be earned only by an honest facing of the worst, but the moral of the sequence is that it is possible to break through the constraint of Little Ease by the communion of sexuality.

Gunn offers a further elaboration of this secular redemption in 'The Geysers', also in *Jack Straw's Castle*, where a multisexual orgy in a bath-house in Sonoma County, California, is made an emblem of human community, although one achieved only with ambivalent difficulty and danger, since the final 'yielding' of self may also be an Orphic tearing apart by the other(s). But the most simply relaxed statement of the theme in his work is probably the title poem of *Touch* (1967). Its stealthy free verse lines melt lapsingly into one another in mimetic representation of a cold, isolated human body slowly moving towards and penetrating a warm, sleepy other body in bed: no Conradian, *doppelgänger* 'secret sharer' now, but a manifest sharer. The mutuality of sexual sharing provokes a near-identity of the two subjectivities in which an ultimate privacy emblematises or actually provokes an ultimate communality:

> What is more, the place is
> not found but seeps
> from our touch in
> continuous creation, dark
> enclosing cocoon round
> ourselves alone, dark
> wide realm where we
> walk with everyone.

This is, if anywhere in Gunn, the true 'place' of liberation, the place in which sexual tenderness creatively remakes a human community. The place does not wait discovery, it waits being brought into being by mutually generous human wills. If this is an oneiric utopian community of sleep and touch, it nevertheless bears full knowledge of those dystopias of twentieth-century Little Ease ranged against it, since 'Touch' has previously imagined its (presumably Jewish) 'you' thinking of its 'I' as 'the nearest human being to / hold on to in a / dreamed pogrom'.

It is hard to read 'Touch' now without thinking of Aids and the sexual miseries and human tragedies of San Francisco in the 1980s. Gunn has made this his subject (how could he not?) in the sequence of poems to which I have already referred. That Little Ease should again constrict ease in this unpredictably appalling way makes these poems an integral but extremely sad coda to the themes I have been defining in Thom Gunn. The image of the isolated statue in 'The Missing' takes its edge not only from its revision of the figure of the 'pose' but from its being the antithesis of the communal vision of 'Touch'. Gunn is left in the cold isolation of his own statue, its 'chill contour' trapping him in 'unwholeness'. It is a poem hollowed out by its inability to bring the contours of his own earlier work into properly developed relief.

Notes

1. Donald Davie, 'English and American in *Briggflatts*', in *The Poet in the Imaginary Museum: Essays of Two Decades* (Manchester: Carcanet, 1977) pp. 285–92.

2. Donald Davie, *Collected Poems 1950–1970* (London: Routledge and Kegan Paul, 1972), p. 301.

3. In George Dekker (ed.), *Donald Davie and the Responsibilities of Literature* (Manchester: Carcanet Press, 1983), p. 47.

4. Davie, *Collected Poems 1950–1970*, p. 301.

5. Charles Tomlinson, *Some Americans: A Personal Record* (Berkeley: University of California Press, 1980), p. 13.

6. David Jones, *The Anathemata* (London: Faber and Faber, 1952), p. 19.

7. William Carlos Williams, *Paterson* (New York: New Directions, 1963), p. 2.

8. Thom Gunn, *The Occasions of Poetry: Essays in Criticism and Autobiography* (London: Faber and Faber, 1982), p. 173.

9. At the time of writing, this poem was unpublished, and I am grateful to Thom Gunn for showing me a copy of it. It has since appeared in *The Man with Night Sweats* (London: Faber and Faber, 1992).

10. But see Gregory Woods, *Articulate Flesh: Male Homo-Eroticism and Modern Poetry* (New Haven and London: Yale University Press, 1987), pp. 212–13, for the suggestion that 'will' in Gunn, as in Shakespeare's sonnets, is a pun on 'phallus'.

11. *The Occasions of Poetry*, p. 67.

Chapter 9
Negotiations
Ted Hughes and Geoffrey Hill

'To The Sea', the opening poem of Philip Larkin's *High Windows* (1974), is a member of the group of Larkinian post-imperial pastorals I have categorised above. 'Half an annual pleasure, half a rite', the poem's seaside holiday is one from which Larkin is alienated ('Strange to it now, I watch the cloudless scene'), but which retains the power to compel him with its nostalgias of remembered childhood and, more significantly, with its suffusion in habitual, inherited decencies:

> It may be that through habit these do best,
> Coming to water clumsily undressed
> Yearly; teaching their children by a sort
> Of clowning; helping the old, too, as they ought.

The seaside becomes a littoral pastoral, a *paysage moralisé* in which the continuity of petit-bourgeois probities is evoked and sanctioned by their detached celebrant; 'as they ought' is the pat of approval, betrayed into condescension by its imitation of slightly prissy rectitude. The pastoral is a mode of idealistic exclusion: 'To The Sea' contains transistor radios, but not mods-and-rockers rioters or any other reminder of those social discontinuities which, in the 1960s and 1970s, were drawing vast numbers of English holiday-makers to cheap foreign resorts. 'As they ought' may, in that context, be regarded as a recommendation in the face of inevitable attrition.

The early work of Geoffrey Hill is also, beneath the glaze and polish of symbolic transformation, much preoccupied with the English seaside. This is largely because, as 'Requiem for the Plantaganet Kings' has it, the 'possessed' sea often 'evacuates its dead', those dead with whom Hill's work is much taken up; but it is partly too because the seaside, far from acting as Larkinian nostalgic pastoral, acts as the locus in Hill's work of a strong anti-bourgeois animus. In the second of his 'Two Formal Elegies (For the Jews in Europe)' in *For the Unfallen* (1959) holiday-makers become an emblem of post-war European forgetfulness of the Nazi holocaust:

> For all that must be gone through, their long death
> Documented and safe, we have enough
> Witnesses (our world being witness-proof).
> The sea flickers, roars, in its wide hearth.
> Here, yearly, the pushing midlanders stand
> To warm themselves; men, brawny with life,
> Women who expect life. They relieve
> Their thickening bodies, settle on scraped sand.

The word 'midlanders' punningly confuses those who come from the 'midlands' of England with those from middle Europe who may have been involved in Nazi crimes; the emphasis on 'life', animal-like and generative, is ironically insistent in this lament for the dead; and the animal imagery is reinforced by the pun on 'relieve', which suggests public urination as well as rest, and by the final phrase in which the holiday-makers are perceived, subliminally, as birds of prey. The whole is replete with a disgust which makes it a dystopian underside to Larkin's utopian fantasy.

Ted Hughes is not much happier on the beach. It is where he discovers the jawbone of 'Relic' with its lesson in the voracious ('In that darkness camaraderie does not hold; / Nothing touches but, clutching, devours'); it is where the terrifying eponyms of 'Ghost Crabs' emerge, 'An invisible disgorging of the sea's cold / Over the man who strolls along the sands'; and it is where, in 'Postcard from Torquay' in *Moortown* (1979), a German yachtsman, xenophobically anti-English, becomes the agent of a savage criticism of contemporary English mercenariness and servility when he stalks off,

> Commandant – at home
> On the first morning of Occupation –
>
> To arrange, with lofty carrying words,
> His costly yacht's descent
> Into that swell of tourist effluent
> And holiday turds.

It would be difficult to say that the near-apoplexy there is definitely not Hughes's own; but even if it is not, the lines represent a conception of the English seaside horribly remote from Larkin's. The pathos of his 'clumsily undressed' enablers of decent English traditions is counteracted here by a sullying scatology and by the hyperbole of the metaphor for the German tourist which implies that England, having heroically repelled invasion during the war, now entertains it, willingly and unperturbedly.

In their study of the carnivalesque in European culture, *The Poetics and Politics of Transgression*, Peter Stallybrass and Allon White note that the seaside was the primary peripheral or liminal site (always partially legitimated) to which carnival moved as it was repressed in its traditional forms by bourgeois legalism in the nineteenth century.[1] In Larkin's poem the site of carnival is reconstructed as a scene of instruction: it produces a moral *exemplum*, provides a lesson in the good life, is recuperated for a bourgeois hegemony. In Hill and in Hughes it is the site of extreme disturbance and distress: it is where we speak to the dead, or are possessed by them; it is where 'we' are invaded by 'them'. Hill and Hughes are, of course, very different kinds of poet; but a fundamental effort of both, which profoundly reorients English poetry at the end of the 1950s, is an undermining of the discourses of English civility and decorum in which the Movement had its being, in the interests of a response to the historical realities of post-war Europe.

Hughes is copious, prolific, in the bulk of his work given to free forms and latterly to works realised in co-operation with others (in particular the American artist Leonard Baskin); and a large part of his effort has been dedicated to what he has described, recalling the terms of his essay on Keith Douglas, as a 'general all-purpose style . . . . the dream of an ideal vernacular'. This has its origins, probably, in Hughes's valorising of dialect – in his own case the dialect of West Yorkshire – over what he calls 'the terrible, suffocating, maternal octopus of ancient English poetic tradition'. 'Whatever other speech you grow into,' he says, 'your dialect stays alive in a sort of inner freedom, a separate little self'; and this is accompanied by considerable class venom in his earliest prose.[2] Hill is punctilious, exiguous, hieratic and formidably post-Empsonian in his knotted intricacy and ambiguity; he is given to traditional metres, careful syllabics and forms such as the sonnet and the rhyming quatrain or (when he writes in free forms such as the prose-poem) to quasi-liturgical, incantatory rhythms. Hughes is impelled in much of his work towards the creation or discovery of some provisionally sustaining myth as an alternative to what he reads as the irretrievable corruption and barrenness of English Christianity, and this myth tends to catch up into itself transformatively, or possibly to elide, actual historical circumstance and event. Hill's is a much more specifically and narrowly focused *oeuvre* which vividly mediates a series of significant historical moments – in particular Anglo-Saxon Mercia, nineteenth-century British imperialism and the First World War – in which the orthodox theologies and liturgies of European Christianity are heavily implicated and exposed. Behind Hughes and Hill it is possible to sense the pressure and presence of those two apparently implacably opposed figures from an earlier moment in English literary and cultural history, Lawrence and Eliot.

In the fascination with the apparent end of Christianity and with crucially defining phases of modern English and European history, both Hughes and Hill inscribe a major moment in the history of poetry in the period: they are the first English poets of post-war European catastrophe. Both born in the late 1930s, they came to maturity during the immediately post-war period when Europeans were faced with the two realities which have been most signally formative of the modern historical consciousness and conscience: the Nazi concentration camps and the atomic bomb. Hughes's imagination is permanently haunted by the First World War, in which his father was a combatant. It is the subject of a clutch of poems at the end of *The Hawk in the Rain* (1957), and is figured in the nightmare short play 'The Wound' in *Wodwo* (1967), in that volume's outstanding poem 'Out', in some of the incidental imagery of *Crow* (1970), and in some of the poems evoking the West Yorkshire landscape of his birth, *Remains of Elmet* (1979). The First World War, the war of the father, does duty in Hughes, as it were, for the rest of the horrors of the century. Through his father's subsequently guilty, quasi-posthumous existence, it is almost as though Hughes has inherited that war genetically, becoming his father's *doppelgänger* :

> While I, small and four,
> Lay on the carpet as his luckless double,
> His memory's buried, immovable anchor,
> Among jawbones and blown-off boots, tree-stumps, shell-cases
> and craters,
> Under rain that goes on drumming its rods and thickening
> Its kingdom, which the sun has abandoned, and where nobody
> Can ever again move from shelter.

In Hill there is a more direct address to the matter of the concentration camps themselves. *For the Unfallen* – a book whose title itself reminds us, in its negative, that we are all now merely survivors, and that the condition is temporary – has the 'Two Formal Elegies (For the Jews in Europe)', and several poems in *King Log* (1968) reiterate the theme: 'Ovid in the Third Reich' – the self-exculpating monologue of a death-camp commandant; '"Domaine Public"', written in memory of Robert Desnos, the poet who died in Terezin in 1945; 'I Had Hope When Violence Was Ceas't', the brief, horrified monologue of an inmate; and 'September Song', a strenuously self-doubting poem preoccupied with the moral implications of making poems from such material. There is a wilful decidedness in their taking on of this subject matter; it is clearly done in the face of such sentiments as Davie's in 'Rejoinder to a Critic': 'How dare we now be anything but numb?'

This involvement in modern European history may be read as the originating impulse behind much in the poetries of Hughes and Hill. It prompts their interest in some of the work of the 1940s rejected or ignored by the poets of the Movement (Dylan Thomas, and Robert Graves's *The White Goddess* in Hughes's case; Sidney Keyes in Hill's; and, as I have shown in Part Two, Keith Douglas in both). It leads them, particularly in the 1960s and 1970s, to pursue a close involvement with modern and contemporary European poetry. Hughes co-edited the journal *Modern Poetry in Translation* in the 1970s and has translated the work of the Hungarian Janos Pilinszky and contributed an introduction to Anne Pennington's translations of the Yugoslav Vasko Popa. Hill has clearly been influenced by the French poets St-John Perse (whose long prose-poem *Anabase* was published in a translation by Eliot in 1931) and Yves Bonnefoy; his work makes specific reference to such other modern European poets as Osip Mandelstam and Paul Celan; and one of his later lengthy sequences, *The Mystery of the Charity of Charles Péguy* (1983), is titled for, and written in perturbed celebration of, the French Catholic poet killed in the First World War.

Such interests and affiliations are given notable extempore expression by Hughes in an interview:

> One of the things [the *New Lines*] poets had in common I think was the post-war mood of having had enough . . . enough rhetoric, enough overweening push of any kind, enough of the dark gods, enough of the id, enough of the Angelic powers and the heroic efforts to make new worlds. They'd seen it all turn into death camps and atomic bombs. All they wanted was to get back into civvies and get home to the wife and kids and for the rest of their lives not a thing was going to interfere with a nice cigarette and a nice view of the park. The second war after all was a colossal negative revelation. In a sense it meant they recoiled to some essential English strengths. But it set them dead against negotiation with anything outside the cosiest arrangement of society. They wanted it cosy. It was an heroic position . . . Now I came a bit later. I hadn't had enough. I was all for opening negotiations with whatever happened to be out there.[3]

In his tackling of 'whatever might be out there', Hughes writes, essentially, two separable kinds of poem. The first, running through his entire career, and reaching its apogee, to my mind, in the 'Moortown' sequence (1979), is the individual lyric which revises a tradition of English 'nature' poetry, and specifically animal poetry, towards a discovery within the natural world of forces, energies and instincts which always implicitly, and sometimes explicitly, criticise the rational human intellect. The degree and kind of criticism is not always easy to decipher, since the almost exclusive diversion of the central theme of violence onto the animal world offers a latitude which would clearly be

impossible if Hughes addressed the human social or political spheres
more directly. Nevertheless, his work has frequently been criticised for
its apparent admiration of the energy of animal instinctual violence as an
alternative to what he appears to read as a debased contemporary
culture. The condemnation is clear enough in his prose writings and
interviews, and in those poems which do handle the social world more
straightforwardly ('A Motorbike' and 'Postcard from Torquay', for
instance, in *Moortown*). And it is notoriously hard to defend the poem
'Hawk Roosting' (from *Lupercal*) against charges that it unironically
celebrates the bird's will to domination by superior ability in violence.

However, this is by no means the whole story of Ted Hughes's
nature poetry, which frequently has a still, quiet intensity of scrutiny,
reverential and amazed before the recognition of otherness. It also often
has a hard pathos deriving from the way Hughes's celebration of natural
vitality is crossed with his appalled, fascinated, occasionally apparently
near-fetishistic sense of mortality. There are poems in which natural
energy or effort is evoked with a kind of desperation, in the anguished
acknowledgement that, however intense the present power might be, it
cannot long survive; and it is notable that elegy itself – most memorably
in *Wodwo* and the 'Moortown' sequence – is a generic constant in
Hughes. 'The Rat's Dance' in *Wodwo* is one such poem. Almost
unbearably, it evokes a rat caught and dying in a trap, and dying against
everything in his nature ('Trying to uproot itself into each escaping
screech') until:

> The rat understands suddenly. It bows and is still,
> With a little beseeching of blood on its nose-end.

One of Hughes's characteristic procedures is on display in those
unexpected anthropomorphisms which attach a human pathos to the rat's
extinction: it 'understands', in a word which suddenly, alarmingly
transforms an effort of instinct into an apparent effort of will or moral
intelligence, just as the phrase 'beseeching of blood' appears to give the
rat a power of prayer to this force stronger than itself.

The anthropomorphisms suggest, of course, that Hughes's animal
poems are also human allegories; and in this sense they are at one with
the second type of characteristic Hughes poem, the longer sequence
with mythical or metaphysical ambitions, of a kind possibly encouraged
by Vasko Popa's long poem-cycles, *Earth Erect* and *Wolf Salt*.[4] On four
of them from the late 1960s and 1970s Hughes's reputation is probably
still most securely based: *Wodwo* (properly considered the first sequence,
I think, though more usually read as a collection of individual pieces),
Crow (1970), *Gaudete* (1977), and *Cave Birds* (1978). The human
meaning in these poems is a speculatively metaphysical one which
assumes specifically theological or parodistic-theological expression at

particular points; and the speculations are supported by the driven, wild eloquence of Hughes's prose writings and interviews of the time. The aim is towards a mythical synthesis garnered from eclectic and esoteric sources (including Graves's *The White Goddess*, Egyptian mythology, Amerindian Trickster legend, Elizabethan alchemy and shamanistic tradition) which might act as an imaginative substitute for the doctrinal and symbolic hollowness of contemporary Christianity. The ambition is therefore very large, but such syntheses seem extremely late in time; Blake had his visions, Yeats had his *Vision*, but Hughes has not codified his intimations into system, nor has he pursued them very far into his later work. In contemporary poetry the vatic is itself liable to seem hollow very quickly; and in Ted Hughes's work we may have witnessed its final disappearance as a possibility for English poetry. The last poem of *Cave Birds*, embracing provisionality, knows that there can be no grand finale, no final closure, since 'At the end of the ritual / up comes a goblin'.

If his symbols are not developed into a symbology, however, the four central works deriving from them do share a fundamental necessity and compunction: they supply the opportunity for the development of Hughes's central theme into fictions which give permission to the usually forbidden and taboo. Agencies of licence, these provisional myths provoke powerfully disruptive or transgressive texts which oppose religious and sexual orthodoxies in something of the spirit of Bakhtinian carnival. Their central figures literally 'transgress', having their beings astride the boundaries between two worlds. The creature inhabiting the title poem of *Wodwo* is the seeker of an identity between air and water, 'no threads / fastening me to anything'; Lumb, the protagonist of *Gaudete*, is an Anglican priest and a spirit changeling; Crow and the cave birds are – strikingly in Baskin's accompanying drawings – fusions of anthropoid and ornithoid characteristics, the taloned and feathered possessors of bulkily protruberant human genitalia. Situated at the threshold of transgression, these figures draw disturbingly into themselves some of the darkest political, psychological and sexual material. In a startling variant of the *doppelgänger* motif, their dual nature twins the social self with the atavistic other which, in Hughes's schema, always accompanies it: a point he makes with astonishing force in an essay on William Golding, where he displays sympathy for the anthropologist Eugene Marais's theory that man is not the apogee but the accident of evolution, the improperly adapted miscarriage of a Neanderthalian baboon, 'a jittery Ariel among the Calibans'.[5]

It is a new and strange recension of Modernist neo-primitivism and, perhaps, a weird re-introduction of the concept of Original Sin into genetic theory; and, as Hughes gracefully admits in that essay, the idea has its comic side. In *Crow* the idea of God perpetually accompanied, perhaps superseded, by the *doppelgänger* Crow and in *Gaudete* the idea of an Anglican vicar redeeming his parish by a changeling irruption of frenzied fucking also have their comic sides, and laughter is, of course, an intrinsic element of the carnivalesque. In *Crow* the comedy is slapstick, cartoon, unremittingly violent; if the poem uses the Trickster material collected by the anthropologist Paul Radin, then this is very much a Trickster out of Walt Disney too. The poem's laughter is, however, mocking and derisive. One of its major effects is to insist on the way violence comes to us ready-processed, already assimilated, in contemporary media, and therefore hardly properly assimilable at all; and in this sense *Crow* is very much a poem of the moment of the Vietnam war, whose atrocities were being edited for nightly television viewing when the poem was published in 1970.

In *Gaudete* the comedy is probably less intended and less functional, deriving from the jolting discontinuities between the poem's location and its metaphysic, as if the inhabitants of Dylan Thomas's Llaregyb were suddenly to undergo demonic possession (although there is a tradition, associated particularly with John Cowper Powys, of the rural-erotic-metaphysical in English prose). Nevertheless, it contains some of Hughes's most ravishingly voluptuous writing, but voluptuous almost to a febrile degree. And this is, I think, its point: the febrility of *Gaudete* is the febrility of voyeurism. Originally written, amazingly, as a film scenario, the poem constantly presents us with its characters viewing one another through binoculars, windows, telescopes, cameras. Human sexuality in *Gaudete* comes to us mediated through an editorial lens. In one of his strongest later poems, 'Eclipse' in *Flowers and Insects*, Hughes positions himself as the voyeur, through a magnifying glass, of the mating of a pair of spiders; and one implication of the horrified fascination with which *Crow* and *Gaudete* confront their taboo material may be that the art of poetry is a spectator sport too, in which the reader views the friction of private or dreadful experience against public language. Both poems gain power from what can be sensed within them of sexual and psychological pressure not released but diverted into form; in *Crow* this is primarily a matter of Oedipal stress, in *Gaudete* of adulterous and suicidal sexuality.

The leaner and more clearly coherent *Cave Birds* gains from its decision to expose material of this kind to a less dissipatingly fragmentary and mythical treatment than *Crow* and a less resolutely plotted narrative than *Gaudete*. Subtitled 'an alchemical cave drama', it is an entirely novel sort of interior but objectified psychological drama of regression and release, in which Hughes's poems and Baskin's drawings become genuinely interdependent. The 'cave' of the title may be taken to be the cave of the skull, in which the poem's nightmarish anthropo-ornithoid creatures, standing in the way of any easy transactions between the human subject and society, play out their roles (as summoner, interrogator, plaintiff, judge, accused and executioner) in a psychic trial of guilt, self-condemnation and expiation. The origins of these compunctions in individual catastrophe are perceptible, if oblique, in lines aching with affliction ('I felt life had decided to cancel me / As if it saw better hope for itself elsewhere'; 'I was glad to shut my eyes, and be held'); but the sequence as a whole objectifies, in a ritualistic formal re-enactment, interior states of anxiety, dread, morbidity, desperation, confession and remorse. The exact nature and locus of these feelings, therefore, remains humanly (and personally) unspecified, but achieves psychological and poetic recognition inside the impersonal dramatic dialogue between poet's word and artist's image. The ritual contains the most tender realisation of the *topos* of the 'great mother' in Hughes's work, as the fraught and disintegrative emotions of the sequence are unburdened by the figure of the loving feminine. Suicidally regressive self-abnegation ('Nothingness came close and breathed on me − a frost / A shawl of annihilation has curled me up like a new foetus') is dissolved by the ministrations of the figure named by one poem 'A green mother':

> It is heaven's mother.
> The grave is her breast
> And her milk is endless life.
>
>   You shall see
> How tenderly she has wiped her child's face clean
> Of the bitumen of blood and the smoke of tears.

This reading of *Cave Birds* is perhaps too relentlessly psychologising; it is a poem which opens itself up so malleably to co-operative readerly interpretative effort that there is hardly any agreement among its commentators. The poem 'A green mother' might at least as profitably be read, for instance, as an assuaging but resolutely non-Christian account of an afterlife; and the two most perfect poems in the sequence, 'The knight' and 'Bride and groom lie hidden for three days', may similarly be considered resourceful transformations of the physical facts of death and decay into a nurturing imaginative metaphysics, a reading of death as the 'perfection' and 'revelation' of the body's assimilation into natural process rather than the object of terrified anticipation, a later recension of Dylan Thomas's 'A Refusal to Mourn'. Whether as psychological or as metaphysical drama, however, *Cave Birds* is one of the crucial poems of the period; but it makes Hughes's acceptance of the position of Poet Laureate in 1984 seem in some ways astounding.

For *Cave Birds* presumes the exhaustion of Christianity; and the post of Poet Laureate is, as Neil Roberts has reminded us, one with strong Christian associations.[6] In some of the poems Hughes has published as Laureate the Christian implications of the post are diverted into something continuous with his former work, but weirdly so: a view of monarchy and nationhood as themselves quasi-religious entities, susceptible to an elaborate mythologising which nevertheless keeps one combative eye on the more quotidian views of the tabloid press. Admirers of Hughes's earlier poetry may also be impressed by the ways in which other poems offer a further display of the regal metaphors available in the concept of 'the animal kingdom'. Nevertheless, the sceptical or republican reader may remain stony-hearted when confronted with certain examples of Hughes's patriotic warmth. What psychological compulsion can have induced him, for instance, to celebrate an English royal marriage by writing, among an assortment of regal platitudes, that 'your *I do* has struck a root / Down through the abbey floors'?[7] In the Anglican wedding service in Westminster Abbey Sarah Ferguson said, as everyone in such a service says, not 'I do', but 'I will'. Yet in another poem commemorating a marriage somebody does say 'I do':

> I made a model of you,
> A man in black with a Meinkampf look
>
> And a love of the rack and the screw.
> And I said I do, I do.

Sylvia Plath, scarifyingly, in 'Daddy'.

In Geoffrey Hill the post-war knowledge of horror comes, as in the fourth poem in the sequence 'Of Commerce and Society', in metre, rhyme and meditative calm:

> Statesmen have known visions. And, not alone,
> Artistic men prod dead men from their stone:
> Some of us have heard the dead speak:
> The dead are my obsession this week
>
> But may be lifted away. In summer
> Thunder may strike, or, as a tremor
> Of remote adjustment, pass on the far side
> From us: however deified and defied
>
> By those it does strike. Many have died. Auschwitz,
> Its furnace chambers and lime pits
> Half-erased, is half-dead; a fable
> Unbelievable in fatted marble.
>
> There is, at times, some need to demonstrate
> Jehovah's touchy methods that create
> The connoisseur of blood, the smitten man.
> At times it seems not common to explain.

The poem is typical of Hill in a number of ways. It is about hearing the dead speak, specifically the dead of the European holocaust; and almost all his work is a self-conscious communing with the dead: far more radically than Hughes, the elegiac is his predominant mode, and the locution 'the [adjective] dead' is one of his most characteristic signatures ('the authentic dead', 'the unedifying nude dead', 'the first dead', and so on). Communing poetically with the dead, however, is not a neutral or necessarily innocent act: if 'artistic men' enter this conversation, so do 'statesmen', and the conversation can be a mode of rhetoric as well as a mode of the poetic. The suspicion about fundamental motivation in poetry, as in political power, is Hill's major theme; neither politician nor poet really have a conversation with the dead; they give a voice of their own to the dead, ventriloquising on their behalf, but inevitably using them for their own purposes too, to make policies and to make poems. In Geoffrey Hill the making of poems becomes, self-consciously, an act fraught with potential embarrassment, anxiety and guilt. His is a poetry written under the sign of an undermining sentence from Coleridge's 1796 Notebook which he cites in his critical prose: 'Poetry – excites us to artificial feelings – makes us callous to real ones'.[8] The poem can be given its permission only by the scrupulous scepticism of its unease before its own powers of appropriation and exploitation.

If the scrupulousness is maintained, then the poem is also sanctioned by memorial obligation. It may preserve what time and human inertia or turpitude would destroy: prodding the dead from their stone may ensure that they are not allowed to rest in the 'fatted marble' of official, politically exploitable monuments. Hence those central poem-sequences in which Hill searches out instances and *exempla*, points of centripetal intensity, where the pressures of history and poetry may be registered at their strongest: 'Funeral Music' in *King Log* (1968), evoking the period of the 'Wars of the Roses'; *Mercian Hymns* (1971), which crosses an evocation of the Mercian Anglo-Saxon king Offa with mediated autobiographical material; 'An Apology for the Revival of Christian Architecture in England' from *Tenebrae* (1978), which offers in a series of sonnets a meditation on the historical transformations of what Coleridge in one of the poem's epigraphs calls 'the spiritual, Platonic old England'; and *The Mystery of the Charity of Charles Péguy* (1983), which meditates on the life, writing and death of Péguy partly as the enablement of a consideration of some of the implications of the Christian concept of sacrificial death.

This poem from 'Of Commerce and Society', however, also alerts us to the peculiarities of diction and tone with which Geoffrey Hill is capable of approaching such perturbing and recalcitrant material; the tone of this poem seems hardly appropriate to its occasion. The word 'prod' in the poem's second line is the first marked breach with decorum: you prod cattle from their pen, not dead from their stone, and the word therefore suggests a belittling animalising of the dead. If this, however, is inappropriate to the reverence we usually offer the dead, it may remind us of how little reverence was ever offered to the violently dead, especially the dead of Auschwitz, who were prodded into cattle trucks, and how little reverence may be offered them in their afterlife in political rhetoric or poetic appropriation. In its diction of defamiliarisation the word therefore earns its own expressive appropriateness. But what of the dilettante, almost dandyish insouciance of 'The dead are my obsession this week / But may be lifted away'? It is at one with the adjective given to the methods of Jehovah which Auschwitz may be said to illustrate: 'touchy'. One is usually 'a bit touchy', slightly irritable on a bad day; touchiness does not often kill six million people. And perhaps it is also at one with the foregrounded wordplay which moves by contraction from 'deified' to 'defied' to 'died'.

In Geoffrey Hill, the reader is frequently held up, even snarled up, in exactly such problems of tone, diction, attitude and approach. In this case one reading could probably make a case for 'touchy' similar to the one I made for 'prod': that actually it grows into appropriateness the more you consider what exactly it was that prompted ordinary human beings to commit mass murder. Many of the grander explanations pale beside the greater horror of what Hannah Arendt famously (in relation to Adolph Eichmann) called 'the banality of evil': perhaps the grossest crimes have been committed because people have been a bit 'touchy', and perhaps cultures as well as individuals can be 'touchy'. And 'touchy' is a not inappropriate, if nevertheless comically deflating, epithet for the Old Testament God, or 'Jehovah', who is, after all, prone to murder on his off days. The wordplay could similarly be accounted for by reading it as thematically functional: when thunder 'does strike', some will 'deify' it, others will 'defy' it, but whether they treat it as a god or a fate, they will 'die' regardless. The contraction of the participle, then, enacts, as it compacts, the fate of the Jews under the Nazis.

Yet I cannot personally think that this particular verbal figure 'grows into' any greater appropriateness by being unpacked in this way: anything that is 'play' will seem inappropriate to this occasion. I think one is forced, therefore, to take it as a deliberate inappropriateness, of a kind perhaps not inappropriate to that dilettante or dandyish voice which has already sounded, and which it seems impossible to account for other than by positing the notion of a 'speaker' or 'persona', and by taking the poem as in fact a dramatic monologue, spoken in character by an 'artistic man' addressing the matter of Auschwitz as almost an exercise on a theme, the theme being the title of the sequence, 'Of Commerce and Society', whose subtitle happens to be 'variations on a theme'. This of course ironises the moral issue raised by the poem almost to a vanishing point of uninterpretability: the relationship between art and atrocity is being raised by a poem in which the artist who writes is himself a dilettante dabbler in the darkest matter of twentieth-century experience, 'obsessed' by the dead only for a week at a time. If the 'speaker' is being condemned, it could be said, it is a condemnation audible only to the most subtly attuned literary sensitivity.

Where the poet 'Geoffrey Hill' is in all this is hard to tell – the composer of the variations who is also the instrument-maker – but this kind of imbrication of mode on mode and baroque convolution of address is undoubtedly where Hill's scrupulousness leads him. The procedure – which can occasionally seem not so much a way of proceeding as a way of stopping *better* – reaches its apogee in the sequence 'The Songbook of Sebastian Arrurruz' where, in the poem 'From the Latin', Hill offers a translation from the work of a poet he has himself invented; into which he implants his most strikingly erotic line ('And at night my tongue in your furrow'). It is as though what presses most deeply on the personal life can be allowed to survive in poetry only almost at the vanishing point of formal complication. We are not far here from the involution of the Modernist Portuguese poet Fernando Pessoa, who wrote four quite different kinds of poem under his own name and three heteronyms. He also prepared for publication, in the year of his death, a volume to be called *Cancioneiro* (*Songbook*); and in 1922 he had published his *English Poems*.[9] Hill gives us Sebastian Arrurruz's dates as 1868–1922, and 'From the Latin' was also originally dated 1922. While it is possible that there is a more than merely coincidental relationship between Arrurruz and Pessoa, the date is more obviously Hill's genuflection to the *annus mirabilis* of Modernism, the year of *The Waste Land* and *Ulysses*, those texts to which his own formal ingenuity and linguistic density maintain an allegiance.

The creation of voices in Hill's poems, of speaking subjects who are themselves sometimes knowingly subjected to authorial control, leads to his use of the plurivocal sequence as his major form. In some of his earlier individual lyrics the attempt to compact into a brief space the desired level of irony and ambiguity can, at its extreme, seem implosion rather than revelation, the poem pushed in on top of itself by the effortful tension and stress of ambiguous articulation. In the greater spaciousness of the sequences, and in the opportunities they provide for the dramatisation, rather than the static enactment, of irony, the reader feels liberated into the interpretation of necessary obliquity rather than, as he or she can sometimes feel in the individual lyrics, locked into an almost masochistic self-argument.

In 'Funeral Music' the handling of the sequence makes for an extraordinarily poignant and shocking evocation of a brutal period of English history, as Hill weaves into and out of the voices of three of the earls about to be beheaded. The ironical resonances are at once dramatic, historical and theological:

> If it is without
> Consequence when we vaunt and suffer, or
> If it is not, all echoes are the same
> In such eternity. Then tell me, love,
> How that should comfort us – or anyone
> Dragged half-unnerved out of this worldly place,
> Crying to the end 'I have not finished'.

This speech – climactic, desperate, disappointed – is addressed as a personal epistle of 'last words' to someone beloved, named as 'love' but nowhere otherwise identified. The poignancy therefore derives initially from the dramatisation: the butchered fifteenth-century figure speaks his address to the woman he is leaving. But he also speaks through her to us as readers, and speaks in particular to the poet who is now writing him. Identified as 'contractual ghosts of pity', the poem's 'characters' are therefore held to this contract with a poet, the poet who re-creates them through pity, ventriloquising on their behalf. Hill's sequences consistently construct forms similarly caught between dramatic monologue and lyric meditation. Doing so, they also set in mutually undermining relationship dictions drawn from opposed and antagonistic areas of experience: barbarisms against civilities; mimetic abrasions against oracular eloquence; what the *Péguy* poem calls 'high farce' against 'low tragedy'. In an *oeuvre* making crucial use of the tropes of oxymoron and paradox, Hill may well be regarded as a late poet of the mixed genre castigated by Pope in *The Dunciad* as a 'mazy dance' ('How Tragedy and Comedy embrace; / How Farce and Epic get a jumbled race'). Hill's sequences are as remote from Donald Davie's neo-Augustan recipes for purity of diction as is conceivable; the mixed dictions and registers are an attempt to ensure that the poet does not shirk confrontation and explanation, but that at the same time he continuously undermines any propensity in himself to become a 'connoisseur of blood'.

Sometimes, as in my own efforts with 'Of Commerce and Society' above, it can be extremely difficult to interpret these poems. In the *Péguy* poem, for instance, a number of critics have sensed an objectionably schoolmasterly tone, as Hill parades Péguy too obviously as an example; but the admitted peculiarities of tone are ascribed by Vincent Sherry, one of Hill's finest critics, to the presence in the poem of 'a dramatic interlocutor, resembling, say, the circus barker go-between in Brecht's historical farces'.[10] The notion is a sophisticated one, but (like the concept of the 'Arranger' introduced into criticism of *Ulysses* by David Hayman, which this resembles)[11] it can hardly have occurred to any reader without Sherry's suggestion; and yet, were it accepted, it would clearly make a large difference to any interpretation of the poem. A more savage critical debate has raged over the 'Apology for the Revival of Christian Architecture' sequence, where some critics have accused Hill of reactionary organicist assumptions in his evocation of imperial English nostalgias, but others have, on the contrary, found him retrieving such instances for ironic inspection and scrutiny. It is conceivable that a poetic of such painstakingly involuted self-scrutiny may leave the reader properly chastened but finally unappeased. Taking to a terminal point the Modernist theories of impersonality propounded by Eliot and Joyce, moving Empsonian ambiguity towards utter undecidability, Geoffrey Hill may put us in the position of those petitioners to the figure of 'Music' at the end of his 'Tenebrae': 'when we would accost her with real cries / silver on silver thrills itself to ice'.

Yet the difficulties of interpretation deriving from the clash of dictions, from an undecidability of tone, from the plurivocal play among styles and discourses, are perhaps the inevitable result of as sophisticated a verbal and poetic intelligence as Hill's coping with the conviction that any more univocal English would be pretence and delusion after what history has inflicted on the language. His work seems to embody at its source the conviction that, from where we are now, there is no centre of value to be finally located, no model of utterance which can create an innocent space, no articulation free of guilt or impure motive. Neither can the human subject itself, constituted from warring discourses, discover any single, fixed place of authority, certainly not in any construction a reader may make from the signature and inscription 'Geoffrey Hill'. Which is why, I take it, *Mercian Hymns* twins Hill's own childhood experience with the reign of that early imperial ruler, Offa, positing 'Not strangeness, but strange likeness' between twentieth-century gifted, working-class child and eighth-century ruler, between the body and the body politic, between the high and the low style, between the vernacular and the literary. The result, as in hymn XXVII, is a poetry of compacted interruption in which a word is hardly uttered before it is modified, cancelled, undermined. This is Hill's painful art of vocation and revocation, that art of critical juxtaposition in which mythical allusion, journalistic reportage, word-slippage, bad pun and self-conscious pastiche cross, collide, co-habit and interbreed:

> 'Now when King Offa was alive and dead', they were all there,
>   the funereal gleemen: papal legate and rural dean;
>   Merovingian car-dealers, Welsh mercenaries; a shuffle of
>   house-carls.

> He was defunct. They were perfunctory. The ceremony stood
>   acclaimed. The mob received memorial vouchers and signs.

> After that shadowy, thrashing midsummer hailstorm, Earth
>   lay for a while, the ghost-bride of livid Thor, butcher
>   of strawberries, and the shire-tree dripped red in the
>   arena of its uprooting.

Notes

1. Peter Stallybrass and Allon White, *The Politics and Poetics of Transgression* (London: Methuen, 1986), pp. 179–80.

2. Cited in Ekbert Faas, *Ted Hughes: The Unaccommodated Universe* (Santa Barbara: Black Sparrow Press, 1980), pp. 202–3.

3. ibid., p. 201.

4. See Vasko Popa, *Collected Poems 1943–1976*, translated by Anne Pennington with an introduction by Ted Hughes (Manchester: Carcanet Press, 1978).

5. Ted Hughes, 'Baboons and Neanderthalers: A Rereading of *The Inheritors*', in John Carey (ed.), *William Golding: The Man and His Books* (London: Faber and Faber, 1986), p. 166.

6. See Neil Roberts, 'Ted Hughes and the Laureateship', *Critical Quarterly* vol. 27 no. 2 (1985), pp. 3–5.

7. Ted Hughes, 'The Song of the Honey Bee', in *Rain-Charm for the Duchy and Other Laureate Poems* (London: Faber and Faber, 1992), p. 23.

8. Geoffrey Hill, *The Lords of Limit: Essays on Literature and Ideas* (London: André Deutsch, 1984), p. 4.

9. See Fernando Pessoa, *Selected Poems*, translated by Jonathan Griffin (Harmondsworth: Penguin, 1974).

10. Vincent Sherry, *The Uncommon Tongue: The Poetry and Criticism of Geoffrey Hill* (Ann Arbor: University of Michigan Press, 1987), p. 216.

11. See David Hayman, *Ulysses: The Mechanics of Meaning* (Englewood Cliffs: Prentice-Hall, 1970).

Part Four
From the Sixties

Introduction

In the 'postscript' added to the 1967 reprint of his *Purity of Diction in English Verse* Donald Davie observed that 'the England of the 1950s is in some ways extraordinarily remote already';[1] and his long poem 'England', written at about the same time, anatomises a condition with which he was completely out of sympathy: 'Brutal manners, brutal / simplifications, as / we drag it all down'. Philip Larkin is calmer but also self-excluding in the paradigmatically self-deflating, if satirical, lines of his 'Annus Mirabilis', written in 1967:

> Sexual intercourse began
> In nineteen sixty-three
> (Which was rather late for me) –
> Between the end of the *Chatterley* ban
> And the Beatles' first LP.

The force of Davie's invective focuses on the violence done to his conception of the literary, since 'England' is written with Ted Hughes explicitly in mind. Larkin's cultural signals (the Penguin paperback publication of D.H. Lawrence's *Lady Chatterley's Lover* in 1960; the release of the Beatles' first LP, *With the Beatles*, in 1963) fix the 1960s, rather, as the moment of new licences and permissions in both sexual and artistic behaviour, permissions Larkin was to take advantage of in, for instance, the number of four-letter words he uses in his volume *High Windows* (1974). Whether read as threat or opportunity, whether castigated or mildly satirised, the 1960s clearly presented themselves to these central exponents of the poetic styles of the previous decade as radically alternative and oppositional.

Davie's 'England' exposes in a more exacerbated form an argument he had already pursued in a dialogue with the critic A. Alvarez published in 1962 in the first issue of what was to become one of the most significant little magazines of the 1960s, Ian Hamilton's *the Review* (I discuss it further below).[2] The influential poetry editor and critic of the

Observer, Alvarez powerfully recommended the work of Ted Hughes in his anthology *The New Poetry*, published by Penguin in 1962 and subsequently in a revised and enlarged edition in 1966 (the edition I refer to here). That anthology, with its introductory essay 'The New Poetry or, Beyond the Gentility Principle', remains one of the central documents for an understanding of the evolution of poetry in the period. A very striking book in physical appearance, its cover illustration is Jackson Pollock's *Convergence*; and that American action painting, developed out of the styles of Abstract Expressionism which, in the post-war period, represented a concerted American takeover of the world art culture (and market), is exactly appropriate to the impulse of the anthology, as is the driven extremity of Pollock's own biography. Alvarez marshals his English poets behind four exemplary American figures: John Berryman, Robert Lowell, Anne Sexton and Sylvia Plath. But, as has often been pointed out, the English figures, ranging from Norman MacCaig to Ian Hamilton, have no apprehensible coherence (they include almost all the old Movement poets, for instance, along with Hughes and Hill), and in fact the introduction does not argue any. Prescriptive rather than descriptive, it isolates a central complaint and judgement and recommends a new orientation. Its significance, therefore, lies beyond itself, in the work of some of these poets, and others, as it developed after the mid-1960s.

Alvarez's complaint is that English poetry has, since the experimental Modernism of Eliot and Pound in the 1920s, employed various 'negative feedbacks' as the result of an endemic English 'gentility'. Culminating in the Movement's 'academic-administrative verse', these 'feedbacks' have prevented it from addressing the most urgent modern and contemporary experience: the two world wars; the concentration camps; genocide; the threat of nuclear war; and the terrifying lesson of psychoanalysis that 'the same forces are at work within us'. In the American poets of the mid-century Alvarez discovers a willingness both to learn from the technical achievements of Eliot and to confront the 'forces of disintegration' in the political world and in their own psyches. He calls, therefore, for a 'new seriousness' from English poets which might emulate the work of these Americans, their 'poetry of immense skill and intelligence which coped openly with the quick of their experience, experience sometimes on the edge of disintegration and breakdown'.[3] If there is something vaguely hectoring and disdainful in Alvarez's tone in this introduction, as though he is far superior in sensitivity to any of his English poets, and something suspiciously almost glamorous in his view of extremity, the charge of a disabling gentility is well-founded, and the recommendations were to some extent, although not always in terms Alvarez would have recognised, taken up by some of these poets, and by others, subsequently.

The influence of the Americans, particularly Lowell and Plath, on

English and Irish poets since the 1960s has been wide-ranging. Lowell actually lived in England in the 1970s and a pressure from the post-*Life Studies* (1959) phase of his work, even if sometimes only temporary, is marked on such otherwise different poets as Donald Davie, Seamus Heaney, Derek Mahon and Michael Hofmann. The influence of Plath, who also lived and wrote in England in the late 1950s and early 1960s, is crucial on an entire generation of women poets and, indeed, on the development of feminist theory as well as feminist poetry since the late 1960s (I return to this in Part Five); but her presence may also be sensed more unexpectedly elsewhere: in Heaney's 'Summer Home' sequence in *Wintering Out* (1972), for instance, and in some of the work of Douglas Dunn. In his poem 'The Hour' in *The Happier Life* (1972), which is almost pastiche-Plath in places, Dunn names four o'clock in the morning 'The Sylvia Plath hour'; and there is a sense in which, after the publication of her brilliant and astonishing posthumous volume *Ariel* in 1965, the mid-1960s were altogether, both in America and in Britain, the Sylvia Plath hour. Alvarez in *The New Poetry* made these pressures and contacts significant at an extremely early and prescient point: the anthology includes hitherto unpublished poems by Plath and features Berryman at a stage of his development prior to *The Dream Songs*, the poems on which his reputation most securely rests.

If Alvarez was influential in directing English poetry towards a particularly enabling kind of American writing, he was similarly serviceable in relation to European poetry. As advisory editor of the outstanding Penguin Modern European Poets series, which began in 1963, he was instrumental not only in bringing to the attention of a British readership some of the best modern and contemporary work of Europe, including Eastern Europe, but also in making translation itself a notable feature of the poetic activity of the period. (Lowell, whose volume of translations or versions, *Imitations*, was published in 1962, was also influential in this regard.) For a time in the 1960s and 1970s the Penguin series was accompanied by a number of other forums for the dissemination of poetry in translation, most notably the beautifully produced Cape Editions series edited by Nathaniel Tarn, the Rapp and Carroll Poetry Europe series, the still continuing journal *Modern Poetry in Translation*, begun under the editorship of Ted Hughes and Daniel Weissbort in 1965, and the several Poetry Internationals initiated by Ted Hughes in 1967, at which a large number of international poets convened in London to read their work. There are objections to poetry in translation, and they have been made with great force by a number of poets and critics in the period. One of the most subtle and persuasive is that made with characteristic aphoristic wit by Peter Porter. The problem with translation, he says, is that, 'burdened with so much good will', its relentless well-intentionedness 'upstages us a little'.[4] This may well be the bracingly derogatory way of putting what Seamus Heaney admiringly but perhaps masochistically says in his essay 'The Impact of Translation': that 'because we have not lived the tragic scenario which such [East European] imaginations presented to us as the life appropriate to our times, our capacity to make a complete act of faith in our vernacular poetic possessions has been undermined'.[5]

Between Porter's scepticism and Heaney's faith the argument will continue to run; but it is clear that the act and influence of translation is of central importance to English poetry since the early 1960s. Simply to name some of the finest translations of the period is to register something of their scope and influence: Czeslaw Milosz and Peter Dale Scott's Zbigniew Herbert (1968); Anne Pennington's Vasko Popa (1969); Elaine Feinstein's Marina Tsvetayeva (1971); Michael Hamburger and Christopher Middleton's Paul Celan (1972); Edmund Keeley and Philip Sherrard's C.P. Cavafy (1975); Ted Hughes and Janos Csokits's Janos Pilinszky (1976); Clive Wilmer and George Gomori's Miklos Radnoti (1979); Hans Magnus Enzensberger's own translation of his *The Sinking of the Titanic* (1981); Jon Stallworthy and Peter France's Boris Pasternak (1983). In addition, there have been some outstanding translations by poets of earlier work, notably Peter Dale's Villon (1973) and his Laforgue (1986); Alistair Elliot's eye-openingly erotic Verlaine (1979); Christopher Logue's versions of Homer in *War Music* (1981). At various points in this study I have referred to some of the particular ways in which translation has affected English work; but the dialogue and exchange have been constant and endemic.

When Larkin refers to the Beatles in 'Annus Mirabilis' he is giving the Sixties one of its most obvious new names and locations. In this poem the Beatles represent, along with *Lady Chatterley*, a new sexual permissiveness; and this became a theme in the later Larkin most lucidly crystallised in the title poem of *High Windows*. The Beatles represent other things too, however, which have their part in any history of poetry in the period. At the centre of the explosion of youth culture in the 1960s, they are evoked euphorically by Thom Gunn: 'they stood for a great optimism, barriers seemed to be coming down all over, it was as if World War II had finally drawn to its close, there was an openness and high-spiritedness and relaxation of mood'.[6] This new openness and relaxation are also implicit attacks on English gentility; in what William Scammell has perfectly characterised as their 'uproar and nirvana', the Beatles inscribe a new relationship between popular and 'high' culture.[7] Their music and lyrics were the subject of a kind of criticism never previously employed in relation to popular forms.[8] This partial dissolution of cultural categories – apparent also in relation to the potent and protean 1960s eclecticism of Bob Dylan – has had far-reaching consequences, some of which I return to in the introduction to Part Five.

If the Beatles and Dylan represent this, and were certainly to some extent responsible for it, they were not, however, alone. A notion of poetry as performance as well as print had already begun to develop in the poetry-and-jazz meetings of the late 1950s and early 1960s. Sometimes associated with the Campaign for Nuclear Disarmament, such meetings had radical political alignments and affiliations. With the disillusioning support given to the American involvement in Vietnam by Harold Wilson's Labour government of the mid-1960s, a poetry of the 'Underground', associated with rock music, festivals, 'happenings' and anti-war protest, developed rapidly and found its clearest focus in the 'International Poetry Incarnation' at the Albert Hall in June 1965 and in Michael Horovitz's Penguin anthology *Children of Albion: Poetry of the 'Underground' in Britain* (1969), with its vast (sixty-page) rhapsodic-ecstatic 'Afterwords'. Horovitz's Underground is a capacious one – he includes sixty-three poets – but overwhelmingly male: only four of the sixty-three are women. If this now seems the most obvious limitation on the revolutionary potential of the 1960s Underground, there are many aesthetic limitations too: even the most scathing anti-Vietnam poems – Adrian Mitchell's 'To Whom It May Concern', for instance – seem diminished on the page. A poetry of the deliberately impermanent, much of this work is now probably best regarded as part of the history of the political moment which culminated in the Paris *évènements* of May 1968. In this dissolution of categories the irony may be that it is the songs – in particular, it seems to me, those of Dylan – that have proved permanent, where the poems now seem to fall off the page in their fragile ephemerality.

The 'Underground' nevertheless has a more secure place in the history of poetry in the period, for several reasons. It was organised around a number of small presses which, in the 1960s and early 1970s, published some extremely fine work by British poets, and introduced British readers to a number of writers in the Pound/ Carlos Williams/ Charles Olson tradition of American poetry. These presses included Cape Goliard, which published Olson; Fulcrum, which published Basil Bunting's *Collected Poems* (1968) and David Jones's *The Tribune's Visitation* (1969); Ferry, Trigram and Migrant. The counter-voice in contemporary British poetry was sounded in a number of poets associated with these and other small presses, some of whom Horovitz published in *Children of Albion*, but whose work never sat very cosily there, and who have subsequently gone on to produce arresting and significant poems deliberately outside the cultural 'mainstream' and the commercial publishers of contemporary poetry: Andrew Crozier; J.H. Prynne; Roy Fisher; Lee Harwood; Tom Raworth; and Ian Hamilton Finlay, whose 1960s 'concrete poetry' developed into some striking later artefacts, letterings and horticultural objects. And, through its presence as a regional, extra- or anti-metropolitan kind (particularly in the extremely popular work of the 'Liverpool Poets' – Adrian Henri, Roger McGough and Brian Patten – which was collected as the best-selling volume in the Penguin Modern Poets series, *The Mersey Sound*, in 1967, and in Tom

Pickard and the Mordern Tower poets in Newcastle), it brought to public attention a poetry self-consciously written from the British provinces, preparing the ground for some subsequent work which has become one of the strongest and most influential kinds in English writing since the 1960s.

Such a poetry was one of the focuses of Jon Silkin's little magazine *Stand*, which had originally been started in 1952 but, after a break, returned in 1960 and still continues. Published from Leeds and subsequently from Newcastle, it acted as a major organ of encouragement and dissemination for some provincial or regional writing: Tony Harrison, who was involved in its editing for a while, published there, as did Douglas Dunn. In both these poets, as I indicate below, a regional poetry is also a poetry of working-class origin: both were first-generation grammar-school beneficiaries of the 1944 Butler Education Act, which opened secondary and tertiary education to a far wider class base than previously. When, in 1966, Seamus Heaney published his first book, *Death of a Naturalist*, he was drawing on comparable sources of identity and anxiety. The little magazine edited by James Simmons in Northern Ireland, *The Honest Ulsterman*, began in May 1968 with an issue containing an interview with Roger McGough (citing Dylan and John Lennon) and an editorial, glowing with the Civil Rights meliorism of the period, recommending the 'independence' of the 'regions'. Befitting the apocalyptic date of the journal's origin, these relatively innocuous contents came blazoned with the magazine's short-lived subtitle, 'monthly handbook for a revolution'. But there was, of course, a genuine poetic revolution being promulgated; and the insistent regionalism is confirmed by the second issue which published Harrison along with Heaney and included a piece on Brian Patten and Tom Pickard. It is remarkable, in such a context and in a magazine published in Belfast, that there is no explicit reference to Northern Ireland itself. Only a few months later, on 5 October 1968, the Civil Rights movement met the violent opposition of the Royal Ulster Constabulary in the streets of Derry city; and the results of that confrontation, it could be claimed, have been the single most influential factor on the subsequent history not only of Britain and Ireland, but also of contemporary 'English' poetry.

Notes

1. Donald Davie, *Purity of Diction in English Verse* (London: Routledge and Kegan Paul, 1967), p. 201.

2. The Davie/Alvarez dialogue is reprinted in Ian Hamilton (ed.), *The Modern Poet: Essays from 'the Review'* (London: Macdonald, 1968), pp. 157–76.

3. A. Alvarez (ed.), *The New Poetry* (Harmondsworth: Penguin, revised ed. 1966), pp. 28–9.

4. See Michael Schmidt and Grevel Lindop (eds), *British Poetry Since 1960: A Critical Survey* (Oxford: Carcanet Press, 1972), p. 208.

5. Seamus Heaney, *The Government of the Tongue* (London: Faber and Faber, 1988), p. 44.

6. Thom Gunn, *The Occasions of Poetry* (London: Faber and Faber, 1982), p. 180.

7. See William Scammell, 'Hostages', in *A Second Life* (Liskeard: Harry Chambers/Peterloo Poets, 1982), p. 15.

8. See, in particular, Wilfred Mellers, *Twilight of the Gods* (London: Faber and Faber, 1973).

Chapter 10
Some English Attitudes
Peter Porter, Peter Redgrove, Hugo Williams,
Ian Hamilton, David Harsent

The late 1950s and early 1960s witnessed the rise of two groupings of
poets less significant than the Movement but more genuinely and
straightforwardly interactive, and of notable influence on the poetry of
the following years. 'The Group' organised by Philip Hobsbaum (and
later by Edward Lucie-Smith) and the journal *the Review* edited by Ian
Hamilton share, in their titles, a near-anonymity which may signal
self-effacing tentativeness or its opposite, depending on the degree of
stress placed on the definite article (Hamilton's lower case 'the', in
particular, draws attention to itself in the very act of lowering itself).
This ambiguity seems very revealing of their constitution, premise and
approach, and revealing too about their cultural moment. Although they
share little else in common, both derive from the procedures and style of
the academic study of English Literature in Oxford and Cambridge in
the 1950s and early 1960s. The Group was explicitly linked to the
seminar practices of Cambridge English under F.R. Leavis; *the Review*
implicitly to some conception of the exacting discriminations of a
platonically ideal Oxford tutorial.

The Group

Philip Hobsbaum was a pupil of F.R. Leavis at Downing College,
Cambridge, when he organised meetings of a group of poets there in
1952. The Leavisian discussion of texts in a seminar, with its 'common
pursuit of true judgement', was intended to spill over into these
discussions of their own work among a group of contemporaries. In
London in 1955 these practices were formulated into a weekly meeting
in which participants would discuss work previously circulated in
cyclostyled copies. In 1963 Hobsbaum and Edward Lucie-Smith edited

A Group Anthology which contained, as an 'epilogue', a taped excerpt from the Group's conversation; and Hobsbaum subsequently discussed this kind of close practical criticism of new work by contemporaries in his book *A Theory of Communication* (1970).[1] The pattern was eventually repeated in Belfast when Hobsbaum moved there in 1966. One of the participants, Seamus Heaney, describes this later version in his essay 'The Group' in his critical book *Preoccupations* (1980): Hobsbaum, Heaney recalls, 'emanated energy, generosity, belief in the community, trust in the parochial, the inept, the unprinted'.[2]

This encouraging and entrepreneurial spirit was clearly beneficial to, and helped cement a relationship between otherwise disparate writers. The original London Group contained, among others, Peter Porter, Peter Redgrove, George MacBeth and Alan Brownjohn. It is impossible to trace any common pattern or concern among these poets; and the Group singularly lacked anything like a programme or manifesto. The only shared element in their creativity was the agreement that creativity should be open to rational scrutiny and modifiable by advice. In this, the Group may be regarded as the predecessor of those numerous creative writing 'workshops' which have been such a notable feature of the writerly life since the 1960s; indeed, a brief continuation of the London Group after Hobsbaum's departure was called the 'Poetry Workshop'. The democratising tendency of the word 'workshop' perhaps indicates the most lasting significance of the Group. Providing an arena in which poets of diverse imagination and energy could find advice, confirmation and companionship, it helped to deconstruct further the tail-end 1940s neo-Romantic conception of the poet *maudit* and to push deeper into institutionalisation the more self-deprecatory image of the poet prosecuted by the Movement. If some aspects of the Group now seem a little glumly dutiful or earnest, it nevertheless provided for a handful of young poets of stature, including Porter and Redgrove, a beneficial model and meeting-place.

In the preface to his *Collected Poems* Peter Porter alludes to Louis MacNeice's recommendation to 'leave even not-so-well alone' when collecting your past work.[3] It is a recommendation which dangerously gives hostages to fortune; but it also suggests that Porter sympathises with the large energy and push, the multifarious effort, of MacNeice's *oeuvre*. His own work shares the MacNeician fullness but also the flatulence, the garrulousness as well as the grace and gravity. Its range is exceptional, embracing the satirical vignettes of metropolitan life in the early 1960s which established his initial reputation; historically dense meditations and monologues which cross the contemporary with various types of alternative world; narratives and fiction-poems which may well be regarded as precursory of some of the later, better-known narrative modes of the 1970s and 1980s (particularly those of James Fenton); private and public elegy and lament; and, increasingly as the work progresses, an elaborate self-commentary. This variety of subject matter is unified by two entirely distinctive Porterian characteristics: a pervasive melancholy, despite the spirit and vigour of much of his surface descriptiveness, and an exceptional density of cultural reference and allusion, most notably to music.

The latter is often intimately connected with Porter's reverence for the reality and idea of 'Europe', and in particular of Italy. This is most uncharacteristic of English poetry in this period, but is strongly reminiscent of the Australian poet A.D. Hope; and Porter was born in Australia, moving to England only in his early twenties. The rooting of himself in a cultural homeland in Europe reflects, perhaps, both the aspirations of the autodidact and the emotional needs of the outsider. This can occasionally have its self-indulgence (*'Thank God, / Grâce à Dieu, Gott sei dank* – we are / As international as an opera festival, / We who love Italy', he writes in 'The Cats of Campagnatico', apparently without irony about the exclusiveness of that plural), but it is notable how lacking in the ordinary English class snobberies Porter is. Genuinely outside most of that, his poetry about England has the authority of an always partially detached curiosity. If the poem 'The Last of England' tells us that 'You cannot leave England, it turns / A planet majestically in the mind', Porter nevertheless orbits this planet at a very oblique angle.

In early satires such as 'John Marston Advises Anger' this produces the verve and resonance of a fascinatedly hyperbolic disgust:

> It's a Condé Nast world and so Marston's was.
> His had a real gibbet – our death's out of sight.
> The same thin richness of these worlds remains –
> The flesh-packed jeans, the car-stung appetite
> Volley on his stage, the cage of discontent.

The 'Condé Nast' world of the late 1950s and early 1960s gave Porter, himself at the time an advertising copy-writer (like Peter Redgrove), the occasion and material of much of his most characteristic early work. The appetitiveness of the times, and their duplicities and hypocrisies – quite a different, more jaded and pessimistic picture of the 'swinging Sixties' from that available in the poetry of the 'Underground' – are his themes; and their appurtenances are, everywhere, his decoration. These poems are a roll-call of now outmoded modes: Daks suits, Jensen cars, Dacron swimwear, 'all the democratic sexiness' from which Porter, emotional outsider too, is usually excluded, with a slightly self-pitying regretfulness which would seem indebted to Larkin if it did not also seem so instinctive and natural.

This satire of the metropolitan smart set, however, gradually deepens into a melancholy, Horatian, post-imperial gloom. 'Seaside Resort' in *Preaching to the Converted* (1972) makes its contribution to the English 'littoral' I have already commented on in Larkin, Hughes and Hill, but in its meditative murmur and vague air of helplessness it points back also to the anxious uncertainty of Matthew Arnold in 'Dover Beach'. With 'Empire gone', conscious of 'nothing but the calm of history dying', the poem reflects on a statue of Queen Victoria in an English coastal town:

> I am almost in love
> with the small black Queen in the wind
> and I will not notice that the beach is full
> of mussel shells and crab claws
> and the smell is unimaginable
> yet like your mother's corpse,
> that the torn feather is a terrible
> catastrophe, and I am cold
> and lonely on an unimportant strand.

The imperial nostalgia here, and the post-imperial wistfulness, are criticised by that wilful refusal to recognise the present evidence of the senses ('I will not notice . . .'); the Arnoldian melancholy attaching to death and decay – a kind of lapidary, supine quietism – can be sustained only by ignoring the actual smell of the rot.

It would clearly be simplistic to claim that such a self-critically ambivalent position must be unique to a poet from the old imperial colonies; but the smell here and the 'terrible / catastrophe' harmonise with the view of civilised Australia offered in the fine poem 'Cities of Light' which closes *Fast Forward* (1984). A poem in which an Australian aborigine celebrates those dream-cities which survive in the aborigine imagination even through present economic misery and political oppression, it also envisages the ultimate persistence of these 'cities of light' when the 'quondam cities' of the Australian present have vanished. The end of those cities will occur when 'each surveying colonel will be hauled / Down from his statue in the seasoned park'. This aborigine would clearly not be tempted to fall 'almost in love' with these statues, as the Porter persona falls in 'Seaside Resort'; but Peter Porter, ventriloquiser on his behalf, may presume the intimacy since the smell of Empire is for him too the smell of death in the family: 'like your mother's corpse'.

It is revealing that when you begin to discuss Porter's apparently social poems of moral and political import, you find yourself adducing an element of biography. His work is, throughout, prey to sudden painful autobiographies, from the depiction of himself 'so eagerly unhappy' in childhood, in the early poem 'Eat Early Earthapples', to the elegies for his wife in *The Cost of Seriousness* (1978). Beyond this, however, his poems frequently lurch from apparent social description and anatomisation into much more private, occasionally dreamlike and quasi-surreal encodings. Sometimes poems which begin as though they are by the later Auden end sounding more like John Ashbery; and it is disconcertingly difficult to extract anything as accessible as a meaning from some of these: even his most enthusiastic critics confess to finding Porter at times impenetrably obscure. He occasionally combines ellipsis with a kind of baroque syntactic compaction, a clotted and static contortedness unrelieved by any genuine memorability of line or cadence. This is perhaps given its definition in a poem which intends a statement of the relationship between an autobiography and an art, 'On This Day I Complete My Fortieth Year'.

Its title alludes to the poem in which Byron celebrates the completion of his thirty-sixth year, and Porter's poem could, indeed, be called 'On Not Being Byron'. A witty exercise in the poet's own setting of limits on theories of the autonomy of art, it charts the disadvantages of being Peter Porter with 'the boring sociology of it / and the boring history', rather than being Byron with Newstead Abbey, owls, graves, a club foot and a driven ambisexuality. The rueful Porterian envy focuses, needless to say, on the disadvantage of having the glaring sunlight of Australia rather than 'the European gloom' as your biographical *donnée*. The poem's perhaps disingenuous anti-heroics conclude with Porter's definition of his own work:

> these are the epiphanies of a poor light,
> the ghosts of mid-channel, the banging doors
>   of the state sirocco.

The Joycean word 'epiphanies' is appropriate to a poet who elsewhere displays an interest in Joyce (particularly in the poem 'James Joyce Sings *Il Mio Tesoro*') and a readiness with the pun. The 'poor light' is presumably an index of the unByronic greyness and melancholy which is the characteristic weather and atmosphere of Porter's work. But the phrase could also imply the tendency of a Porter poem to release an epiphany from the poor light of its surrounding difficulties and impenetrabilities. Again and again his work strains towards epigram, aphorism, apophthegm; the title of one poem is 'Apophthegms Come to the Party', and the juxtaposition of moral sobriety and carnival licence may be regarded as the combination which provokes the most satisfying Porterian amplitude and scope. It is an unusual one in contemporary British poetry, as unusual as the influence of Wallace Stevens which it occasionally suggests. Some of the 'epiphanies' which it manages to cast clear are well worth the wait and the effort, none more so than one of the finest moments from his sequence of elegies for his wife in *The Cost of Seriousness*. Echoing the seventeenth-century poet Henry King in its title and form, 'An Exequy' is a poem which may be thought to rival, in English, some of the poems in the greatest modern sequence for a dead wife, the Italian Eugenio Montale's *Xenia*:

> *O scala enigmatica,*
> I'll climb up to that attic where
> The curtain of your life was drawn
> Some time between despair and dawn –
> I'll never know with what halt steps
> You mounted to this plain eclipse
> But each stair now will station me
> A black responsibility
> And point me to that shut-down room,
> 'This be your due appointed tomb.'

Peter Porter has been a very generous critic of Peter Redgrove, and this must be testimony to the mutual supportiveness of the Group (as well as to the catholicity of Porter's taste), since Redgrove's work is as different from Porter's as could well be imagined. He has sometimes been compared to Ted Hughes, who had some early connections with the Group; one or two of Redgrove's 'bestiaries', in particular 'Thrust and Glory' (on a 'great longhaired hog'), stand comparison with Hughes's, and his work certainly has few other points of contact in contemporary British writing. Like Hughes, Redgrove has laboured at the creation of a complex and internally coherent symbolic system or symbology, explicitly anti-Christian and pagan-organicist-pantheistic, and implicitly Gravesian and Jungian, a private imaginative system intruded upon and interrupted dissonantly and intermittently by 'official', public symbols and myths. Some of its central features, in particular its magical feminism, in which the masculine principle is oriented towards the service of a 'Great Mother', are developed outside the poems too in a body of exploratory fiction and discursive prose, notably *The Wise Wound*, co-written with Penelope Shuttle.[4]

The symbology makes for a considerable amount of repetition, and it is sometimes not at all clear why one poem should end, or another begin, where it does. Its essential features may therefore be fairly briefly described. The hostility to Christianity appears to be the familiar one: threatening any full embodiment, the religion is antithetical to the achievement of human potential and to the true realisation of sexuality. The Church is therefore, in the title of one poem, the 'Killing House', and is always associated with death; and, as the title of the poem strategically placed at the beginning of the 1987 selection of his work insists, perhaps a little melodramatically, Redgrove's poetry is 'Against Death'. Christian disembodiment or bodilessness is therefore opposed with what might be thought a kind of somatic eschatology, a celebration of various kinds of repletion discovered in the human body and in the world's body.

Such celebration is at the very centre of Redgrove and is manifested in various forms. In such poems as 'On the Screaming of Gulls' and 'Minerals of Cornwall, Stones of Cornwall', it is a particularity in naming the appearances and appurtenances of the physical world in their correct scientific language which is strongly reminiscent of the Hugh MacDiarmid of 'On a Raised Beach' (as is the tendency of these poems to delight in itemisation and catalogue for their own sake). It is a joy in the richness of variant dictions too, especially the restoration of archaisms like 'swart', 'tippet', 'scatheless', 'peltry' and 'yare'. It is, above all, the development of patterns of imagery and association, through poem after poem, drawn from a relatively small area of reference: insect life, horticulture and a kind of fantasia on domesticity and family relationships (especially paternity). At times in these poems Redgrove is voluptuous, exhilarated and euphoric in a version of that narrowly circumscribed, zany and comic English metaphysical pastoral also to be read out of such earlier productions as Stanley Spencer's paintings, T.F. Powys's *Mr Weston's Good Wine* and some of the films of Powell and Pressburger. As in them too, the English folktale (crossed, in Redgrove, with one of its contemporary recensions, the Hammer horror film), with its alternately comic and frightening sense of the persistence of ancient ritual, is often visibly stirring just beneath the surface.

Insects — called in 'The Widower' 'the small kin' — are perhaps his most exceptional symbol, with a resonance by turns (or even all at once) Blakean, Franciscan and Christopher Smartian. All kinds of 'ephemerids' — flies, wasps, spiders, bees, moths — sustain an empathetic poetry of the minuscule which has one of its climaxes in 'The Funeral', an entirely original kind of maternal elegy in which Redgrove, attending his mother's funeral, sprouts 'birth-wet wings' which he entwines with his father's wings 'ragged and tattered like those of an old moth', effecting in him a lightening of the burden of grief. This metaphor for empathy (which may, stated coldly like this outside the poem in which it figures, seem almost ridiculous) is sanctioned by numerous other instances in the work of this imagery of insect wings, but it clearly occurs here as more than just metaphor. The wings are offered as the transcription of some quasi-visionary experience at one with the poem's final vision of the dead mother herself

> at the door ajar
> On the field of light, looking back over her shoulder,
> Smiling happiness and blessing me, the coherent veil
> Of the radiant field humming with bees that lapped the
> water, and she bent
> And washed her tired face away with dew and became a
> spirit.

The bees there act as the visible (and audible) signal of the other world into which the dead mother is disappearing; their humming is a kind of consolatory psalm, audible to the poet and his father who share, with their newly sprouted wings, the bees' arachnoid features. The insect 'symbol' in the poem therefore proposes a visionary interconnection. A great deal of Redgrove's work takes as theme the elemental struggle between life and death, and the interpenetration of the two ('Sean's Description' memorably offers a 'firm sweet apple' as 'what a dead person really looks like; taste her'); and the almost obsessional theme can become dissipated among its hyperbolic repetitions. Here, however, the visionary interpenetration is managed with a very light hand: the visionary moment is a humanly poignant and selfless one too. Remembering the old woman's exhaustion, the poem grows at its close into an appropriately Dantean allusion: its final, absolving image is a subtle, painful and tender revision of that moment in the *Purgatorio* when Dante washes the face of a dead friend with dew.

This visionary stillness consorts in 'The Funeral', in a way wholly typical of Redgrove, with a mundanity or even bathos: 'back at the house I sobbed my heart out in the little white-tiled loo'. It is this risky element which makes comparisons with Ted Hughes quickly otiose. Such visionary elegies as Hughes's 'The Green Wolf' have an absoluteness of assurance and command; their strength is all in their certainty that they have evolved an exactly appropriate diction and form. Redgrove, on the contrary, has little time for the appropriate; he signally lacks decorum. This can be mere weakness; and, faced with the vastness of his output, it is hard to disagree with the criticisms of his detractors. He is, indeed, repetitive and hypertrophic; his poems frequently lurch for forms they never quite achieve, wildly proliferating a dissipating and centrifugal imagery, drowsing into themselves; he almost entirely lacks the memorable line or the inevitable rhythm and cadence; individual poems can seem little more than a patchwork of motifs. But, as in other poets of 'visionary' orientation (Whitman, Lawrence), the restlessness – which may seem flailing – is the price of the intensity.

The intensity results from both an earnestness and a vulnerability in the pursuit of his central symbols. If the earnestness can seem unintentionally comic (even if you are prepared to admit that it is occasionally intentionally so), the vulnerability will almost always seem a saving grace, exploratory and undogmatic. The result, as in 'The Funeral', is an awkwardly affecting tenderness and an almost childlike confession of confused feeling, uninterrupted by the usual adult defence mechanisms of distance or irony. This is quite different from any *faux-naïf* sophistication, although it may sometimes seem over-ingratiating. For this reason, Redgrove is, it may be, most successful when his eye is led to the margin of his symbology by some originating impulse outside it: when, in 'The Proper Halo', it discovers a congruity with itself in an uncle's comic misunderstandings, or when it is plotted into a politics in such poems as 'Living in Falmouth' or 'Who's Your Daddy', with its uncompromising anti-militarism. The battleship *Ark Royal* in that poem remains obdurately outside the poet's desire to accommodate it inside the nurturing warmth of his characteristic metaphors ('It is not a white spider / Flying in its cracked web of the lake'); and the poem ends by finding metaphors which make the battleship terrifyingly strange, the alien location of a mechanised slaughter which can be included in, but not comprehended by the imaginative generosity of poems like Peter Redgrove's:

> It is the sledge made of dead men's nails,
> The glittering horse of scythes,
> The refrigerator of snowy carcases.

the Review

Ian Hamilton's little magazine of the 1960s and early 1970s, which ran from 1962 to 1972 (subsequently metamorphosing in 1974 into *The New Review*, which survived until 1978), was probably more significant for the level of its critical debate than for the poetry published in its pages: Hamilton himself was one of the fiercest and most decided poetry reviewers of the period. Nevertheless, it established an influential 'house style', pursued most notably by Hamilton himself, David Harsent and Hugo Williams. The most obvious feature of the *Review* style is the brevity of individual poems, a brevity complemented now by the exiguousness of some individual outputs over the years since the 1960s. The brevity is a reflection of the desire to produce the refined, distilled lyric essence of a moment, event or relationship. Clearly deriving some of its impulse from the imagists of early Modernism and, behind them, Japanese haiku and tanka, and having close affinities with some American poetry of the 1960s (James Wright, Robert Bly), this kind of 'miraculous' lyricism (as Hamilton calls it in his preface to his collected work) places all its premium on the emotion itself.[5] Generated from a very narrow range of imagery (especially light, hands and hair), and from, almost always, the use of falling cadences, interior locations and direct vocative addresses to a 'you', these poems tend to a dangerous constancy of tone: they are plangent, melancholy, weary, resigned, passive. Because they are so brief and surrounded by so much white space, great attention is thrown on matters of lineation and even punctuation, which may be as much an atmospheric as a grammatical pointing. In Hamilton's 'Birds line the gutters, and from our window/ We see cats . . .', for instance, the comma – not essential grammatically – seems a kind of tired sigh, an almost theatrical notation.

The slight lyric grace of these poems, however, if it occasionally threatens to collapse into the merely precious, is also a tight-lipped, stoical attempt to distil essential emotion from bewildering and threatening feelings often merely hinted at. In Hamilton's *The Visit* (1970) grief for a father's death is prominent, and the developing knowledge of a wife's insanity turns the volume, almost, into an extended sequence in which individual poems draw sustenance from one another and from their governing context. In Harsent too, madness, suicide and the difficulties and duplicities of domestic life ('We have learned to pretend that we live like this') are permanently within earshot. This can make for an overwrought air of the portentous and minatory, but it also focuses some genuinely perturbing juxtapositions. The usual enclosure within interiors (most frequently bedrooms), for instance, is breached by the flickering television set: in Harsent's 'The Late Late Show' from *After Dark* (1973), a woman gradually retrieving full consciousness (after sleep or drink or drugs or sex, we are not told) is put into the perspective of a concluding couplet which tells us that 'In a corner Cybulski bled / through someone's spotless laundry'; and Hamilton's 'Newscast' similarly ironises interior English comforts with the sudden intrusive displacements of the TV:

> The Vietnam war drags on
> In one corner of the living room.
> The conversation turns
> To take it in.
> Our smoking heads
> Drift back to us
> From the grey fires of South East Asia.

This is the *Review* method at its most satisfactory, and it is commented on by an observation Hamilton makes when discussing a poem by James Wright: 'The image is permitted to come forward but . . . it comes by way of discrimination, it makes energising contact with the "outer world".'[6] In too many *Review* poems the image is not so much discriminatingly energised as locked into a solipsistic or spineless inertia. Here the image of the 'smoking heads' is complexly and horrifyingly extensive, certainly energised by its ambiguity. The leisure of the TV audience with their cigarettes is forcibly crossed with the pain of those suffering the other catastrophic fires of Vietnam. The heads which 'drift' back to the spectators are momentarily almost surreally disembodied, but in Vietnam the surreal nightmare of decapitation is all too real. The languid English conversation might 'take it in', since the

TV insists on being acnowledged, but it cannot fully 'take it in', since the continuation of comfort depends on excluding it (the heads do 'drift back', they don't stay put), and to 'take it in' fully may even imply the admission of culpability and engagement in protest against the Wilson government which supported American foreign policy: an activity and a discourse clearly quite alien to the quietist resignation of this pretty imperturbable community, where the appalling thing happens in wearied cliché ('drags on') and only in 'one corner' of a room – and, by implication, a conversation – in which so many less tedious things are happening. Yet the sensitivity which records this anecdote is implicitly appalled by the juxtapositions enforced upon it: the 'living room' is taken over by the killing fields of that heavily capitalised geography of the other, 'South East Asia'. The poem, then, seems both true to and revealing of the moment of its composition and the character of its perceiving participant; it is a poem in which the English liberal conscience catches itself in the stasis of impotence.

Despite such triumphs of compacted brevity, however, it was perhaps a consciousness of the dangers of monotony that soon impelled the *Review* writers towards more spacious forms and more oblique devices: the sequence, such as Harsent's 'Dreams of the Dead' and 'Moments in the Lifetime of Milady'; and the use of personae, such as Harsent's 'Mr Punch' and Hugo Williams's 'Sonny Jim'. It is revealing that both of these personae, perhaps influenced by the split selves in John Berryman's *Dream Songs*, vent uncivilisable emotions of aggression and hostility which are left in the margins of the more purely lyric work. The persona is essentially a way of diverting the lyric impulse into the obliquity of dramatic presentation. I have already commented on the theatricality of Hamilton's punctuation; and there is also a dramatic element in the frequency of direct address in many *Review* poems. This can sometimes even be alarming, when the 'you' addressed (almost always, we are to assume, the woman with whom the 'I' is having a troubled relationship) is made too presumptuously an object of manipulation: 'You turn to me and when I call you come / Over and kneel beside me'; 'you want to lean / But patiently, upon my arm'. The kneeling and the leaning there are gestures of abnegation, part of a manipulative male fantasy of dominance and instruction. Another way of putting this might be to say that the poet's attitude to his human subjects in these poems is directorial: like a stage director, he places them in attitudes and interior locations and puts words in their mouths ('you say' is a common locution). One of the distinguishing features of Hugo Williams is that he is nervously and self-referentially alert to this dramatising element in the *Review* manner and scrupulous about its potential moral difficulties.

Although *the Review* published his first pamphlet when he was only twenty-three and he is the author of some of the most exiguous of all contemporary poems, Williams is not adequately characterised by the definitions of the *Review* poem which I have offered above. His first volume, *Symptoms of Loss* (1965), derives in part from a Movement manner, which makes it precociously and rather forbiddingly finished. Fortunately, if Williams was so much older then, he has grown younger than that since, ringing the changes on a variety of styles and eventually producing, in *Writing Home* (1985), one of the most striking and memorable individual sequences of the period. His penchant for the louche and the *demi-mondain* is apparent even in that first book, however, in such poems as 'The Pick-up' and 'An Anonymous Affair'; and this in itself helps give his work its exceptionality in contemporary English poetry. Sublimely unafraid of the dandyish or the quasi-camp gesture, he fills the already haiku-like forms of the volume *Some Sweet Day* (1975) with cherry blossom and clouds ('O lovely cherry tree, come true') and makes a mock-Japanese vignette out of an inflatable item of beach furniture in a poem called 'Li-Lo'; and in the poems of erotic frustration, longing and loss which make up the volume *Love-Life* (1979) he appears almost to out-Cavafy Cavafy as his poetry picks up cadences and a mood from that great modern Alexandrian poet as he figures in the well-known English translations of Edmund Keeley and Philip Sherrard (even though Williams's second-person pronouns are, unlike Cavafy's, all unambiguously female).

As this premeditated and scrupulous intertextuality might suggest, Williams's poems – for all that they might initially appear the unmediated, sometimes even sentimental spontaneity of direct autobiographical utterance – are actually sophisticated exercises in a self-aware and performed self-display. The closing lines of 'The White Hair' in *Love-Life* conveniently suggest several of the characteristic attributes of a Williams poem:

> Not day by day,
> But line by line I live, not seeing you.
> The hungry hours of the earth grope through me now
> In their search for images.
> I wish I could pluck you out of me
> As easily as the white hair I saw in the mirror,
> Though even then I noticed my searching right hand
> Start moving in the wrong direction.

The self-referentiality here, as the poet lives along the lines of his poem rather than in computable time, harmonises with numerous references in Williams to the act of composition itself. There is an intensity but also a poised, calm, studied brio in this; the lessons of haiku, from which this poem clearly derives, have been well learned. The poet displays his fictive and formal inventiveness even in the act of implicating them in his suffering. The suffering too, erotic and almost febrile, is the common emotional centre of a Williams poem; but, as often, it is combined with a tone not far from the whimsical. And the final image is entirely distinctive in its almost cinematic quality, its ability to freeze a gesture as a director might freeze a frame: a sudden verbal stasis or gradual slow-motion is an intrinsic element in the Williams repertoire. It is also characteristic in the way it sucks personal suffering, and any actual other human subjectivity, into a sudden, annihilating vacuum of narcissism. The mirror-gazing vanity, or obsession with his own ageing, makes that original 'not seeing you' suddenly and retrospectively ambivalent: it means not just 'not coming into contact with you', but 'not seeing you, seeing myself instead' – which may, of course, explain why he is not seeing her any more, as she fails to live up to the expectations of his own self-regard.

In using such narcissistic tropes, as he frequently does, Williams is displaying an awareness of the ways in which identity is a construction, not a given. If his poetry is, in one sense, all surface, then it persuades us, like some of the work of Roland Barthes, that surfaces are all significance too: his poems might well be regarded as little 'mythologies' (in the Barthesian sense) of the humdrum and the ordinary, teasing out a structure of signification from what appear the inevitable physical and emotional *donnés* of a life. This is at its clearest in *Writing Home*, where his affinities with cinematic technique and his theatrical tropes are brought to their most interesting focus and intensity. It is also the volume in which Williams most frequently gazes at himself in a mirror; and the book's exploration of narcissism and identity is carried forward through a sequence of poems which is, on the surface (and paradoxically, it may be), a subtle, memorable and haunting elegy for his father.

Hugo Williams's father was the well-known English actor and playwright Hugh Williams, who died in 1969 (Hugo's name makes him of course almost, but not quite, his father's mirror image). The title *Writing Home* plays with the fact that the book is partly composed from Hugo Williams's transcription (and presumably partial rewriting) of his father's wartime letters to his mother; those poems, and a number of others in which the son remembers meetings with his father, make the volume dense with the re-created presence and present absence of, clearly, a very memorable man, a 'personality' in the now outmoded sense of that term. But the title presumably also plays with other potential senses: the poet-son remembers writing letters home from school and re-creates their stoically suppressed misery and loss; this volume is a 'writing home' to his own origins, family and past; and it writes out its poet's own familial or genetic 'home' or identity as, scrutinising traces and memories of a father to discover 'What manner of man it was / Who walked in on us that day', he is also attempting to discover 'What manner of man I might be'.

The intimacy with which we feel we have come to know Williams's father in the book, and Hugo's own wary, ironic, fascinated, deeply affectionate relationship with him derive, paradoxically, from the apparent superficiality of the descriptions and evocations. 'Good looks were everything where I came from', the poem 'Waiting To Go On' says; and the recurrent preoccupation of the poems is, indeed, with looks: with dress, hairstyle, expression, gesture, manners, imitation. Like a large number of poems in the book, this one uses a theatrical situation to initiate a figure for the constructions of identity. Here the child tries literally to identify himself with his father when, while his parents are out, he dresses (in front of a mirror) as 'Hugh Williams, even more handsome in Regency!'. As he hears their car returning, he has 'about one minute / to put everything back where I found it / and come downstairs as myself'. The child must be furtive when he plays the part (of the father) he wants to be; but he is acting too when he plays the publicly acceptable role (of the son) he is expected to be. Such theatrical tropes convey a whole relationship between father and son: the father plays a part in his wartime letters, at once stoic and appalled, just as he plays Shakespeare in the Tunisian desert; for a punishment the father makes his son walk out of the room backwards bowing and saying 'Goodnight, my liege'; the son is a 'hero of the subplot' while his parents carry the plot; and so on. And they are pursued to an ultimate point, when the father's cremation is represented as his final performance.

These figures carry over into play and pastiche emotions of anxiety, guilt, dread, loss and desire, which come across all the more vibrantly for this almost insouciant performance. Yet they also make it plain that these emotions are an element in the relationship between father and son, not the whole of it. If the sometimes baffled and overwhelmed intensity of the sequence occasionally makes it seem that we are being offered studies in a pathology, the generosity of its own performed recall – which so energetically brings a father back, posthumously, on stage – insists that we are witnesses of a celebration. When the final poem in the book, 'Now That I Hear Trains', recalls the father pushing the son on his new bike along a beach, it concludes: 'When I looked over my shoulder / he was nowhere to be seen'. But of course he is now to be seen, mirrored in these poems, returned home in what may be the only conceivable immortality, that of his son's 'writing home'. *Writing Home* is a volume which brings some of the techniques of the *Review* poem (and some of its themes too, since a dead father also haunts the work of both Hamilton and Harsent) to a new complexity and clarification in images whose precise and tactful, but also self-revealing discriminations make energising contact with a whole complex of significant emotion and consciousness. It should be said in conclusion, in case this sounds too grandiloquent, that the poems are also frequently very funny.

Notes

1. See Philip Hobsbaum and Edward Lucie-Smith, *A Group Anthology* (London: Oxford University Press, 1963) and Philip Hobsbaum, *A Theory of Communication* (London and Basingstoke: Macmillan, 1970).

2. Seamus Heaney, *Preoccupations: Selected Prose 1968–1978* (London: Faber and Faber, 1980), p. 29.

3. Peter Porter, *Collected Poems* (Oxford: Oxford University Press, 1984), p. v.

4. Peter Redgrove and Penelope Shuttle, *The Wise Wound: Menstruation and Everywoman* (London: Gollancz, 1978).

5. Ian Hamilton, *Fifty Poems* (London: Faber and Faber, 1988), p. x.

6. Ian Hamilton, *A Poetry Chronicle: Essays and Reviews* (London: Faber and Faber, 1973), p. 125.

Chapter 11
Barbarians and Rhubarbarians
Douglas Dunn and Tony Harrison

As I have already observed, the Butler Education Act of 1944, by providing for a secondary and tertiary education for working-class children, most of whom would otherwise have had no such access, brought a range of new class and regional interests, histories and attachments into British poetry in the 1960s. As it did into many of the arts, of course: witness the work of David Mercer, Dennis Potter, David Storey, and numerous others. In some of the poetry, as in the novels and plays, a besetting preoccupation is with difference: cultural (and usually economic) difference between the educated child and his (and it usually is 'his') parents; geographical difference between the child's new place (often southern or well-travelled cosmopolitan) and the originating home (often northern) – so that the theme of the 'return home' is endemic to this work; and the difference made to the educated consciousness by the stresses and anxieties of such divorce from origin and the pull in two directions which it provokes. Although some of these matters are handled interestingly in the poetry of Ken Smith, whose *Fox Running* (1980) is outstanding,[1] and although they are handled, along with other kinds of difference too, in work from Northern Ireland since the late 1960s (in particular that of Seamus Heaney and Paul Muldoon), they may be observed most notably in British poetry in the work of Douglas Dunn and Tony Harrison.

Douglas Dunn made his initial reputation with the volume *Terry Street* in 1969. Terry Street was a working-class terrace in Hull, off which Dunn himself lived while a mature student of English Literature in the city's university. The sequence of poems dealing with the terrace is a notable contribution to an urban realism in some English poetry of the 1960s. The place is evoked with uneasy sympathy and disquiet, with a tenderness towards the reduced but resilient lives carried on there (particularly the lives of women), but with a dourly unillusioned sense of the actual nature of the reduction, reminiscent at times of that extraordinary English novel of working-class life, Henry Green's *Living*. The poignancy of empathy is balanced against the disgust of recognition;

if 'Children bounce balls / Up into their dreams of sand, and the sea they have not seen', nevertheless 'The litter of pop rhetoric blows down Terry Street, / Bounces past their feet into their lives'. The sequence appears to hover unresolvedly, then, between empathy and satire, and the uncertainties and ambivalences of his own view are themselves figured in some of the characteristic attitudes into which Dunn places himself, attitudes in which the observer is himself observed, the explainer explained:

> This time they see me at my window, among books,
> A specimen under glass, being protected,
> And laugh at me watching them.
> They minuet to Mozart playing loudly
>
> On the afternoon Third. They mock me thus,
> They mime my culture. A landlord stares.
> All he has worked for is being destroyed.
> The slum rent-masters are at one with Pop.

The implicit presumption with which Dunn observes and criticises is itself implicitly criticised here; the books and music of his high culture fail to protect him from the lacerating mockery of the objects of his scrutiny. Those whom he would judgementally objectfy as specimens, instances, cases objectify him in turn; and the poem ('Young Women in Rollers' is its almost caricaturing title) generously and savingly includes the two-way transit.

The title poem of Dunn's fifth volume, *St Kilda's Parliament* (1981), concludes with a very striking instance of a similar kind of perceptual reciprocity. The poem is actually titled in full 'St Kilda's Parliament: 1879–1979' and bears the motto, '*The photographer revisits his picture*'. The island of St Kilda in the Hebrides is no longer inhabited, and this photograph of its former inhabitants is therefore the representation of a vanished community (the word 'community' is a significant one in Dunn). The poem is a fiction in which, from the perspective of the poem's own present moment, the photographer meditates on the alternative and remote lives led by his nineteenth-century Hebridean subjects. After a career spent covering the political and cultural life of the intervening hundred years ('the emaciated dead, the lost empires'), this fantasy photographer has now returned to the unromanticised islanders of his 1879 photograph; and his subjects refuse subjection:

> Here I whittle time, like a dry stick,
> From sunrise to sunset, among the groans
> And sighings of a tongue I cannot speak,
> Outside a parliament, looking at them,

As they, too, must always look at me
Looking through my apparatus at them
Looking. Benevolent, or malign? But who,
At this late stage, could tell, or think it worth it?
For I was there, and am, and I forget.

The photographer is excluded from his subjects here by culture, geography, language and time: a more radical and fundamental version of the exclusion represented by the figure of the poet framed behind his bookish window in the *Terry Street* poem. But that very exclusion sets the terms of the contract the photographer enters into with his subject people; his ability to look at them and use this apparatus of observation, which they cannot do themselves, may appropriate them to his artistic purpose but it also translates them beyond themselves, into a temporal future beyond their dead past, into the stasis of survival. Raising the necessary moral question about all such appropriations – 'Benevolent, or malign?', ambiguously asked of both the islanders and the photographer – the poem gives this crucial preoccupation a memorable realisation; and it also suggests that the best art intricates the artist, possibly despite himself, in the lives of those he uses. In 'St Kilda's Parliament: 1879–1979', his material reclaims the photographer; across the gap of a century he is pulled back to the strange, unsettling but altogether compelling world of his human subjects. They have gone; he has forgotten; only the art itself, this photograph, survives, opaque but tantalising the contemporary viewer with interpretative possibility.

The concern with what I have called here 'perceptual reciprocity', and its compelling treatment in different poems by Douglas Dunn, is unsurprising from a writer whose work is so densely populated, so dependent on the observation of the lives of others. Like the subjects of *Terry Street* and 'St Kilda's Parliament', these lives are almost always those of the excluded, rejected, alienated. In his weirdly serious–comic half-palinode 'Remembering Lunch', also in *St Kilda's Parliament*, Dunn satirises his 'pretence of being a John Buchan of the underdog'; but however the stance is ironised, the underdog is always at the centre of focus in Dunn's lens. *Terry Street* represents, in the context of his subsequent work, a displacement of his own Scottish working-class background onto the 'backwaters' of Hull; and that background itself features prominently in a large number of anecdotal poems anatomising class resentment and – another significant Dunn word – 'grudge'. 'Guerrillas' from *The Happier Life* (1972) is one such poem, but it also summons, in its conclusion, the other lives with which Dunn's poetry characteristically deals. The poem concerns the resentment felt by Dunn and his fellow schoolchildren at the wealthy farmers' children who shared their classrooms, favourites of the teachers and owners of the land. The literal poem of class antagonism is moralised, in conclusion, into a poem of more than merely present resentments, a poem which complicates its emotions in the resonances of local history. The young Dunn and his friends act as subversives or 'guerillas' on the others' farms:

> Outlaws from dark woods and quarries,
> We plundered all we envied and had not got,
> As if the disinherited from farther back
> Came to our blood like a knife to a hand.

Those 'disinherited from farther back' supply the immediate material of much of Dunn's work, most notably of the sequence 'Barbarian Pastorals' in the volume *Barbarians* (1979): here Dunn's class resentments and antagonisms are not so much displaced into, but placed by a rediscovered and deconstructed history.

Prior to *Barbarians* Dunn's forms were predominantly free verse and loosely iambic stanzas. With this volume, however, and in this sequence, his writing explodes into a new exoticism of stanzaic shaping and elaborate rhyme scheme. Given the reduced lives and histories which are the material of these poems, such luxuriant metrical patterns make irony a principle of form; the barbarians – 'the disinherited from farther back' – now inherit, or occupy, the civilised garden of English poetic decorum. It is no doubt with something of this irony in mind that Dunn has described these poems as operating the 'stylistic ploy of Peasant Baroque (or, The Scholarship Boy's Revenge)'.[2] The forms are not merely ironic, however, but enabling: they offer the oportunity for emotions of resentment, indignation and (perhaps) self-righteousness to be diverted into performance and display; and they summon a utopian space within the shapes of literary language itself in which the currently excluded and dispossessed may figure their own potential future possession.

The word 'barbarian' derives from the Greeks' name for one who did not speak their language, 'bar-bar' being their onomatopoeic representation of the strangers' tongues. Those who speak strangely – not in the accents of civility – in the sequence 'Barbarian Pastorals' include the 'monstrous proletariat' discovered in Africa by the Roman geographer Pomponius Mela; the gardeners of a great house in a fictional county of England in 1789, year of the French Revolution; a peasant self-improver in Renfrewshire in 1820, labouring at his Latin and remembering the ruling-class poet William Motherwell; a supplicant artist being kept waiting forever by the lady of another country house; a young Scottish Orangeman ('He is, but does not know it, destitute'); and Dunn himself, caught in America by the military draft in December 1965, a barbarian in danger of being sent to Vietnam along with hundreds of thousands of working-class Americans. This exceptional sequence, which is at the centre of Dunn's achievement, continues beyond its bounds in the volume *Barbarians* with additional poems in *St*

Kilda's Parliament dealing with the eighteenth-century Scottish rural schoolmaster poet John Wilson; the late-eighteenth-century and early-nineteenth-century Scottish peasant poet Robert Tannahill; and the Edinburgh lower-class boy 'Green Breeks' who features in an episode from Lockhart's *Memoirs of Sir Walter Scott*. The 'peasant baroque' in Douglas Dunn is predominantly turned, then, towards Scotland, and appropriately so in the Great Britain of the late 1970s and 1980s when Scotland is so scandalously marginalised by the political and economic policies of the succeeding governments of Margaret Thatcher. In Dunn's later work these 'pastorals' are accompanied by such publicly turned poems on the fate of Scotland as 'Witch-girl' and 'An Address on the Destitution of Scotland'.

If there is occasionally something Calvinist and kirk-elderly about the strenuousness of his social engagement, however, the altogether surprising, capacious and released is also liable to happen at almost any moment in Dunn's books. His is a libertarian socialism in which a yearning for the purely fictive, and for various types of imaginative repletion, also have their place: in such poems as the bitter-sweet 'Billie 'n' Me', for instance, in which he fantasises a relationship with Billie Holiday, becoming a kind of Frank O'Hara of Hull, and in 'The Musical Orchard' in which he sounds almost like Jacques Prévert. Not the least significant element in this is a quietly feminist anti-machismo present in all his work. This rises to something like explicitness in such poems as 'The Sportsmen' ('They will be murdered in bedrooms, / Their cars pressed into squares of scrap') and the delicious 'Ratatouille' ('Neither will it invade Afghanistan / Or boycott the Olympic Games in a huff'); but it is also a vibrantly informing presence in *Elegies* (1985), a volume of poems commemorating the tragically early death of his wife, where 'Dining' asserts that 'it feels / As if I have become a woman hidden in me'. This element in Dunn reaches its apogee in the sequence *Europa's Lover* (1982) which imagines Europe itself, in its beneficent and oneiric aspects, as a woman. Descanting on themes from European history in a style at once phantasmagorically gnomic and lucidly precise, and therefore effecting the most secure bridge Dunn has yet erected between the almost separable kinds of poetry he has written, the sequence culminates in an assertion of identity and self-renewing effort in which the feminised figure speaks, in support of Albert Camus (author of the quoted sentence), against the history of European Fascism:

> 'Sleep with me. You will be my many children,
> My messenger and my amanuensis.
> You have nothing to lose. Give me your life
> Again, and again, as I invent my cause.
> I am my own mother and my daughters.
> I love my people. "Our Europe is not yours."'

Together we will say that again, as, once,
It was said by one of my sons to another son
In the days of souls without names smouldering
In the years of the counting of rings and teeth.'

Dunn's *Barbarians* contains a pungent brief vignette entitled 'Glasgow Schoolboys, Running Backwards':

High wind . . . They turn their backs to it, and push.
Their crazy strides are chopped in little steps.
And all their lives, like that, they'll have to rush
Forwards in reverse, always holding their caps.

The poem freezes and frames a pose or a gesture which is then made the focus of a comment on the class system, the literal pushing against the wind and holding of caps made an emblem of the boys' lack of any future other than struggle and servitude, and the poet's empathy understatedly signalled by the almost audible sigh of those inevitabilities of time and obligation: 'all their lives' and 'have to'. In the way it uses an almost theatrical gesture as origin and emblem, the poem is remarkably close to the procedures of Tony Harrison; in its understatement remarkably distant. When Harrison published his *Dramatic Verse* as a Penguin paperback in 1986, he retitled it *Theatre Works*; and, in a poet so prominently given to ingenious wordplay and pun, we should probably read the title as part of a polemic: the theatre of Tony Harrison *works*, it shoulders a burden, it makes a case, it engages in a struggle. His *Selected Poems* could similarly have been called *Poetry Works*. From the beginning of his career but most prominently in the long sequence-in-progress of sixteen-line or 'Meredithian' sonnets, *The School of Eloquence* (1978), and in such related long poems as *v.* (1985), Harrison's crucial theme and occasion have been the experience of his Leeds working-class background and his grammar-school and university, Classics-educated divorce from that original, oppressed culture. His entire *oeuvre*, indeed, far more obviously than Dunn's, could take as its subtitle 'The Scholarship Boy's Revenge'; and, in its points of stress and self-blindness, as well as in its overt programme, it is marked indelibly with the imprint of the disintegratively ambivalent benefits for the working class of the 1944 Education Act.

Harrison's class allegiance is made both clear and complex in the epigraphs to *The School of Eloquence*: one, from E.P. Thompson's *The Making of the English Working Class* (1963), indicates how the title of the sequence is taken from a code-name for the radical organisation known as the 'London Corresponding Society' which was suppressed by law in 1799, the year after the French Revolution; and the other, from Milton's *Ad Patrem*, registers filial gratitude to a father who 'scorned the sacred Muses'. Harrison thereby intricates himself in a class loyalty imposed on him genetically: the recognition of paternity is the recognition of an oppressed history. But his own divorce from that oppression is also cunningly implied by the Milton quotation: from one of Milton's Latin poems, it addresses his father in a tongue he could never understand, the tongue that carries a whole freight of European literary and cultural tradition, but carries it exclusively, for those with the privilege of education. The irony is that this tongue, Latin, is likely to be as opaque to the majority of Harrison's even highly literate contemporary readers as it is to Harrison's father; but the English tongue, and its poetic forms and structures, are (of course) not. The Latin, therefore, stands to all of Harrison's readers who lack the privilege of his own (now virtually extinct) classical education as Harrison's own use of their apparently shared tongue stands to his father. It is a lesson to the usual reader, opening the book, in the alienation, incapacity and anxiety which the use of any language may involve for those not privy to its class and cultural encodings, and it subtly insists that language in Tony Harrison is the site of class struggle. Both the pathos and the political venom of his work derive from the fact that in articulating a filial fidelity Harrison is also articulating a utopian and culturally impossible desire: 'I'd like to be the poet my father reads!'

That line appears in the second of two sonnets in *The School of Eloquence* under the common title 'The Rhubarbarians'. Harrison derives the word from his father's information that Leeds is the source of most of England's rhubarb and from the fact, well-known to Tony Harrison the successful dramatist, that when a stage crowd engages in *sotto voce* conversation, it says 'rhubarb-rhubarb'. The Leeds working classes are therefore the 'rhubarbarians': they are those who mumble at the side of recorded history, like Dunn's more lexicographically correct 'barbarians'; they are those who feed on the commonest and bitterest of all garden fruits; they are those whose ancestors are, in the first of these two sonnets, cut down as Luddites by the '*tusky-tusky*' of the pikes of the bosses' troops (as a footnote tells us, 'tusky' is the Leeds word for rhubarb). Harrison's work insistently confronts the probities and civilities of middle-class English poetic language with the rougher outsider energies and inarticulacies of these rhubarbarians. His iambics clash, grind and grapple, abetted by alliterative effects reminiscent of Anglo-Saxon and medieval forms, as they precariously maintain control; they are the visible and audible location of the battle declared in the opening poem of *The School of Eloquence* ('On Not Being Milton'): 'Articulation is the tongue-tied's fighting'.

As representative of the tongue-tied, bringing to the articulation of poetry accents it has commonly rejected or oppressed, Harrison imagines his poetry under the patronage of the linguistically dispossessed. A prefatory, epigrammatic quatrain to *The School of Eloquence* entitled

'Heredity' derives his talent for poetry from his uncles Joe and Harry –
'one was a stammerer, the other dumb', and other tropes and figures of
ambiguously difficult articulation also inhabit his work: Fracastorius, the
tongueless poet in 'The White Queen'; the simile for the fruit given to
him by Jane Fonda in 'Guava Libre' ('Lips cropped off a poet. That's
more like. / That's almost the sort of poet I think I am'); the stutterer
Demosthenes, training himself into oratory by shouting against the sea,
his mouth full of pebbles, in 'Them & [uz]'. Dedicated to Richard
Hoggart, author of *The Uses of Literacy* (1957), the earliest and classic
account of working-class reading habits, and Leon Cortez, a stand-up
comedian who 'translated' Shakespeare into Cockney, the two sonnets
under that title chart Harrison's progress from school to the beginnings
of literary fame in a way that writes the fundamental oppositions of the
sequence in miniature.

The first sonnet evokes Harrison's grammar-school English teacher
attempting to instil Received Pronunciation in the working-class,
non-standard English child as he reads Keats's 'Ode to a Nightingale':
'*mi 'art aches*' for 'my heart aches'. Exclusion is the lot of the
rhubarbarian Harrison: 'I played the drunken porter in *Macbeth*'. The
second sonnet is Harrison's revenge and manifesto: 'So right, yer
buggers, then! We'll occupy / your lousy leasehold poetry'. The
metaphor knows that poetry is property; and if property is theft, then
this thief will steal some of it back again, on behalf of the dispossessed
community of that 'we'. Indeed, he steals it in the very act of making
his declaration, since the demotic 'yer buggers' is an occupying raid on
standard English, a raid on behalf of the inarticulate. 'Them & [uz]' is
under no illusions, however, about the difficulties of the struggle it
engages. Its most forceful tropes are tropes of vomiting and
engorgement: the child Harrison has his 'mouth all stuffed with glottals,
great / lumps to hawk up and spit out', and the man achieves his success
only by performing an act of masticating rapine: 'I chewed up
Littererchewer and spat the bones'. The outraged effortfulness is the only
conceivable response to a class enemy who will always effortlessly rob
you again, engaging in its own endless raids of recuperation: when
Harrison thinks he has at last won out by converting his despised
teacher's name for him, 'T.W.', into the language of home, 'Tony', *The
Times*, in its first reference to him, 'automatically made Tony Anthony'.

The individual sonnets of *The School of Eloquence* are plotted around
such emblematic episodes and incidents. Harrison is a very cunning,
ingenious and inventive shaper of his experience and reading into
well-turned and tailored individual poems; the sixteen-liner is skilfully
manipulated for its polemical and anecdotal potential. There are
numerous poems of his whose central moments stay in the mind like the
moments of good short stories: the young Harrison's head sticking out of
the terrace skylight window to tell his friends he's '*gorra Latin prose*' and

can't go out; the terror of the convict winched down a Castleton cave to test its depth for a wager by the 'stout upholders of our law and order'; the last apple pie baked by Harrison's mother and eaten by father and son after her death; the father buying the son *Poems from the Yorkshire Dales* when he's decided to die; and his cremation, going into an oven 'not unlike those he fuelled all his life' as a 'baker's man'. Like John Berryman's *Dream Songs*, the sequence is a very self-conscious performance of the dramatised self, the self addressing an audience and interrupted by the characters of its own creating consciousness. But it is precisely the element of performance in these poems that seems to me to raise some doubts about the Harrison undertaking.

In 'Punchline', Harrison notes that the traditional way out of the working class was by becoming a boxer or a stand-up comedian: both performers on display. His own sequence more or less self-consciously aligns itself with this 'tradition' when the poem 'Turns' offers us Harrison wearing his father's cap. Doing a 'turn' in it before the mirror, he imagines it making him look more working-class, before the poem turns to his father's collapse in the street, his cap turned up beside him as though he has been doing a 'turn', a comic or musical routine, for money. The sonnet's final quatrain reads:

> He never begged. For nowt! Death's reticence
> crowns his life's, and *me*, I'm opening my trap
> to busk the class that broke him for the pence
> that splash like brackish tears into our cap.

'Trap' there is undoubtedly a dangerous pun: when the *School of Eloquence* poem opens its mouth it also opens a snare; and these lines pointedly acknowledge their own potential connivance in the culture game: they perform for the paying guests. Harrison's pawkily ironic awareness of the potential traps lying in wait for his own work does not always, however, save him from some of the dangers of writing, always, a popular, even populist, performance poetry, doing a 'turn'. This may well be the inevitable product of Harrison's being, in Terry Eagleton's peculiarly almost oxymoronic phrase, a 'natural Bakhtinian';[3] but it does have its drawbacks: and, indeed, the reader may well think of Kipling long before Bakhtin when reading Harrison, diametrically opposed as their politics are (in 'Next Door' the nine-year-old Harrison is given his first book, *The Kipling Treasury*, by a neighbour). The natural Bakhtinian will probably deny the very existence of a more intimate or 'private' poetic voice, asserting that the notion of such a space of non-contamination is an ideological dupe, that all voices are in fact caught up into and cut across by other voices. Nevertheless, Harrison's constant lack of that perhaps delusive register does mean that the emotions of his work can seem uncomplicatedly simple and unsubtle;

that it rarely reads as well or as affectingly a second time round; that it tends to turn its human characters into caricatures – a gesture or two serves for both father and mother; that it can seem self-advertising, as it constantly measures the gap between Harrison's origin and his achievement. It is obviously necessary for this sequence immersed in personal history and heritage to convey a strong sense of Harrison's success, but it needs great reserves of tact to balance pride in class against personal hubris.

His strongest work is therefore arguably that in which the fiction or plot makes such self-contemplation and inwardness irrelevant or unnecessary. One such poem is *v.* (1985), which gained great media attention when it was broadcast as a television programme in 1987, ostensibly because of its use of four-letter words. The poem, in a lengthy set of iambic quatrains of a declamatory and occasionally almost doggerel kind, is plotted around an encounter between Harrison-as-poet and a skinhead in a Leeds graveyard. Harrison is visiting his parents' grave and is horrified to find it desecrated by spraypaint writing the word 'United' (for 'Leeds United', the local football team). His fantasised dialogue with the guilty skinhead, who becomes a second self or *doppelgänger* of Harrison's, swells to a kind of 'state of England' inclusiveness, pivoted around the 'v' of the poem's title. That letter, sprayed on the gravestones, is initially the 'versus' of local football competition, a word which puns throughout on Harrison's own 'verses'; but it stands also for the more apparently united England of Harrison's childhood, represented by Churchill's wartime V sign. As the poem progresses, the letter takes on numerous other oppositional significations: middle and working class; the Coal Board and the National Union of Mineworkers prior to the Miners' Strike in 1985; north and south; man and woman; Ulster and Eire; employed and unemployed. Arguing a political case for the spraying of gravestones – the jobless resentfully desecrate the tombs of those whose jobs proudly accompany their names on their headstones – the skinhead insists that the act of desecration is the assertion of an identity in the only kind of public writing available, his version of the need answered in Harrison himself by having his name in Broadway lights. In the poem's strongest insistence of *doppelgänger* empathy, 'poet' too is 'a crude four-letter word', and the skinhead insists that 'A book, you stupid cunt, 's not worth a fuck'. The poem's relentless use of expletives brings to a newly vigorous articulation the hitherto inarticulate: there are moments in *v.* when the four-letter words rise to a great poignancy of anger and incapacity. The poem is a central document of the remnants of the industrial working-class North of England in the mid-1980s, a country dangerous, derelict, despairing, on the dole, driven into an apparent permanence of division and decay.

Notes

1. See Ken Smith, *The Poet Reclining: Selected Poems 1962–1980* (Newcastle upon Tyne: Bloodaxe Books, 1982).

2. 'Douglas Dunn writes', *The Poetry Book Society Bulletin*, no. 100, Spring 1979.

3. Terry Eagleton, 'Antagonisms', *Poetry Review*, vol. 76 nos. 1–2 (1986), p. 21.

Chapter 12

Varieties of Neo-Modernism

Christopher Middleton, Roy Fisher, J.H. Prynne

The work of Dunn and Harrison draws part of its strength from a political opposition and antagonism. Opposition and antagonism, which are also certainly in part political but which register themselves more immediately as functions of an aesthetics and a publishing history, are also keynotes of a large amount of British poetry since the 1960s which has, as part of its policy, refused a coherent label, but which it is possible to think of as the 'neo-Modern'. I take this term from Frank Kermode who, in his essay 'The Modern', first published in the mid-1960s, and reprinted in *Modern Essays* (1971), proposed a 'discrimination of Modernisms' into the 'palaeo-Modernist' and the 'neo-Modernist'.[1] The discrimination has not much taken, largely because of the subsequent use of the term 'postmodern' (to which I return in the introduction to Part Five), although Alan Young employed it again in 1980 in an essay which includes an account of Christopher Middleton.[2] Kermode (and Young) use the discrimination to apply to different attitudes to the Modernist conception of 'order'. I want here to appropriate it newly to differentiate this work from both the 'Modernist' and the 'postmodern', so that it may be made to indicate three essential characteristics: a turning against what these poets read as a played-out native humanist or empiricist tradition; a deliberate indebtedness to the work (poetic, critical and aesthetic) of Ezra Pound and, through him, of an American writing whose central figure is Charles Olson; and a readiness for an exploratory or experimental formal inventiveness not common in post-war British poetry.

The 'Pound tradition' in recent British poetry is distinguishable into two separate forms, which may be defined as 'Pound/Eliot' and 'Pound/Williams/Olson'. The former includes David Jones and Basil Bunting and has found its primary outlet and focus in William Cookson's magazine *Agenda* (which has produced some remarkable special issues on the work of Jones, Bunting and Hugh MacDiarmid); and it includes the poetry of C.H. Sisson, much extolled by *PN Review* and the Carcanet press (to both of which I refer in the introduction to

Part Five). The latter is much more fugitive, deliberately ignoring 'mainstream' British publishers, and choosing instead publication by little magazine and small press. Andrew Crozier, who has been one of the foremost theorists of this work, has castigated the 'mainstream' of post-war British poetry for its 'figures of empirical lyricism': dully and routinely operating a metaphorical poetry in which the poet's subjectivity is the primary focus of interest, this work becomes in fact an element of rhetoric and a feature of marketing and advertising, in which the poet's personality and 'development' are the focus of primary critical interest.[3] Crozier believes that the way the sensibility of the Movement in the 1950s was allowed to set the agenda for subsequent British poetry was partly a function of the accidental lack of opportunity for further publication of those poets who had begun their careers in the 1940s; and he has, consequently, consistently defended some of the work of the 1940s (in particular that of W.S. Graham and Nicholas Moore) against its received idea. What he finds of value in such work, and what he believes the contemporary poetry he is defending maintains a continuity with, is a salutary selflessness and refusal of the hubris of 'personality': these poetries are laudable for their 'displacement of the discursive centrality of the self' and for their desire to treat the person as 'a site in which experience is to be acted out as conflict'.[4] Even if one does not accept his view of the poetry of the 1940s, the theory he expounds in these critical essays is a bracing alternative to what can sometimes seem a too ready accommodation by some contemporary poets of the 'market' value placed on their work. Since, however, some of the poets Crozier presumably has in mind (Tom Raworth, Lee Harwood, Douglas Oliver) have in fact, in the late 1980s, been given a kind of commercial publication which must be the envy of many poets of the 'thrills and frills' persuasion, it remains to be seen whether the ascetic purity argued for by Crozier can survive.[5]

Christopher Middleton's hostility to what he reads as a contemporary English empiricism (resulting, variously, in 'anecdotage' and in the egotism of the 'confessional') is registered at several points in his collections of essays, *Bolshevism in Art* (1978) and *The Pursuit of the Kingfisher* (1983), particularly in the brilliantly suggestive and inventive 'Reflections on a Viking Prow' and the more openly self-preoccupied 'For Marton, Erwin and Miklos'. 'Reflections on a Viking Prow' takes issue with 'the humanistic solecisms' and 'the scripts of subjective expression' and seeks to replace the egotistical 'confessional' with the more self-effacing but ultimately self-revelatory 'configural'. Theorising intuitions and local perceptions in something of the way Roland Barthes does in some of his earlier work (and not at all embarrassed by the comparison), Middleton combats the idea of the poem as self-expression with a ramifying conception of the poem as structure, in a way continuous with both post-structuralist theorising of the sign and with an

English Ruskinian tradition. It is continuous also with some of the theorising of the high Modernist moment: like Eliot, Pound and David Jones (to whose concept of the 'sacramental' his essay alludes), he has his own modern version of the Fall, a 'nightmare of designification' to be resisted only by another recension of Modernist impersonality which might place a new relation between subject and object into the structure of a text. Only when that structure becomes 'radiant' and 'polysemous' may the object be enabled to resist designification:

> The regard resting on the object is . . . the key to
> self-affirmation: a self reclaims itself from nonentity and, as the
> object reveals itself in a certain light, that self can gaze into its
> own depths as an agent of interiority . . . . Between 'I am' and
> 'This is' there can be strange ligatures – a magico-grammatical
> tissue links first and third persons singular.[6]

Middleton's own ligature 'magico-grammatical' may imply that there is a kind of nostalgia in him, despite his explicit disclaimers, for a lost divinity. The vanished god leaves sacramental traces in the world to be reclaimed by the text in a kind of late Platonic semiotics; the god may be brought down or back by a calling-forth of disregarded but still immanent spirits. Officially, however, this new relation is turned not towards theology but towards a ludic politics. The poem effects a revision of attitudes by subverting cliché and stereotype; it '*infuriates* the world into showing its hand'. For Middleton, poetry is a 'limit to enslavement' and thereby 'exigent': 'I decipher the dreams of the victims who had no chance to speak'. In 'For Marton, Erwin and Miklos' he defines these new orientations in his work as a 'body-consciousness', in which he might appear 'a scatty hermit feeling out the formal relations between cobwebs and starlight'; and, in less self-parodistic vein, he defines the procedures resulting from such a consciousness:

> This exigent poetry tends to have archipelagic structures. Its
> movement tends to be a dance, not a walk. It is a poetry balanced
> over gulfs of silence, a poetry of surprises, of enigmas, scrutiny
> followed by vertiginous distance, a poetry of broken uncertain
> surfaces, of foregrounded hinterlands.[7]

Naming Apollinaire, Eliot and the Pound of *Homage to Sextus Propertius* as the precursors of such a poetry, Middleton is defining and refining a neo-Modernism here, drawing something lost or abandoned back into English poetry in the same critical act in which he becomes his own best interpreter.

Such a poetry in Middleton himself characteristically begins with an object situated in a place which is then, as the poem drifts from contemplation to association, scrutinised into some newly defining self-relation or self-revelation. The atmospheres of particular places – Portcothan, Avebury, Anatolia, Texas – are made an intimate part of the revelatory power of specific objects: a male torso; paintings by Bonnard, Toulouse-Lautrec and Delacroix; a cart with apples; 'Le Nu Provençal'; an old woman at the county dump; a wild horse; 'Ibeji', an African figurine on a desk; a photograph of an old wine press; a snail on the doorstep. With a cool and steady avoidance of the potential ingratiation of a single 'voice', these poems seem genuinely, tentatively and humbly at the service of their objects rather than their poet's personality. The result is a poetry of great experimental variety, as individual poems work to preserve individual objects against designification by defining individuating verbal shapes and textures. Within these verbal forms the contemplative poetic intelligence, the mind-in-action, becomes the true object of the poem's knowledge. Displaying a sensibility both refinedly ascetic and refinedly epicurean, Middleton's poems waver – or 'dance' – between surface and depth, affection and recoil, closeness and distance, image and discourse, place and displacement, intimacy and estrangement: binaries which are, in his work, independent of hierarchy, the one testing and tempering the other in an oscillating movement.

Certain states of being and consciousness predominate as the locations for these perceptions. In the earlier work, perhaps in a way closer to the English Romantics than Middleton would wish to admit, childhood is a condition frequently returned to; and there is also a recurrent interest in the pre-industrial and the non-European: all come together in the poem 'Navajo Children' which ends as an instruction in difference ('But how / could you get any / more thin, small, far'). Animals also feature frequently, making the work seem occasionally almost a kind of bestiary with allegorical resonance. And what originates as apparently literal or realistic description may at any moment twist into the quasi-surreal: dream and waking, where the resources of the unconscious may be tapped, are also common states and tropes in the work. The slippage between different modes of being and behaving is a kind of alertness in which Middleton guards against the conventionality of a subject/object perceptual relationship. He appears to aspire to the condition described in 'Ginestra', where 'Metaphor and fact refuse to mix'; his self-image as a poet might be the state desired by 'An Englishman in Texas' – 'But let him move once, / free, of himself, into some few things'.

The deceptively casual 'Snail on the Doorstep' from *Carminalenia* (1980) typifies the procedure. In a structure loosened from punctuation and from conventional syntax, the poem begins as a set of apparently random impressions of a snail and its defining context of weather, time and situation – although, significantly, the mode is an interrogative of scrutiny, inquiry, inspection (though lacking its mark of interrogation): 'Is it rain or dusk'. In the second stanza metaphor and fact are collocated, though they do not quite mix, in two lines of parallelising or analogising: 'Snail on a doorstep far south / A radio knob you want to turn it'. The line break there is a break between metaphor and fact too: we see the connection in the very refusal to insist it; and that refusal makes it also a disconnection. It is as though the Poundian image or ideogram is holding at bay the kind of foregrounded metaphoricity employed by the 'Martian' poets of the 1970s and 1980s. This throws attention on the consciousness or sensibility which refuses to make the connection, in lines which indicate why the snail might, however briefly, be perceived as the knob of a radio: 'you want to turn it . . . / For news and think another catastrophe / News counts the decay / And substance of sacred things'. This is a mind which subtly and alertly returns to the word 'catastrophe' something of its original force in Greek tragedy, that terrible reversal of fortune which is indeed the 'decay . . . of sacred things'. The stanzas that follow then sway under the yoke of these lines, implying such questions as: is this, then, a 'sacred' snail; and, what might a 'sacred' object be in a modern poem?

> Snail on the doorstep knees cracking
> Light from nowhere
> Point like a pyramid strikes the shell
> Strikes the ultimate
> Spiral centre
>
> It is this expanse only an expanding
> Centre of the spiral
> The light stops where it started
> But the snail on the doorstep
> Uncoils in the light and blooms
>
> The pyramid whispering expands
> It follows the infinite curve of space
> It ends where it started
> If this were not a snail
> There could be no universe
>
> If this were not a snail
> Another door would not let out
> These children
> They would not have crept
> Under the mulberry on tiptoe
> Fingers to their lips
>
> All the snails would roll
> Hightailing it away from them

Startled horns aswish to test
Cooler air
Not spirals like the sun

Refusing the first metaphor (the snail as radio knob), the poem refuses any easy assimilation of its object of contemplation to the metaphor-making consciousness which contemplates it, insisting on the difference of the systems of which object and consciousness are part; enforcing a difference between metaphor and fact, the poem calls uneasy, sceptical attention to the act of perception which is its occasion. Instead of following initial similitude, this poem brings the snail into relation with other systems of which it may be part – the implied large sacred systems of ancient Egypt (the pyramid) and the Celtic or Native American (the spiral) – but this perceiving consciousness is unable to locate any specific source for its nonetheless desired sacred transfigurations: if any sacred light strikes this object it is a 'Light from nowhere'. That perception prompts this perceiver to acknowledge the sheer natural power of the snail, as, responding to the light, it 'blooms' (as naturally, almost photosynthetically, as a plant); and the syntactical ambivalence of the lines, together with their lack of punctuation, allow this natural blooming a translucence onto the imaginative blooming which is the perception/poem itself: a printed 'expanse' in which the snail's 'expanding' is recorded. Under the poet's eye, as it is witnessed in his language, the snail blooms into a 'radiant' or 'polysemous' variant of itself.

And in this variant it is an instruction in a perfect resistance of selfhood, proposing in its own pyramidal and spiral shape an almost Hopkinsian lesson in the containment and stasis of natural form (it is significant that, in his prose, one of Middleton's few native English exemplars is Hopkins). Rather than following the linear progress of the kind of poem that might have developed from the initial metaphor, this poem instead figures curving and circularity as the finest, resistant shapes of perception. Nothing in the universe is changed by the poet's light, by the gaze of the text, but rather than seeming an intolerable, totalitarian imposition of some quasi-divine order, this is instead a liberating (or 'expanding') awareness of a potential new relation between self and world. To name a snail a snail (and not, for instance, a radio knob, or any other thing) is to be released into the joyful recognition of a world of natural process and procedure in which, suddenly, children figure again as the poignant notation of the desire for a universe cleansed of the jaded imposition of the clichés of consciousness. That note of desire and joy, the hope of a new plenitude, is registered at its most intense when the poem's own language finally takes on the childlikeness of that local vernacular 'Hightailing' and 'aswish', the poem itself suddenly hightailing it away from its readers, aswish with its own certitude and self-esteem. A poet's dream of the newly secularised sacred, 'Snail on the Doorstep' inherits a 'neo-Modernist' perceptual clarity of focus from both William Carlos Williams and Paul Klee; it manages to 'translate' them into English poetry with a bravura and panache lending weight to the more assertive declarations of 'How to Listen to Birds': if a note or two 'Concentrates the practised world / Into some new thing', in the accepted Romantic and post-Romantic mode, then this is also

> at a variance so fine
> It modifies the whole
> Machine of being: this
> Is not unpolitical.

As in Middleton, one of the signs of Roy Fisher's neo-modernity is his deft combination of verse and prose forms in some of his poetry. Middleton is a fine, and different, writer in his prose-poems: the volume *Pataxanadu* (1977), for instance, plays intricate formal and thematic games in a way reminiscent of Borges. Fisher's long prose piece *The Ship's Orchestra* (1966) provides him with a similar opportunity, running an elaborate formal descant on themes only briefly hinted at in the poems and, in particular, giving free rein to a strain of Surrealism kept under much tighter control there. The long sequence *City* is more typical in the way its prose complements the verse with its own descriptive and analytic rigour; and it also indicates something of the way in which Fisher may be thought an even more surprising figure than Middleton in post-war English poetry. It brings no exotic foreign locations into its form, but is actually as pointedly and punctiliously located in the post-war English urban-provincial as the work of Philip Larkin. The city is never actually named but, in common with the location of most of Fisher's work (most notably the sequences 'Wonders of Obligation' and *A Furnace*), it is quite clearly Birmingham; and the English industrial Midlands is the constant object of its perceptual effort:

> Brick-dust in sunlight. That is what I see now in the city, a dry
> epic flavour, whose air is human breath. A place of walls made
> straight with plumbline and trowel, to dessicate and crumble in
> the sun and smoke. Blistered paint on cisterns and girders,
> cracking to show the priming. Old men spit on the paving slabs,
> little boys urinate; and the sun dries it as it dries out patches of
> damp on plaster facings to leave misshapen stains. I look for
> things here that make old men and dead men seem young.
> Things which have escaped, the landscapes of many childhoods.

The punctiliousness of Fisher's exact and distinguished prose here is the register of a desire to get this 'city' into his poem, to remake it in the place of writing; and, as elsewhere in the *oeuvre*, the form taken by this desire may be felt to owe something to such comparable modern American efforts as those made by Carlos Williams, Charles Olson and Ed Dorn. The characteristic note of repining struck by the final sentences, however, seems English Romantic in origin, and makes Fisher – like Middleton – a more peculiar combination of the local and the 'other' of literary Modernism than some of his own declarations of scope and intent in interviews, which emphasise the 'effect of indeterminacy' in his work, would tend to suggest.[8] It is not entirely surprising to find him, in the preface to *A Furnace* (1986), acknowledging both a formal and thematic indebtedness to the work of John Cowper Powys, that extraordinary late-Romantic exotic and nature-mystic. Although Fisher's later work differs from his earlier in being more overtly and persistently concerned with local histories as well as topographies, I think it is possible to sense, throughout, a bizarre and individuating combination of an English provincial realism, a formal and philosophical neo-Modernism and a will towards a kind of contemporary sublime.

At the end of the passage I have quoted from *City* the city becomes, in a move characteristic of Fisher, a city of the mind too, carried across from the physical to the psychological by the metaphoric potential of the poetic act. In some of his work a social realism predominates, even to the extent of issuing in an extractable morality. In 'For Realism', for instance, Fisher as the child of a Birmingham working-class family lets his attention fall onto the rebuilding of the city, typical of many English midland and northern cities, in the 1960s, when the old terraced houses made way during a campaign of 'urban development' for new blocks of high-rise flats. The poem is lent a darker irony from our contemporary perspective, after we have witnessed the subsequent decay (and frequent demolition) of that hideously deformed 1960s exercise in architectural and social engineering:

> A conscience
> builds, late, on the ridge. A realism
> tries to record, before they're gone,
> what silver filth these drains have run.

The 'conscience' there is the 'social conscience' of those planners, architects and social workers responsible for such 'development', and it is silently condemned by the way the poet's own 'realism' is opposed to it. This 'conscience' has all the hallmarks of certitude, single vision, authority; this 'realism' writes itself in the quite different metaphoric and oxymoronic energies of the phrase 'silver filth', which acknowledges that the conscience has its reasons (the terraces were, after all, 'filth'), but not its rationale (it sees filth as only filth, and as no other thing). Only the poem may penetrate beyond the 'conscience' to find a language for the lost community and culture.

In a peculiar essay on Fisher Donald Davie appears to decide that this poem reveals the desire for an anti-democratic and authoritarian politics (which is, however, he thinks, itself tempered by a democratic realism elsewhere in the work).[9] I can't see this: the politics of 'For Realism' seem to me locatable closer to anarchism than to authoritarianism. In fact, the poem is surely almost explicitly anti-authoritarian in that the 'conscience' it satirises derives from a source of authority (in the state) which we may recognise as representative of all such sources. It strikes a blow 'for realism' against the culpable blindness of all who would presume authority. If this is to interpret the poem correctly, it would certainly be in harmony with what we may understand of Fisher's poetic elsewhere. *City*, for instance, is a long poem which resists the authority of organic coherence or closure; its separate elements remain obdurately separate, refusing to strain for the potentially specious or spurious glamour of interrelationship. At a more intimate and local level, this seems to me the case with the shorter poems too; and it is undoubtedly the major reason for Fisher's reputation as a 'difficult' writer and (even after his publication by a very 'mainstream' publisher, Oxford University Press), a largely unassimilated one. He is a poet in whom the experiential facts of observation and perception are often disconcertingly unsettled by their becoming facets of a perceiving consciousness itself. Social commentary, we might say, is always placed at risk by poetic meta-commentary; landscape, by displacement into mindscape; fact, by reverie.

Unlike Middleton, Fisher has no significant body of prose theory to argue the case for this personal anti-empiricism; but, as in Wallace Stevens, a number of his poems are their own meta-commentary, glossing the effort and procedure. This is 'It is Writing' in its entirety:

> Because it could do it well
> the poem wants to glorify suffering.
> I mistrust it.
>
> I mistrust the poem in its hour of success,
> a thing capable of being
> tempted by ethics into the wonderful.

This is undoubtedly Fisher's version of Middleton's antagonism to the 'humanistic solecisms'. The poem is not to be a site of transformation or transcendence, a location in which a subdued human passivity registers its diminishments, accepting them by apparently overcoming them in the scene of writing: this 'ethics' is no 'success' at all, and makes the poem only a place of self-recognition or specious consolation. Much of Fisher's work, as a result – it sometimes seems almost dutifully – refuses this temptation. The refusal is a kind of self-limitation and a kind of chastity:

the poems characteristically give the impression of something undeclared, held in check, warily resistant to declaration. I think this is true even of some of the earlier poems which are in general more replete with the ordinary satisfactions of imaginative work than the sometimes etiolated and abrasive or even rebarbative later poems. There is, for instance, 'Experimenting', from the sequence 'Interiors with Various Figures'. Like others in the sequence, the poem evokes inexplicitly the 'interior' of a sexual occasion from the viewpoint of an 'I' regarding a 'she'. Fragments of scene, location, gesture are juxtaposed with fragments of wary, even hostile, dialogue and quotation:

> Experimenting, experimenting,
>> with long damp fingers twisting
>> all the time and in the dusk
> White like unlit electric bulbs she said
> 'This green goes with this purple,' the hands going,
> The question pleased: 'Agree?'

Such poems seem to combine something of the atmosphere and occasion of Eliot's 'Portrait of a Lady' ('slowly twisting the lilac stalks') with a new disorientation derived from the theories of *ostranenie* ('making strange') of the Russian formalists. The combination of these two Modernisms results in a slow-motion, filmic, sometimes hallucinatory calm in Fisher. The relations of his various figures in their confining interiors seem attenuated, dispersed among objects into which their speech fades and reappears with poignant unpredictability: a 'Portrait of a Lady' done by Lucian Freud, almost.

All of this occasionally threatens to tumble his poems into chasms of irresolvability, incertitude and indeterminacy, their images and statements appearing to maintain only the most tenuous and brittle congruence. The terms in which he praises the jazz musician Joe Sullivan in the elegy for him which entitled one of Fisher's volumes, 'The Thing About Joe Sullivan', are almost certainly self-referential too: he could 'amble and stride over / gulfs of his own leaving'; he traces 'the rapid and perverse / tracks that ordinary feelings / make when they get driven / hard enough against time'. Nevertheless these exquisite vanishings and dissolvings are also frequently transfused by a strain of the late-Romantic never openly admitted to but none the less powerfully present. This has the effect of casting up, suddenly and unexpectedly, a particular figure, notation or image (usually associated, more or less explicitly, with loss) with a striking inevitability. The conclusion of the first in the sequence 'Handsworth Liberties' defines this while also performing it:

> It all
> radiates outwards

in a lightheaded air
without image;

there is a world.
It has been made
out of the tracks of waves
broken against the rim
and coming back awry; at the final
flicker they are old grass and fences.
With special intensity
they gather and break out
through birch-bark knuckles.

In a sequence developed, once more, out of images from a specific urban-industrial location, these lines appear to want to restore to this place something of the intensity of feeling associated with more 'natural' places in the history of English Romanticism; the poem, we might say, places Handsworth, for all the manifest discontinuities, into an edgy continuity with the Derwent and the Duddon in Wordsworth. In the terms of the poem 'Some Loss', if there is 'blankness' there is also 'grace', 'the insistence of the essential, / the sublime made lyrical / at the loss of what's forgotten'.

The work of J.H. Prynne, which probably draws on some sources similar to Fisher's (Olson, Ed Dorn), also has its conception of 'place'. Prynne's notion of place, however, is much less specifically topographical than Fisher's: the term, reiterated in a number of poems, seems, rather, to point towards some utopian or metaphysical realm in which present contradiction may be reconciled into harmony, in which alienation may reassemble itself into pleasure. Since he is so notoriously difficult, it may be useful for me to say what I mean by this in a close reading of a passage from the first poem printed in his *Poems*, 'The Numbers', from the volume *Kitchen Poems* (1968):

The whole thing it is, the difficult
matter: to shrink the confines
down. To signals, so that I come
back to this, we are
                small / in the rain,
                open or without it,
                the light in de-
light, as with pleasure amongst not merely
the word, one amongst them; but the
skin over the points, of the bone.
That's where we have it & should
                diminish: I am no

                    more, than custom,
                    which is the vital
   & signal, again, as if we tie into
   so many voices. Wish for them:
   elect the principal, we must take
   aim. *That* now is the life, which
                        is diffuse, out of
                        how we are too
                        surrounded, unhopeful.

The 'open' form of this, derived from American, post-Poundian sources,
and particularly, I presume, from Olson's theories of 'composition by
field', is typical of Prynne, relying on a combination of long and short
lines in a typographical arrangement of some pictorial delicacy and grace
which also draws attention to the play of syntax and voice. This passage
is, indeed, in part itself about that play; the poem is the space in which a
difficult matter must be compacted, but if it is to have any cultural
resonance it must itself play among the voices of that culture's 'custom'.
The poem is the place in which, out of the conflicting voices of a
society, a difficult articulation, dependent on choice or decision or
'election', must be made. The deictic 'that', italicised (in a way
strongly reminiscent of Dorn), is the poem putting its finger on the place
or point where a diffuseness may be properly concentrated, in the face
of the forces which always oppose such concentration, effort and
intensity.

   The poem's title, 'The Numbers', draws together, punningly, some of
the elements affecting that concentration: the measures of the poem
itself; the costing or accounting of those things necessary to choice; the
intrication of aesthetic artefacts like poems in a set of economic
circumstances. The 'place' which the poems attempt to locate is the
place of opposition to unthinking social valuations (what Roland Barthes
calls the 'doxa'); the poem may effect a kind of dilation, an opening up
into light of the customary world. A number of poems in *The White
Stones* (1969) locate this as a place of 'love' which is partly a personal
love, but which also appears to take on quasi-mystical resonance, even in
the act of explicitly denying formal notions of the 'mystical'. 'The Holy
City' perhaps names this place in one of its most apprehensible and
accessible forms:

   Where we go is a loved side of the temple,
   a place for repose, a concrete path.
   There's no mystic moment involved: just
                   that we are
                   is how, each
                   severally, we're

                    carried into
     the wind which makes no decision and is
     a tide, not taken. I saw it
                    and love is
                    when, how &
                    because we
                    do: you
     could call it Ierusalem or feel it
     as you walk, even quite jauntily, over the grass.

If this is a city made by human relationship or by the human imagination – the body's city or the poem's city – it is also a redeemed city in which 'love' may figure as the identity of a human community, the new 'Ierusalem'. Alert, probably, to both Blake's Jerusalem and Joyce's New Bloomusalem in *Ulysses*, the word indicates something of the scope of Prynne's enterprise and design. Spelt as it is, it is one of many instances in his work of a use of medieval linguistic forms, and elsewhere there is a manifest interest in medieval monasticism. This element figures in the work, I think, not in any pseudo-medievalising way, but as a register of difference: the 'Ierusalem' will be, before it is anything else, a linguistic place in which a variety of dictions may register, clash and possibly harmonise. In 'Break It' – whose title presumably alludes to Pound's reminiscence in the *Cantos*: 'To break the pentameter, that was the first heave' – Prynne sets his face against 'all / the acrid wavering of language, so full / of convenient turns of extinction'; and his poems unite the medieval and the scientific, the languages of monasticism and of geology, in the hope that a community distinct from this linguistic 'extinction' may be registered there. Such conjunctions imply a politics too, since the hope is that they will tie 'the ligatures to / revise governance' ('The Numbers').

   This is wholly in tune with the effort of the high Modernist moment; and Prynne expresses the classic Modernist angst most explicitly at the beginning of 'Airport Poem: Ethics of Survival': 'The century roar is a desert carrying / too much away; the plane skids off / with an easy hopeless departure'. His work occasionally makes reference to the specifics of 'the century': Vietnam, 'the cabinet of Mr Heath', the march on the Pentagon, the murder of Lee Harvey Oswald, and what he reads as the 'silliness' of the doxa of the 1960s in the poem 'Questions for the Time Being'. But he is not so historically referential as Pound, Olson or Dorn. Rather, his political consciousness registers as a taking up of the human dimension into a vaster cosmological scale, particularly in the outstanding poems 'The Glacial Question, Unsolved', a poem on geology, and 'Aristeas, in Seven Years', a poem on shamanism. In these, Prynne seems to me close to some native British exemplars, David Jones and Basil Bunting, although as far as I am aware (and strangely enough), the connection has not been made. In poems which attempt to compress into their forms a great density of technical information, poems which are grand orchestrations of the single voice or script, the urge to some kind of 'epic' capacity which was so much a feature of the Modernist moment seems to embody itself in one (perhaps final) native British form.

Since *Brass* (1970), however, a great deal of Prynne's work has come to me to seem almost impenetrably opaque. It is surely dangerous for any poetry to resist the intelligence as well as this later Prynne does. Without its team of dedicated explicators, on the model of Poundian academic scholarship, it is difficult to know where this kind of work will find its audience, except in the Cambridge where Prynne teaches and has created an enthusiastic local following. If this is the kind of neo-Modern hermetic impasse to which traditional English humanists and empiricists have traditionally consigned the works of the British neo-Modern, then it is hard to know how to argue with them. Except to acknowledge, of course, one's own intellectual and practical limitations and bear testimony to the satisfactions of the work one does (more or less) understand. In doing that, I want to look finally at 'Moon Poem' which offers a perhaps surprising continuity between Prynne's neo-Modernism and a native English Romanticism.

David Trotter has explored some of the ways in which the Blake of the Prophetic Books figures in Prynne;[10] but the presence behind 'Moon Poem' is, I think, not Blake but Coleridge, and specifically the Coleridge of 'Frost at Midnight'. 'The night is already quiet and I am / bound in the rise and fall', the poem opens, setting in motion both an atmosphere of withdrawn self-contemplative solitude, associated with the word 'quiet', and a set of figures (moonlight, winter, diffusing warmth, silence, night) which also feature in Coleridge's great poem. Written in February 1798, 'Frost at Midnight' deliberately abstracts itself into its solitude out of the clamour of that revolutionary year, the same year in which Coleridge was to write 'France: An Ode' ('When France in wrath her giant limbs upreared'): the poem's concluding image of natural reciprocity, as the poet-father contemplates his infant son in the firelight, figures a longed-for and impossible stability which everything outside this solitude denies. It is a stability performed by 'the secret ministry of frost', a ritual or ceremonial. Prynne's poem, published in 1969 after that other year of revolutions, 1968, explicitly reads a political morality out of its situation: the 'rise and fall' of the quiet night is an unease in which he is 'learning to wish always for more', but learning too to 'hold to the gradual in / this, as no revolution but a slow change / like the image of snow'. The disbelief in the revolution of 1968 is no disbelief in the possibility of social change, but the recommendation of a gradualism, of the patient extension of 'a community of wish'. The poem saves itself from the charge of privileged quietism by confessing its own place of origin as a version of pastoral rather than a confrontation with *realpolitick*, possible perhaps only to those not directly afflicted, and yet maintaining the efficacy of the poet's song as at least the place where such charged intricacies of sympathy and decision may be made and recorded. The final lines may be said to join together in their own ceremonial utterance another Coleridgean figure, that of the Aeolian harp, with that other psalmic harp of the Biblical King David; but their atmosphere, tone and imagery are perfectly consonant with the conclusion of 'Frost at Midnight'. In these fine lines, is it possible that we are offered a neo-Modern conversation poem?

> The consequence of this
> pastoral desire is prolonged
> as our condition, but
> I know there is more than the mere wish to
> wander at large, since the wish itself diffuses
> beyond this and will never end: these are songs
> in the night under no affliction, knowing that
> the wish is gift to the
> spirit, is where we may
> dwell as we would
> go over and over within the life of the heart
> and the grace which is open to both east and west.
> These are psalms for the harp and the shining
> stone: the negligence and still passion of night.

Notes

1. Frank Kermode, 'The Modern', in *Modern Essays* (London: Fontana, 1971), pp. 39–70.

2. See Alan Young, 'Three neo-moderns: Ian Hamilton Finlay, Edwin Morgan, Christopher Middleton', in Peter Jones and Michael Schmidt (eds), *British Poetry Since 1970: A Critical Survey* (Manchester: Carcanet Press, 1980), pp. 112–24.

3. Andrew Crozier, 'Thrills and frills: poetry as figures of empirical lyricism', in Alan Sinfield (ed.), *Society and Literature 1945–1970* (London: Methuen, 1983), pp. 199–233.

4. ibid. p. 228.

5. I am thinking here of the series of Paladin paperbacks in which the collected poems of these writers have been given prominence.

6. Christopher Middleton, 'Reflections on a Viking Prow', in *Bolshevism in Art and other expository writings* (Manchester: Carcanet Press, 1978) p. 46.

7. *The Pursuit of the Kingfisher* (Manchester: Carcanet Press, 1983), p. 48.

8. See, for instance, Roy Fisher, *Nineteen Poems and an Interview* (Pensnett: Grosseteste, 1975).

9. See Donald Davie, 'Roy Fisher: An Appreciation', in *Thomas Hardy and British Poetry* (London: Routledge and Kegan Paul, 1973), pp. 152–72.

10. See David Trotter, *The Making of the Reader: Language and Subjectivity in Modern American, English and Irish Poetry* (London and Basingstoke: Macmillan, 1984), pp. 218–30.

Chapter 13
The Poetry of Northern Ireland
Seamus Heaney, Michael Longley, Derek Mahon

Seamus Heaney's first book, *Death of a Naturalist*, was published by Faber and Faber in London in 1966. The date marks the beginning of an altered relationship between Irish and English poetry which has had immense significance in the years since. Before 1966, contemporary Irish poetry was of course known to English readers: MacNeice had remained a force (although it was hardly noticed that he was Irish); and Austin Clarke, Patrick Kavanagh, Thomas Kinsella, John Montague and Richard Murphy maintained or established reputations. But, in the late 1960s, it was that poetically enriching but politically disintegrative juncture between the time, the place and the poet that made out of Seamus Heaney the crucial point of intersection between two previously separable if not entirely separate traditions. The juncture is nakedly apparent in *Death of a Naturalist*, where the influences of an education in English literature (Wordsworth, Hopkins, Ted Hughes, the Movement) inform Heaney's attempt to write out his own rural background, but jostle with a desire to write out also his condition as a Northern Irish Catholic. The poem 'At A Potato Digging', which makes contemporary Irish agricultural labour transparent to the tragic and brutalising historical moment of the 1845 Irish famine, and the prophetic poem 'Docker' ('That fist would drop a hammer on a Catholic – / Oh yes, that kind of thing could start again') insist on expressing a history of oppression and a present phase of sectarian stasis which derive from the unique experience of Heaney's own place and time, but which, once 'that kind of thing' did indeed 'start again' in 1968, two years after the publication of *Death of a Naturalist*, seemed all the more pressing too on an English audience. Famously, the book's opening poem, 'Digging', attempts to breach the distance between Heaney's writing and his origins by making his pen a metaphoric spade, his poetry a form of agricultural labour (and, eventually in his work, an excavation); but the pen is also, in the poem's opening lines, 'snug as a gun'. *Death of a Naturalist* foresees that this instrument of writing will bring to light matters darker and deeper than the notations of rurality which form the specific material of many of its poems.

Heaney's was the first full volume by that remarkable constellation of writers from Northern Ireland who began publication in the late 1960s. As I have already indicated, the 1960s were exceptionally energising elsewhere too; and it is worth observing that the new Northern Irish poetry precedes the beginnings of the new Northern Irish 'Troubles': the Belfast Festival of 1965 published the first three pamphlets by Heaney, Derek Mahon and Michael Longley. Nevertheless, the involvement of these writers in the cultural and political situation which produced the crisis of the North, and their responses to it within their work, form a crucial new element in poetry in English in the 1960s; they are the first articulators of that unfinished business which has, even in its periods of apparent stagnation and stasis, come to set the political tone and tenor of the way we all live now in these islands. Their poetry, sometimes apparently despite its own deepest desires, bears the burden of involvement and implication as necessity, not predilection.

Heaney's essay 'Feeling into Words' in *Preoccupations* (1980) offers an account of the first phase of his career which describes the moment after 1968 at which it became necessary to articulate something more than that narcissistic mirror-gazing stare which informs all poetry at some level, no doubt, and which explicitly offers an aesthetic rationale in 'Personal Helicon', the poem which concludes *Death of a Naturalist* ('I rhyme / To see myself, to set the darkness echoing'). Under the pressure of Northern violence, poetry had to make a case for itself, had to be in some sense accountable and responsible. Citing Yeats's discovery of 'befitting emblems of adversity' during the Irish Civil War of the 1920s, Heaney expresses the poet's task after 1968 as the search for 'symbols adequate to our predicament'.[1] Beginning with *Wintering Out* in 1972, his work may be read as an evolving exfoliation of the relationship between the 'self' referred to in 'Personal Helicon' and the community implied by the word 'our' in that quotation from 'Feeling into Words': the community which is, at different points in his work, the inhabitants of Northern Ireland and the inhabitants of the whole island of Ireland, but which is crucially the Catholics of the North. The realisation made in the immediate aftermath of the first shock of violence is that 'seeing yourself' adequately is to see much more than yourself; it is to explore the network of attachments, allegiances and affiliations which entangle you in your moment and your place; it is, perhaps, to register the process in which a 'self' recognises itself as a 'subject'. It is a realisation manifest in the way the 'darkness' of 'Personal Helicon' translates itself into 'the dark that wombed me' in the poem 'Antaeus' which opens Part I of *North* (1975).

Heaney's strength as a poet, however, lies not only in such difficult and rigorous self-recognitions but in the buoyant intelligence and energy of the metaphors, images, fictions and symbols – adequate to a series of predicaments and organised into memorably individuating cadences –

with which he articulates them. *Wintering Out* (1972) employs modes of obliquity and implication, reading a history and a politics out of language itself, the English language as it is spoken and written in Co. Derry, Heaney's original place in Northern Ireland. The book draws out of etymology, and out of a contemplation of the linguistic suppressions, fractures and persistences of an English tongue which has uprooted its native Irish precursor from this territory, a resonant sense of the inheritance of a colonial culture; and it becomes thereby, as I claim in the introduction to Part Five, the seminal single volume of the post-1970 period of English poetry. 'The Tollund Man' in that book initiates what is probably the best-known of those 'fictions' along which the contemporary is directed or diverted in Heaney's work, those 'bog poems' which figure centrally in *North*, in which Northern Irish sectarian violence is related to sacrificial ritual murders in the preservative peat bogs of Iron Age Jutland, a myth of juxtaposition and interpenetration — of present and past, civility and barbarity, sexuality and death, male and female — derived from Heaney's reading of P.V. Glob's book *The Bog People*.

Field Work (1979) contemplates the North from a position of withdrawal, composing a kind of luxuriant but anxious pastoral and a series of personal and national elegies in which the constant preoccupation with the kind of action a poem might represent is moved into another register: not the curt, clipped, lyrically disruptive and deliberate shapes of much of *Wintering Out* and *North*, but a more capacious, extended and socialised address. *Station Island* (1984) and *The Haw Lantern* (1987) annotate Heaney's modified, eventually even satirical attitude to his first allegiances, his painful revision of received impressions and opinions, his uncertainties, hesitations and waverings about the relationship between poetry and the public life; and they do so in forms other than the individual lyric which has been the staple of his work. There is the dramatised narrative of the 'Station Island' sequence; the mask or persona of 'Sweeney Redivivus'; the parable kind of *The Haw Lantern*, indebted partly to Auden, partly to such contemporary East European poets as Zbigniew Herbert and Czeslaw Milosz. These later poems also encode a desire to move beyond the characteristic post-symbolist inquiry into the nature of poetry itself which is to be found in much of Heaney, towards an even more strongly foregrounded but enigmatic and hermetic preoccupation with the nature of writerly inscription, which draws on some of the perspectives and vocabulary of modern literary theory. It is hardly surprising that a poetic *oeuvre* which opens up with an evocation of the implement of its own composition should eventually move into such writerly self-involvements and hermeneutic codings.

These are the essential contours of Heaney's writing, the outlines of a shape which has remarkable coherence, density and solidity; and to sketch them like this is to become aware of two crucially defining characteristics of his procedure. The first is that the Heaney *oeuvre* is a densely recessive one: it ponders deeply a relatively small number of major images and symbols drawn primarily from a rural childhood, revolving them under the light of a constantly varying (and, I suppose, sophisticating) gaze until, yielding the history of an individual sensibility, they yield also the history of a place and a people. Bog, mud, stone, water, birdflight, vocable, calligraphy: all are meditated again and again into a well-founded and integrated corpus in which poem complements poem; poem qualifies, modifies, argues with and frustrates poem; poem calls to poem over a span of years and circumstance. This process is at its most visible in 'Sweeney Redivivus' where the self-reference is sharply specific, the pen-spade of 'Digging' metamorphosing into 'the shaft of the pen' of 'The First Gloss', taken hold of in a move towards a 'margin'; and where another kind of judgemental sharpness is directed too, in 'The First Kingdom', at the rural world celebrated in *Death of a Naturalist*:

> And seed, breed and generation still
> they are holding on, every bit
> as pious and exacting and demeaned.

But even where this process is less visible it is still quietly operating. It is essentially a Yeatsian process, though it lacks Yeats's intransigence of command and egotistical authoritativeness. But it possesses some of the same satisfactions: Seamus Heaney is a poet (and, despite some generic experimentation, like Yeats a poet of the individual lyric) who manifestly 'develops', and develops in response to recognisable features of a political and intellectual biography. A growing scepticism about the premises on which Irish nationalism is predicated, combined with a firm, if revisionist, commitment to an alternative Irish future, is clearly registered, and registered as perturbation, in the work. So is a sometimes almost astonishing willingness to display the stylistic effects of his reading: Hughes in the first book, Robert Lowell in *Field Work*, Auden and the Europeans (and also Edwin Muir) in *The Haw Lantern*. This obviously has dangers of derivativeness not always entirely avoided; but it also suggests something essential about Heaney's poetry: it is a poetry discovering itself in action, tracing the graph of an essential biography, engaging its readers in the existential decisions of a life always turned out towards public accountability as well as inward to its own compunctions, obligations and necessities. The readiness to accept stylistic mentors is testimony to a genuine tentativeness and humility in the Heaney attitude, but perhaps also to a more autocratic certainty that a recognisable *timbre* of his own will survive, by transforming, the inherited manner and mode. The short, swift 'Widgeon' in *Station Island* may be read as a little allegory of both the tentativeness and the assurance, as it meditates its anecdote into parable: the person plucking a wild duck discovers the bird's voice box and 'blew upon it / unexpectedly / his own small widgeon cries'. There is an authentic sense of the 'unexpectedness' of Heaney's own continued gift and scope in his work, but an equal and opposite assurance of the incremental effort being enunciated. As in Yeats, the eventual Heaney *Collected* will be a harmonic resolution of the various motifs and motives; the graph of the life's work will almost certainly seem an astonishingly decided and well-plotted one, the product of one of the most penetrating and assured poetic intelligences of the period.

The second characteristic procedure recognisable in the contours of the career is the aim of engaging Northern experience not directly but by refracting it through some exterior or alien material. The etymological and archaeological delectation of *Wintering Out* and *North*; the self-conscious and self-correcting mythologising of the bog poems; the confrontation with Dante, and with some of the essential features of the English lyric tradition, in *Field Work*; the recuperation of the dream-vision poem in 'Station Island' and the ventriloquising through the medieval Irish figure of Sweeney (hero of the long poem Heaney has translated as *Sweeney Astray*) in 'Sweeney Redivivus'; the renovating reorientations of the parable-poems in *The Haw Lantern*: all are modes of indirection, feeling their way along the lines of sometimes imaginatively daring fictions. They are also modes of location: they evolve strategies for addressing the North unpredictably but with a view to placing it adequately inside an outer history and inside the history of a sensibility. The result is a kind of poetry in which the matter of contemporary British and Irish political history at its most urgent and terrifying is run along the very private lines of an interior sensibility and personality. The major impact of Heaney's work on both British and Irish poetry since 1970 has lain in this discovery of a mode of inheriting and transforming a tradition in such a way as to meet and accommodate pressing contemporary need, without slackness or inertia, but with a sensibility and awareness fully awake to the complexities of the matter in hand.[2]

In his critical work Seamus Heaney has continuously celebrated the achievement of Patrick Kavanagh, an Irish writer of the generation immediately preceding Heaney's own. There are those (and I am one of them) who fail to find in Kavanagh the degree of interest Heaney finds there, and who therefore read Heaney's interest in Kavanagh as the strategic filling-in of a gapped Irish tradition: rural, Catholic and almost-Northern (he was born in Co. Monaghan), Kavanagh acts as an enabling device for Heaney, an earlier poetic exemplar involved with some of the same issues on almost the same ground, and therefore also a kind of insulation against the towering reputation of the Irish but very differently Irish Yeats. For Michael Longley and Derek Mahon –

Northern Protestant, urban poets – there is no doubt, as I suggested in Part One, that Louis MacNeice acts in some similarly exemplary ways; and the poetry of both shows interesting inheritances.

In Michael Longley, who has edited a selection of MacNeice, the influence is a matter of tone and resource: although he is not at all as copious, he has, within the smaller compass of his work, a similar suddenness of variation. Even within individual poems Longley sometimes bewilderingly swerves between realism and fantasy, personal lyric and mythopoeia, narrative and parable, genuinely topographical and imaginary location. The metamorphoses of tone and mode tend to foreground the poetic act itself, the making of the poem; the occasions of Longley's poems are caught up more obviously than is usually the case into the generative capacities of language and form themselves, mediations handled sometimes with an almost erotically delighted intensity. This makes Longley a strange poet of political event; and indeed his address to the matter of the North has been, crucially, a series of variations on that genre in which private grief and public speech have traditionally met in mutually complicating ways, the elegy.

The necessity of establishing credentials before presuming to speak for the Northern dead is a moral compunction articulated in Longley's elegies as a disruption of elegiac decorums or an oddly unsettling variation of register. In 'Wounds' the murdered Irish dead are approached only by way of an evocation of his father's death (as a 'belated casualty' of the war in which the 'Ulster division' fought on the Somme). The poem's unblaming bafflement before the public sorrow is earned and licensed by the personal pain; the authority of familial continuity sanctions contemporary reference. And the poem's veerings of tone and effect – from the almost surreal image of the padre 'Resettling kilts with his swagger-stick . . . / Over a landscape of dead buttocks' to the plangency of Longley's recall of his dying father ('I touched his hand, his thin head I touched') – ensure that in this elegist's hands the form is jolted out of its customary poignancies into something less certain and therefore perhaps more genuinely responsive to this exceptional situation.

Longley's approach to the violence of the North is, altogether, tentative, reticent and unpresuming. It is developed unforcedly and organically out of his usual poetic procedures: an estimation of the natural world as solace but reminder of transience; a wry but self-implicating sense of human oddness and angularity, reflected in moments of narrative comedy; an interest in historical, classical and mythical occasion as it can be subtly appropriated to quirky contemporary transformation. These ways of indirection work well in 'Peace (after Tibullus)', where an implicit relation is established between sexual and political violence and between classical Rome and contemporary Ireland. The poem's pastoral, cornucopian conclusion is a register of erotic tenderness and desire which takes on a deeper power of potential assuagement from its political context:

> But punch-ups,
> Physical violence, are out: you might as well
> Pack your kit-bag, goose-step a thousand miles away
> From the female sex. As for me, I want a woman
> To come and fondle my ears of wheat and let apples
> Overflow between her breasts. I shall call her Peace.

At the opposite pole from this, the elegiac sequence 'Wreaths' also mixes modes, but now to gruesome effect. The three poems of the sequence elegise three of the usual victims of sectarian atrocity, their usualness foregrounded by the titles of the poems which establish them only as functions of their jobs, their services to the state: 'The Civil Servant', 'The Greengrocer', 'The Linen Workers'. The implication of the titles is presumably that in Northern Ireland nobody is truly invisible behind a function, since your job can place you in front of a bullet. The poem on the civil servant culminates in an evocation of the grief of his widow, which is all the more panic-stricken for its punctilious control and precise hysteria: she 'took a hammer and chisel / And removed the black keys from his piano'.

The final poem in the sequence, 'The Linen Workers', is one of the strangest poems even Michael Longley has written, and one of his strongest. Unlike some of his work, this poem does not move out from realism towards some less easily apprehensible mode, but originates in the element of fantasy and moves only in its concluding stanzas towards the incident of massacre commemorated by its title. The initial fantasy is a cruel, horrifying and absurd cadenza on Christ's teeth:

> Christ's teeth ascended with him into heaven:
> Through a cavity in one of his molars
> The wind whistles: he is fastened for ever
> By his exposed canines to a wintry sky.

The power of the conceit derives partly from what may be read rationally through its intense compression: the hollow absurdity of the vicious, dog-eat-dog religion which resurrects itself in these sectarian murders; its unrelentingness, as it eternally fastens people to its desolation. Its force is also constituted, however, from its sheer imaginative energy, the near-derangement of its representation. There is a hint in it of one of Dali's surreal Christs hanging suspended above the earth, but its hallucinatory strangeness is much crueller than Dali's almost-reverence: Christ is a viciously grinning death's-head. The canine teeth hang over the poem that follows, since it owes its weirdly compelling structure to the discovery of analogues for those teeth, first in the 'deadly grin' of his father's false teeth in their tumbler, and only then in the set of false teeth that falls to the ground after the killing:

> When they massacred the ten linen workers
> There fell on the road beside them spectacles,
> Wallets, small change, and a set of dentures:
> Blood, food particles, the bread, the wine.
>
> Before I can bury my father once again
> I must polish the spectacles, balance them
> Upon his nose, fill his pockets with money
> And into his dead mouth slip the set of teeth.

Like 'Wounds', then, but much more disorientatingly, this poem owes its fidelity of feeling to the establishment of an authenticating relationship between public and private. The linen workers, killed in a particularly notorious incident and therefore immediately caught up into the Northern media and propaganda machines, are here restored to a decent burial within a poem which elegises them by elegising a father. The linen workers are felt for because the father is felt for; and the poem knows that a public elegy can only be written from such private sources when the public horror is seen to invade the private grief. In setting those eucharistic emblems, 'the bread, the wine' as equivalences of the ordinary things that fall with the dead, the poem is perhaps offering a more consolatory image of the religion than the nightmare one with which it opens; but the true consolation of this quite selfless elegy is the gesture of human decency with which it closes.

In Derek Mahon a profound scepticism about the value of poetry in the face of such terrors is accompanied by a sense of loss registered in several ways: as a self-consciously rearguard insistence on the disappearance of the gods; as a usually unemphatic, but convinced historical apocalypticism; and as an imaginative haunting by desolate or deserted marine topographies. These absences and emptinesses are paradoxically allied with great stylistic zest; the wit, complication and finish of his work, and its consistent images of light, are partly, no doubt, indebted to MacNeice, whom Mahon commemorates in 'In Carrowdore Churchyard'. In that poem Mahon instances MacNeice's 'fragile, solving ambiguity', but he clearly acts for Mahon too as an exemplar of estrangement: uniquely among the contemporary Northern poets who have registered the influence, Mahon has taken on something of MacNeice's visitor's or tourist's attitude to Ireland. MacNeice's at least partly outsider status when he comments on Ireland seems to Mahon a liberation rather than a limitation, one that he, as a Belfast Protestant educated in Trinity College, Dublin, but spending long periods of his life outside Ireland, clearly feels sympathetic towards. Significantly outsiders of various kinds are commemorated in Mahon's work: the poets of the 1890s, Marilyn Monroe, De Quincey, Van Gogh, Malcolm Lowry, François Villon.

Mahon's other major literary allegiances and affiliations also strongly suggest the desire to perceive home from away, origins from destinations, place from displacement. Samuel Beckett, that Irish European whom MacNeice also admired, is a central presence in the work. What he calls 'Beckett's bleak *reductio*' encourages in Mahon a minimalism observable particularly in one of his most characteristic structures, the narrow, three-line stanza. Beckett also acts, obviously, as an exemplar of complex silences and despairs. And, as a native Irish Protestant who followed James Joyce into self-imposed French exile, he undoubtedly acts as mentor to the Francophile Mahon who has translated a number of French poets, including Corbière, Nerval, Rimbaud and particularly Philippe Jacottet, and who has written, in 'Death and the Sun', a complexly self-involving elegy for Albert Camus. The Francophilia is the major strand in a large network of cultural allusion in Mahon: in particular to other modern European poetry (Rilke, Brecht, Pasternak, Cavafy) and to European painting (Munch, Van Gogh, Renoir, and outstanding poems on Pieter de Hooch's *Courtyards in Delft* and Uccello's *The Hunt by Night*). Mahon's is also a much-travelled cosmopolitan poetry and its Irishness, like MacNeice's, is defined in relation to other places, especially America, rural Surrey and London.

His essential contribution to contemporary poetry lies in this extremely sophisticated enmeshing of his Irish material in a large situating context in which the material itself registers with a newly estranged clarity and poise. 'Penshurst Place' and 'Courtyards in Delft' may be regarded as paradigms of such relationships and juxtapositions. In the former the famous home of the Sidneys, celebrated effusively by Ben Jonson in 'To Penshurst' as a pastoral idyll of the good life, is discovered less idealisingly as the home of 'intrigue and venery' as well as lute music, where the courtiers and dogs have 'bad dreams' which include 'The Spanish ships around Kinsale, / The screech owl and the nightingale': the English idyll rudely disturbed by the Irish battle. 'Courtyards in Delft' begins by evoking de Hooch's painting (of 1659) with leisurely, knowledgeable attentiveness, cataloguing a domestic scrupulousness which resolutely represses any sexual or political complexity until the final stanzas suddenly and, at first, almost comically offer us the young Mahon himself as an inhabitant of the painting's light, ease and restraint:

> I lived there as a boy and know the coal
> Glittering in its shed, late-afternoon

Lambency informing the deal table,
The ceiling cradled in a radiant spoon.
I must be lying low in a room there,
A strange child with a taste for verse,
While my hard-nosed companions dream of war
On parched veldt and fields of rain-swept gorse;

For the pale light of that provincial town
Will spread itself, like ink or oil,
Over the not yet accurate linen
Map of the world which occupies one wall
And punish nature in the name of God.
If only, now, the Maenads, as of right,
Came smashing crockery, with fire and sword,
We could sleep easier in our beds at night.

Mahon's sensing of an identity between de Hooch's Delft and his own childhood Belfast is dependent not only on the fact that both are the scenes of dissenting, Orange Protestantism, but that both repress any admission of the political violence on which their respective social stabilities depend: repressions which return, with a vengeance, in post-1968 Belfast, in modern South Africa. The painting is read, then, as a text in which the violence and civilised repressions of Protestantism and colonialism, and their ultimate destruction in chaos and apocalypse, are present but barely visible to the naked eye, though easily interpretable by one who has witnessed such cultures from within. The poem is effectively companioned by the later 'Death and the Sun' where Camus's 'plague' is superimposed on the plague of violence lying in wait for the Belfast in whose peace the young Mahon first reads his existential hero.

The painting which secretes rather than confesses its political or historical resonance may also be regarded as a paradigm of the Derek Mahon poem; his work, like Heaney's, argues with itself about its own function and capacity in relation to the contemporary violence. 'Rage for Order' offers a poet 'indulging' a Stevensian dream of imaginative coherence from a Larkinian 'high window' above 'the scorched gable end and the burnt-out buses'; but the 'dying art' still has 'desperate ironies' which may prove essential. And 'The Last of the Fire Kings' offers a representative for the poet caught up in political event: the figure of one of those tribal kings from Frazer's The Golden Bough who, instead of waiting patiently to be ritually murdered by his successor, decides to commit suicide 'Rather than perpetuate / The barbarous cycle'. His people, he knows, will not permit his liberating gesture ('rightly perhaps') –

Demanding that I inhabit,
Like them, a world of

Sirens, bin-lids
And bricked-up windows –

Not to release them
From the ancient curse
But to die their creature and be thankful.

The poem poses at its most nakedly binary in Mahon the terms of the essential opposition: poet against people; free poem against commitment to tribal (or sectarian) *mores*; sophisticated self-sacrifice against atavistic feeling.

The poem in which these oppositions are placed is itself, like most of Mahon's work, a carefully and meticulously posed work of art. Its Frazerian fiction; its exquisite, almost exiguous, stanzaic shape; its perfect cadences; its almost pedantic allusiveness; its lapidary diction: all contribute to the effect of a profoundly meditated poetic structure. The essential theatre of Mahon's work derives from the way such carefully wrought forms are made to contain his sometimes extreme material; the sophistications of procedure and manner can implode into great emotional dereliction when they seem a mere veneer on abandonment and loss. This is perhaps particularly the case in two characteristic kinds of Mahon poem: the 'science fiction' poem (such as 'An Image from Beckett', 'Lives' and 'Going Home') which plays with ideas of metempsychosis, inhabiting characters or objects which can view the present in some larger post-historical perspective (the prospect of nuclear or ecological disaster haunts all of Mahon's later work); and the poems of desolate places, especially desolate Irish places (such as 'North Wind: Portrush', 'Rathlin Island', 'A Garage in Co. Cork' and, above all, 'A Disused Shed in Co. Wicklow'). Both kinds sometimes make use of what Mahon calls 'the mute phenomena', the elements, attributes and detritus of the physical world which surround us and which we ignore, but out of which various kinds of morality and metaphysic may be read.

'A Disused Shed in Co. Wicklow' is dedicated to J.G. Farrell, author of the fine novel *Troubles* (1970), a historical novel set in Ireland in the 1920s. The novel brilliantly evokes the fate of the Anglo-Irish by describing the gradual ruin of a hotel which is in any case burnt to the ground by Irish republicans in the closing, apocalyptic pages. Mahon's poem sets its 'disused shed' 'Deep in the grounds of a burnt-out hotel', and the mushrooms growing inside the shed are said to 'have been waiting for us in a foetor / Of vegetable sweat since civil war days'. The poem therefore takes its basic fiction from literature and is intertextual with the Farrell novel; but it uses that fiction as the opportunity for a fantasy which gradually swells with inclusiveness. The shed's mushrooms – overcrowded, patient, prone to nightmare, expectant of release – become emblematic of lives lived under duress, of the imprisoned, the decaying and the forgotten; and their fate is therefore complexly interwoven with that of the class or caste which visibly falls out of history in Farrell's book. In the final stanzas, however, their significance is opened out beyond Ireland into a resonant historical lament and plea:

> A half century, without visitors, in the dark –
> Poor preparation for the cracking lock
> And creak of hinges. Magi, moonmen,
> Powdery prisoners of the old regime,
> Web-throated, stalked like triffids, racked by drought
> And insomnia, only the ghost of a scream
> At the flash-bulb firing squad we wake them with
> Shows there is life yet in their feverish forms.
> Grown beyond nature now, soft food for worms,
> They lift frail heads in gravity and good faith.
>
> They are begging us, you see, in their wordless way,
> To do something, to speak on their behalf
> Or at least not to close the door again.
> Lost people of Treblinka and Pompeii!
> 'Save us, save us,' they seem to say,
> 'Let the god not abandon us
> Who have come so far in darkness and in pain.
> We too had our lives to live.
> You with your light meter and relaxed itinerary,
> Let not our naive labours have been in vain!'

The discoverer who speaks in the voice which speaks the poem is, with light meter and relaxed itinerary, a tourist who happens to have stumbled across these mushrooms accidentally, perhaps on a tour to interesting Irish historical locations. It is here that the attitude of tourist, or visitor, which Mahon admires in MacNeice, is given one of its most notable expressions in his own work. The poet, like the tourist, is inevitably an accidental intruder on sufferings which are not his own, but he knows they are not his own and will not claim otherwise. If he is an empathetic tourist he will, however, convey the suffering he discovers to other historical sufferings he knows of and will convey his experience to an audience. This is at least to respond to the least the mushrooms ask: that the door be not closed again, that the 'lost people' of history be given contemporary witness, that the poet-photographer emulate their own gravity and their own good faith.

Notes

1. Seamus Heaney, *Preoccupations: Selected Prose 1968–1978* (London: Faber and Faber, 1980), p. 56.

2. I have written extensively on Heaney elsewhere, particularly in my *Seamus Heaney* (London: Faber and Faber, 1986).

Part Five
Since 1970

Introduction: Towards the Postmodern?

Seamus Heaney's *Wintering Out*, published in 1972, opens with a poem called 'Fodder'. Its first lines, however, are a correction of the title, introduced by a conjunction of differentiation:

> Or, as we said,
> *fother*, I open
> my arms for it
> again.

As the book opens, the book's arms open to include the dialect or vernacular pronunciation which the poem's more official title excludes in its standard English: the italicised word *'fother'* is the register of the speech of a community not adequately represented by 'correct' pronunciation. The poem, like many to follow in the volume, will bring newly to articulation the speech and idiom of that community, significantly enabling an often disabling local dialect or vernacular. The poem will say it 'as we said' it: in, it may be, the language of the 'father', a word subliminally also present in the vernacular 'fother'. The word as well as the remembered object named by the word are reached for 'for comfort', as some assuagement for the 'long nights' evoked in the poem's final verse which are, presumably, continuous with that 'morning' named in the volume's dedicatory poem, in which the 'new camp for the internees' figures prominently. 'Fodder', that is to say, is a poem implicitly fraught with the political circumstances of Northern Ireland in the early 1970s. *Wintering Out* and the book which followed it in 1975, *North*, bring, in their different ways, the first shock and terror of that conflict into British poetry. In that period in the early 1970s which saw the IRA terror campaigns on the British mainland, with the bombing of the Tower of London in July 1974 and the Birmingham pub bombing of November that year (with its long sequel undermining confidence in the British judicial system), and the responses of British state security which included the 1974 Prevention of Terrorism Act and the increasing use of the Metropolitan Police Special Patrol Group, these volumes by Heaney may be regarded as necessary responses to the urgencies of the moment; and they decisively reoriented the course of British poetry, not only by articulating the matter of the North of Ireland, but also by their influence on a younger generation of British and Irish writers.

In introducing a lexicon and a register of pronunciation distinct from 'received' or standard English, and in taking etymology itself as theme and preoccupation, these volumes may also be read as paradigms of the decisive shift in cultural consciousness after the 1960s. The erosion of cultural and political consensus manifest in that decade, and incarnate in the changes in the Tory party after Edward Heath's performance during the miners' strike of 1974, had, by the mid-1970s, become normative in British life: with the first of her three governments after the election of 1979, Margaret Thatcher began to dissolve the remnants of consensus into a new political doctrine, an explicit ideology eventually aggrandised with her own name, as 'Thatcherism'. Both politically and culturally this acted as a force of polarisation, as it became apparent that Thatcherism involved the dismantling of the Welfare State erected by the post-war consensus. The poetry of regionalism which had begun to develop in the 1960s took on a new impetus and force as a result of the developing division of the country into an economically and culturally advantaged South and a deprived and disadvantaged North: one of the divisions crucially articulated, as I have already observed, in Tony Harrison's *v.* (1985).

That book was published by Bloodaxe Books, established by Neil Astley in Newcastle in 1978. Along with Michael Schmidt's Carcanet Press and journal *PN Review*, established in the late 1960s and early 1970s first outside Oxford but subsequently in Manchester, these initially smaller but later highly successful presses reoriented the publishing of poetry in Britain away from what had been an almost exclusively metropolitan centre. Carcanet initiated the careers of a number of contemporary writers (such as Neil Powell, Clive Wilmer and Dick Davis), but it would be true to say that it is more notable for bringing back into, or sustaining, in print a large number of poets of an older generation (such as Donald Davie, Christopher Middleton and C.H. Sisson), and for its American and foreign poetry in translation. The editorial views of *PN Review* have been conservative and Anglican, but its poetry and critical pages have always been far more catholic in taste than the editorial line would suggest. Bloodaxe Books has also performed very useful services to American and European poetry but has published a more notable crop of younger writers, often with some regional focus, such as Ciaran Carson from Northern Ireland and Simon Armitage from Huddersfield.

Within the academy too, however, the processes of fragmentation became increasingly visible and articulate from the early 1970s, as the Arnoldian–Leavisite conensus of the 1950s collapsed under the new orientations of such British literary and cultural critics as Richard Hoggart and Raymond Williams, and subsequently under the pressure of foreign literary theory: Barthes, Benjamin, Bakhtin, Derrida, Foucault, Kristeva. A crucial aim and effect of this theorising was to place under sceptical scrutiny all previous conceptions of a unified or organic 'tradition' or 'narrative' or 'history' of literary culture. Traditions are fractured by division; narratives are subverted; histories are interrupted (by 'her stories', for instance): all are subject to processes of deconstruction which may reveal their construction as systems of power and control.

It is in this context that Heaney's 'as we said', and his alternative lexicon, take on their paradigmatic force. A great deal of the most interesting poetry of those writers who began to publish after 1970 is written as in some sense oppositional or antagonistic to an idea of a dominant cultural or political or linguistic system. Heaney's uses of a Co. Derry vernacular are followed in the poetry of Northern Ireland by such contemporary vernacular variants as those of Paul Muldoon and Ciaran Carson, which signal the presence of an Irish idiom, lexis and technical or formal indebtedness below the surface of their English, and of Tom Paulin, whose work self-consciously employs a lexicon which he attributes to an Ulster vernacular origin, but which some of his critics ascribe to a Joycean or Audenesque tendency to neologism. (In 1990 Paulin published his *Faber Book of Vernacular Verse* which gives some of these matters a sharper edge and focus and attempts to recuperate a partly hidden history for them.) Peter Reading, in some of his poems of what Paulin has called 'Junk Britain', focuses an outraged critique of Thatcherism through the demotic speech and orthography of an oppressed working class or underclass. Blake Morrison, in 'The Ballad of the Yorkshire Ripper', employs a Yorkshire vernacular in a way which both criticises an endemic cultural machismo and celebrates an alternative dialectical tenderness and sensitivity.

If these British and Irish variants make their contributions to a 'new English', they are part of a movement or orientation which also signally includes the work of those Westindian-British poets represented in such anthologies as James Berry's *News for Babylon: The Chatto Book of Westindian British Poetry* (1984), Paula Burnett's *Penguin Book of Caribbean Verse* (1986), and Fred D'Aguiar's section of *The New British Poetry 1968–88* (1988), the succeeding generations from those black communities established in Britain in the processes of post-war immigration. The fractures and junctures of language and identity when the black writer uses the language of his colonial oppressor, articulating the displacements of a hitherto largely unarticulated history, are significantly paraded by the title of Berry's volume, 'Babylon' being the land of exile in Rastafarian mythology, and by Grace Nichols's epigraph poem in the Burnett anthology:

> I have crossed an ocean
> I have lost my tongue
> from the root of the old one
> a new one has sprung

The 'new one' may be an individually accented and inflected version of standard English, as it is in many of the poems of Berry himself and of E.A. Markham, or it may be various types of *patois*, Caribbean Creole and phonetically reproduced lexical variants, sometimes known as 'Nation language'. In the work of 'Dub poets' like Benjamin Zephaniah and Linton Kwesi Johnson (in a way that connects them with the punk and new wave music of the mid-1970s and later, and influenced by the reggae of Bob Marley) these linguistic resources are combined with music; and in performance some of their work takes on an extra charge of venom and denunciation, as the repressed history of servitude and oppression meets the contemporary squalor of black urban experience in Thatcherite Britain, with its SUS laws, its riot police, its recrudescence of the explicit racism of the National Front, its endemic mass unemployment, its increasingly Draconian immigration laws. It is a poetry in which England becomes Kwesi Johnson's 'Inglan':

> w'en me jus' come to Landan toun
> mi use to work pan di andahgroun
> but workin' pan di andahgroun
> y'u don't get fi know your way aroun'
>
> Inglan is a bitch
> dere's no escapin' it
> Inglan is a bitch
> dere's no runnin' whey fram it

If anger, resentment, hostility and anguish are unsurprisingly prominent among the emotions catalogued in these poems, they are by no means its sole *raison d'être*; and the variety of means and modes in some of its finest exemplars brings a newly energising element into the plurality of voice and writing in contemporary poetry. Of particular note are Markham's 'Lambchop' poems of the mid-1970s, Grace Nichols's long poem 'I is a Long Memoried Woman' (1983), Fred D'Aguiar's 'Mama Dot' sequence (1985) and some of Berry's work, including his exile's lament 'Lucy's Letter', with its double sigh of plangency and resilience ('Things harness me here. I long / For we labrish bad'). The most subtle poems in this new kind are not fixated on a lost past but are exploratory of a new black British identity, one conscious of coming, in the later 1980s, fully into possession of its own 'other' cultural and linguistic resources: witness, in particular, the bravura wit and aplomb of John Agard's 'Listen Mr Oxford Don':

> I ent serving no jail sentence
> I slashing suffix in self-defence
> I bashing future with present tense
> and if necessary
>
> I making de Queen's English accessory
> to my offence

These alternative Englishes, inscribed with strong class, regional or racial affiliations and identifications and prominently signalled by lexical variation or deviance, are complemented, in much contemporary poetry by women, with uses of English which challenge a perceived masculinist dominance in the 'man-made language' of the (presumed) cultural norm. In my section on women's poetry below I locate what is in effect a conception of an *écriture féminine*, along the lines of some French feminist models, in the syntactical and lexical patterns of Medbh McGuckian and, to some degree, in the procedures of Denise Riley, and I also attempt to describe some of the implications and effects of a more 'traditional' women's poetry in Carol Rumens and Anne Stevenson. Like the other categories into which the critic may construct the contemporary, the category of the 'womanly' or the 'feminist' is not a hermetically sealed and self-identified one, but one riven by faction and fraction, permeable to the alternative and the unorthodox, waiting for its future. It is clear, however, that writing by women constitutes one of the most notable elements in contemporary British poetry: feminist theorising since the late 1960s, both in Britain and abroad, both social and literary-cultural, and the presence, example and writing of Sylvia Plath, have manifestly provoked a new conception of how the experience and desire of women may be articulated in the contemporary poem. In the 1970s and 1980s a whole range of women poets began to establish themselves, partly through a number of anthologies: Lillian Mohin's *One Foot on the Mountain* (1979); Carol Rumens's *Making for the Open: Post-Feminist Poetry* (1985); Jeni Couzyn's *The Bloodaxe Book of Contemporary Women Poets* (1985); and Fleur Adcock's *The Faber Book of Twentieth-Century Women's Poetry* (1987).

If the decentring impulse of Heaney's *Wintering Out* may be read as paradigmatic of the variations and deviations which I describe here, this was a significance recognised by one of the most prominent anthologies of the period, the *Penguin Book of Contemporary British Poetry* edited by Blake Morrison and Andrew Motion in 1982, in which Heaney is placed first and named as originary: 'the new spirit in British poetry began to make itself felt in Northern Ireland during the late 1960s and early 1970s'.[1] The anthology was, even as these things go, an exceptionally controversial one; and Heaney himself entered the debate when, in 1983, he published, as the second pamphlet from the newly founded Field Day company in Derry, his poem *An Open Letter*, in which he refuses the national identity 'British' imposed on him by the anthology's title, and does so from a situation explicitly read as post-colonial: 'This "British" word / Sticks deep in native and *colon* / Like Arthur's sword' – an insistence emphasised by the fact that the poem uses the 'wee habbie' stanza form of that other 'stranger', the Scots Burns.[2] Some critics thought this response a bit over-earnest; but it does make an essential point about the way a national and cultural identity is problematised in a great deal of the poetry of these islands since the early 1970s. The centrifugal spirit of the time may well be better realised by the Paladin anthology *The New British Poetry 1968–88* (1988) which required four editors working independently to tell four separate stories.

The Motion/Morrison volume has, however, been influential in some of its characterisations, discovering in the poetry it prints a new 'ludic and literary self-consciousness', a 'preference for metaphor and poetic bizarrerie to metonymy and plain speech' and a kind of self-perception and self-dramatisation completely at odds with the recommendations of Alvarez in *The New Poetry*. These are poems in which the poets seem 'not inhabitants of their own lives so much as intrigued observers, not victims but onlookers, not poets working in a confessional white heat but dramatists and story-tellers'. The 'departure' represented by this work is one which 'may be said to exhibit something of the spirit of post-modernism'.[3] The term is not defined any more particularly; but it is one that has come increasingly into currency since the mid-1970s. It has seemed to some critics merely modish; and its most significant theorists themselves betray (or revel in) varying degrees of hesitation and uncertainty about its use. The uncertainty turns on what precise relationship to Modernism it proposes, and on whether most of what may be described as 'postmodern' is in fact already contained within Modernism itself: so that theories of the postmodern would, in the end, be offering little more than an anxiety about a relationship to Modernism and, possibly, an awe of it, a sense that so many possibilities were realised there and then that all that remains in culture now is to trail along in the shadows of the giants.[4]

Throughout this study I have attempted to define various attitudes to Modernism taken up by succeeding generations of British writers; and in Part Four I have used the term 'neo-Modern' to refer to a poetry self-consciously and even combatively parading a relationship to a particular kind of Modernist model, that associated with the Pound–Olson–Williams line of American poetry; despite its lack of currency, it still seems to me a useful term for this kind of 'writing after Modernism'. I also think, however, that the term 'postmodern' may be genuinely useful in defining a series of attributes shared by contemporary work which may be much less self-consciously or 'officially' indebted to or accommodating of, Modernism. In one influential view of postmodernism, indeed, it becomes less an optional mode or model, and more the definition of a historical phase or phenomenon. In this kind of theorising everything in contemporary culture is recuperable by the postmodern, which is read as the cultural arm, as it were, of contemporary post-industrial, multinational capitalism. The 'postmodern debate' then becomes the name for the way in which the contemporary theorises itself; and, particularly in some American models (in the L=A=N=G=U=A=G=E poets, for instance), the interaction of theory and 'imaginative' writing is intense and endemic. Britain is not yet quite America, however; so, without necessarily subscribing to this view, I want to suggest how some elements of the work discussed in this section may be usefully considered as postmodern.

What I have been describing already as the fragmentation of a purportedly once unified or organic tradition into separate and often mutually hostile variant kinds is, on one reading, itself the most profound feature of the postmodern: in Jean-François Lyotard's influential *The Postmodern Condition: A Report on Knowledge* (1979) he posits the end of the 'master narrative' as the essential condition of the postmodern. The concept or construction of a 'national' literary tradition would be one such master narrative; and it seems clear that an essential spirit in contemporary writing is to write against any such totalisation, to disrupt it with other kinds of narrative: those of class, gender, ethnic origin, race and religion. The postmodern anti-essentialist critique of the depth model of identity and culture, and its alternative position that both are to be viewed in conditions of protean construction, as a play among signifiers, are reflected in several ways in contemporary poetry: in the preoccupation with surface in 'Martian' poetry, a surface whose alienating strangeness can only be gradually assimilated, or brought into internal coherence, by the systematising, analogising intellect; in the way brand names and commodities feature so frequently in the work of Ciaran Carson, as though identity is partly dispersed into processes of commodification, or even as though identity has itself been commodified; in the use of images of a British imperial past in Andrew Motion and James Fenton, where the images are present precisely as images – as simulacra, structures already much read and interpreted, drained and depleted of significances they once carried in history; in the temporal confusions or interminglings in Fenton, where the uncertainty of historical period contributes further to the impression of *bricollage*, to the sense that the past is being not so much re-invented as newly dreamt through a contemporary consciousness; and in the temporal transparencies of Paul Muldoon where, for instance, an Irish early-medieval voyage narrative is read through a pastiche of the twentieth-century Californian of Raymond Chandler.

Pastiche and parody are usually identified as features of the postmodern; and they abound in the poetry of the period. In addition to Muldoon's 'Immramm' and 'The More a Man Has the More a Man Wants', notable examples would include: Anne Stevenson's American family letters in *Correspondences*; Craig Raine's pidgin or semi-Creole in 'Gauguin'; Peter Reading's versions of demotic writing in 'Ukulele Music'; Christopher Reid's 'translations' from an unspecified Eastern European language in *Katerina Brac*; Fenton's vaguely 1930s-Audenesque minatory, throughout his work; Carson's formal mimesis of endlessly digressive and delaying Irish storytelling. Although parody and pastiche are also prominent features of Modernist writing (in Joyce's *Ulysses*, for instance, and Eliot's *The Waste Land*), there is often a genuine distinction to be made between the way they figure there and the way they figure in contemporary work. It is a distinction made most satisfactorily, to my mind, in Brian McHale's *Postmodernist Fiction* (1987). The move from Modernism to postmodernism, he argues, is a move from epistemology to ontology. Concerned with the problems of knowledge, Modernism's technical experimentations, such as parody and pastiche, are always ultimately recuperable by a concept of psychology. The 'Nausicaa' episode of *Ulysses*, we might say, is written as pastiche women's magazine fiction because Gerty MacDowell's subjectivity has been largely constructed from such materials; and Eliot's juxtaposition of parodistic fragments in *The Waste Land* reflects a mind in the process of disintegration. Concerned with the problems of being, the experimentations of postmodernism decentre subjectivity more radically. As Steven Connor puts it (after McHale) 'subjectivity gives way to textuality'.[5] This seems to me a useful way of thinking about, for instance, the virtually uninterpretable dispersal of the matter of contemporary Northern Ireland into a range of textual traces (including Walt Disney, Gertrude Stein, Nathaniel Hawthorne, *Sir Gawain and the Green Knight* and the Trickster cycle of the Winnebago Indians) in Muldoon's 'The More a Man Has the More a Man Wants' and the persona-cipher of Christopher Reid's *Katerina Brac*, whose subjectivity, such as we have of it, is manifestly an intertextual construct dependent on the history of poetic translation in the period and especially indebted to the Penguin Modern European Poets series.

The parodies and pastiches of some of these texts draw material from popular or mass culture into the preserve of the 'high culture' of the poem; and it is a marked feature of the postmodern that it breaks down distinctions between high and low culture. In Joyce's 'Nausicaa' the pastiche acts as the vehicle of irony and (albeit partly sympathetic) judgement, placing Gerty at a certain perspectival remove from the reader; in the parodies and pastiches of postmodernism there is no comparable interpretative hold. In Muldoon's 'Immramm', for instance, it is not at all clear that the hip Chandleresque patter is intended as judgemental commentary on the odd and oddly inconsequential exploits of the narrator; and Muldoon's work is a great promiscuous riot of cultural reference in which the 'high' (Robert Frost, Ovid's *Metamorphoses*) mingles on the same plane with the 'low' (the Clancy Brothers, 'Johnny B. Goode'). His poems, we might say, enter a realm of pastiche in which such cultural distinctions are manifestly eroded; or, further, the poems are constructed partly with the point of eroding such distinctions, and occasionally in contradistinction to some poems which observe the more traditional pieties and decorums (Seamus Heaney's, for instance). Pastiche is not the only meeting-place of the high and low in contemporary writing, however: other conjunctions would include the use of popular genres in some of the 'narrative' poems of the period (the thriller, the chase and the western in Muldoon, and the murder mystery in Motion's 'Dangerous Play') and the interconnections between some of Fenton's poems and his journalism, and his setting of themes of contemporary disintegration and terror to the rhythms of children's songs, nursery rhymes, ballads and jingles in *Manila Envelope* (1989), in a way reminiscent of some of Bob Dylan's *Basement Tapes* material.

In discussing some of this poetry, as I do below, I should emphasise what a selective range of work I am dealing with from the period since 1970. If postmodern theory is an attempt to write the history of the contemporary, then its uncertainties, anxieties and discursive fractures are hardly surprising; and the same plea may be entered by the critic of contemporary poetry. The poems I discuss here seem to me in some ways representative of significant elements in the history of the period; and they are poems I read with pleasure. Given that these poets are in mid-career, the categories into which I divide their work are also provisional; other categories and alignments would clearly have been possible. To name one outstanding instance, the work of Paul Muldoon, discussed under the 'Northern Ireland' rubric, has also been at the centre of the 'new narrative' in contemporary poetry. But such hesitations, anxieties and provisionalities are, I hope, reasonable attitudes for any historian of the contemporary.

Notes

1. Blake Morrison and Andrew Motion (eds), *The Penguin Book of Contemporary British Poetry* (Harmondsworth: Penguin Books, 1982), p. 12.

2. Seamus Heaney, *An Open Letter* (Derry: Field Day Theatre Company, 1983), p. 7.

3. *The Peguin Book of Contemporary British Poetry*, p. 20.

4. My view of the postmodern is indebted in particular to: Steven Connor, *Postmodernist Culture: An Introduction to Theories of the Contemporary* (Oxford: Basil Blackwell, 1989); Linda Hutcheon, *A Poetics of Postmodernism: History, Theory, Fiction* (New York and London: Routledge, 1988); Fredric Jameson, *Postmodernism or, The Cultural Logic of Late Capitalism* (London and New York: Verso, 1991); Richard Kearney, *The Wake of Imagination: Ideas of Creativity in Western Culture* (London: Hutchinson, 1988); Jean-François Lyotard, *The Postmodern Condition: A Report on Knowledge* (1979; Manchester: Manchester University Press, 1984); Brian McHale, *Postmodernist Fiction* (New York and London: Methuen, 1987).

5. Connor, *Postmodernist Culture*, p. 125.

Chapter 14
In Ireland or Someplace: A Second Generation from Northern Ireland

Paul Muldoon, Tom Paulin, Ciaran Carson

Now, in the dream of our own plenitude,
I want to go back
and rap it as milk, jism, cinnamon,
when it might be a quick blow-job
in a 6-motel,
or a small fear just
in a small town
in Ireland or someplace.

(Tom Paulin, 'Mount Stewart')

The work of the second generation of writers from Northern Ireland has been produced in the wake not only of an earlier initiatory achievement, but also of the continuing situation in the North. Beginning at a point beyond the brief period of Civil Rights optimism, it has had to cope from its origins with the greater depredations of the province after the early 1970s. In making this dual response – both aesthetic and social – this work has issued persuasive technical invitations to the poetry of the present English moment and articulated with powerful and subtle resource the tensions of its Irish context. In some respects this may be regarded as an almost explicitly shared undertaking: Muldoon dedicates *Quoof* (1983) to Carson; Paulin concludes his critical book *Ireland and the English Crisis* (1984) with a celebration of Muldoon's long poem 'Immramm'; and the lengthiest contemporary section in Muldoon's anthology, *The Faber Book of Contemporary Irish Poetry* (1986), is devoted to Paulin.

For all three poets the work of Seamus Heaney figures as both authority and embarrassment, and therefore to some extent a determinant of their own poetic strategies. In the tradition of Irish 'answer poetry', perhaps, in which different poets engage in a verse dialogue with one another, they all at particular moments encode a response to the immensely successful elder poet. Muldoon has a series of references, wry and gently satirical, which suggest both the respect of engagement and the wily, mischievous divorce from allegiance and affiliation. The literary joke in the middle of the long poem 'The More a Man Has the More a Man Wants' in *Quoof* is a paradigm of this sometimes almost secret debate in Muldoon. The poem's hero, Gallogly, takes sustenance during his adventures:

> Gallogly lies down in the sheugh
> to munch
> through a Beauty of
> Bath. He repeats himself, *Bath*,
> under his garlic-breath.
> *Sheugh*, he says. *Sheugh*.
> He is finding that first 'sh'
> increasingly difficult to manage.
> *Sh*-leeps. A milkmaid sinks
> her bare foot
> to the ankle
> in a simmering dung hill
> and fills the slot
> with beastlings for him to drink.

Gallogly, hero of this complex, learned and intertextual poem, is here pronouncing the Northern Irish dialect word for 'ditch', 'sheugh'. In Heaney's placename poem 'Broagh', pronunciation of 'that last / *gh* the strangers found / difficult to manage' is made a tentative instance of solidarity and potential community between Catholic and Protestant who inhabit the same small territorial patch; in Muldoon the final 'gh' of 'sheugh' seems easy, while the initial 'sh' comes across as stage-Irish, the sign not of community but of stereotype. Muldoon's reference then (which is followed by an allusion to a moment in the medieval Irish poem which Heaney has translated as *Sweeney Astray*) presumably implies obliquely that Heaney's preoccupation with Northern placename and dialect can itself be recuperated by a dangerous and phoney kind of 'Irishness' from which Muldoon himself, formed by a cultural complex almost identical to Heaney's (Northern, rural, Catholic, Queen's University-educated), instinctively withdraws.

There are comparable moments in Paulin and Carson. Where Muldoon is all sly insinuation, Paulin is abrasive and abrupt. In 'And Where Do You Stand on the National Question?' in *Liberty Tree* (1983), a conversation with a 'flinty mandarin' provokes a negative self-definition:

> Your Lagan Jacobins, they've gone
> with *The Northern Star*. I've heard
> Hewitt and Heaney trace us back
> to the Antrim weavers –
> I can't come from *that*.

The implication that Heaney's (and John Hewitt's, that elder Ulster Protestant poet's) definition of Ulster Protestant identity is mistaken and perhaps presumptuous is grounded in Paulin's restless, anxious, combative effort at his own definition of that identity, and of judgement upon it and aspiration for it, throughout his work. The poem 'At Maas', for instance, adapts a trope from Heaney – that of the symbolic voice of some inanimate object offering advice to the poet – in order to make a most unHeaney-like gesture of negation and dismissal. In Heaney's 'North' the poet is instructed in the difficult consolations of poetry by the 'swimming tongue' of a Viking longship. In 'At Maas' (Maas is a village in Co. Donegal) Paulin puts his ear to the ground and hears only 'the *chthon-chthon* / that spells *must*', the atavistic instruction in processes of historical inevitability; and the poem's own counsel is offered not by the barbaric Viking but by the civility of a Georgian mansion, a civility capable of recognising the almost posthumous state it inhabits:

> . . . the Adam form
> through the trees
> says, 'Take up your pen,
> make a new barm
> and try the whole thing again.

   To claim to recognise that '*chthon-chthon*' (derived from the word *chthonic*, 'coming from under the earth'), as Paulin may be implying the Heaney of *North* claims, is of course a dangerous activity for the poet. The land can only speak in the voice you choose to give it, and that may be a voice which excludes less desirable voices which will not cease their clamour because the poet refuses to acknowledge them. Ciaran Carson has been one of the strongest critics of this strain of 'chthonic' recognition in Heaney, and his refusal of assent to *North* when he reviewed it in the *Honest Ulsterman* has been given currency in much subsequent critical debate.[1] In his poem 'The Irish for No' (from the volume of the same name published in 1987), references to Heaney's early work are juxtaposed with references to Keats, and both are made to co-habit, in the poem's 'Mish-mash. Hotch-potch', with the savagery of topical reference:

> What's all this to the Belfast business-man who drilled
> Thirteen holes in his head with a Black & Decker? It was just
>   a normal morning

> When they came. The tennis-court shone with dew or frost, a
>   little before dawn.
> The border, it seemed, was not yet crossed: the Milky Way
>   trailed snowy brambles,
> The stars clustered thick as blackberries. They opened the door
>   into the dark:
> *The murmurous haunt of flies on summer eves.* Empty jam-jars.

It would be too heavy-handed to describe this collage of references as straightforwardly satirical at Heaney's expense; but the allusions do seem to imply a sense of unease and limitation. The grotesquerie of the Belfast suicide and the unspecific minatory narrative in which 'they' are presumably coming with some underhand purpose in mind (murder, kidnapping) consort oddly with and imply some judgement on the sensorial opulence of Heaney's early work. Heaney's second volume, *Door into the Dark*, was published in 1969, the second year of the 'Troubles'. Carson's poem finds behind the door not contemporary terror but the luxuriousness of Keats's 'Ode to a Nightingale'; and those 'jam-jars' which are, in Heaney's 'Death of a ' Naturalist' and 'Blackberry-Picking', full of frogspawn and blackberries are, in Carson, ominously or disappointedly 'empty'. Although the reasons are not spelt out or insisted, the passage appears to find Heaney's poetic of late-Romantic plenitude and expansiveness wanting in the dark of contemporary social and political attrition.[2]

It has become something of a convention in criticism of Muldoon and Paulin to suggest that they form an antithesis: Seamus Deane discovers in them 'a battle between a poetry of denial (Muldoon) and of commitment (Paulin)', and Edna Longley's celebration of Muldoon is part of an argument in which Paulin is derogated.[3] (Carson has not, at the time of writing, been adduced as a significant presence in these debates since his publishing history until the late 1980s was such an odd one: he published a well-regarded, if still only 'promising' volume called *The New Estate* in 1976, but, apart from a short pamphlet, maintained a silence of over ten years until the universally acclaimed *The Irish for No*.) It would be foolish to claim, against Deane and Longley, that there are not clearly distinguishable tones, attitudes and forms of behaviour among these poets; but the sharing of this muted intertextual debate with Heaney may be regarded as a point of energising origin for all of them, an origin which links acknowledgement and deviation.

The will towards this primary liberation is the ground of a genuine spirit of liberation in their work as a whole. In circumventing Heaney they are circumventing conceptions of obligation and responsibility, the deliberate shouldering of a burden, and even perhaps of authority and patriarchy which his work embodies – and embodies, of course, in relation to the matter of Northern Ireland. Although Heaney's later work consistently longs for various kinds of liberation, the longing is itself made the focus of anxious and guilty self-debate. It occasionally seems as if he has to punish himself into liberation, and then punish himself for such an act of presumption; and the various anxieties of the work do not include the anxiety that his own anxieties may not be of interest to the reader. It is taken for granted that the poet's debate with himself is of public moment, that he is a genuine antenna of the culture. Whereas in their various resistances to the Heaney procedure Muldoon, Paulin and Carson sustain a more self-effacing liberation and write a poetry which manages to circumvent the iron oppositions, antitheses, polarites and dualities of Northern Ireland since 1968 – to circumvent those binary divisions not by an irresponsibility or carelessness but by embracing them in the serious playfulness and pluralism of (in all three cases) a genuinely innovative writing. The single authoritative centre and 'voice' of a Heaney poem is decisively rejected in favour of complex and complexly ironic kinds of fragmentation, intertextuality, formal experimentation, analogising, synthesising, tale-telling and gaming in which 'Ireland' is offered a series of alternative identities. In the energy and cunning of its behaviour, this work offers an always implicit and sometimes explicit challenge to the stasis of the contemporary Irish present; in the terms of my epigraph from Paulin, it searches out the 'someplace' of difference within the 'Ireland' of present political and cultural construction, and does this in the imaginary noplace, the 'utopia', of writing itself.

Muldoon is the most insouciant and zestfully ludic of the three, creating a poetry that conceals far more than it reveals, a poetry predicated on a kind of epistemological uncertainty and tolerance. 'Who's to know what's knowable?' he asks in 'Our Lady of Ardboe':

> Milk from the Virgin Mother's breast,
> A feather off the Holy Ghost?
> The fairy thorn? The holy well?

The sceptical questioning produces a guarded alertness to his own procedures and solicitations, an awareness of the potential self-delusion and duplicity of any obvious investment in attitude or opinion, a knowing fear of the suasions and snares of language itself; and the tolerance results in a fascination with metamorphosis and simultaneity. Muldoon is clearly at home in the Irish language; he has translated the work of the contemporary Irish-language poets Michael Davitt and Nuala Ni Dhomhnaill, and the old Irish poem *Immramma Mael Duin* is the exotically parodied and plundered source for his own long poem 'Immramm'. It is possible to sense the presence of this other language in some of the forms of Muldoon's English, in particular in his audacious assonantal rhyming (the poem 'Quoof' goes so far as to rhyme 'English' with 'language') and his constant use of the present habitual 'would', a tense in the Irish language which, as Edna Longley has said, makes in Muldoon's English for a profound 'distrust of the definitive'.[4] This ghostly presence of a second language within the language actually written is only the primary conjunction in a poetry driven by the collocation, juxtaposition and interpenetration of things usually held separate and distinct: Muldoon's work is hybrid, heterogeneous, Ovidianly metamorphic, lubricated by the dangers and deliciousness of 'mixed marriage' (the title of one poem) and miscegenation (nowhere more clearly, perhaps, than at the point in 'Immramm' where the white cat of the original is transmogrified into the 'black cat' – the black jazz musician – of the Muldoon). If his work veers and swerves, melds and meshes, pirouettes and counterpoints, it is almost inordinately in control of itself too, finely and tactfully setting a frame around its postmodern canvas. Like the hare dislodged by Sir Alfred McAlpine at the end of 'I Remember Sir Alfred', Muldoon's work too 'goes by leaps and bounds / Across the grazing, / Here and there, / This way and that, by singleminded swervings.'

Many of Muldoon's singleminded swervings veer towards, and pull back from the political. In 'Gathering Mushrooms' the mushrooms alternate as the fungoid focus of Muldoon's affectionate recall of his father, a mushroom-farmer in Co. Armagh, and as the less domesticated 'psilocybin', the hallucinogenic catalyst of disturbing drug-visions. As the latter, they induce the poem's closing hallucination, in which Muldoon's head becomes a horse's head which 'shook its dirty-fair mane / and spoke this verse'. The 'verse', given the whole of the concluding stanza to itself (a stanza which is a typically Muldoonian 'deconstructed sonnet'), consists of a plea for recognition and support from a prisoner behind concrete and barbed wire. The verse ends:

> If we never live to see the day we leap
> into our true domain,
> lie down with us now and wrap
> yourself in the soiled grey blanket of Irish rain
> that will, one day, bleach itself white.
> Lie down with us and wait.

The IRA hunger-strikers who died in Long Kesh internment camp in 1981 (beginning with Bobby Sands, who did write 'verse', on toilet paper)[5] are given their plea here, and their due. The lines seem genuinely moving, articulated with sympathy and respect. But there are lurking ironies here too: in the apparent endlessness of the longing for that utopian 'true domain'; in the indictment implicit in the word 'soiled' (the blankets of the hunger-strikers were literally soiled with their own excrement, but the ferocity of their violence has perhaps more generally soiled the Irish weather or atmosphere); and in the posture requested by the final invitation – if you lie down you may stay down, and if you wait you do only what has been done so often already in Irish experience and literature (the *topos* of 'waiting' is brilliantly telescoped by Muldoon himself, in the poem 'Lull', into the phrase 'that eternal interim').

The verse is also, in the terms of the hallucination, spoken by a horse with a dirty-fair mane. If that recalls the matted hair of the unwashed prisoners on the 'dirty protest' in the early 1980s, the fiction of hallucination makes this Paul Muldoon's own head too; Muldoon, that is to say, spontaneously ventriloquises for an IRA prisoner at a moment when rational control has lapsed. The fiction of the poem allows him, therefore, both the acknowledgement of a culturally conditioned intimacy of involvement with the traditions of Irish Republican politics and, *at the same time*, a distancing of himself from them. The poem has traced a graph of both filiation and detachment, of empathy and scruple; its poetics of oblique implication has implied something of what it is to be 'implicated'. Anecdote, reminiscence, respectful pastiche and the register of distorted consciousness are collated in such a way as to render the most intimate textures and contours of psychological and political response. This is what a poetry singleminded in its swervings may be like, reaping the moral and aesthetic benefits of metamorphosis and simultaneity.

Collations, collusions and collisions create in Muldoon an extraordinarily open and free poetic space, the width of reference paradoxically making for a sometimes almost paper-thinness of poetic texture. In 'Immramm' an ancient Irish voyage-tale melts into the hip patois of Raymond Chandler, conveyed in exuberantly Byronic stanzaic shapes; in 'Crossing the Line' the medieval Welsh *Mabinogion* (itself Ovidian in the fluidity of its Celtic shape-shifting personae) passes savage comment on the Anglo-Irish Agreement of 1985 ('Pryderi's gifts of hounds and horses / turn out to have been fungus'); in 'Meeting the British' an eighteenth-century encounter between a British general and a tribe of Canadian Indians – the general leaving the gift of 'two blankets embroidered with smallpox' – acts as an implicit analogue for other imperial and colonial encounters in which the British also bear the Greekest of gifts; in '7, Middagh Street' the inhabitants of the house in New York occupied by W.H. Auden when he first went to America perform an elaborate verbal gavotte (in a kind of postmodern rendering of the Renaissance form of the *corona di sonnetti*, such as John Donne employs in 'La Corona') to a tune written by Auden himself in his elegy for Yeats (the tune of 'For poetry makes nothing happen . . .'); in 'The More a Man Has the More a Man Wants' the Trickster legends of the Winnebago Indians supply a framework for a reading of Northern Ireland in its contemporary crisis. Recondite and usual, ancient and postmodern, swerving over a line-break from Irish history to

Amerindian mythology, from Celtic lore to the cinema of Malik and the painting of Klee, from sexual encounter to political parable, from local parish to cosmopolitan metropolis, from sushi to Duns Scotus, Muldoon's work is immensely adroit and nimble, quick-witted and a bit superior, challenging the reader to keep up with it. If it is occasionally in danger of smirking at its own cleverness, of degenerating from epistemological uncertainty to mere knowingness (nowhere more than in his longest poem, *Madoc*, of 1990), or of becoming exiguous almost to uninterpretable vanishing point, its playful intertextuality is also a genuine tolerance, a seeking out of the alternative, the speculative, the untested (several poems deal with abrupt, enigmatic or inexplicable departures). 'Our Lady of Ardboe', having asked its epistemological question, answers it like this:

> Our simple wish for there being more to life
> Than a job, a car, a house, a wife –
> The fixity of running water.

In its freedom and simultaneity Paul Muldoon's work offers, always, an implicit poetic challenge to the fixed position; and, in that, it may be regarded as offering itself as an aesthetic paradigm of a better future Anglo-Irish politics.

At first sight and in his earlier work Tom Paulin may indeed seem the antithesis of Muldoon: he appears to write there an earnest, dour, tight-lipped, fricative poetry signalling an engaged Ulster conscience confessing rather than performing itself in verse. Those earlier poems strenuously grapple with the political realities of the North and do so in a discourse continuous with that of the political debate and polemic in which Paulin has also engaged. The poems attempt a diagnosis (or post-mortem?) of what one of their titles calls the 'Cadaver Politic'. Taking off from the title of Paulin's first book, *A State of Justice* (1977), they consistently probe the nature of the 'state' and employ a vocabulary of publicly available terms which gradually take on more private and metaphoric significance: the word 'state' itself, 'stillness' and 'history', 'spirit', 'form' and 'society'. Paulin is unafraid of abstraction, explicitly desiring 'some undoctrinaire / Statement of what should be' ('A New Society'), and insistent about what should not be: in 'A Partial State', from *The Strange Museum* (1980), the mottoes of Belfast's public buildings are 'emblems of failure' which tell us that '*What the wrong gods established / no army can ever save*'. Their settings, what 'The Hyperboreans' calls their 'theoretical locations', are exactly appropriate to these grim politico-poetic meditations: dispiriting urban wastelands, the bleak disenchantments of dank maritime areas, the grey afternoon light of border towns.

The danger that this might all become almost self-parodyingly lugubrious or morose is diminished by an alternative element in earlier Paulin which has to do with the ease, grace and delight discovered outside the hyperborean: in 'the first freshness' of tender sexual relationship; in the spontaneity and voluptuousness of Indian culture and ceremony; in the sudden release of energy into the near-nonsense of the poem 'Pings on the Great Globe' in *The Strange Museum*; and in the assuagement and seductiveness of certain kinds of less obviously engaged art. In Paulin's first two volumes these concerns are kept more or less distinct; and the poem-sequence 'The Other Voice' in *The Strange Museum* is a kind of dialogue or debate between them. The poem opens with moments of biography (a visit to an Anglican schoolmaster; a 1960s socialist cell in Belfast; some camp donnish advice in a garden) which witness cultural affiliations and divisions; and it then enlarges into a meditation on one major historical testament to the antithesis underlying these divisions: the time of revolutionary Russia and its exemplary figures of Trotsky and Mandelstam. When Trotsky's heroism and earned revolutionary fervour, his self-sacrificial commitment to the historical process, diminish, in Paulin's savage account, into the contemporary 'glossy brutalism' of 'a regiment of clones', Mandelstam, the great Russian symbolist (or 'Acmeist') poet killed by Stalin comes to speak in the poem for an art 'free of history'. 'The Other Voice' offers no explicit choice between Trotskyan engagement and Mandelstam's hermetic aestheticism, but Mandelstam does get the poem's last word, a word which gives the 'word' itself a quasi-religious primacy ('Beyond dust and rhetoric, / In the meadows of the spirit / I kiss the Word'). The sixth section of the poem, evoking Mandelstam for the first time, conjures his presence out of a dream of release from the effort of Northern responsibility, and bends its knee to Mandelstam as Mandelstam bends his knee to the Word:

What does a poem serve?
Only the pure circle of itself.
Now, between two coasts,

The servants of the state
Doze to the drum of engines.
Hammered stars, a dark dream,

The hard night in a dead bowl.
Where a free light wakes
To its spacious language

Choice is still possible.
I dream of a subtle voice,
Stare in a mirror and pray

To a shadow wandering
Beyond the cold shores
And tides of the Baltic.

This seems crucial to an understanding of the sudden near-discontinuity in Paulin's work between *The Strange Museum* and *Liberty Tree* (1983). That dream of a subtle Mandelstamian voice opposing itself to the 'dark dream' of the state registers a greater willingness to trust the potentially self-aggrandising and narcissistic freedom of an art untrammelled by political obligation. The irony is, of course, that however untrammelled Mandelstam's own subtle voice may have been, he was inevitably drawn into political satire in his writing and he died a victim of the Stalinist state after his final terrible years as an 'internal exile' of that state. Nevertheless, Paulin does appear to make here the choice of a more 'spacious language'; he begins in *Liberty Tree* to write in forms which house together in the same poem some of the contrary impulses of earlier individual lyrics. In doing so, he creates a poetry of striking individuality in which the desire for an untrammelled art visibly and audibly engages in a prolonged, protean battle with the sometimes angry, sometimes almost exhausted effort at responsibility.

The new spaciousness and freedom derive from a number of sources: a greater willingness to take as theme the apparently inconsequential or arbitrary, particularly marked in *Fivemiletown* (1987); a relaxing of obvious formal control to the extent that some poems break their lines throughout only in accordance with the grammatical phrase; a readiness to parade, without explication, a wide range of literary and historical reference; an explicit use of the language of post-structuralist theory (Barthes, Derrida, de Man); a frequent elision and slippage between the political and the sexual; a new wildness of comedy or grotesquerie in the use of narrative and a foregrounding of elements of riddle and nonsense; and a reliance on the colloquial and idiomatic and on what Paulin apparently considers Northern dialect, what some of his critics think neologism (words like 'fremd', 'senna', 'biffy', 'bistre', 'glooby', 'screggy', 'stramash', 'dayclean'). Combined with the fundamental preoccupation of a large number of his poems not now with the North alone, but with the effort of defining a Protestant consciousness and inheritance, this all makes for an agitatedly analogising poetry in which categories slip and slide and different historical epochs and colonial topographies are collided.

Its scope is extensive and surprising. In 'The Book of Juniper' Paulin's location of value in a revised eighteenth-century Protestant republicanism finds emblems for itself in a series of meditations on the juniper plant, culminating in the utopian vision of an army 'carrying branches / of green juniper' through Ireland towards an oneiric future in a 'sweet / equal republic'. But there are also the less idealistic Protestant collocations of 'Off the Back of a Lorry' where such instances as 'a jumbo double / fried peanut butter / sandwich Elvis scoffed / during the last / diapered days' combine to form 'a gritty / sort of prod baroque / I must return to / like my own boke'; the whoopingly revivalist shape of 'I Am Nature' in which the American action painter Jackson Pollock is identified in his 'Scotch-Irish . . . scrake' and related to the Northern Irish scrake and perturbation of the billiards-player Hurricane Higgins; the bitterness of 'Desertmartin' in *Liberty Tree* which draws Paisleyism into a like condemnation with 'Masculine Islam, the rule of the Just . . . / A theology of rifle-butts and executions'; and the empathy of 'An Ulster Unionist Walks the Streets of London' which appreciates the pathos and terror (which give rise to terrorism) of those apparently abandoned by the systems which once sustained them.

The notation of identity in Paulin has, therefore, both its despairs and its desires. The free space of the poem becomes the field in which the one might merge into the other, but only with the greatest circumspection and unease: the utopian desire of 'The Book of Juniper' faces the historical hopelessness of the 'mild and patient prisoner / pecking through granite with a teaspoon' in 'Of Difference Does it Make' (Paulin's version, it may be, of the 'eternal interim'). But the desire of Paulin's work is that something better than what we are might be derived from a proper scrutiny of what we have been, that the educated historical sense might recognise a more adequate future locked somewhere in the texts and wrong turnings of its Presbyterian tradition, in the almost forgotten emblematic names of 'Munro, Hope, Porter and McCracken' chanted reverently in 'Father of History'. The 'other voice' of his poetry hears itself most clearly in the reason, proportion and formality of the eighteenth-century Linen Hall library in Belfast. In 'To the Linen Hall', the poem which closes *Liberty Tree*, that voice is given its tongue:

> Our shaping brightness
> is a style and discipline
> that finds its tongue
> in the woody desk-dawns
> of fretting scholars
> who pray, invisibly,
> to taste the true vine
> and hum gently
> in holy sweetness.

This is perhaps less the actual Linen Hall than the Linen Hall of utopian writing, a place possible at present only in the poem, not the *polis*: not the historically identified and constructed 'Ireland' but the imaginary, renewable potential of a still unconstructed 'someplace'.

In both Muldoon and Paulin the writtenness of their work is tested and cut across by a strong sense of orality: the desire to evoke the texture and stress of speech may be a major reason for Muldoon's Chandleresque pastiche and for Paulin's vernacular/neologising. In Ciaran Carson the attempt to bring the density and pressure of the oral into the written is still more prominent. His first language is Irish, and he has retained a vocational interest in traditional Irish music and storytelling; and *The Irish for No* makes a punctilious acknowledgement to 'John Campbell of Mullaghbawn whose storytelling suggested some of the narrative procedures of some of these poems'. The book exhilaratedly plays with the tensions between a sophisticated literary awareness (containing some almost arch literary in-jokes, for instance) and the Irish tall tale or yarn. In doing so, it redeems the digressive Irish oral story from any connotations of stage-Irishry and it manages a great variety and subtlety of effect, ranging from pathos and near-tragedy to the comic surreal. It also finds an energisingly innovative shape in which to handle the permanent themes of Irish identity and consciousness and the experience of the North, but – personalised as reverie – some more intimate themes of private memory, desire, sexuality, loss and creativity too (as in the mesmerising 'Calvin Klein's *Obsession*' which yokes weirdly together the disparate worlds of Edward Thomas, Andy Warhol and Frank Ifield).

The book's structure is exceptionally lucid. Following an introductory poem, it has three sections, the opening and closing ones containing four long poems, the central section having sixteen nine-line poems which share with the longer pieces an exceptionally long line, derived partly from the example of the contemporary American poet C.K. Williams. The central section, explicitly about 'the collapsing city' of Belfast, maps the contours of its topography of violence, sectarian hatred and British Army occupation and surveillance; it contains poems about, *inter alia*, bombings, demolitions, August 1969, an IRA murder, an interrogation. Their procedures are quasi-reportage, with a reiteration of numerous Belfast street names and buildings (or ex-buildings), but their tone is baffled, hopeless, almost unbelieving; the combination gives them something of the careful and studied hyper-realism of de Chirico, the vertiginous nightmare encodings of Kafka. At the climax of the sequence the poet sets himself in a biblical rôle which haunts the entire book. 'Slate Street School' remembers his first day back at school, as a child, in a winter term. The falling snow provided a teacher then with the opportunity for some catechetical instruction ('*each flake as it brushes to the ground is yet another soul released*'); and the poem constructed out of these memories supplies the poet now with his terrifying self-image:

And I am the avenging Archangel, stooping over mills and
    factories and barracks.

I will bury the dark city of Belfast forever under snow: inches,
    feet, yards, chains, miles.

The anger and desperation of that derive from the fact that the
apocalyptic angel chants his vengeful intention in the rote of the
schoolchild. In this city with its satanic mills and intimidating barracks,
the apocalypse happens in the child's classroom; his beginning all too
clearly knows his end.

The long poems folded about this section range more widely in their
imaginative links and associations. The zestful digressive energy of these
story-poems – by turns hilarious, pathetic, erotic – cuts a kind of psychic
and social cross-section through Irish life, exposing both private and
public neurosis and repression; they are drawn towards not only the
atrocities of Belfast but the mental breakdowns and used-up, debased
lives of particular characters. Their technique is to beguile the reader by
their insouciance, their air of vague distraction, their apparently
undesigning relaxedness, until the secrets at their hearts are revealed, or
occasionally just less concealed, with a sudden startling force. The
remarkable 'Dresden', for instance, opens with a sidling, raconteurial
charm, all ease and anecdotal invitation:

Horse Boyle was called Horse Boyle because of his brother Mule;
Though why Mule was called Mule is anybody's guess. I stayed
    there once,
Or rather, I nearly stayed there once. But that's another story.

All ease, but all disguise too: the naming of people and parts is
all-important in these poems but here the nickname has an
undiscoverable origin and points towards an epistemological recession of,
ultimately, vertiginous extent: 'anybody's guess' is nobody's certainty.
This accompanies an announcement of narrative undecidability: what
appears to be the opening of this story ('I stayed there once')
immediately modifies itself, only then to erase itself completely ('But
that's another story'). The apparently casual ease of an unhurried
introduction to a long story in fact exposes depths of hermeneutic
difficulty; and 'Dresden' falls further into them as it proceeds – by fits
and starts, windings and withdrawals – to tell its actual story, in the act
of telling several other stories. The narrator reports Horse Boyle's story
of 'Young Flynn', a callow IRA volunteer who attempts to smuggle
gelignite over the border on a bus. A policeman boards the bus because
his bicycle tyre is punctured and Flynn, terrified, quite unnecessarily
confesses. The yarn then meanders through Flynn's self-education in jail
until it veers again into a memory of Boyle's schoolteacher Master
McGinty 'back before the Troubles'. Only towards its close does the
poem reveal its true story and explain its title; 'really Horse's story', it is

the story of how, an Irish immigrant in Manchester during the war, he joined the RAF and became a rear gunner over Dresden:

> As he remembered it, long afterwards, he could hear, or almost
>   hear
> Between the rapid desultory thunderclaps, a thousand tinkling
>   echoes –
> All across the map of Dresden, store-rooms full of china
>   shivered, teetered
> And collapsed, an avalanche of porcelain, slushing and
>   cascading: cherubs,
> Shepherdesses, figurines of Hope and Peace and Victory,
>   delicate bone fragments.
> He recalled in particular a figure from his childhood, a
>   milkmaid
> Standing on the mantelpiece. Each night as they knelt down
>   for the rosary,
> His eyes would wander up to where she seemed to beckon to him,
>   smiling,
> Offering him, eternally, her pitcher of milk, her mouth of rose
>   and cream.

The narrative suddenly pulls itself all together at this point, as these 'thousand tinkling echoes' of Dresden chime with others less noticed on a first reading: the noise of the 'baroque pyramid of empty baked bean tins' outside Horse's caravan; the tinkling bell in the shop entered in memory early in the poem; the 'mortar bomb attack in Mullaghbawn' reported by Horse, who owns the place's only TV set; Flynn's undetonated bomb; 'the grate / And scrape' of spade against stone in Carrick; and the poem's final 'scraping' and 'tittering' as the drunken Mule returns through the tin-stacks. The 'delicate bone fragments' of Dresden, fragments of china and fragments of human bodies, have, that is to say, their uninsistent analogues elsewhere in the poem's careful weaving through apparent digression. The story of Horse Boyle – the stories he tells and the story which tells him – is therefore an entirely, but not obviously connected story about some typical patterns of Irish experience: involuntary emigration; service in the British armed forces for want of anything else to do; involuntary recruitment to the IRA; a life of sexless, vaguely alcoholic smallmindedness, meanness and seediness at home; and the kitsch consolation of an eroticised intercessory feminine religious presence.

When the narrator of 'Dresden' leaves Horse Boyle's caravan (and the story and the poem) 'through the steeples of rust, the gate that was a broken bed', it is hard to say what is left unbroken: not this man, certainly, or this place. The poem constitutes a subtle performance of the

fragmentations of personal and national identity; and the sole opposition
to its despairs is the performance itself, the unstoppable flow of Horse
Boyle's, and the narrator's, storytelling. This is no metaphysical,
Beckettian heroics of writerly obligation, but the seeking of the only
possible consolation in a society which renders you incapable of action: a
compulsion to speak and to go on speaking, in stories which, even as
they tell your truth, also distort you, and others, with gossip, rumour,
evasion and subterfuge.

If that is the sole alternative 'plenitude' in Carson, then he is perhaps
the most thoroughgoing postmodernist among his generation of
Northern Irish poets. Both Muldoon and Paulin are, ultimately, willing
to place more trust in the imagination and its desires, and therefore in
the potential for difference, than Carson. The introductory poem to *The
Irish for No* is called 'Turn Again'. Initiating the book's numerous
cartographic tropes, it describes a map of Belfast which shows only what
does not exist – a bridge that was never built, a bridge that collapsed:

> Today's plan is already yesterday's – the streets that were
> there are gone.
> And the shape of the jails cannot be shown for security reasons.

Turn again in contemporary Belfast, the implication must be, and you
turn only into another map already written for you; you turn, indeed,
into that unperspectived flat surface which writes you, projects you
according to an already outdated plan. In 'Turn Again' the only
possibility of changing history is the possibility of throwing off your own
shadow. This has its connections with what seems a genuine interest in
and use of serialism and precognition in Carson's work (one of the long
poems is actually called 'Serial'); but it is also the most desolate image of
subjugation and subordination in these three poets.

Notes

1. See Ciaron Carson, 'Escaped from the Massacre?', *The Honest Ulsterman*, 50
   (Winter 1975), pp. 183–6. Reprinted in Tony Curtis (ed.), *The Art of
   Seamus Heaney* (revised ed., Bridgend: Seren Books, 1985).

2. This paragraph is a version of what I say in my essay 'One Step Forward,
   Two Steps Back: Ciaran Carson's *The Irish for No*', in Neil Corcoran (ed.),
   The Chosen Ground: Essays on the Contemporary Poetry of Northern Ireland
   (Bridgend: Seren Books, 1992), pp. 211–33, where I pursue some of these
   issues further in relation to Carson's work.

3. Seamus Deane, *A Short History of Irish Literature* (London: Hutchinson, 1986), p. 244, and Edna Longley, *Poetry in the Wars* (Newcastle upon Tyne: Bloodaxe Books, 1986), pp. 185–210.

4. Longley, *Poetry in the Wars*, p. 222.

5. See Bobby Sands, *Skylark Sing Your Lonely Song* (Dublin and Cork: The Mercier Press, 1982).

Chapter 15
A Pen Mislaid: Some Varieties of Women's Poetry

Medbh McGuckian, Anne Stevenson, Carol Rumens, Denise Riley

The first poem in Paul Muldoon's selection from Medbh McGuckian in his *Faber Book of Contemporary Irish Poetry* is a poem from a pamphlet, *Single Ladies*, which she has not included in any of her full-length books. Muldoon is nevertheless astute in recognising its appropriateness as an introduction to her work. The poem is called 'Smoke':

> They set the whins on fire along the road.
> I wonder what controls it, can the wind hold
> That snake of orange motion to the hills,
> Away from the houses?
>
> They seem so sure what they can do.
> I am unable even
> To contain myself, I run
> Till the fawn smoke settles on the earth.

The word 'whins' identifies this as a poem from Northern Ireland, where this is the word for 'gorse'. With that identification in mind, it is possible to be unsettled by the word 'orange', which may take on an allegorised political resonance (coded for the Orangemen of Northern Ireland). This agricultural act, the burning of the gorse, may act as emblem of a sectarian politics: the Orange fire rages devastatingly against the Green gorse, and the poem's 'wonder' (or terror) is that nothing can control it, that the 'houses' too − location of the intimate, domestic, 'private' − may be consumed. If this is the allegorical reading proposed by the poem's first stanza, however, the second shifts this politics onto a different ground. This is not to be another Northern Irish poem of sectarian division, but a poem of another kind of division or difference: that between a 'they' and an 'I', an authoritative certainty, self-assurance and self-definition and a driven, ecstatic, unlimited refusal of such closure. The conflagration released by the poem's 'they' is answered by the joyful self-delight of its 'I', awaiting the moment of a future 'settlement' beyond this present perturbation.

If this poem has its origin, then, in a specific political situation and context, it opens itself out into a less specific one: from sectarian division into an implicit masculinism/feminism opposition. It moves, we might say, from a literal geo-political border towards this other border of gender identity, a border patrolled by masculinist authority and taboo but open to transgression by feminist refusal of 'containment'. This is very much the border territory of Medbh McGuckian's poetry; and it is a territory manifest, most immediately, in the actual textures of her language: in her grammar, syntax, diction and imagery. She writes characteristically in long periodic sentences, rolling and flowing over the line-breaks, hard to unravel into meaning without the reader's frequent return across the involuted lines of text. She uses a sometimes esoteric diction, alert to virtually lost etymologies, and occasionally drawing on a foreign lexis, even for some central concepts (the Spanish 'querencia', the Persian 'balakhana', for instance). And her images and metaphors derive from a relatively compact area of domesticity, maternity, horticulture, weather and the traditionally 'static / Occupations' (as 'The Standing' puts it) of women confined to a house (sometimes in more or less unannounced dramatic monologues or ventriloquisings on behalf of nineteenth-century women, with their needlework, embroidery, portrait painting and so on).

The expression 'my poems' is a familiar one in her work; and an exposed self-referentiality occasionally defines the results of these formal decisions. In 'Prie-Dieu', for instance, she defends her 'untutored' and 'always / Sexed' discourse:

> This oblique trance is my natural
> Way of speaking, I have jilted
> All the foursquare houses, and
> My courtyard has a Spanish air,
> Defiant as a tomboy . . .

The difficulties of her syntax and diction are necessitated by their intrinsic foreignness to the culture in which they are articulated; they position themselves outside the claims of the bourgeois morality represented by those 'foursquare houses' and outside the conceptions of gender and sexuality which would define a young girl as 'tomboy' when she engages in activities 'inappropriate' to her sex.

This poem, 'Prie-Dieu', makes it clear that this new poetic language is employed as the space in which a number of inexplicit and secret meanings may be encoded. It is a poem about the loss of Catholic faith and the consequent repositioning of herself in relation to the mother through whom, in childhood, she acquired the dominating and constricting forms of that faith ('The world that is dead in me, my mother's / Sleeping-hide'). Hence, when it defines its own alternative speech as 'natural', the poem is registering a wry, ironical awareness of the provisionality of our distinctions between the 'natural' and the 'acculturated'; a deconstructive gesture against the way an ideology operates by claiming for itself the inevitability of the natural; and a celebration of the value of a secularism developed, with personal difficulty, in opposition to an inherited religion. The method of a McGuckian poem is evolved to create a space in which some subjects (marriage, pregnancy, maternity) may be articulated with a new intimacy, and in which others (masturbation, menstruation, bisexuality) may, breaching taboos, be articulated exceptionally. The poem 'Slips' makes the method continuous with that slippage of language associated by Freud with subconscious revelation, slips of the tongue and slips of the pen. Including, like much of her work, an imagery of apples (which inevitably drags along in its wake Genesis-motifs of Eve, temptation and fall), and references to a matrilineal line of grandmother and mother, the poem ends by offering an interlocutor the poem's own episodes or anecdotes as a series of duplicities –

Tricks you might guess from this unfastened button,
A pen mislaid, a word misread,
My hair coming down in the middle of a conversation.

The eroticism of that is the air breathed by a large number of her poems, dealing as they do with an 'always sexed' experience; but it is also a metaphor for the controlled licence and permission given to her pen by this language, easily misread by an unthinking masculinist presumption.

With this level of quasi-allegorical import, it is not surprising that one of the most frequently reiterated motifs in the poems is that of the 'letter'. The letter from the other – friend or lover, male or female, it is never explicitly declared – acts as a figure both of almost ineffable desire and of the absence in writing of the embodiment of such desire. The letter is, variously in different poems, delivered but unread; it is the sign of a secret, complicit compact not to be revealed to a third (but interested) party; it comes bearing news of experience unrecapturable by its addressee and therefore the focus of both envy and jealousy; it is kept tantalisingly enclosed in its envelope, a kind of ritual of erotic stimulation and delay. The poles represented by the letter in McGuckian may be read out of 'Ode to a Poetess' and 'On Not Being Listened To'.

In the former it features as an image of plaintive *jouissance*, 'the never-to-be-repeated awakening / Of a letter's morning freshness', where the word 'awakening' is perhaps derived from that earlier text of womanly self-transcendence, with its many early-morning scenes of marine light and new possibility, Kate Chopin's *The Awakening*. The latter's title voices the familiar feminist complaint that women are silenced by masculinist practice and history (as Kate Chopin was silenced by the hostile reception given to *The Awakening*); this silence is represented in the poem's final line by 'the closed throat of the envelope'. Between the possibility and the foreclosure, the letters of Medbh McGuckian's own poems weave their complex and resistant but enticing text: they too act as letters in which an identity has not yet been successfully defined but lies awaiting its moment of satisfactory articulation.

This provisionality of self-identity, the strong sense conveyed by these poems that they represent the stages of an identity in process – making it up as it goes along, catching up with itself, following in its own footsteps – is given one of its most notable metaphors in her best-known poem, 'The Flitting'. In Northern Ireland a 'flitting' can mean a house removal, but this flitting connects with an elaborate imagery of birdflight in McGuckian: flitting from one house to another, but flitting also between stabilities of identity and identification ('Catholic' and 'Protestant', perhaps, as well as 'male' and 'female'). It seems entirely appropriate that the poem should include a delicate evocation of what is clearly (but only implicitly) Vermeer's *Girl with a Pearl Earring*. To hide the blemishes on the walls of her new house McGuckian hangs reproductions of a number of Dutch paintings, including this great canvas by a male painter much given – not coincidentally, I presume – to secret narratives often connected with the reception or reading of letters by women. Now, at this late stage of her history, the girl with the pearl earring is in turn gazed at by this woman poet who reads an analogy for herself out of Vermeer. In Vermeer the girl with the pearl earring gazes out from the canvas with an expression uninterpretably caught between erotic invitation and shy reproach at being intruded on. McGuckian catches her up into her own hermetic horticultural figures and makes her the locus of darker longings and desires:

> She seems a garden escape in her unconscious
> Solidarity with darkness, clove-scented
> As an orchid taking fifteen years to bloom,
> And turning clockwise as the honeysuckle.
> Who knows what importance
> She attaches to the hours?
> Her narrative secretes its own values, as mine might
> If I painted the half of me that welcomes death . . .

Such lines may be thought to take a stage further the possibilities for a contemporary women's writing opened up by Sylvia Plath in her *Ariel* poems. Anne Stevenson, herself an American by birth and education, began writing in the 1960s; but it is since the early 1970s, and in England, that she has made her real reputation. It is one that explicitly places itself into relationship with the Plath work and machine. The author of the controversial Plath biography, *Bitter Fame* (1989), Stevenson also made Plath her primary example and *point d'appui* when she contributed an illuminating piece dealing with her own work to the well-known symposium edited by Mary Jacobus in 1979 as *Women Writing and Writing About Women*. Called 'Writing As A Woman', it presents Esther Greenwood's position in Plath's novel *The Bell Jar* as analogous to Stevenson's own suffocating position in the 'appalling numbness' of an early marriage, and she defines her character Kay Boyd in the sequence *Correspondences: A Family History in Letters* (1974), already admittedly a form of self-representation, as 'a sort of Esther Greenwood'.[1] This makes it all the more surprising, then, that she refuses to define herself as 'a specifically feminist poet', asserting a principled opposition to the positions taken by the doyenne of American feminist poet-critics, Adrienne Rich: 'A good writer's position should be bisexual or trans-sexual'.[2] Elsewhere she has been willing to employ the orthodox Eliotic language of the poetic 'tradition' as though, contributable to alike by women as well as men, it can still exist without the fractures of gender. And indeed the generality of her poems – even those which quite specifically deal with what we might think the feminist themes of marriage, maternity and the resented or disabling confinement in a domestic space (such poems as 'The Mother', 'The Suburb' and 'The Price') – accommodate themselves with ease to a 'tradition' of the Anglo-American anecdotal-meditative lyric.

Throughout her career Stevenson writes with intelligence and force within this tradition, managing a deft transformation into lyric meditativeness of material dependent upon an engagement with some of the central issues and debates of the period. There is, for instance, her excellent poem 'Where The Animals Go' which organises into its spirited fiction or *humoresque* both a concern with human treatment (or mistreatment) of animal life and a baffled secular hope for religious transcendence, imaged as a Platonic sublime, the animals 'crowding in together, / each into the haunches of its archetype':

> There, sexed as here, they're without hurt or fear.
> Heaven is honeycombed with their arrivals and entries.
> Two of each Butterfly. Two of each Beetle.
> A great Cowness sways on her full uddered way.
> All kinds of cat watch over the hive like churches.
> Their pricked ears, pinnacles. Their gold eyes, windows.

It is not insignificant, however, that even in this paradisal fiction – the paradise which has been inherited only after the suffering of butchery – the animals are imagined still 'sexed'. Much as her official pronouncements reject the public labels, Anne Stevenson does prominently 'write as a woman', making a point here (as I cannot imagine a male poet doing in such a poem) of the fact of gender difference. That fact becomes a matter of specifically literary resentment in 'From the Men of Letters', a monologue by successful male literati congratulating themselves on their having secured 'a room in language'. The metaphor of occupying an attractive hotel while the 'crippled' live 'swarming and unnamed' in the rubble outside registers the writers' arrogance and self-esteem, which are prey, however, to the vulnerability of the realisation that the 'crippled' are also their material:

> When they throw their arms
> around our words
> and weep
>
> we are horribly embarrassed.
> How will their experience
> forgive our tall books?

The question, spoken in these languidly privileged voices, is a disingenuous one, inspired far more by the embarrassment than by the desire for forgiveness; and this judgemental irony is clearly the creation of a consciousness which itself stands to one side of this discourse, outside this 'room in language'. It would be too melodramatic to insist that this consciousness, which is a woman's, is therefore to be identified with the 'crippled' and anonymous outsiders, those not admitted to the privileged hotel of Literature; but not much too melodramatic in the light of what is certainly Stevenson's most overtly feminist poem, the narrative sequence to which I have already referred, *Correspondences: A Family History in Letters*.

The poem's punning title compacts the various kinds of 'correspondences' with which it is concerned. It is, first of all, an epistolary poem, a poem-in-letters, on the model of the eighteenth-century epistolary novel, in which the fortunes of a prominent New England family are traced from the moment of their first setting out (in the person of the clergyman Adam Ezekiel Chandler) from Yorkshire in 1789, to the letter dated 4 July 1972, from the poet Kay Boyle in London to her father in Vermont, on the fourth anniversary of her mother's death. Within this sequence of correspondence other metaphoric correspondences gradually assume an intelligible and significant shape. There are correspondences-with-a-difference of situation and character between people separated in history: in particular, the figures of the prodigal son and the woman torn between the rival claims of writing and family. There are elaborate correspondences between the origins of this family in Puritan/Calvinist theology and its continuance and end in American capitalism and public-spiritedness; so much so that the sequence acts, in part, as a critique of the way a theology-turned-economics infiltrates and largely corrupts many areas of public and private life. The hippy radicalism of the late 1960s, inherited by one of the last scions of the Chandler family, is an ironic commentary on and reversal of the work ethic to which the family, allied to the family of the 'Arbeiters' (German, of course, for 'workers'), has been committed throughout its history.

There is, above all, a series of correspondences and non-correspondences between the Chandlers in their public and in their private lives. Indeed, the sequence as a whole leaks the one into the other by the fiction in which these private historical records become public when the family archive is opened up. This casts a ray of intensely ironic light on the discrepancy between two of the poem's four sections, 'In the Hand of the Lord 1829–1939' and 'Women in Marriage 1931–1968'. The exclusively male world of public affairs in the former, in which the family is prominent in the realms of church, business, the academy and medicine is contrasted with the female world of the latter, in which women keep their most intense lives secret from their husbands: these are lives shared with lovers, with sons, with writing, and (despairingly) with the bottle. The poet Kay Boyle brings these worlds together in various ways. As woman, divorcée and poet, she has brought the world of domestic and familial suffering into the public discourse of the published poem. The effort involved in this has led her to the brink of mental disintegration (her strongest link to Plath's Esther Greenwood in *The Bell Jar*); and the sequence marks no optimistic or utopian feminist progression. Indeed, I take the date of Kay's final letter – 4 July 1972, the fourth anniversary of her mother's death, and Independence Day – to mark a jaded irony at the expense of the kinds of 'independence' America has made possible to some of its subjects during the course of its history.

The choice of this date, which may in some ways seem to overplay its hand with an almost melodramatic insistence, alerts us to the way the sequence has itself been a duel between independence and interdependence, between the need for women to organise a life not economically dependent on men and the way they are nevertheless compelled into a familial interdependence with men as fathers, lovers, husbands, children. The potential for both is registered in Kay's final letter to her father, which is a refusal to return to the family plot in Vermont, and a reminder to the reader, no doubt, that a sequence such as this is possible only for a poet who has displaced herself from the origins she is now both recreating and effacing: refusing to return to the family plot is the ultimate signifier of her refusal to be plotted by the family, her final unwillingness to 'correspond'. Giving a new twist to the Jamesian theme, *Correspondences* is a poem which rewrites an American origin from an uprooted English perspective: it is an Anglo-American poem in the most thoroughgoing and radical sense.

It is hard to believe that Anne Stevenson thinks that a poem like this can accommodate itself with any real ease to an idea of a single, unfractured 'tradition'; the reconstruction of a past from the fragmentary letters which inscribe it writes a 'family history' anew and in the interests of that most 'untraditional' of things, the construction of a viable female identity which may withstand the limitations everywhere written into the family it describes. The poem itself, however, appears to know its own nature better than the poet does; and in one of its finest sections, the letter written by Kay to her sister after their mother's death, there is a sudden and unforeseeable swerve into a use of myth continuous with various other feminist appropriations of mythical material in contemporary literature. The myth of Demeter and Persephone here incarnates exactly that ambivalent sense of interdependence and independence characteristic of the relationships between mothers and daughters throughout the sequence, expressing the daughter's gratitude for a life and an inheritance mixed with sorrow for the mother's thwarted, sacrificial life and painful regret for an example that must be rejected:

> But the mother smiled and smiled.
>   She was brilliantly consumed, a sacrifice
>   sufficient for each summer.
>
> Should any daughter blame her?
>   The mother made her choice.
>   She said her 'no' smiling.
>
> She burned the kissed letters.
>   She spat out the aching seeds.
>   She chose to live in the light.
>
> Would you wake her again from the ground
>   where at last she sleeps
>   plentifully?

Carol Rumens, editor of the controversial anthology *Making for the Open: Post-Feminist Poetry* (1985), is, like Stevenson, sceptical of the 'feminist' label. Hostile to gender 'separatism', she intends her term 'post-feminist' to represent 'a tiny gesture towards the day when gender tags become obsolete'; and she finds a 'moral dimension' in the fact that such poems as Charlotte Mew's 'The Farmer's Bride' and John Berryman's 'Homage to Mistress Bradstreet' succeed so well in understanding the contours and sensibility of the other gender. She has a point – although not one, perhaps, that seems quite so well-founded when we remember that Mew and Berryman are both notoriously problematic sexual pathologies (and suicides): there may be strong, and describable, psycho-sexual reasons why they found it possible to read themselves so successfully into the other gender. Be that as it may, Rumens's line makes her antipathetic to conceptions of a women's poetry, in a women's language, for women. Defending women's role in a 'tradition' jointly available to both men and women, she maintains the efficacy of poetry as 'a kind of moral corrective to politics, even – or perhaps particularly – at its least overtly political'.[3]

Whatever doubts we may have about the brisk persuadedness of her opinions here, they are continuous with her own work. For Carol Rumens, the rejection of conceptions of a womanly writing is at one with the search for a lucid, elegant and well-worked style of her own in which matters of social as well as personal import may be articulated with honesty and clarity; the language of her poems is almost always the attempt at a shared discourse, at an extreme from the inward-turned, self-involved and self-constructing language of a McGuckian. The control is often, however, the control of a fierce anger, as in the monologue 'Houses by Day' which unrelentingly re-creates the drugged, apathetic listlessness of a wife in a 'high mid-sixties' marriage:

> The tight ring dragged on my thickening finger.
>
> The trauma of marriage swallowed me. I became
> a ghost whose buried rage hoists furniture,
> whose stultified self rattles in the attic.
>
> Adjusted now, I have learned my role is to wait
> for the key in the lock, to serve the first, clean kiss,
> and light up at a flick of my clitoris.

In these bitterly self-mocking lines the wife is made a ghost of herself as her true life lies hidden; and they are themselves ghosted by the presence of that 'madwoman in the attic', the first Mrs Rochester in *Jane Eyre*, confined until whatever has been repressed in her returns as the vengeful conflagration which puts an end to the master's house. If this allusion flits across the poem's face, then it adds a further dimension to what we may in any case read as a minatory note in the final lines. This adjustment under duress – in which she serves a kiss like a plate of food and lights up sexually with all the spontaneity and emotional interest of an electric light bulb – may be only temporary, and the word 'wait', hovering ominously at its line-break, may signal the eventual emergence of a more destructive rôle than this adjusted and subjected one.

In many of her earlier poems, particularly those more taken up with the evocation of urban living, Rumens resembles Peter Porter: there is the same almost bug-eye for detail, and a similar urge to the satiric. In such poems as 'Eviction', however, she is also, more explicitly, a witness to the victimisation of the losers in this urban jungle of the late 1960s and early 1970s. Such socio-political vignettes provide a staple form in Rumens, and, as in Porter, they derive from the Auden line in modern English poetry; and Auden figures often in reference in Rumens's poetry and prose. When she writes in the introduction to *Making for the Open* of a non-gendered 'tradition' to which women as well as men poets should be regarded as contributary, she is thinking primarily of this Auden tradition of social observation and commentary, of the portrayal of the personal life as the nexus of socio-political interrelationship; and the penultimate sentence of her introduction does indeed cite one of Auden's best-known poems ('September 1st, 1939') in support of her contention that 'we must re-imagine one another – across all the barriers of gender and nationality – or die, not, of course, only in the individual sense but with the real likelihood of finally extinguishing all life on our planet.'[4]

It is in this context of the apocalyptic that we should read the development of Rumens's poetry since *Unplayed Music* (1981) and more particularly from *Direct Dialling* (1985), where she moves out from the almost exclusively English social and political world into a larger preoccupation with post-war East European experience, including Jewish experience. One of the most notable of these poems, the sequence 'Outside Osweicim', is subtitled 'a poem for voices'. The voice of its own title refuses the more familiar German word for the poem's placename: Auschwitz. In temporarily removing the spotlight from the placename, the Polish word also proposes newly to our attention that what happened in this place was never ascribable only to a German nationalism but to an anti-semitism then endemic to the continent of Europe. And not only 'then', of course: the reality of European anti-semitism is still all too apparent (witness some of Lech Walesa's crude, gallery-playing speeches in the Polish presidential elections of 1990, for instance). 'Outside Osweicim' is, then, not so much a poem about Auschwitz as a poem about the way the place and what happened there persist in history and in human psychology. Its 'voices' are those of the lost who must nevertheless be constantly re-invented, and who may become newly audible in poems historically and geographically distant from them; who may become so, or who must become so, since we must re-imagine one another or die:

> It puzzles the secular light, this polyphony
> of dim cries. I wasn't there, I heard nothing,
> yet the air is so full of them, I could sing them all.

The poem, which ends with another voice, that of an anonymous, beautiful, disappeared eighteen-year-old girl, is met and complemented by the ending of 'A Prague Dusk, August 21st 1983', where male figures of totalitarian oppression are met with an image of oppositional release, desire and delight, an almost oneiric image of satisfied maternity:

> Going home on the metro
> the children chatter
> but the mother is almost asleep.
> Some sweet, unscripted dream
> is drifting across her face,
> follows the droop of her arm
> to the grasses that nod in her lap.

Medbh McGuckian and Carol Rumens, different as their languages are and as their sense of 'women's poetry' appears to be, are both nevertheless poets in whom certain norms and conventions remain untransgressed: specifically the norms and conventions of bourgeois (married) heterosexuality. Rumens's embittered satiric attacks on the institution of marriage are accompanied by poems in which the basic orientation towards a male partner remains fixed and established. However deeply McGuckian's language may be fractured and impelled by transgressive impulses and desires, her work remains preoccupied with a relationship with a man/husband and a house, and proffers such relationships as consolatory as well as limiting: 'I wanted curtainings, and cushionings; / The grass is no bed after dark'. A large amount of the poetry deriving from the new feminisms after about 1970, however, takes at least part of its urge and energy from the desire to inscribe radical alternatives to such conventions and norms, celebrating such possibilities as lesbianism, planned single parenthood, communal living. Denise Riley is a fine poet in this alternative line, whose work is continuous with an evolving body of theoretical feminist prose writing.

There would be a truth in saying that the work of McGuckian and Rumens is, for all its differences, predominantly concerned with the 'experience' of women. Denise Riley's is preoccupied not so much with the representation of experience as with the forms taken by representation itself. Concerned to occupy a space between the usual signifiers and signifieds of 'femininity' and 'womanliness', her attempt is to discover a form and a language in which the ways in which women have been conventionally represented in writing may be undermined, satirised and overcome. Frequently, inverted commas seal off not only speech and quotation but alternative or opposed kinds of discourse, making the poems sites in which a kind of counter-discourse plays with or argues with or interrupts an expected discourse. This is true of the work as a whole too, not just of single poems, since many poems go untitled: the effect is to make separate pieces interdependently self-commenting. One of these poems, which appears to deal with a lesbian relationship and auto-eroticism, concludes ' "She" is I'. The sudden self-identification with the poem's narrativised or fictionalised third person deconstructs the conventions of poetic anecdotage and lyrical impulse, collapsing them together in a moment which is both poignant with self-revelation and dedicated to the exposure of one of the conventions of the relationship between writer and reader.

A number of such 'betweens', of binary oppositions both held apart and brought together in reconciliation or violent juxtaposition, figure in Riley's work: 'I' and 'she'; 'love' and 'economics'; the 'she-husband'; the 'infant' who 'has always been older than twenty-eight'; the quotation from a twenty-year-old exercise book in 'Making a Liberty Belle' which, in its stereotype of 'femininity', reads so differently in this poem, inside inverted commas, from the way it read then. The poems slip and slide around these categories and conventions, disturbing them into new relationships and alignments. It is not for nothing that the title of her first book is *Marxism for Infants* (1977): the politics of these poems are, by and large, the politics of the domestic space, in which children figure prominently, but it is a politics which gives a new charge to the old axiom that 'the personal is the political'. Indeed, the examination of these categories is made under a radical consciousness that the category 'woman' is continuous with the category 'colonised': 'A note on sex and "the reclaiming of language"' features a figure named 'The Savage' in an allegory in which stereotypes of both 'woman' and 'savage' (in the Western anthropological tradition from Frazer to Lévi-Strauss) are explored and exposed in a context which sets this exploration at the centre of a new poetic effort:

> She will be discovered
> as meaning is flocking densely around the words seeking a way
> any way in between the gaps, like a fertilisation
>
> The work is
> e.g. to write 'she' and for that to be a statement
> of fact only and not a strong image
> of everything which is not-you, which sees you
>
> The new land is colonised, though its prospects are empty
>
> The Savage weeps as landing at the airport
> she is asked to buy wood carvings, which represent herself

The act of representation here – figuring a woman in image or language – is an act of misrepresentation, the act of an aggressively appropriative dominant culture or civilisation, naming the other by removing from it any reality in which it might actually recognise itself. That kind of naming is the way a mercantile capitalism will operate, disciplining into marketable image (those 'wood carvings') what would otherwise remain unadoptable as threat or licence.

I have no idea whether the kinds of criticism Carol Rumens makes of a politicised poetry in *Making for the Open* are intended to apply to poems like this (although Riley does not figure in the anthology). If they are, however, it is possibly worth noting here my own certainty that these lines are indeed poetry and not some other thing. They have a seriousness of address to the matter in hand which registers as a delicate, tentative rhythmic progression in which the 'work' which the poem recommends is visibly and audibly carried on in the poem itself, with a movement 'seeking a way / any way in between the gaps'. The poem's form, moving between a kind of speedy annotation and a more intensely lyric plangency, is a reticulation in which various types of discourse and counter-discourse may coalesce. The reader, working to create 'meaning', is made part of this effort or 'work'; but the writer has done the work too, since the poem has a strong anecdotal and allegorical element, neither laboured nor insisted. There is also, for all the discursive play in Riley, a characteristic signature: the poems have a sort of trustfully hesitant invocation, as though, deriving from a complicated and taxing loneliness, they are nevertheless confident of finding an auditor or interlocutor. The conclusion of an untitled poem on living alone with children may seem a motto for this aspect of her work – 'It looked impossible but I was not / disheartened'.

This is all as far from a propagandist platform poetry as I can well imagine, a kind Riley is herself ironic about in 'To the islands' ('writing politics is a luscious glow / and gives a quick buzz to your style'). The politics of her poems contend with the intimately apprehended knowledge expressed in 'Ah, so': 'disturb the text; you don't disturb the world'. This is at one with the effort of the rest of Denise Riley's work which, variously, offers translations of Hölderlin (that poet of another counter-discourse, alienated from the theism of his time and ultimately classified as insane) and a body of poetry working towards a language of the feminist-utopian out of a well-charted poetics of present difficulties and impossibilities. It seems as well to end with one such utopian moment, figured in a way continuous with such feminist-suicidal-proleptic-utopian moments as the endings of Edith Wharton's *The House of Mirth*, and Kate Chopin's *The Awakening*: the last lines of 'The Cloud Rose':

> In rain-divided air to rise
> to what she may, and is not said to, be
> In the air a shadow of a child circled attentively

in the cloudless air
in the unimaged air
in that dry air of no flower I long to breathe

Notes

1. Mary Jacobus (ed.), *Women Writing and Writing About Women* (Beckenham: Croom Helm, 1979), p. 172.

2. ibid., p. 174.

3. Carol Rumens, *Making for the Open: Post-Feminist Poetry* (London: Chatto and Windus, 1985), p. xviii.

4. ibid.

Chapter 16
Grammars of Civilization?
The 'Martian' Poetry of Craig Raine and Christopher Reid

Explaining his choices for the *New Statesman's* Prudence Farmer Award in 1978, James Fenton entitled his article 'Of the Martian School'.[1] The only members named by Fenton were the prize's two winners, Craig Raine and Christopher Reid; but, perhaps in self-fulfilling prophecy, the manner and style described there subsequently became a notable feature of the work of other writers too: 'Martian' simile is discoverable in such poets who began publishing in the late 1970s and early 1980s as David Sweetman, Michael Hofmann, Philip Gross and Blake Morrison. Fenton's name for the manner, cannily attention-grabbing and mnemonic, has also stuck; although, perhaps not very accurately, what it seeks to convey is a sense of the radically unfamiliar and alien.

Fenton derives it from Craig Raine's poem 'A Martian Sends A Postcard Home', which subsequently provided the title for his second book in 1979. The poem's eponymous Martian is a visitor to Earth seeing everything for the first time; but since he is provided with no particular character or attributes, he is more cipher than persona, representative of Raine's interest in the 'innocent eye', the cleansed perception, the unprejudiced observation. The originality of the mode of perception means that the reader has to work to unravel the objects contained within the Martian's descriptions; he offers similes and metaphors wrapped up in that most ancient of poetic devices, the riddle:

> In homes, a haunted apparatus sleeps,
> that snores when you pick it up.
>
> If the ghost cries, they carry it
> to their lips and soothe it to sleep
>
> with sounds. And yet, they wake it up
> deliberately, by tickling with a finger.

What am I? A telephone, the reader answers, but only after a pause: a pause in which we have already probably registered what we will take fuller stock of on subsequent readings. That there is tenderness, wonder, delight and a kind of timidity in the Martian's encounter with this everyday object. The routinely functional, the virtually invisible, has become a partner in relationship; the object has, as it were, become a subject, animated into a newly destabilised oddness and accuracy by a novel use of that most hackneyed of poetic means, the pathetic fallacy. The pathos is not wholly fallacious either, since, turning the telephone into ghost and baby, it reminds us of the inestimably beneficial thing a telephone is: the agent of our contact, across a distance, with other people.

This perceptual revision, usually heavily dependent on an exuberant use of visual simile and metaphor, is the essence of the Martian style, and it has led some critics to align it with that process of 'defamiliarisation' theorised by the Russian formalists of the 1920s, Shklovsky in particular, and developed into a poetic by the young Boris Pasternak. At its finest, it delays perception until, the reader's intelligence having detonated the perception, the object appears newly vivid in the flash. One of the finest examples in Christopher Reid comes at the end of 'Baldanders', a poem about a weightlifter: coincidentally, this too involves a telephone. The weightlifter on his catasta is perceived in the moment before his lift:

> Glazed, like a mantelpiece frog,
> he strains to become
>
> the World Champion (somebody, answer it!)
> Human Telephone.

The weightlifter crouched to his weights is shaped something like a frog and a telephone, and he gleams with sweat and oil, as pottery gleams with its glaze; and the wit of the lines is partly dependent on this perception of physical relationship, a perception itself dependent on a sharpened and refined visual, tactile and spatial sense. It depends also, however, on the exasperated, almost demented demand of the parenthesis, which, with a brio of compaction, relates the effortful, straining desperation of the weightlifter to the ordinary strains and exasperations of domestic or office life, and registers with a kind of affectionate, uncondescending amusement the entertaining absurdity of the endeavour: who would put himself through such hell to be a champion telephone; but, equally, who would not admire the spectacle?

The telephone as the apparatus shared by these poems may serve to suggest the essentially domestic range of the Martian gaze; which is why in one major respect Fenton's coinage could hardly be less appropriate.

What is rendered strange in this poetry is usually an aspect of the ordinary life, something deeply and intimately familiar. If there is a ghost in the machine, the machine is nevertheless situated 'in homes'. The poems are themselves quite open about this element of their constitution, spelling it out in implied rationale and principle: when one of Raine's poems explores 'the great indoors', for instance, and occupies 'the museum of ordinary art', and when Reid celebrates in a suburban garden 'our peaceable kingdom'. Endeavouring to remove the automatism of perception is not an insignificant task for art; and according to Shklovsky this is in itself 'an aesthetic end'.[2] His formalism, on the other hand, was a deliberate engagement with the over-politicisation of art by the new Soviet state, and in that context an exaggerated emphasis on the transformative self-delight of art, to the exclusion of all other functions, is readily understandable. Some readers of Raine and Reid, however, have found their procedures less intrinsically satisfying and less obviously relatable to any larger context of purpose or meaning: once you have said 'a telephone', such readers would argue, you might well say 'so what?'

The major stylistic ploy of the Martian – its highly ornate, ingenious and riddling use of visual simile and metaphor – does have its limits. When it operates at less than full pressure, it can become an exhaustingly reflex St Vitus's Dance of perceptual acrobatics, a mere parade of star turns; and even at its best it has its element of the *tour-de-force*. Poems can become just catalogues of simile, their subject matter apparently chosen only for its amenability to spectacular treatment (a zoo, a school sports day, a farm, a train journey). Reid is, indeed, probably knowingly ironising this in his title 'Disneyland': the poem has a matador cock, an odalisque cow and an Indian-goddess crab. Poems of extended simile, such as Raine's 'In Modern Dress', in which domestic scenes are re-created as Elizabethan pantomime, pall after a reading or two, the effortful ingenuity of the poet's calculating intellect too manifestly substituting for any more reliably poetic impulse or origin. And when human beings are the objects of perception, the method can seem to condescend and patronise, reifying them into elements of a mannered performance, just as some metaphors drawn from the human world can be shamefully lacking in compassion: the 'paraplegic legs' of mosquitoes and a pear tree 'pruned like a leper' in Raine, for instance, are cases where the perception of visual similarity should have ceded to moral compunction. Nevertheless, the story of the Martian manner is one of an increasing subtilising of an original cleverness, in which the field of implication of the characteristic tension between familiar and strange is rendered wider, more complex and more emotionally intricate; the visual is regarded as our mode of entry into true sympathy and a true sense of things, and it may act as a kind of secular salvation.

Both poets draw to some extent on the language of an abandoned

Christianity for this underlying recognition, and on a range of similes and metaphors of reading in which the world is perceived as a book, a text of hermetic arcana to be carefully interpreted and decoded. Occasionally, one or other of these languages accompanies a central Martian motif, one of the most traditional in English poetry, the *memento mori*. When Craig Raine lays a lawn with his young daughter, the 'crumbling tomes' of the sods compose a 'Domesday Book'; a walk in the country is also a walk through a kind of Dantean inferno; and even in the 'Book of the Market', it is a case of 'Everywhere, *memento mori*'. The domesday book of everyday life can be read even more clearly in a graveyard, and that is a not infrequent site of the Martian imagination. Some of Raine's most memorable earlier lines derive from reading a notice in a cemetery which forbids small children from attending funerals; the poet-reader gives the notice an ironic and dreadful further clause:

> unless a father pays the bill
> for a satin box of buried treasure –
> the feel of a fontanelle, buttocks
> tender as a soft-boiled egg, and all
> the inventory of little flesh.

The intimacy of the simile there is an intense moment of, in this case, tactile perception of similarity, but it is also manifestly serving a complex emotional purpose, poising a vibrant rendering of temporary physical presence in a context of devastatingly permanent absence, and earning its pathos in a way that makes the word 'little' in the final line perhaps an unnecessary over-solicitation of sympathy. Such lines suggest that Raine's energetic verbal performances elsewhere are self-consciously a ballast against intimations of mortality; in the poem 'Rich', he codifies this as a celebration of Nature personified as a feminine presence: 'I woo her with words / against the day of divorce'. The weddings of his work, the joinings of what has hitherto been disjunct, are always celebrated within earshot of its funerals; the epithalamial is muted in the elegiac.

In Christopher Reid, the figurative use of the language of sacramental and petitionary Christianity is much more insistently foregrounded than in Raine, and it is not used with any simple irony. The consolations of the domestic, of relationship, of art itself are often figured as the gifts of a natural bounty and beneficence, transformative and salving, but arbitrarily available in a world always threatening to resolve into nothingness. In 'A Whole School of Bourgeois Primitives' the suburban garden is the site of 'the sacraments and luxuries / we could not do without'; in 'From An Idea By Toulouse-Lautrec' a meal is a ritual of appeasement, a 'syncretic eucharist'; in 'Pump, Cutlery, Capital P' the ability to interpret motorway signs is 'A Whitsun-gift'. These brief, epiphanic benedictions may be read as almost explicit responses to Wallace Stevens's query in 'Sunday Morning' (that classic post-Arnoldian statement of transcendental absence and sublunary repletion), 'And shall the earth / Seem all of paradise that we shall know?' Their frequently Stevensian titles are not the only indication that Reid's poems are offered as a kind of supplement to these late-Romantic metaphysical concerns; and one of his finest, 'Magnum Opus', introduces the Martian trope of reading into the formerly sacred ground itself, inspecting the 'great work' of a cathedral.

'A huge and implausible fiction', it is read for what it has once contained of human consolation and philosophy, but what survives now only as an unbelievable narrative, punningly evoked as 'the tall tale of the cross'. The poem's casual, offhand tone, its itemisation of unharmonious or absurd details and its demythologising historical sense mark it as a phase in English post-Christian consciousness well beyond Larkin's 'Church Going', a phase which the last stanza of Larkin's poem explicitly refuses to envisage. 'A serious house on serious earth it is,' says Larkin (or the Larkin-persona), '. . . And that much never can be obsolete'. But yes it can, Reid appears to imply with his 'ambiguous ground', his final stanzas possibly an almost conscious rebuke to the Larkinian near-sententiousness:

> The organ, modulating
> on currents of reverie,
> seemed like accommodating
> all secularity,
> with grave rumpuses, flytings
> of fanfares and fugal whoopee,
>
> when the frilly choir entered,
> blasé and epicene.
> I recall a young woman who fainted,
> my neighbour's atonal keen
> and the brute baby that ranted
> against the preaching dean.

The notation of the intrusion of a theatrical secularity, camp and preposterous, into the once sacred space is nevertheless unobtrusively balanced here against the potentially more 'serious' implications of the closing details. The 'atonal keen' is a humorous description of dreadful out-of-key hymn-singing, but it is also a reminder that the 'keen' of human sorrow was once adequately succoured by this still persisting liturgy; and the fact that the baby is 'brute' is a reminder that this place once convinced human beings that they shared a fate different from that of the brutes. However mutedly, the lines therefore inscribe loss as well as amused frivolity; and it is unsurprising that, when Reid elsewhere confronts the even more intransigent alienness of 'Three Sacred Places in Japan', he should utter a sort of prayer of his own:

> Green seaweed wraiths, a beer-can, drunk,
> are tugged by the tide . . . You Nothings, bless
> me in my next-to-nothingness!

The disregarded flotsam and jetsam of the Japanese seaboard, rather than the tall tale of the cross, seem the entirely suitable recipients of a Martian prayer. Sacraments now are to be found a long way outside the church doors and they come as unlooked-for accident and interruption.

The tropes of the world as book and the world as sacrament evoke ideals of order which Martian poems may ironise but to which they owe a ghostly or elegiac allegiance. The end of Reid's 'The Ambassador' enforces both the irony and the allegiance. The poem imagines its eponymous ambassador attempting to understand the strangeness of what appears to be another planet, but what is actually a child's playroom ('Life in this narrow neck / of the galaxy reads like a rebus'); but the given world ends up as inscrutable as it begins, with the ambassador lost, unhappy and far from home. Nevertheless, he articulates what sounds like a major statement of principle at the poem's conclusion:

> but at heart I still adhere
> to the maxim, that through a studious
> reading of chaos we may
> arrive at the grammar of civilization.

Prompted by his interviewer, John Haffenden, Reid has discussed the 'sham personae' of some of his poems: the ambassador here is, he maintains, 'a way of escaping the perils of my own sententiousness'.[3] The ambassador-persona, that is to say, is pompously self-deceiving in ignoring the evidence of his senses in favour of the maintenance of a dignified *parti-pris*; and 'The Ambassador' is a poem about the uninterpretability, by an adult, of the world of a child and, by inference, the essential uninterpretability of all 'other' experience. It is certainly central to the Martian method that the terms of simile always summon unlikeness even as they propose likeness, holding all experience in a kind of permanently ambivalent pun. Yet Reid surely protests too much here. If the ambassador is duped in believing the search for a 'grammar of civilization' to be meaningful, the poem in which he appears offers a more complex and less sententious, because self-ironising, justification for such a search. In the shapes and forms of its own grammatical and structural relations, it dramatises a small but available and valid morality: that we presume understanding of others, particularly of our children, at our (and their) peril; that presumptuousness and a *parti-pris* are the enemies of enlightenment; that the generous will to empathy may disguise the desire to dominate.

Some of the best later work of both Raine and Reid develops exactly such an ambivalent civilised grammar out of subjects even more apparently remote from the processes of ordinary perception and understanding than young children. In *Rich*, Raine extends the Martian manner into an engagement with such extremes of ordinary experience as widowerhood and the aftermath of a stroke, and into experiences transcribable only in forms of incompetent or incorrect English: pidgin in 'Gauguin', and an exile's broken English in 'Purge'. In *Katerina Brac* Reid writes an entire volume in another 'sham persona', that of an East European woman poet in a post-war totalitarian state: her English is therefore an English of translation, and the book is, among other things, a commentary written in the margins of the Penguin Modern European Poets series of the 1960s and 1970s. Reid brilliantly mimics the hesitations, the odd flatnesses and sudden intensities, the failures of accurate idiom endemic to modern poems in English translation. He conveys with remarkable accuracy their quality of an almost tangible but ghostly absence, as if the poem's English contains the shadow of what pre-existed it. These forms which make the English language strange to itself are one of the most arresting directions in which the Martian preoccupation with strangeness and familiarity has moved.

If there is an innate potential for cosiness in some of the earlier Martian-domestic poems, these later recensions of the style emphasise, much more disturbingly, the dislocating weirdness of which it is also capable, as the language awry and askew registers the perturbation of desolating experience. In Raine's 'Gauguin', the woman's pidgin painfully re-creates sexual fascination and longing, handled as a kind of neologistic voyeurism ('till he cry like a candle / and heflame blow out'), until it climaxes in an italicised cry of loss and lack: '*Handmake Kodak man, come back, / my secrets are sorry with oil*', where the pidgin neologisms or euphemisms have great poignancy, Gauguin not reduced but strangely magnified when he is regarded as the imitator of photographs, and the final line a beautiful but unflinchingly regretful evocation of masturbation. And in 'Purge', the linguistic contortions and zanily inventive pseudo-idioms, fractured and nakedly vulnerable, are the linguistic and grammatical signs for the experience of political terror: less a grammar of civilization here than the civilized mimesis of a grammar of barbarism:

> I have been by the garden
> since dawn, with a silver fork
> (a wedding gift from formerly
> when our love was little in years).

> I have buried the past,
> making my possessions shy
>
> and now I have a headache in my heart.

The language of *Katerina Brac*, while never so formally incorrect, is
rarely idiomatically fluent. Its opening poem 'Pale-Blue Butterflies', for
instance, offers this:

> I'm sure that I was not alone
> in feeling, as I do each year,
> that this would be the perfect time
> to mend the whole of one's life.

The first line makes us ask why 'I am' is elided, but not 'I was not'; the
fourth is a bold attempt at idiomatic or even proverbial expression
flawed only in that the idiom 'to mend one's life' does not exist in
English, and even if it did 'the whole of' would be redundant and
'one's' here, after the repeated personal pronouns in the opening line,
would still be impossibly stilted. The awkwardness which never resolves
into settled idiom, tone or even style of elision is endemic to the book.
The tone, however, even if unsettled, is recognisable: wan, etiolated,
wistful, its falling cadence the register of stasis, it is early-Eliotic, and
almost specifically *Portrait of a Lady*-like. Clearly, Katerina Brac is a
minor poet, no major twentieth-century East European woman poet
such as Anna Akhmatova or Marina Tsvetayeva; but the book's central
irony is that this recognisably *haute-bourgeoise*, early-Modernist sensibility
is locked into the post-war intransigences of Eastern Europe. In
'Pale-Blue Butterflies', for instance, the frail, even slightly precious
notation of the seasonal arrival of butterflies ('lighting on our favourite
blooms, / as detachable as earrings') is undercut by the information that
they come 'without official notification' and by the fact that Katerina,
for all that she manages to sound like an idle Eliotic *dame du salon*,
actually sees these butterflies in the moments when she raises her head
from the back-breaking task of picking strawberries to sell in town at
'the official market price'. The repetition of the word 'official' is the
indication of the way the once privileged delicacy of this sensibility is
manhandled by the exigencies of an unremittingly ubiquitous state
bureaucracy.

Katerina Brac retains some of the earlier Martian metaphoric
invention, but with a new and genuinely disorienting defamiliarisation.
The poem 'Tin Lily', for instance, imagines the loudspeaker on a van as
the eponymous lily 'strafing the boulevards' with official instructions,
and concludes in what might be thought a nightmare transcription of the
Martian aesthetic into a terrifying political morality:

This is not surrealism,
but an image of the new reality,
a counterblast to Copernicus.

Something similar happens in 'Little Man', a portrait of the anonymous official himself, whose silhouette is 'eerily imitated' by the 'knot and swell' of his tie. But it also turns to new poetic profit the essential Martian spirit of the ludic and the libertarian (the sequence includes a gently empathetic poem on the patron saint of these qualities, Apollinaire), particularly in the way the 'sham persona', which risks the various dangers inherent in a male poet's assuming the female rôle, becomes a vehicle for a wry gender revision or re-inscription, as in 'Son of Memory' with its opening line, 'So the Muse of History is a man!' and its working-out of the conceit, at once humorous and desolate, that this daughter of Memory is a man in drag ('It's hard to trust a living soul / when even mythology is suspect'). At such moments the serious playfulness of *Katerina Brac* is a long way from the clever flash and dazzle of the earlier Martian manner, reaching towards an altogether more painful and alert inclusiveness.

Notes

1. James Fenton, 'Of the Martian School', *New Statesman*, 20 October 1978, p. 520.

2. See Victor Shklovsky, 'Art as Technique', in Lee T. Lemon and Marion J. Reis (eds), *Russian Formalist Criticism: Four Essays* (Lincoln and London: University of Nebraska Press, 1965), p. 12.

3. John Haffenden, 'An Interview with Christopher Reid', *Poetry Review*, vol. 72 no. 3 (September 1982), p. 21.

Chapter 17
Hiding in Fictions: Some New Narrative Poems

James Fenton, Andrew Motion, Peter Reading, Blake Morrison

> (Verse is *not* Fiction –
> ask any librarian)
>
> (Peter Reading, Fiction, 1979)

The first poem in Andrew Motion's selected volume, *Dangerous Play* (1984), is called 'Open Secrets'. In its opening stanzas (contained within inverted commas) a son describes how his father has vented his anger on a maid called Florrie and how the boy has discovered from her, during a moment of sexual intimacy, how his father has taken five shots to kill a stag that day, the final shot being fired by his gillie, McDermot, who is given the stag to keep quiet about this lapse in English upper-class machismo. Together after dark in McDermot's barn, the poem's son-narrator and Florrie hear the stag next door 'dribbling and pinging blood in a metal bucket'. With that, the poem's inverted commas close and its final stanza moves out of this narrative into another narrative, the narrative of a writer addressing the person he lives with and re-positioning Florrie and the boy as figures of his own imagination:

> Just now, prolonging my journey home to you, I killed
> an hour where my road lay over a moor, and made this up.
> Florrie I sat on a grass-grown crumbling stack of peat
> with the boy by her side, and as soon as she whispered
> *Come on. We've done it before*, I made him imagine
> his father gralloching the stag, slitting the stomach
> and sliding his hands inside for warmth. He was never
> myself, this boy, but I know if I tell you his story
> you'll think we are one and the same: both of us hiding
> in fictions which say what we cannot admit to ourselves.

Perhaps almost too explicitly, this poem spells out some of the *raisons d'être* of the 'new' narrative poetry, the poetry of 'secret narratives' (as the title of one of Motion's books has it), practised by a number of poets in the 1980s. The poem's 'open secrets' are, firstly, the secrets of the father and master of the house – secrets to do with his incompetence and inadequacy – which are known to the servants and betrayed to the son: that nexus of guilt and repression familiar from many narratives of the English upper classes. But the 'open secrets' are also those writerly repressions, reticences and inarticulacies rendered public in poetry not by lyric confession but through the deflections of story, plot and characterisation. 'Open Secrets' theorises its own central paradox: that only through hiding in a fiction can its writer/narrator reveal himself, but that this revelation is also the opportunity for further concealment. The invented narrative of class guilt, with its linkage of filiality, sexuality and violent death, may be not only a deflection of, but a diversion from the implied 'real' narrative, which would be an account of why this writer is 'prolonging' a journey home: which would therefore, probably, turn out to be a story of the erosion or breakdown of a relationship.

Such paradoxes of revelation and concealment, of confession and deception, are at the heart of the new narrative poetry which derives its impetus partly from a suspicion of and reaction against those American confessional modes (with their apparent cult of suicidal extremism) recommended by Alvarez in *The New Poetry*. James Fenton's 'Letter to John Fuller' pokes more than mild fun at Alvarez:

> He tells you, in the sombrest notes,
> If poets want to get their oats
> The first step is to slit their throats.
>   The way to divide
> The sheep of poetry from the goats
>   Is suicide.
>
> Hardy and Hopkins hacked off their honkers.
> Auden took laudanum in Yonkers.
> Yeats ate a fatal plate of conkers.
>   On Margate Sands
> Eliot was found stark staring bonkers
>   Slashing his hands.

Fenton's instances here are all poets who had more than their share of psychological and emotional disturbance, but who (Fenton's implication would be) deflected it with grace, tact and energetic inventiveness rather than advertising it as a kind of moral superiority. The rejection of the Alvarez extremism can lead him towards a kind of wilfully callow whimsy, most obviously in his 'light verse' collaboration with John

Fuller, *Partingtime Hall* (1987); but, perhaps partly under Fuller's own tutelage, it also lies behind his development of a mode of poetic representation more interested in the possibilities for poetry of novelistic fiction than those of psychoanalytic therapy. The kinds of narrative to which Fenton and, after him, other poets have been attracted include sensational and sentimental material of a kind that would not be out of place in Victorian fiction or some of the contemporary popular genres. Fenton's own work treats of international war, the displacement of populations and the psychology of murderers. Andrew Motion has his sensational murder too in 'Dangerous Play' and elsewhere handles a colonial incident with appalling fatalities ('Bathing at Glymenopoulo'), a young English woman's witnessing of a German pilot's crash ('The Letter'), and a history of colonial courtship, death in childbirth and grief (*Independence*). Peter Reading is drawn to actual (or very skilfully pastiched) eighteenth- and nineteenth-century narratives of shipwreck, that great subject of Victorian genre painting and poetry, from Felicia Hemans to Gerard Manley Hopkins. Blake Morrison writes, in 'The Inquisitor', a long poem of espionage which refers to Conrad and derives partly from motifs in the work of John le Carré; and, in 'The Ballad of the Yorkshire Ripper', a sensation tale whose 'hero' is, in a sense, already written into the culture in the nineteenth century by the correspondence between his cognomen and that of the most notorious of Victorian murderers, Jack the Ripper.

These narratives are never offered 'straight', however, but in contexts, perspectives or ventriloquised voices which ironise them and engage the reader in the task of interpretation. They tend not towards closure but cancellation, not towards gradual revelation but towards a kind of implosion; and their narrators, whose roles as storytellers are usually foregrounded as they tell their tales, are characteristically ill-defined, dubious, uncertain about their own stories, morally ambivalent. They are frequently strangers or aliens or in some other way separate from the communities in which their stories are set. Andrew Motion leaving Belfast at the end of his well-known poem of that title 'as much a stranger as I came' may be regarded as paradigmatic. His own narrator in *Independence* tells his story of India only when he is back in an alienating England, and his perspective is taken through 'a hole / in the misted silvery glass'; he becomes voyeur to his own past. Reading's plural narrators include drunks, lunatics, survivors of shipwreck and cannibalism and, outstandingly (in 'Ukulele Music'), the charlady mother of a disgustingly delinquent son. Morrison's narrator in his 'Ripper' poem is a 'Bessy' (cissy? homosexual?) in a Yorkshire community whose dialect is predicated on the values of an insecure male aggression towards women. Fenton's narrators and characters include, prominently, lonely children with a bewilderedly partial comprehension of their own circumstances; in such poems a principle of almost dramatic irony may operate, in which the reader gradually comes into possession of more information than the narrators themselves. The ironies in Reading are more savage, and a matter of structure: appallingly violent, repulsive or desperate material is conveyed in organisations of pedantic, if arbitrary, fastidiousness. In C (1984), for instance, the progress of various cancers is written in '100 100-word units', and it is the irony of incongruity and discrepancy which fascinates Reading's aghast but systematic imagination.

For all their dangerous play with their narratives, however, these are poems which frequently and almost solemnly declare their sources; they characteristically come bristling with acknowledgements. Motion tells us that 'the source for "Dangerous Play" is James Fox's White Mischief; Fenton directs us to Korean Patterns by Paul S. Crane (Seoul, 4th ed. 1978) as one of the texts from which 'material [is] drawn' for 'Chosun', and has a sequence of 'found' poems, 'Exempla 1968–1970'; Reading constantly quotes newspaper headlines and reports of contemporary horrors, and offers apparently 'found' narratives from such serendipitous places as 'A lady's album of 1826 / in my possession'; and Morrison tells us that 'The Inquisitor' 'alludes to or borrows material from a number of sources' (such as The Book of Lech Walesa and Rupert Cornwell's God's Banker), and that 'The Ballad of the Yorkshire Ripper' 'is much indebted to Gordon Burn's excellent study of Peter Sutcliffe, Somebody's Husband, Somebody's Son' and 'some of the dialect in the poem was taken from Richard Blakeborough's Wit, Character, Folklore and Customs of the North Riding of Yorkshire (1911)'. There is an almost pedantically dutiful scholarliness about some of these recherché attributions (as if the poets fear being caught out in plagiarism by an exceptionally scrupulous examiner with access to a copyright library); but they also indicate one further major element of the genre. Turning outward from lapidary polish and self-delight, these poems self-consciously spill back over into the world and the texts from which they derive and to which they address themselves; this is a poetry always enmeshed in circumstance, time, place and society.

This 'worldliness' (in the sense in which Edward Said uses the word in his book The World, the Text and the Critic) makes it more than usually topical. Fenton feeds his work with some of his experiences as a journalist (particularly as a war correspondent in Cambodia in the early 1970s). Morrison's subjects include the American bombing of Libya in 1986, Sara Tisdall's 1984 trial under the Official Secrets Act and, in the finest sequence of 'The Inquisitor', the Falklands/Malvinas war of 1981. Reading's unstanchable prolificacy (since 1974 he has published a volume almost every year) makes his work almost uncannily correspondent with the newspapers of its contemporary moment: the shooting down by the Russians of the Korean airliner KA 007 in September 1983, for instance, figures significantly in 'Ukulele Music', published in 1985; and his poem 'Cub', which concerns a cub reporter for Reuters witnessing an attack 'in parched mad bloody Lebanon' by a cub Arab terrorist (aged twelve) resulted in a number of vituperative attacks in letters to the *TLS*, where it was published, and in *The Times*. (Reading's typical response was to include the poem as part of his 'Ukulele Music' sequence and to embed there a quotation from, and castigation of his critics: 'when I want you to chirp-up, matey, I'll rattle the cage'.) The clear political dimension of this topicality becomes most explicit in direct attacks on Margaret Thatcher in the work of Reading and Morrison. Reading's *Stet* discovers 'Great Britain's / satrapess gloatingly self-applauding' over the Falklands war; and Morrison's 'The Inquisitor', again in the context of the Falklands, contains this revolted satirical vignette:

> Her Jerusalem's made of sterling.
> Her voice rings like a grocery-till, softened
> With the pity she's hardened from the land.
> Her grail's religious: coming from the flatlands
> She dreams of death on a high green hill.
> Nothing can countermand the Iron Will.

I turn now to a reading of some representative poems of this new narrative in the context of some other work by their authors.

What they do not say: James Fenton's 'Nest of Vampires'

James Fenton's plangently cadenced sequence 'A German Requiem' is apparently entirely simple in diction and syntax and straightforward in technique, but it is in fact a poem preoccupied with opacity. It summons an extremely vivid sense of the psychological and cultural repressions of present-day Germany by considering the absences, duplicities and reticences of everyday speech and behaviour; the literally 'unspeakable' Nazi past is the pressure behind every line of a poem in which the only eloquence is 'the eloquence of young cemeteries'. This is the secret narrative behind the memorable smile in the final poem of the sequence:

> His wife nods, and a secret smile,
> Like a breeze with enough strength to carry one dry leaf
> Over two pavingstones, passes from chair to chair.
> Even the inquirer is charmed.
> He forgets to pursue the point.

> It is not what he wants to know.
> It is what he wants not to know.
> It is not what they say.
> It is what they do not say.

The 'inquirer' here, diverted from his research by the sinister charm of the implicit narrative he has almost unwittingly stumbled on, may be taken as a figure for the reader's own position in relation to the narratives in Fenton's poetry. His narrators are, indeed, often themselves in something like this position too: journalist, anthropologist, half-ignorant child – all markedly without *parti-pris* – become semioticians before a set of data, scrutinising them into some ambivalent and partial revelation. The invitation to the reader is to interpret their interpretations or, at least, to rest as content as possible in irresolution, incompletion and lack of closure.

This involves an almost inevitable readerly insecurity which harmonises with the poems' air of vague menace, their coiled, minatory defensiveness. There is a lot in this of 1930s Auden, something of Eliot's sinister hint and gesture, and something of the intermittent and cryptic narrative drift of John Ashbery; but these figure less as 'influences' on Fenton's poems than as properties of them, to be handled almost as he handles the material of his 'found' poems: fragments for instruction or delight, shapes useful to a design, but not allegiances pledged or sources transformed. This has two results: the poems have a certain static quality, an air of contrivance, a sense of worked architectonic structure; and his *oeuvre* notably lacks the unified coherence of individual personality. So little do his poems resemble one another in any way, indeed, that he might be thought to have given a new twist to the Poundian injunction to 'make it new'; each poem seems to embody a sense of how boring it would be to have anything like it done again.

'Nest of Vampires' is narrated by one of Fenton's several child-narrators. The scion, it seems, of an aristocratic family, he tells his story while the family home, an English country house set in parkland, is being dismantled. The 'story' itself is a rudimentary one: he catalogues some features of the house's interior and exterior furnishings, reports a disturbed parental quarrel about money, tells us that he hates the house and that the local children hate him, and suddenly reveals that he has been searching in the house for 'a clue' (though he does not specify to what). The poem concludes with his strolling beyond the house's lodge speculating on the emptiness of the villages and his father's loss of all his money:

> I keep meeting a demented beggar
>   Who mutters about the mouldiwarps
>
> With tears in his eyes. The house is all packed up

Except for one mirror which could not be moved.
In its reflections the brilliant lawns stretch down.
  'Where's that wretched boy?' I'm going now
  And soon I am going to find out.

Fenton spells out some of the poem's implications in interviews.[1] An historical poem, it is set fairly close to the Act of Enclosure (although 'the period is deliberately confused'), and the beggar weeping for the mouldiwarps (moles) is a John Clare figure; part of the poem's inspiration is the passage in which Clare writes 'and hang the little mouldiwarps like to traitors every one' (Fenton is in fact conflating separate lines from Clare's great poem 'Remembrances' in which he laments the effect of enclosures on his own life: 'Enclosure like a Buonaparte let not a thing remain'). The child's 'guilty secret' is 'the class system . . . He's going to find out that he is part of a ruined nobility that has devastated the countryside.' Fenton then self-deprecatingly ironises this as 'a typical late 1960s E.P. Thompson reading'; but if this is intended to register some embarrassment at its own slightly self-righteous ideological purity, it also strongly implies that this is only one possible 'reading' among many.

Fenton's own reading suggests his ability to collapse a large English social history into a set of vividly charged images; but it seems at least as significant that it virtually denies its own authoritativeness. Indeed, it contradicts itself in asserting a particular period for its setting and then insisting on a 'confusion' of periods. This implies, I think, a rather different relationship between the poem's serious moral/political import and its ludic elements than Fenton's reading willingly admits. When you read the poem, your uncertainty about period is in fact extremely unsettling; this is, initially, its salient feature. It therefore comes as some news that the enclosures are involved here at all. Although a knowledgeable reader of English poetry would probably pick up the Clare reference, and that would bring enclosures to mind, they are certainly not very foregroundedly inscribed in the poem, and that makes it hard to read in quite the specific Thompsonian-radical way Fenton proposes. Its nature as literary *bricollage* seems to make any potential political allegory both more extensive and more wryly implicative than this; its details actually compose a summary of, and a terminal point for the English country house poem.

The title 'Nest of Vampires' bathes the poem in a lurid, quasi-Gothic glow, and may also half-allude to the title of François Mauriac's *Le Noeud de Vipères*, whose plot turns viciously and chillingly on avarice within the family of a French chateau. The vampires of Fenton's country house have lived by sucking the blood not only of the tenants of their estate but also of the peoples they have colonised: the boy describes, in the poem's opening stanzas, the bric-à-brac of imperial plunder as it is being removed from the house. This house is, perhaps, a version of Marvell's Appleton House or Jonson's Penshurst or Yeats's Coole Park, swept clean of the subterfuge and patronised sycophancy which idealised those English and Anglo-Irish seats, emptied of their celebratory recognitions in English and Anglo-Irish literature. But the house is also, surely, a metonym for post-imperial England itself. With the money gone, the son is willingly, even eagerly disinherited, and in quest of some new social organisation and self-knowledge. Yet that 'mirror which could not be moved' stands in the way of any simply optimistic reading of the poem's close. Reflecting the house's 'brilliant lawns', is it an emblem for a disabling English narcissism, an inability to take one's eyes away from the imagined glories of an imperial past and the comforts and splendours made possible by the British Empire? Or for the inevitability of a present moment which will seem the reversed image of a vanished past, all reality drained out into a fantasy of unfulfillable desire? The mirror may be allowed to stand too as an emblem for Fenton's own work: brilliant as it is, slightly forbidding and unaccommodating, giving back a strange and perturbing likeness of the world we think we inhabit.

Writing into the dark: Andrew Motion's *Independence*

When Andrew Motion interviewed James Fenton for *Poetry Review* in 1982 he asked a question which seems more revealing of his own attitude to narrative than it is entirely useful to an understanding of Fenton's: 'Is narrative for you . . . a way of drawing on strong personal feelings but at the same time freeing yourself from them?' Fenton's response deflects the question with an elegant phrase: 'When you're actually engaged in the practice of writing itself, you must always be writing into the dark'.[2] The phrase may be a good way in to Motion's own work, which seems more biographically dependent and more willing to confess that dependence than some other narrative poetry.

Motion recounts the crucial fact of his biography in the autobiographical prose sketch 'Skating'. His mother suffered a riding accident in his early adolescence; the resulting brain damage put her into a coma from which she never recovered and she died ten years later without ever leaving hospital. The incident and its afterlife in Motion's development figure recurrently in his work, particularly in the lyric sequence 'Anniversaries'. He has, clearly, had 'strong personal feelings' and the desire to free himself from them. His narratives characteristically involve death (often violent death), loss and grief, and they even link horses and death ('Bathing at

Glymenopoulo') and establish a relation between sex and death (Motion learnt of his mother's accident while anticipating his first sexual experience with a girl; the heroine of *Independence* dies in childbirth). These almost therapeutic narrative patterns are foregrounded by Motion himself in the careful plotting of his selected poems, *Dangerous Play*, to include lyric and narrative work, organised around the autobiographical prose recollection. Motion's narratives – fittingly for a writer who has also made an independent reputation as a biographer – do indeed make 'dangerous play' with the circumstances of his own life. Peculiarly located along the line from lyric to narrative, they attempt, it may be, to write something generically original, the 'lyric narrative'.

Their predominant emotions are melancholy and their predominant perspective is the saddened backward glance. Motion's work has, in these respects, its clear affiliations with Edward Thomas and Philip Larkin; and, like Larkin, he is an elegist of empire, drawn to vignettes of England's imperial and colonial past. The narrator of *Independence* is a colonial businessman recently returned from India. Insomniac in his father-in-law's house on the English coast, he smears a hole in the misted bedroom window and 'sees' through it into the life he has left, which he proceeds to describe to an unnamed auditor, gradually identifiable as his dead wife. His story, which has affinities with some of the prose narratives of Paul Scott and J.G. Farrell, enmeshes his personal life in the public life of India prior to independence. As a carpet dealer, he is located functionally in a commercial network of exploitative transactions between imperial power and native resource; he is eventually forced to become 'independent' of them as India becomes independent of British rule. His personal story is a tale of romantic love and loss: he courts and marries the boss's daughter (in Independence week) but she dies in childbirth while he is away on a business trip.

This story is almost archetypal in its contours but vividly realised in its local detail. Its scenes have the intense memorability of similar scenes from good short stories, perhaps all the more lucidly particularised by the fragmentary obliquity of the narrative method, the lack of contextualising commentary. The wife's death gives the poem's title a further ambiguity: the narrator is the victim of an undesired and desolating 'independence' from the woman he has loved; and the story he is telling here is one phase of what we are to read as an ongoing haunting of his imagination by this material. The lines in which his wife and child become ghosts to him have a disturbingly Gothic tremor and their near-morbidity is the poem's deepest emotional complex:

> I was hardly listening,
> lost in the first moment
> I brought you to life
> underground: your hair set,

>powder soft on your cheek,
>and the dress slinking
>back from your bare arms
>as you stretch and show me
>our slippery mottled child.

The almost queasy eroticism of this is strongly reminiscent of some of Motion's poems on his mother, particularly 'In the Attic', in which he caresses her clothes – 'all your unfinished lives / fading through dark summers, / entering my head as dust' – and 'The House Through', where the mother is herself the narrating ghost, 'slipping my miniature / into his head'.

The difficulty with this is that Motion's colonial settings appear to imply that the fixation is the culture's as well as the individual's. Some critics have taken the Indian material in *Independence* as mere décor, cinematic backdrop. I think the insistence on the hero's economic dependence on the country, and some of its re-created detail – the train, for instance, with its 'windows barred, and the packed / vanishing faces of refugees' – tend to make that a myopic view. But it is still hard to feel that this historical narrative poem manages to situate its period in any very fruitful relation to the present moment of its composition. The elegiac tone in Motion tends to suggest nothing more convinced or complicated about Britain's imperial past than the pain of its loss. In this respect *Independence* is lacking at just the point where, it may be, Motion's best-known poem, 'Anne Frank Huis', is lacking too: at the point where personal emotion should connect with present political fact. 'Anne Frank Huis' is a poem which certainly registers with great sensitivity the melancholy which must be part of any civilised response to a visit to the house in Amsterdam in which the Frank family were hidden until their eventual capture by the Nazis, and it climaxes in the comparison of his freedom with her incarceration which is the generously empathetic fruit of this characteristic conversation with a ghost. Looking at the pictures of 'Princess Elizabeth' which Anne posted above her bed, he concludes:

>And those who stoop to see them find
>not only patience missing its reward,
>but one enduring wish for chances
>
>like my own: to leave as simply
>as I do, and walk at ease
>up dusty tree-lined avenues, or watch
>a silent barge come clear of bridges
>settling their reflections in the blue canal.

What he 'finds', then, is worth finding; the poem has genuinely, if perhaps slightly too exquisitely, felt out the reality of individual human suffering in history. But what it has failed to find is precisely what the custodians of the Anne Frank House in Amsterdam would wish him to have found, the political dimension of that anguish. When you climb down the stairs from the hiding place of the family you are confronted, on the house's ground floor, with a permanent exhibition of anti-fascist material. In a gesture of deconstructive anti-pathos, this locates the experience of the Frank family as part of an ongoing European history which included in the early 1980s (when I visited the house) the British National Front, for instance, and the rise of Le Pen in France. Motion's poem, with its concluding image of the lonely flâneur, tends to deflect this potential political point into an interiorised, solipsistic melancholy. 'Anne Frank Huis' therefore throws into relief the tensions implicit in Motion's work. Very convincingly portraying its feelings of loss, it is in danger of reading the world as a kind of permanent correlative of interior emotion, its narratives all too manifestly and limitedly the scripts of the individual psyche.

Junk Britain: Peter Reading's 'Ukulele Music'

The sequence 'Ukulele Music' forms Book I of Peter Reading's longest book, also called *Ukulele Music*, published in 1985. Since his first volume, *For the Municipality's Elderly* (1974), Reading has worked primarily in sequences which sew a thread of narrative or plot around a single central preoccupation: old age in that first book; adultery in *The Prison Cell and Barrel Mystery* (1976); mental illness in *Tom o' Bedlam's Beauties* (1981); cancer in *C* (1984). But these single themes are filtered through multiple narrators speaking a babble of different accents and dialects, writing a plurality of Englishes ranging from upper-class formality to lower-class demotic and solecism. Acutely attuned to the frequencies of English class and the peculiarities of English province and locale (his Shropshire is as memorable as Housman's), Reading writes strangely intermittent Bakhtinian polyphonies, the voices seeming to emerge from a buzzy radio static, the hiss of permanent interference, the cacophony of crossed signals; and the writings apparently recuperated from original sources are similarly threatened by illegibility, indecipherably worn out with age. The last line of *Final Demands* (1988) is actually the wordless transcription of metrical feet, scrawled through with a negating cross; the poem, like the lives it evokes, is placed under the 'final demand' of erasure.

If this has its pathos, however, Reading also has a relished Beckettian disgust for the activities of 'H. sap.' (he adopts Beckett's characteristic plosive of abhorrence, 'Pah!', at moments of particular stress). The disgust derives from what Tom Paulin has called Reading's 'amazed and unflinching discovery of a subject few English poets have been able to confront – Junk Britain'.[3] In 'Ukulele Music', Junk Britain is exceptionally to the fore, in contexts which invite a complex series of situating judgements. The sequence has three central characters. The charlady Viv writes misspelt, solecistic and semi-literate but nevertheless vibrant and poignant letters to her employer, a poet. The letters concern her tribulations with her family who are involved, both as perpetrators and victims, in some of the horrific incidents related in individual poems by the poet-employer: her son twists a broken bottle into a baby's eye; her sister is a member of the bus queue showered with lemonade bottles from a pedestrian bridge – incidents narrated against a background of urban deprivation and mass unemployment. The poem's third character is the figure whom Viv calls 'the Capting'; he is, we are to presume, the 'author' of the poem's central section of narratives about disasters at sea (including an account of the atom bomb test on Bikini Atoll in 1954, written in a pastiche which appears to date it a hundred years earlier). Viv also, however, realises that she is herself written ('maybe we're better off here in his WRITINGS, orrible though they / often is sometimes, than THERE – out in that awful real-life'), and Reading's intertextual play is the source of much of the poem's imaginative exuberance. One of the paradoxes of his work, of which it is lucidly self-aware, is that its grim occasions provoke it into greater and greater feats of 'prestidigital' invention, particularly in his adoption of resolutely unEnglish classical verse forms – the distich and alcmanic in 'Ukulele Music'.

Throughout the sequence, giving it its title, the absurdly encouraging instructions from a beginner's manual for the ukulele cut across the pathos, terror, violence and squalor of the narratives being recited. Deriving from a George Formby song played by one of Viv's children, the trivial, out-of-tune 'plinkplinka plinkplinka plonk' of the ukulele comes to represent this poetry's own judgement upon itself: that it is a footling and trivial performance, counting its feet into classical distichs as it both records and recoils from the 'junk' of its material. Formby's permanently grinning, happy-go-lucky, music-hall, idealised Lancashire working-class Englishness, accommodating and malleable, is jammed up against the kind of brutalised underclass world that also figures in Edward Bond's play *Saved*; and the buoyant Formby ukulele suffers a hollow and tinny diminuendo. In tune with that, the Capting's sea-voyages climax in the poem's third section in a post-holocaustal voyage. Junk Britain's ship of state goes down, definitively, to the final strummings of the ukulele; and, in a way that recalls Hans Magnus Enzensberger's *The Sinking of the Titanic* (published in his own English translation in 1981), Reading's sequence inscribes satire, allegory, prophecy, self-justification and self-commentary in a poetic text which may well come to seem definitive of its particular moment, the British mid-1980s.

The maritime material brings to a pitch of particular intensity and complication Reading's frequent collocation of past and present. In 'Ukulele Music' the imperial maritime tradition of 'Great Britain' is set over against its present seedily avaricious commercialism, but is also viewed as underminingly continuous with it. The Capting's shipwreck narratives are narratives of loss and failure, of arrogant plunder, pettiness and rank-pulling, of the imperial disruption of local cultures and ecologies; but they nevertheless all climax in the dignified celebration of a heroic capacity to keep singing in the face of adversity. These sea shanties – work-songs, not idle songs, the songs of people with jobs getting on with the job – compose a richer and potentially more humane music than the tinklings of the ukulele; but the poem leaves it entirely open which music is more appropriate to our own present and future. A climactic passage, indeed, binds together the voyage of the post-apocalyptic ship, the Capting's marine language, the instructions of the ukulele manual, and a commentary on the poem's own form. It is a passage of extraordinary mimic energy, even in the catalogue of Reading pastiche: classical in its distichs but acknowledging English medieval origins in its alliterative clang and clash. This is its conclusion, as the ship reaches its port, a set of fallout shelters:

> Wend your luff, messmates, and let go the skysail halliards, mister,
> cut the brace pennants and stays, reef the fore-topgallant in,
>
> falling barometer, send down the skysail yard from aloft, sir,
> strum with felt pick back and forth, lightly across all four strings,
>
> all sail should be double-gasketted, stow the mainsail and crossjack,
> make yr pentameters taut: two-and-a-half feet times two,
>
> bend ye now three lower storm-staysails and a storm spanker, mister,
> take in the three upper tops, close-reef the foresail, F sharp,
>
> tighten the B string and place finger at the back of the second
> fret of the A string and keep spondees and dactyls close-clewed,
>
> trim yr heroic hexameter (or it may be dactylic),
> splice the pentameter aft, finger yr frets as ye go . . .

The revision of Homeric epic simile here, with its interweaving of the good running of a ship, the playing of a ukulele and the making of classical metres, seems to offer an ultimately undermining irony in Peter Reading. For all his depreciation of the capacity of an art like poetry to act as any kind of ballast against the depredations of the reality his contemporaries must inhabit, an art as inventive, restless and exploratory as his is its own justification; and it is justified because it is hard work. 'Ukulele Music' is a sea shanty sung to ukulele accompaniment, the work-song of a Stakhanovite producer of text writing from the despair of a society which has denied work to millions. This poetry of unemployment ends by asking some unanswerable questions, this one above all:

> And shall it, now, be counted
> as ye dignified defiance
> in us towards our fateful
> merciless element,
> or gull naivete,
> cousin to recklessness,
> that, e'en in pitching Gulphward,
> our salt kind brings forth chanteys?

The phrase 'our salt kind' is redolent of the discourse of Newbolt and Masefield; with its pride of national and even racial solidarity and exclusivity, it has a whole imperial history behind it. But it figures in these lines in this poem as perhaps the palest hope that 'our salt kind' might acknowledge the true nature of its present condition, not wallow in a crippling nostalgia for a vanished imperial past (although 'pitching Gulphward' may seem an astonishingly prophetic gesture in a poem of 1985, reaching out towards the Gulf war of 1990). The only conceivable alternative to apocalypse might be to envisage a time when 'chanteys' may be sung without any taint of imperialistic swagger, in recognition of the guilt of an imperial past, the reality of a pluralist and multiracial present, and while those singing them have the benefit of employment.

Cleaning up streets: Blake Morrison's 'The Ballad of the Yorkshire Ripper'

Blake Morrison's England is a country of secrets and repressions, the antagonisms of family and class, the atmosphere of duplicity and betrayal. The settings and tenor of much of his work recall 1930s Auden as much as Fenton does, and Morrison's articulacy about the allegiance extends as far as a rewriting of Auden's classic 'Night Mail' poem (to include 'a town sleeping in now there's nothing to get up for'). Morrison's work too has its Yorkshire country houses comfortably hiding the bourgeoisie from the proletariat working in their factories (or not working in their streets); and he is percipient in his conveying of the newly polarised class relations in the North of England in the 1980s, which harmonise recognisably and depressingly with those of the Auden 1930s. 'The Ballad of the Yorkshire Ripper' is set in, and offers its commentary on, this England.

Peter Sutcliffe, christened 'the Yorkshire Ripper' by the press, terrorised women in West and South Yorkshire in the late 1970s, murdering thirteen of them before he was finally arrested in the winter of 1980. The poem tells his story in ballad metre and in a version of Yorkshire dialect drawn only partly from Morrison's knowledge of it (he was born in Skipton, close to the Ripper's centre of activities, though into the middle not the working class), partly from the glossary in the text by Richard Blakeborough which I have already mentioned. It seems particularly important that Morrison should declare his sources for his dialect usage here since there is, inevitably, the scope for condescension when a middle-class writer apes non-standard English speech. Morrison's poem earns the permission for its imitation by an ingenuity which is also a morality: the meaning of his narrative turns on the potential of the dialect itself to articulate opposed views of the world and, specifically, of relations between the sexes.

The unnamed male narrator comes from the same culture as Sutcliffe, his intimacy with it signalled by his use of the vernacular. But the commentary he offers on his horrifying tale makes it plain that he does not share the aggressive male presumptions of his time and place. He reads the narrative he tells as an indictment of his own culture: Sutcliffe's desire to kill women (to 'clean up streets', as he put it) is the terminal point of a line of logic stretching from the casual victimisation of women implicit in the 'men-talk' of ordinary dialect usage. The indictment includes the specifically religious conditioning of the culture with its Pauline God:

> An ah look on em as equals.
> But mates all say they're not,
> that men must have t'owerance
> or world will go to rot.
>
> Lad-loupin molls an gadabouts,
> fellow-fond an sly,
> flappy-skets an drabbletails
> oo'll bleed a bloke bone-dry . . .
>
> An some o t'same in Bible

where Paul screams fit to bust
ow men are fallen creatures
but womenfolk are t'wust.

Now I reckon this fired Peter,
an men-talk were is goad,
an culprit were our belderin God
an is ancient, bullyin road.

The vernacular words here – 'flappy-skets', 'drabbletails' – have the
air of a kind of medieval flyting, reminding us of the way dialect
preserves tones (both of rancour and of tenderness) which have lapsed
from 'polite' speech; and they are words well worth recuperating for
modern poetry. They are also, however, charged with the culture's
violently and fearfully patriarchal misogyny and repression of female
desire. On behalf of his own revisionist position, the ballad's narrator
heroically endures the accusation that he is a 'Bessy', and the vernacular
redeems itself in the poem's closing sequence, where it acts as the agency
of an extremely delicate and reverential linguistic resurrection:

Ah love em for misen, like,
their skimmerin lips an eyes,
their ankles light as jinnyspins,
their seggy whisps an sighs,

tiny tarn o t'navel,
chinabowl o t'ead,
steppin cairns o t'backbone,
an all e left for dead . . .

An I don't walk appily out no more
now lasses fear lad's tread,
an mi mates call me a Bessy,
an ah dream of all Pete's dead,

an ow they come again to me,
an we croodle out o eye
in nests o fern an floss-seave
an fillytails in t'sky,

an ah mend em all wi kindness
as we kittle out on t'fells
an learn us t'ease o human love
until there in't owt else.

The lovely dialect here – graceful, tactful, erotically charged without the will to dominance, a speech markedly not seeking 't'owerance' ('the upper hand') – incarnates a vibrant alternative to the murderous aggression of a Sutcliffe and to the macho struggle between the case's first detective, George Oldfield, and the phoney 'Ripper' who taunted him with cassette tapes for months, a diversion of police energy which ensured Sutcliffe's survival on the streets.

The alternative is made credible in the poem by the unidealised character of this narrator who, despite his professed feminism, is manifestly drawn to the Ripper and his crimes in something more than the mere spirit of objective reportage. The poem contains lines which made it controversial on its first publication in the *London Review of Books* in July 1985; and their glibly revolting metaphors and similes do manifestly set this speaker at a distance from the civilised decencies and probities. The point is, I think, that he is himself genuinely and clearly implicated in the culture which he also labours to set himself apart from; the man who understands the Ripper is the man who heroically wills himself outwards from all of that into the possibility of a different future, and shows in the richness of his dialect how that future, as well as this present, is latent in the language both men actually speak. This narrative in dialect is therefore also a narrative about dialect; and it composes a subtle poetic contribution to a developing politics of sexuality.

Notes

1.   Fenton's comments are made in 'An Interview with James Fenton', *Poetry Review*, vol. 72 no. 2 (June 1982), pp. 17–23, and 'James Fenton in conversation with Grevel Lindop', *PN Review*, 40, vol. 11 no. 2 (1984), pp. 27–33.

2.   'An Interview with James Fenton', p. 21.

3.   Tom Paulin, 'Junk Britain: Peter Reading', in *Minotaur: Poetry and the Nation State*, (London: Faber and Faber, 1992), p. 287.

Chronology

Note: non-British texts appear in square brackets.

DATE	POETRY	OTHER WORKS	HISTORICAL/CULTURAL EVENTS
1940	Auden *Another Time* Eliot *East Coker* Empson *The Gathering Storm*	Greene *The Power and the Glory* Koestler *Darkness at Noon* Orwell *Inside the Whale*	Evacuation from Dunkirk The London Blitz Churchill becomes PM of Coalition (–1945)
1941	Auden *New Year Letter* Eliot *The Dry Salvages* MacNeice *Plant and Phantom*	Warner *The Aerodrome* Woolf *Between the Acts*	Siege of Leningrad America enters the war after Japanese bombing of Pearl Harbour Blitz on Coventry
1942	Eliot *Little Gidding* Lewis *Raiders' Dawn*	C.S. Lewis *The Screwtape Letters* Waugh *Put Out More Flags*	Fall of Singapore Battle of Alamein Beveridge Report on schemes of social insurance

DATE	POETRY	OTHER WORKS	HISTORICAL/CULTURAL EVENTS
1943	Eliot *Four Quartets* (in US, 1944 in Britain) Muir *The Narrow Place* Dylan Thomas *New Poems*	Green *Caught* Greene *The Ministry of Fear*	Surrender of German army at Stalingrad Fall of Mussolini Part-time work made compulsory for British women
1944	Auden *For the Time Being* Barker *Eros in Dogma* MacNeice *Springboard*	Cary *The Horse's Mouth* Hartley *The Shrimp and the Anemone* Powell and Pressburger *A Canterbury Tale* [film]	D Day landings in Normandy Butler Education Act
1945	Larkin *The North Ship* Lewis *Ha! Ha! Among the Trumpets*	Green *Loving* Orwell *Animal Farm* Waugh *Brideshead Revisited*	Hitler's suicide and German unconditional surrender Surrender of Japan after atomic bombs dropped on Hiroshima and Nagasaki Nuremberg trials of war criminals Labour wins General Election and Attlee becomes PM (−1951)
1946	Muir *The Voyage* Dylan Thomas *Deaths and Entrances*	Green *Back* Larkin *Jill*	Beveridge scheme implemented by National Insurance Act National Health Act Bank of England and coal industry nationalised
1947	Edith Sitwell *The Shadow of Cain*	Graves *The White Goddess*	Nationalisation of electrical industry and road and rail transport

DATE	POETRY	OTHER WORKS	HISTORICAL/CULTURAL EVENTS
		Lowry *Under the Volcano*	Partition of India First British nuclear reactor built, at Harwell
1948	Auden *The Age of Anxiety*	Eliot *Notes Towards the Definition of Culture* Leavis *The Great Tradition*	Communist coup in Czechoslovakia Zionist Jews declare state of Israel in Palestine after end of British mandate Assassination of Ghandi in India
1949	Empson *Collected Poems* [in U.S.] Muir *The Labyrinth*	Bowen *The Heat of the Day* Eliot *The Cocktail Party* Orwell *Nineteen Eighty-Four*	Devaluation of the pound Eire secedes from the British Empire
1950	Barker *The True Confession of George Barker* Andrew Young *Collected Poems*	Cooper *Scenes from Provincial Life* Lessing *The Grass is Singing*	Nationalisation of iron and steel industry announced American troops enter Korea
1951	Auden *Nones* Douglas *Collected Poems*	Forster *Two Cheers for Democracy* Greene *The End of the Affair* Powell *A Question of Upbringing*	Conservatives win General Election: Churchill becomes PM (–1955) Defection of Burgess and Maclean Festival of Britain
1952	Graham *The White Threshold*	Leavis *The Common Pursuit*	Death of George VI and accession of Elizabeth II

DATE	POETRY	OTHER WORKS	HISTORICAL/CULTURAL EVENTS
	Jones *The Anathemata*	Waugh *Men at Arms* Wilson *Hemlock and After*	Contraceptive pill first made First British atomic bomb exploded
1953	Graves *Poems 1953* Charlotte Mew (d. 1923) *Collected Poems*	Beckett *Watt* Wain *Hurry On Down*	Coronation of Elizabeth II Armistice in Korea Everest scaled by Hillary and Tensing
1954	Barker *A Vision of Beasts and Gods* Gunn *Fighting Terms* MacNeice *Autumn Sequel*	Amis *Lucky Jim* Golding *Lord of the Flies* Murdoch *Under the Net*	End of food rationing Roger Bannister runs the four-minute mile Marlon Brando hugely influential in *On the Waterfront* (film)
1955	Auden *The Shield of Achilles* Empson *Collected Poems* (British edn) Graham *The Nightfishing* Larkin *The Less Deceived*	Beckett *Molloy* and *Waiting for Godot* Golding *The Inheritors* Waugh *Officers and Gentlemen*	Anthony Eden becomes PM (–1957) Increase of West Indian immigration to Britain Commercial television begins broadcasting
1956	Conquest (ed.) *New Lines* Muir *One Foot in Eden*	Beckett *Malone Dies* Golding *Pincher Martin* Osborne *Look Back in Anger* Wilson *The Outsider*	British invasion of, and withdrawal from Suez Suppression of anti-Soviet revolt in Hungary First CND march to Aldermaston Beginnings of rock-'n'-roll; Presley's *Heartbreak Hotel*

DATE	POETRY	OTHER WORKS	HISTORICAL/CULTURAL EVENTS
1957	Davie *A Winter Talent* Gunn *The Sense of Movement* Hughes *The Hawk in the Rain* Smith *Not Waving But Drowning*	Braine *Room at the Top* Murdoch *The Sandcastle*	Macmillan takes over from Eden as PM (–1963) Wolfenden Report (on homosexuality and prostitution) Ghana and Malaya granted independence
1958	R.S. Thomas *Poetry for Supper*	Pinter *The Birthday Party* Sillitoe *Saturday Night and Sunday Morning*	Race riots in Notting Hill First high-rise housing estate built
1959	Jennings *A Sense of the World* Hill *For the Unfallen* [Lowell, *Life Studies*]	Arden *Sergeant Musgrave's Dance* Waterhouse *Billy Liar* Wesker *Roots*	First motorway opened
1960	Auden *Homage to Clio* Hughes *Lupercal*	Barstow *A Kind of Loving* Pinter *The Caretaker* Storey *This Sporting Life*	Independence of Nigeria Kennedy becomes President of the USA The *Lady Chatterley* trial
1961	Gunn *My Sad Captains*	Naipaul *A House for Mr Biswas*	Berlin Wall built South Africa withdraws from the Commonwealth

DATE	POETRY, DRAMA, FICTION	OTHER 'WORKS'	HISTORICAL/CULTURAL EVENTS
	MacNeice *Solstices*	Spark *The Prime of Miss Jean Brodie*	Beginning of expansion in British universities
		New English Bible (New Testament)	
1962	Alvarez (ed.) *The New Poetry*	Burgess *A Clockwork Orange*	Cuban missile crisis Commonwealth Immigrants Act
	Middleton *Torse 3*	Lessing *The Golden Notebook*	End of post-war National Service
		Wesker *Chips with Everything*	
1963	Hobsbaum and Lucie-Smith (eds.) *A Group Anthology*	le Carré *The Spy Who Came in From the Cold*	Kennedy assassinated Profumo scandal; Macmillan's resignation;
	MacNeice *The Burning Perch*	[Plath, *The Bell Jar*] The Beatles' first L.P.	Douglas-Home PM (−1964)
	Tomlinson *A Peopled Landscape*		
1964	Douglas *Selected Poems* (ed. Ted Hughes)	Golding *The Spire* Orton *Entertaining Mr Sloane*	Labour wins General Election and Harold Wilson becomes P.M. (−1970)
	Larkin *The Whitsun Weddings*		Commons vote to end death penalty USA increasingly embroiled in Vietnam
	Silkin *Flower Poems*		BBC2 begins broadcasting
1965	[Plath *Ariel*]	Bond *Saved*	Rhodesia makes unilateral declaration of independence
		[Bob Dylan's *Bringing It All Back Home* LP]	Race Relations Board established Discovery of North Sea gas

DATE	POETRY, DRAMA, FICTION	OTHER 'WORKS'	HISTORICAL/CULTURAL EVENTS
1966	Fisher *The Ship's Orchestra* Heaney *Death of a Naturalist* Smith *The Frog Prince*	Orton *Loot* Rhys *Wide Sargasso Sea* Scott *The Jewel in the Crown*	Pay and wages freeze Aberfan mining disaster England wins football World Cup

1967	Gunn
	Touch
	
	Hughes
	Wodwo
		Stoppard
		Rosencrantz and
		  Guildenstern Are Dead
			Anti-Vietnam war
			  demonstrations across
			  Europe
			British troops withdraw
			  from Aden
			Six Day War between
			  Israel and Arab states
			Legalisation of
			  homosexual acts
			  between consenting
			  adults, and of abortion

1968	Bunting
	Collected Poems
	
	Hill
	King Log
		Bond
		Early Morning
			Assassination of Martin
			  Luther King
			Russian invasion of
			  Czechoslovakia
			French students riot in
			  Paris
			Violent police action at
			  anti-war demo in
			  London
			Enoch Powell's
			  inflammatory speech
			  about immigration
			Censorship of theatre
			  by Lord Chamberlain
			  abolished

1969	Auden
	City Without Walls
	
	Dunn
	Terry Street
	
	Heaney
	Door into the Dark
		Fowles
		The French Lieutenant's
		  Woman
			Legal age of majority
			  reduced from 21 to 18
			Divorce Reform Act
			Beginnings of conflict
			  in Northern Ireland
			US moon landing

DATE	POETRY	OTHER WORKS	HISTORICAL/CULTURAL EVENTS
1970	Graham *Malcolm Mooney's Land* Harrison *The Loiners* Hughes *Crow*	Farrell *Troubles* [Kate Millett *Sexual Politics*]	Conservatives win General Election; Edward Heath becomes PM (–1974) Strikes in protest at Industrial Relations Bill; power cuts Introduction of internment without trial in Northern Ireland
1971	Gunn *Moly* Hill *Mercian Hymns*	Greer *The Female Eunuch*	Introduction of decimal currency
1972	Heaney *Wintering Out* Smith *Scorpion and Other Poems* R.S. Thomas *H'm*	Berger *G.* Storey *Pasmore*	Miners' strike Thirteen killed by British troops on 'Bloody Sunday' in Northern Ireland; introduction of direct rule from London Britain joins Common Market
1973	Enright *The Terrible Shears* Muldoon *New Weather*	Murdoch *The Black Prince*	IRA bombs in England 'Three Day Week' as a result of miners' overtime ban Cease-fire in Vietnam Watergate affair in US
1974	Jones *The Sleeping Lord* Larkin *High Windows* Stevenson *Correspondences* Tomlinson *The Way In*	Stoppard *Travesties*	Heath loses General Election; minority Labour government under Wilson; second election increases majority (–1979) IRA bomb in Birmingham pub kills 16

DATE	POETRY	OTHER WORKS	HISTORICAL/CULTURAL EVENTS
1975	Heaney *North* Mahon *The Snow Party*	Bradbury *The History Man* Griffiths *Comedians* McEwan *First Love, Last Rites*	25% inflation; increasing unemployment Equal Opportunities Commission established Margaret Thatcher becomes leader of Conservatives
1976	Gunn *Jack Straw's Castle* Sisson *Anchises*	Brenton *Weapons of Happiness* [Ashbery *Self-Portrait in a Convex Mirror*]	Callaghan becomes PM (−1979) Assassination of British ambassador to Dublin
1977	Davie *In the Stopping Train* Graham *Implements in Their Places* Hughes *Gaudete* Paulin *A State of Justice*	Johnston *Shadows on Our Skin* Pym *Quartet in Autumn* Scott *Staying On* *Never Mind the Bollocks, Here's the Sex Pistols* LP	'Lib-Lab Pact' Violent clashes at Grunwick picket lines Virago Press publishes first title
1978	Harrison *The School of Eloquence* Hill *Tenebrae* Hughes *Cave Birds* Porter *The Cost of Seriousness*	Hare *Plenty*	Soviet-backed coup in Afghanistan
1979	Heaney *Field Work*	Golding *Darkness Visible*	The 'winter of discontent'

DATE	POETRY	OTHER WORKS	HISTORICAL/CULTURAL EVENTS
	Hughes *Moortown*	Naipaul *A Bend in the River*	Conservatives win General Election; Margaret Thatcher becomes PM (–1990)
	Raine *A Martian Sends a Postcard Home*		IRA assassinate Airey Neave and Lord Mountbatten
1980	Kwesi Johnson *Inglan Is a Bitch*	Brenton *The Romans in Britain*	Tories announce privatisation schemes Unemployment at over 2,000,000
	Muldoon *Why Brownlee Left*		
	Ken Smith *Fox Running*		
1981	Fenton *A German Requiem*	Rushdie *Midnight's Children*	Split in Labour Party; formation of Social Democratic Party
	Motion *Independence*	D.M. Thomas *The White Hotel*	Deaths of nine IRA hunger strikers in the Maze Prison
1982	McGuckian *The Flower Master*	Mo *Sour Sweet*	The Malvinas/ Falklands war Proposals for devolution in Northern Ireland
	Mahon *The Hunt by Night*		
	Prynne *Poems*		
1983	Fenton *The Memory of War*	Swift *Waterland*	Thatcher wins landslide victory for second term
	Hill *The Mystery of the Charity of Charles Péguy*		IRA car bomb at Harrods Deployment of Cruise missiles at Greenham Common
	Muldoon *Quoof*		
	Paulin *Liberty Tree*		

DATE	POETRY	OTHER WORKS	HISTORICAL/CULTURAL EVENTS
1984	Heaney *Station Island*	Martin Amis *Money*	The miners' strike led by Arthur Scargill
	Raine *Rich*	Ballard *Empire of the Sun*	
	Reading *C.*	Barnes *Flaubert's Parrot*	
		Carter *Nights at the Circus*	
1985	Dunn *Elegies*	Ackroyd *Hawksmoor*	Anglo-Irish Agreement Heysel Football Stadium disaster
	Harrison *v.*	Winterson *Oranges Are not the Only Fruit*	
	Reading *Ukulele Music*		
	Reid *Katerina Brac*		
	Williams *Writing Home*		
1986	Fisher *A Furnace*	Ishiguro *An Artist of the Floating World*	Signing of the Anglo-Irish Agreement British bases used in US bombing of Libya Parliamentary inquiry into rising problem of AIDS
	Hofmann *Acrimony*		
	Middleton *Two Horse Wagon Going By*		
1987	Carson *The Irish for No*	McEwan *The Child in Time*	Thatcher wins third (and final) term of office Re-opening of case of Birmingham six Violent clashes at News International premises in Wapping
	Heaney *The Haw Lantern*		
	Morrison *The Ballad of the Yorkshire Ripper*		
	Paulin *Fivemiletown*		

DATE	POETRY	OTHER WORKS	HISTORICAL/CULTURAL EVENTS
1988	McGuckian *On Ballycastle Beach*	Hollinghurst *The Swimming Pool Library* Lodge *Nice Work* Rushdie *The Satanic Verses*	Ayatollah Khomeini announces *fatwa* (death sentence) on Salman Rushdie for presumed offence to Islam in *Satanic Verses*; Rushdie goes into hiding Three IRA members shot in Gibraltar
1989	Armitage *Zoom!* Fenton *Manila Envelope* Reading *Perduta Gente* Rumens *From Berlin to Heaven*	Ishiguro *The Remains of the Day*	Release of Guildford Four Hillsborough Football Stadium disaster Tienanmen Square demonstrations in China
1990	Carson *Belfast Confetti* Muldoon *Madoc – A Mystery*	Byatt *Possession*	Re-unification of Germany Margaret Thatcher replaced by John Major as leader of Conservative Party
1991	Heaney *Seeing Things* Motion *Love in a Life* O'Brien *HMS Glasshouse* Reid *In the Echoey Tunnel*	Martin Amis *Time's Arrow* Barker *Regeneration* Carter *Wise Children* Golding *To the ends of the Earth: A Sea Trilogy*	The Gulf War End of the Soviet Union Yugoslavia slides into civil war

General Bibliographies

(i)   Critical Works
(ii)   Bibliographies and reference books
(iii)   Literary, historical, political and cultural contexts
(iv)   Anthologies

Note: Each section is arranged alphabetically. Place of publication is London, unless otherwise stated.

(i) Critical Works

Barker, Jonathan (ed.)	*Thirty Years of the Poetry Book Society 1956–1986* (1988). (A useful compilation of some of the pieces written by poets on individual volumes of theirs selected as 'Choices' of the PBS; complements the book edited by Eric W. White, below.)
Bedient, Calvin	*Eight Contemporary Poets* (1974). (Especially useful for accounts of poets not extensively commented on elsewhere, including Stevie Smith and W.S. Graham.)
Berke, Roberta	*Bounds Out of Bounds: A Compass for Recent American and British Poetry* (New York, 1981). (A helpful survey.)
Brown, Merle E.	*Double Lyric: Divisiveness and Communal Creativity in Recent English Poetry* (1980). (A theory of contemporary poetry as 'dramatic, divisive conflict', pursued in relation to Hill, Larkin, Silkin, Gunn and Tomlinson.)
Brown, Terence	*Northern Voices: Poets from Ulster* (Dublin, 1975). (A book which illuminatingly sets some contemporary work from Northern Ireland in a longer Ulster context.)

Corcoran, Neil (ed.)   *The Chosen Ground: Essays on the Contemporary Poetry of Northern Ireland* (Bridgend, 1992). (Ten essays on this work written from a variety of critical and theoretical positions.)

Davie, Donald   *Thomas Hardy and British Poetry* (1973). (A peculiar and in some ways contradictory book, but notable for a conspectus of the period by one of its most significant poets and critics.)

Davie, Donald   *Under Briggflatts: A History of Poetry in Great Britain 1960–1988* (Manchester, 1989). (Despite its title, it is actually largely a collection of first reviews and, as such, is lively, engaged and combative in the way of Davie's literary journalism, with the tin cans of contemporary controversy tied to its tail.)

Dodsworth, Martin (ed.)   *The Survival of Poetry: A Contemporary Survey* (1970). (A still notable and worthwhile collection.)

Easthope, Antony and John O. Thompson (eds.)   *Contemporary Poetry Meets Modern Theory* (1991). (A collection which attempts to unsettle some cherished categories.)

Forrest-Thomson, Veronica   *Poetic Artifice: A theory of twentieth-century poetry* (Manchester, 1978). (A polemical theory of the devices of artifice in modern and contemporary poetry, hostile to all forms of 'naturalisation' in the criticism of it.)

Haffenden, John   *Viewpoints: Poets in Conversation* (1981). (A useful collection of interviews with ten poets of the period.)

Hamilton, Ian   *A Poetry Chronicle: Essays and Reviews* (1973). (A collection by an influential critic and editor, including essays on 'The Forties' and 'The Making of the Movement'.)

Hamilton, Ian (ed.)   *The Modern Poet: Essays from 'the Review'* (1968). (A collection drawn from the notable little magazine of the 1960s.)

Homberger, Eric   *The Art of the Real: Poetry in England and America Since 1939* (1977). (A survey with the aim of closely relating poetry, society and history in the period.)

Jones, Peter and Michael Schmidt (eds.)   *British Poetry Since 1970: A Critical Survey* (Manchester, 1980). (A fine collection of essays, together with a very useful bibliography of individual volumes published during the 1970s.)

King, P.R.   *Nine Contemporary Poets: A Critical Introduction* (1979). (Includes accounts of Larkin, Tomlinson and Gunn.)

Larrissy, Edward   *Reading Twentieth-Century Poetry: The Language of Gender and Objects* (1990). (A reading, influenced by Lacanian theory, of some modern and contemporary poets – including Tomlinson, Hughes, Heaney and Raine.)

Longley, Edna — *Poetry in the Wars* (Newcastle upon Tyne, 1986). (A collection of essays by one of the most searching poetry critics of the period; particularly notable essays on Douglas, Heaney, Mahon and Muldoon.)

Lucas, John — *Modern English Poetry: From Hardy to Hughes* (1986). (The final chapter, 'Healers in Our Native Land?', offers a spirited account of poetry in the period.)

Mole, John — *Passing Judgements: Poetry in the Eighties* (Bristol, 1989). (A collection of Mole's uncommonly sharp and measured reviews for *Encounter* in the 1980s and, as such, an excellent survey of the decade.)

Montefiore, Jan — *Feminism and Poetry: Language, Experience, Identity in Women's Writing* (1987). (A lucid account which brings poetry and French feminist theory together and contains useful sections on Anne Stevenson and Stevie Smith.)

Morrison, Blake — *The Movement: English Poetry and Fiction of the 1950s* (1980). (An excellent account of 'The Movement', reading it as a chapter of English social as well as literary history.)

Orr, Peter (ed.) — *The Poet Speaks* (1966). (An interesting collection of interviews with a large number of poets, including Jones, Middleton, Porter, Smith and Tomlinson.)

Perkins, David — *A History of Modern Poetry: Modernism and After* (1987). (A lengthy and helpful account of many poets of the period – both British and American – centred on attitudes to Modernism.)

Powell, Neil — *Carpenters of Light: Some Contemporary English Poets* (Manchester, 1979). (An account of a number of contemporaries – including Gunn, Davie and Larkin – 'in the light of an English tradition'.

Press, John — *A Map of Modern English Verse* (1969). (A 'source book' for a study of the period from Modernism to the 1960s, with useful selections from fugitive writings.)

Press, John — *Rule and Energy: Trends in British Poetry Since the Second World War* (1963). (A map of the contemporary as it appeared to a knowledgeable commentator in the early 1960s.)

Raban, Jonathan — *The Society of the Poem* (1971). (Still reads as a very lively and provocative account of some of the poetry of the period and illuminatingly reveals, as well as places, some critical attitudes at the end of the 1960s.)

Rawson, C.J. — *The Yearbook of English Studies*, 'British Poetry Since 1945 Special Number', vol. 17 (1987). (A varied collection of scholarly articles.)

Robinson, Alan — *Instabilities in Contemporary British Poetry* (1988). (A scrupulously intelligent account of a number of poets, including Fenton, Hill, Dunn and Paulin.)

Rosenthal, M.L. and Sally M. Gall — *The Modern Poetic Sequence: The Genius of Modern Poetry* (New York, 1983). (A very large book covering a very large number of 'sequences' and attempting to account for their frequency in the period.)

Schmidt, Michael and Grevel Lindop (eds.) — *British Poetry Since 1960: A Critical Survey* (South Hinksey, 1972). (A valuable collection of essays on individual poets and groupings, together with interviews and a useful bibliography of work published in the 1960s.)

Schmidt, Michael — *An Introduction to Fifty Modern British Poets* (1979). (A helpfully orienting and always sharply decided overview of the century, written as fifty individual critical essays.)

Shires, Linda M. — *British Poetry of the Second World War* (1985). (Particularly valuable for its recovery of social context and of little magazine contributions of the time.)

Smith, Stan — *Inviolable Voice: History and Twentieth-Century Poetry* (Dublin, 1982). (A study of the inescapability of the category of 'history' in any genuine critical account of the poetry of the period, with a particularly relevant chapter entitled 'Margins of Tolerance: Responses to Post-War Decline'.)

Thurley, Geoffrey — *The Ironic Harvest: English poetry in the twentieth century* (1974). (A register of hostility to what is read as the dominant ironist mode of modern poetry, and a plea on behalf of some of the alternatives to it.)

Thwaite, Anthony — *Poetry Today: A Critical Guide to British Poetry 1960–1984* (1985). (A brief but astute survey.)

Tolley, A.T. — *The Poetry of the Forties* (Manchester, 1985). (Useful for restoring a sense of the variety of the period.)

Trotter, David — *The Making of the Reader: Language and Subjectivity in Modern American, English and Irish Poetry* (1984). (A complex, wide-ranging and compelling study, offering among many other worthwhile things a subtle account of the way the reader is both addressed and constructed in modern poems.)

White, Eric W. — *Poetry Book Society: The First Twenty-Five Years* (1979). (A very useful collection of the pieces written by poets on winning the PBS 'Choice' for individual volumes.)

(ii) Bibliographies and Reference Books

Alexander, Harriet Semmes	*American and British Poetry: A Guide to the Criticism 1925–1978* (Manchester, 1984).
Barker, Jonathan (ed.)	*The Poetry Library of the Arts Council: Short-Title Catalogue* (1981).
Chevalier, Tracy (ed.)	*Contemporary Poets* (5th edn, 1991). (A very handy bibliographical and biographical guide, together with helpful critical essays.)
Ford, Boris (ed.)	*The New Pelican Guide to English Literature: A Guide for Readers* (1984). (Part 8, 'The Present', is a useful short bibliography for the period.)
Sherry, Vincent B. Jr. (ed.)	*Dictionary of Literary Biography* (Detroit, 1984), vol. 27 (*Poets of Great Britain and Ireland, 1945–1960*), and vol. 40 (*Poets of Great Britian and Ireland Since 1960*). (Substantial critical biographies of individual writers, often with exceptionally interesting illustrative material from manuscripts and dustjackets.)
Sullivan, Alvin (ed.)	*British Literary Magazines: The Modern Age, 1914–1984* (1986). (An illuminating guide to the places of first publication of numerous poems of the period.)

(iii) Literary, historical, political and cultural contexts

(A very selective listing from the vast amount of reading under this rubric in the period. I itemise texts I have found particularly useful in taking the measure of a particular moment, phase or topic; texts which have had a broad influence in their time; and some texts made use of in the poetry itself.)

Allsop, Kenneth	*The Angry Decade: A Survey of the Cultural Revolt of the 1950s* (1958). (A revealing and lively account of the period by a writer acquainted with most of the writers he discusses; and therefore more a contribution to the debate than a disinterested conspectus.)
Appleyard, Brian	*The Pleasures of Peace: Art and Imagination in Post-war Britain* (1989). (A lively if sometimes rather irritatingly decided conspectus.)

Calder, Angus	*The People's War* (1969). (A classic account.)
Calder, Angus	*The Myth of the Blitz* (1991). (An attempted deconstruction of some cherished attitudes and beliefs.)
Calvocoressi, Peter	*The British Experience 1945–75* (1978). (Very readable social and political history.)
Connor, Steven	*Postmodernist Culture: An Introduction to Theories of the Contemporary* (1989). (An approachable, if almost necessarily at times tendentious account of a difficult phenomenon.)
Cox, C.B. and A.E. Dyson (eds.)	*The Twentieth Century Mind, vol. 3: 1945–1965* (1972). (Useful general essays on culture and thought, including one on poetry.)
Ford, Boris (ed.)	*The New Pelican Guide to English Literature, vol. 8: The Present* (1983). (Particularly useful accounts of 'The Social and Cultural Setting' and 'The Literary Scene'.)
Hartley, Anthony	*A State of England* (1963). (A valuable testing of the temperature of English society and culture between the 1950s and 1960s.)
Hewison, Robert	*Under Siege: Literary Life in London 1939–1945* (1977). (This and the following two books compose an indispensably well-organised cultural sociology of the period.)
Hewison, Robert	*In Anger: Culture in the Cold War 1945–1960* (1981).
Hewison, Robert	*Too Much: Art and Society in the Sixties, 1960–75* (1986).
Hoggart, Richard	*The Uses of Literacy* (1957). (Not only an account of working-class reading but a representative sociology of roots and origins.)
Jacobus, Mary (ed.)	*Women Writing and Writing About Women* (1979). (A valuable collection of individual essays charting some of the impacts of post-1960s feminism.)
Jameson, Fredric	*Postmodernism or, The Cultural Logic of Late Capitalism* (1991). (An astonishingly knowledgeable account of the phenomenon.)
Maclaren-Ross, Julian	*Memoirs of the Forties* (1965). (A revealing account of the period, as much in its style as in its material, by an active participant.)
Marwick, Arthur	*British Society Since 1945* (1982) (A readable social history.)
Mellor, David (ed.)	*A Paradise Lost: The Neo-Romantic Imagination in Britain 1935–55* (1987). (A well-illustrated collection of essays defining a significant and in some ways still potent phase of British culture.)

Melly, George	*Revolt into Style* (1972). (A very readable and spirited account of post-1950s popular culture.)
Sinfield, Alan (ed.)	*Society and Literature 1945–1970* (1983). (A very useful collection of essays, including Andrew Crozier's account of poetry in the period.)
Sinfield, Alan	*Literature, Politics and Culture in Postwar Britain* (1989). (A wide-ranging cultural survey and critique.)
Sked, Alan and Chris Cook	*Post-War Britain: A Political History* (1979; 3rd edn 1990). (An exceptionally helpful, lucid and well-organised survey.)
Stanford, Derek	*Inside the Forties: Literary Memoirs 1937–1957* (1977). (A spirited insider's view.)

(iv) Anthologies

Allnutt, Gillian *et. al.* (eds.)	*The New British Poetry 1968–88* (1988) (Poetry opposed to the 'mainstream', edited into four separate sections.)
Allott, Kenneth (ed.)	*The Penguin Book of Contemporary Verse, 1918–60* (2nd edn 1962). (Contains helpful introductory notes on individual poets.)
Alvarez, A. (ed.)	*The New Poetry* (1962; revised and enlarged edn, 1966). (Controversial and variously influential.)
Astley, Neil (ed.)	*Poetry with an Edge* (Newcastle upon Tyne, 1988). (Poets publishing with Bloodaxe, one of the most significant British presses of the 1980s.)
Berry, James (ed.)	*News for Babylon: The Chatto Book of Westindian-British Poetry* (1984). (A pioneering collection.)
Burnett, Paula (ed.)	*The Penguin Book of Caribbean Verse in English* (1986). (Contains a long, illuminating introduction and helpful notes and glossary.)
Conquest, Robert (ed.)	*New Lines* (1956). (The anthology which propagandised on behalf of the 'Movement'.)
Crozier, Andrew and Tim Longville (eds.)	*A Various Art* (Manchester, 1987). (Poetry of a self-consciously 'alternative' tradition.)
Enright, D.J. (ed.)	*The Oxford Book of Contemporary Verse 1945–1980* (1980). (Poetry chosen with a strongly individual editorial inflection.)

Gardner, Brian (ed.) — *The Terrible Rain: The War Poets 1939–1945* (1966). (Comprehensive and well-organised, with helpful biographical notes.)

Germain, Edward B. (ed.) — *Surrealist Poetry in English* (1978). (A comprehensive account of the fate of Surrealism in English verse.)

Heath-Stubbs, John and David Wright (eds.) — *The Faber Book of Twentieth-Century Verse* (3rd edn 1975). (Basic survey anthology.)

Horovitz, Michael (ed.) — *Children of Albion: Poetry of the Underground in Britain* (1969). (A revealing document of the 1960s.)

Larkin, Philip (ed.) — *The Oxford Book of Twentieth-Century English Verse* (1973). (Larkin's characteristically individual and anti-Modernist account of the period.)

Lucie-Smith, Edward (ed.) — *British Poetry Since 1945* (1970; revised edn 1985). (Catholic and very helpfully organised and annotated.)

Markham, E.A. (ed.) — *Hinterland: Caribbean Poetry from the West Indies and Britain* (1989). (With a lengthy, spirited and original introductory essay.)

Mohin, Lillian (ed.) — *One Foot on the Mountain: an anthology of British feminist poetry* (1979). (A radical alternative to the Carol Rumens anthology below.)

Morrison, Blake and Andrew Motion (eds.) — *The Penguin Book of Contemporary British Poetry* (1982). (Controversially propagandising for a poetry which 'extends the imaginative franchise'.)

Ormsby, Frank (ed.) — *Poets from the North of Ireland* (1979; revised edn 1990). (With a long, illuminating introduction.)

Reilly, Catherine (ed.) — *Chaos of the Night: Women's Poetry and Verse of the Second World War* (1984). (A compelling recovery of some lost material.)

Roberts, Michael (ed.) — *The Faber Book of Modern Verse* (3rd edn, revised with a new supplement of poems chosen by Donald Hall, 1965). (An extremely influential anthology, in its various editions.)

Rumens, Carol (ed.) — *Making for the Open: Post-Feminist Poetry* (1985; revised edn 1987). (Controversial and influential.)

Schmidt, Michael (ed.) — *Eleven British Poets* (1980). (A handy compilation.)

Schmidt, Michael (ed.) — *Some Contemporary Poets of Britain and Ireland* (Manchester, 1983). (A riposte of a kind to the Morrison and Motion anthology of 1982.)

Silkin, Jon (ed.) — *Poetry of the Committed Individual: A 'Stand' Anthology* (1973). (A useful overview of the kind of poetry argued for and supported by one of the longest-running little magazines of the period.)

Skelton, Robin (ed.)   *Poetry of the Forties* (1968). (Exceptionally
well-organised and intelligently introduced.)

Summerfield, Geoffrey   *Worlds: Seven Modern Poets* (1974). (Contains some
(ed.)   excellent photographs as well as helpful notes.)

Individual Authors

Notes on biography, major works, and suggested further reading

AGARD, John (1949–) Born in Guyana and emigrated to England in 1977. He works as a lecturer for the Commonwealth Institute. His books include *Shoot Me With Flowers* (1973), *Limbo Dancer in Dark Glasses* (1983) and several books for children.

AUDEN, W(ystan) H(ugh) (1907–73) Born in York and educated at Oxford. He travelled extensively during the 1930s, including a visit to Iceland with Louis MacNeice, recounted in *Letters from Iceland* (1937), and to China with Christopher Isherwood, recounted in *Journey to a War* (1939). In 1938 he emigrated to the United States and was naturalised as an American citizen in 1946. During the 1930s in England he worked as a schoolmaster, co-founded the Group Theatre and worked with the GPO Film Unit (producing the famous film *Night Mail* in 1936). In America he was attached to various universities. In 1953 he was elected Professor of Poetry at Oxford. In his later life he lived part of the year on the island of Ischia and then in Austria (in the house commemorated in *About the House*, 1965), and in his last years he lived briefly once more in Christ Church College, Oxford. *Poems* (1930) was followed by numerous other volumes, including *Look, Stranger!* (1936), *Another Time* (1940), *New Year Letter* (1941), *For the Time Being* (1944), *The Age of Anxiety* (1947), *Nones* (1951), *The Shield of Achilles* (1955), *Homage to Clio* (1960), *City Without Walls and Other Poems* (1969) and *Thank You, Fog* (1974). The *Collected Poems* (ed. Edward Mendelson) was published in 1976 and *The English Auden* in 1977. He also published a number of verse plays, including *On the Frontier* (1938) (written with Christopher Isherwood) and a number of opera libretti (written with Chester Kallman). His numerous critical writings are partly collected in *The Dyer's Hand and Other Essays* (1963) and *Forewords and Afterwords* (1973).

> See: Carpenter, Humphrey, *W.H. Auden: A Biography* (1981).
> Bahlke, George W., *The Later Auden* (New Brunswick, 1970).
> Boly, John R., *Reading Auden: The Returns of Caliban* (1991).
> Callan, Edward, *Carnival of Intellect* (Oxford, 1983).

Fuller, John, *A Reader's Guide to W.H. Auden* (1970).
Haffenden, John (ed.), *W.H. Auden: The Critical Heritage* (1983).
Smith, Stan, *W.H. Auden* (Oxford, 1985).
Spears, Monroe K., *The Poetry of Auden: The Disenchanted Island* (New York, 1963).
Spender, Stephen (ed.), *W. H. Auden: A Tribute* (1975).

BARKER, George (1913–1991) Born in Loughton, Essex and educated at Regent Street Polytechnic, London. He lived in Japan and in America for a while in the 1940s, where he had a relationship with the writer Elizabeth Smart which became the subject of her famous novel *By Grand Central Station I Sat Down and Wept* (1945). He lived in Rome in the 1960s and then in Norfolk for many years. *Poems* (1935) initiated a very lengthy career in which he published numerous other books, including *Calamiterror* (1937), *The True Confession of George Barker* (1950), *The View from a Blind I* (1962) and *Anno Domini* (1983). His *Collected Poems* (ed. Robert Fraser) was published in 1987. He also wrote several radio plays and some fiction; his critical prose was collected as *Essays* in 1970.

See: 'George Barker at Seventy' (ed. Robert Fraser), *PN Review* vol. 9 no. 5, pp. 39–66.
Heath-Stubbs, John and Martin Green (eds.), *Homage to George Barker on His Sixtieth Birthday* (1973).

BERRY, James (1925–) Born in Fair Prospect, Jamaica and moved to England in 1948. He worked for the Post Office in London until 1977 and has subsequently held posts as writer-in-residence. His work offers a view of London as experienced by the first generation of Jamaican immigrants and is occasionally written in a Creolised English. His publications include *Fractured Circles* (1979), *Lucy's Letters and Loving* (1982) and *Chain of Days* (1985). He has also published short stories and is editor of the influential anthology *News for Babylon: The Chatto Book of Westindian-British Poetry* (1984).

BUNTING, Basil (1900–85) Born into a Quaker family at Scotswood, Newcastle upon Tyne and studied briefly at the London School of Economics. He was jailed as a conscientious objector during the First World War. After the war he worked for a while as a music critic and lived a cosmopolitan, or vagrant, life in Paris (where he worked with Ford Madox Ford on the *Transatlantic Review*), America, the Canary Islands and Italy, spending some time close to Ezra Pound in Rapallo and earning a living by working on sailing boats. During the Second World War he joined the RAF and was subsequently sent to Persia as an interpreter. In 1945 he returned there as a vice-consul in the British Embassy in Teheran and subsequently as a journalist for *The Times*. He returned to Northumberland in the early 1950s, remaining there until his death. A long period of poetic silence ended in the 1960s, partly under the influence of the Newcastle poet Tom Pickard; and in his latter years he was a visiting writer at several American and Canadian universities, and held a fellowship at Newcastle University. His first volume, *Redimiculum Matellarum* (1930) was published in Milan; and Pound's *Active Anthology* (1933) contained fifty pages of Bunting. Other volumes include *Poems 1950* (Galveston, 1950), *Loquitur* (1965), and *Briggflatts* (1966). His *Collected Poems* was published in 1968 and in a new edition in 1977. The *Uncollected Poems* (ed. Richard Caddell) was published in 1991.

See: *Agenda*, Basil Bunting Special Issue, vol.16 no.1 (1978).

Forde, Sister Victoria, *The Poetry of Basil Bunting* (Newcastle upon Tyne, 1991).

Makin, Peter, *Bunting: The Shaping of his Verse* (Oxford, 1992).

Terrell, Carroll F. (ed.), *Basil Bunting: Man and Poet* (Orono, 1981).

CARSON, Ciaran (1948–) Born into an Irish-speaking family in Belfast, where he was educated at Queen's University. After working briefly as a civil servant and a teacher he became Traditional Arts Officer for the Arts Council of Northern Ireland; his *Pocket Guide to Irish Traditional Music* was published in 1986. His first book, *The New Estate*, was published in 1976 (and in a new, enlarged edition in 1988) and was followed, after a long delay, by *The Irish for No* (Newcastle upon Tyne, 1987) and *Belfast Confetti* (Newcastle upon Tyne, 1990).

See: 'Ciaran Carson interviewed by Randy Brandes', *The Irish Review*, no. 8 (1990), pp. 77–90.

Corcoran, Neil, 'One Step Forward, Two Steps Back: Ciaran Carson's *The Irish for No*', in his *The Chosen Ground: Essays on the Contemporary Poetry of Northern Ireland* (Bridgend, 1992), pp. 213–33.

D'AGUIAR, Fred (1960–) Born in London of Guyanese parents and spent his early years in Guyana. He was educated at the University of Kent. He trained and worked as a psychiatric nurse before taking up several writing fellowships. He edits the magazine *Artrage*. His work finds newly inventive and exploratory ways of shaping a contemporary black British poetry, employing both oral and vernacular 'Nation language' forms and standard English, and having frequent recourse to the materials of Guyanese childhood memory. He has published *Mama Dot* (1985) and *Airy Hall* (1989). He has also had plays, including *High Life* (1987), staged, and has edited part of the anthology *The New British Poetry 1968–1988* (1988).

DAVIE, Donald (1922–) Born in Barnsley, Yorkshire and educated at Cambridge. He served in the Royal Navy during the Second World War. He has taught at Trinity College Dublin and the Universities of Cambridge, Essex, Stanford (California) and Vanderbilt (Tennessee). His first volume, *A Winter Talent and Other Poems* (Manchester, 1957), has been followed by many others, including *Events and Wisdoms* (1964), *Essex Poems* (1969), *The Shires* (1972), *In the Stopping Train and Other Poems* (Manchester, 1977) and *Three for Water Music* (Manchester, 1981). The most recent of several editions of his *Collected Poems* was published in 1991. His version of poems by Boris Pasternak, *The Poems of Doctor Zhivago*, was published in 1965. He has also published a large amount of influential literary criticism, including *Purity of Diction in English Verse* (1952), *Articulate Energy: An Inquiry into the Syntax of English Poetry* (1955) (both of which were implicitly offered as statements of principle for the 'Movement' of the 1950s), *Ezra Pound: Poet as Sculptor* (1964), *Thomas Hardy and British Poetry* (1973), *The Poet in the Imaginary Museum: Essays of Two Decades* (Manchester, 1977), *A Gathered Church: The Literature of the English Dissenting Interest 1700–1930* (1978) and *Under Briggflatts: A History of Poetry in Great Britain 1960–1988* (Manchester, 1989). His editorial work includes *The New Oxford Book of Christian Verse* (1981). A volume of autobiography, *These the Companions*, was published in 1982.

See: *Agenda*, Donald Davie issue, vol.14 no.2 (1976).

Bedient, Calvin, 'Donald Davie', in his *Eight Contemporary Poets* (1974), pp. 23–50.

Dekker, George (ed.), *Donald Davie and the Responsibilities of Literature* (Manchester, 1983).

Stead, C.K., 'After 1950 – Some Reflections on the Case of Donald Davie', in his *Pound, Yeats, Eliot and the Modernist Movement* (1986), pp. 325–53.

DOUGLAS, Keith (1920–44) Born in Tunbridge Wells, Kent, and educated at Oxford, where the poet Edmund Blunden was his tutor. His parents separated before he was six. He served in the Second Derbyshire Yeomanry as a tank officer in the Middle East and subsequently took part in the Normandy landings, where he was killed. His *Collected Poems* (ed. John Waller and G.S. Fraser) was published in 1951; a *Selected Poems* was edited, with an introduction, by Ted Hughes in 1964; and the *Complete Poems* (ed. Desmond Graham) appeared in 1978. His prose account of his time in the Middle East was published in 1946 as *Alamein to Zem Zem* (revised edn 1979). *A Prose Miscellany* (ed. Desmond Graham) was published in 1985; it contains the important essay 'Poets in This War'.

See: Graham, Desmond, *Keith Douglas 1920–1944: A Biography* (1974).

Hill, Geoffrey, '"I in Another Place": Homage to Keith Douglas', *Stand*, vol.6 no.4 (1964–5), pp. 6–13.

Longley, Edna, '"Shit or Bust": The Importance of Keith Douglas', in her *Poetry in the Wars* (Newcastle upon Tyne, 1986), pp. 94–112.

Scammell, William, *Keith Douglas: A Study* (1988).

DUNN, Douglas (1942–) Born in Inchinnan, Renfrewshire, and educated at the Scottish School of Librarianship and, as a mature student, at the University of Hull. He worked as a librarian in various institutions, including the Akron Public Library, Ohio and the Brynmor Jones Library at the University of Hull. He has subsequently lived as a freelance writer, with writing fellowships at the Universities of Hull, Dundee and New England, New South Wales. He is currently a Professor in the University of St Andrews. His first book, *Terry Street* (1969), has been followed by *The Happier Life* (1972), *Love or Nothing* (1974), *Barbarians* (1979), *St Kilda's Parliament* (1981), *Europa's Lover* (Newcastle upon Tyne, 1982), *Elegies* (1985) (written on the tragically early death of his first wife) and *Northlight* (1988). His *Selected Poems 1964–1983* was published in 1986. He has also published a volume of short stories, *Secret Villages* (1985) and a translation of Racine's *Andromache* (1990). His 'An Autobiographical Essay: Little Golden Rules', in *Poetry Review*, vol.72 no.4 (1983), pp. 5–10, is of considerable interest.

See: Interview, in John Haffenden, *Viewpoints: Poets in Conversation* (1981), pp. 11–34.

Ash, John, 'Pleasures of Invention, Rigours of Responsibility: Some Notes on the Poetry of Douglas Dunn', *PN Review*, 34 (1983), pp. 43–6.

King, P.R., *Nine Contemporary Poets: A Critical Introduction* (1979), pp. 221–8.

Robinson, Alan, 'The Mastering Eye: Douglas Dunn's Social Perceptions', in his *Instabilities in Contemporary British Poetry* (1988), pp. 82–99.

ELIOT, T(homas) S(tearns) (1888–1965) Born in St Louis, Missouri and educated at Harvard University. He subsequently studied in Munich, Paris and Oxford, working on a dissertation on the philosopher F.H. Bradley (published in 1964 as *Knowledge and Experience in the Philosophy of F.H. Bradley*). He worked as a teacher and as a clerk in Lloyds Bank, later becoming a director of the publishers Faber and Gwyer (subsequently Faber and Faber). He was naturalised as a British citizen and baptised into the Church of England in 1927. He founded the journal *The Criterion* in 1922. He won the Nobel Prize for Literature in 1948, the same year in which he was awarded the Order of Merit. His first volume, *Prufrock and Other Observations* (1917), was followed by *Poems* (1920), *The Waste Land* (1922), *Ash-Wednesday* (1930) and *Sweeney Agonistes* (1932). *Burnt Norton* was published in 1935, followed by *East Coker* in 1940, *The Dry Salvages* in 1941 and *Little Gidding* in 1942. The sequence was published as *Four Quartets* in 1943. The *Collected Poems 1909–1935* appeared in 1936 and the *Collected Poems 1909–1962* in 1963. One of the most influential critics of the century, he also published a large amount of literary and cultural criticism, including *The Sacred Wood* (1920), *For Lancelot Andrewes: Essays on Style and Order* (1928), *The Idea of a Christian Society* (1939), *Notes Towards the Definition of Culture* (1948) and *To Criticize the Critic and Other Writings* (1965). His *Selected Essays* was published in 1932 (revised edn 1950). He also published a number of verse plays, including *Murder in the Cathedral* (1935), *The Family Reunion* (1939) and *The Cocktail Party* (1950). His translation of St. John Perse's *Anabase* was published in 1930. *The Complete Poems and Plays of T.S. Eliot* was published in 1969. The first volume of his *Letters* (ed. Valerie Eliot) appeared in 1988.

See: Ackroyd, Peter, *T.S. Eliot* (1984) (biography).
  Gordon, Lyndall, *Eliot's Early Years* (1977) (biography).
  Gordon, Lyndall, *Eliot's New Life* (1988) (biography).
  Bush, Ronald, *T.S. Eliot: A Study in Character and Style* (Oxford, 1983).
  Dyson, A.E. (ed.), *T.S. Eliot: 'Four Quartets': A Casebook* (1969).
  Ellis, Steve, *The English Eliot: Design, language and landscape in 'Four Quartets'* (1991).
  Gardner, Helen, *The Composition of 'Four Quartets'* (1978).
  Kenner, Hugh, *The Invisible Poet: T.S. Eliot* (1960).
  Moody, A.D., *Thomas Stearns Eliot: Poet* (1979).

ENRIGHT, D.J. (1920–) Born in Leamington, Warwickshire, and educated at Cambridge. He taught at various universities abroad, including Alexandria, Kobe (in Japan), Bangkok and Singapore. He briefly edited the magazine *Encounter* and worked as a director of Chatto and Windus, publishers. His numerous volumes include *The Laughing Hyena and Other Poems* (1953), *Some Men Are Brothers* (1960), *The Terrible Shears: Scenes from a Twenties Childhood* (1973), *A Faust Book* (1979) and *Instant Chronicles* (1985). His *Collected Poems 1987* was published in 1987. He is also the author of four novels, including *Academic Year* (1955); a large body of critical work, including *Man Is an Onion* (1972) and *A Mania for Sentences* (1983); and a volume of autobiography, *Memoirs of a Mendicant Professor* (1969).

See: Simms, Jacqueline (ed.), *Life by Other Means: Essays on D.J. Enright* (1990).
  Walsh, William, *D.J. Enright: Poet of Humanism* (1974)

FENTON, James (1949–) Born in Lincoln and educated at Oxford. He has worked as a literary and political journalist for various newspapers and journals, spending lengthy periods in Indo-China, Germany and the Far East. His first full-length collection was *Terminal Moraine* (1972) and he published *A German Requiem* in 1981. He has made a point of publishing with small presses, collecting his work in *The Memory of War and Children in Exile: Poems 1968–83* (1983). *Manila Envelope* was privately published in Manila in 1989. He has also published *You Were Marvellous* (theatre reviews) (1983) and *All the Wrong Places: Adrift in the Politics of Asia* (1989). 'A Manifesto Against Manifestoes' (*Poetry Review*, vol. 73 no. 3, 1983, pp. 12–16) is his useful and humourous statement of principles.

See: 'An Interview with James Fenton' (with Andrew Motion), *Poetry Review*, vol.72 no.2 (1982), pp. 17–23.
'James Fenton in conversation with Grevel Lindop', *PN Review*, 40 (vol.11 no.2), 1984, pp. 27–33.
Robinson, Alan, 'James Fenton's "Narratives"': Some Reflections on Postmodernism', in his *Instabilities in Contemporary British Poetry* (1988), pp. 1–15.

FISHER, Roy (1930–) Born in Handsworth, Birmingham, and educated at Birmingham University. He lectured at colleges of education in or near Birmingham and, between 1972 and 1982, at the University of Keele. Throughout this period he also played piano with jazz bands and, since 1982, he has been a freelance writer and musician. Often publishing with small presses, he is himself a director of Migrant Press, which published his first book, *City* (1961). Subsequent volumes include *The Ship's Orchestra* (1966), *Matrix* (1971), *The Thing About Joe Sullivan* (Manchester, 1978) and *A Furnace* (Oxford, 1986). His *Poems 1955–1987* was published in 1988.

See: Interview, in Roy Fisher, *Nineteen Poems and an Interview* (Pensnett, 1973).
Davie, Donald, 'Roy Fisher: An Appreciation', in his *Thomas Hardy and British Poetry* (1973), pp. 152–72.
Weatherhead, A. Kingsley, 'Roy Fisher', in his *The British Dissonance* (1983), pp. 29–55.

FULLER, Roy (1912–90) Born in Failsworth, Lancashire, he served in the Royal Navy during the Second World War and wrote a number of poems of the war. He subsequently worked as a solicitor and as director of a large building society. From 1968 to 1973 he was Professor of Poetry at Oxford. Influenced early by Auden, his poetry is almost always formal and restrained, registering personal and political unease in the accents of civility, and firmly pledged to a long-maintained socialism. His many books include *The Middle of a War* (1942), *Brutus's Orchard* (1957), *Buff* (1965), *From the Joke Shop* (1975) and *Consolations* (1987). His *New and Collected Poems 1934–1984* was published in 1985. He also published a number of novels, including *The Ruined Boys* (1959); three volumes of memoirs; and two collections of his Oxford lectures on poetry.

See: Austin, Allan E., *Roy Fuller* (Boston, 1979).

GRAHAM, W(illiam) S(ydney) (1918–) Born in Greenock, on Clydeside, Scotland, and educated at the Workers' Educational Association College, Newbattle Abbey, Dalkeith, for a year. He spent some of his early life in Ireland and America, subsequently living in London and then in a cottage in Cornwall, where he survived on a kind of permanently poverty-stricken patronage. His wife, Nessie Dunsmuir, figures by name in a number of his poems. In Cornwall he was part of a set that included a number of painters (the most notable being Roger Hilton), who also appear frequently in his work. *Cage Without Grievance* (1942) was followed by *2nd Poems* (1945), *The White Threshold* (1952), *The Nightfishing* (1955), *Malcolm Mooney's Land* (1970) and *Implements in Their Places* (1977). The *Collected Poems 1942–1977* was published in 1979.

See: Interview, 'I Would Say I Was a Happy Man' (with John Haffenden), *Poetry Review*, vol.76 nos.1/2 (1986), pp. 67–74.

Bedient, Calvin, 'W.S. Graham', in his *Eight Contemporary Poets* (1974), pp. 159–80.

Edinburgh Review, special issue on Graham, no.75 (1987).

Grant, Damian, 'Walls of Glass: the poetry of W.S. Graham', in Peter Jones and Michael Schmidt, (eds.), *British Poetry Since 1970: A Critical Survey* (1980), pp. 22–38.

Lopez, Tony, *The Poetry of W.S. Graham* (1989).

Punter, David, 'W.S. Graham: constructing a white space', in his *The Hidden Script: Writing and the Unconscious* (1985), pp. 131 – 53.

GUNN, Thom (1929–) Born in Gravesend, Kent, and educated at Cambridge. After his national service in the Army he spent six months in Paris. In the early 1950s he studied at Stanford University, California with the American poet and critic Yvor Winters. He has taught at the University of California at Berkeley, spending time in London in 1964–5 but otherwise living in San Francisco, the location of numerous later poems. His first full-length collection, *Fighting Terms* (Oxford, 1954), has been followed by *The Sense of Movement* (1957), *My Sad Captains and Other Poems* (1961), *Positives* (1966) (a collaboration with his photographer brother Ander), *Touch* (1967), *Moly* (1971), *Jack Straw's Castle* (1976), *The Passages of Joy* (1983) and *The Man with Night Sweats* (1992). His earlier work was associated with both the 'Movement' and with Ted Hughes (a joint selection of their poetry was published in 1962). His essays were collected as *The Occasions of Poetry: Essays in Criticism and Autobiography* in 1982 and he has produced selections of the poems of Fulke Greville and Ben Jonson.

See: Interview, in John Haffenden, *Viewpoints: Poets in Conversation* (1981), pp. 35–56.

Dyson, A.E. (ed.), *Three Contemporary Poets: Thom Gunn, Ted Hughes and R.S. Thomas* (1990) (a 'casebook' of critical essays).

Giles, Paul, 'Landscapes of repetition: the self-parodic nature of Thom Gunn's later work', *Critical Quarterly*, vol.29 no.2 (1987), pp. 85–99.

King, P.R., *Nine Contemporary Poets* (1979), pp. 77–106.

PN Review, 'Thom Gunn at Sixty' issue, vol.16 no.2 (1989).

Powell, Neil, 'Thom Gunn: A Pierglass for Poets', in his *Carpenters of Light* (Manchester, 1979), pp. 19–59.

Woods, Gregory, 'Thom Gunn', in his *Articulate Flesh: Male Homoeroticism in Modern Poetry* (1987), pp. 212–31.

HAMILTON, Ian (1938–) Born in King's Lynn, Norfolk and educated at Oxford. He was co-founder and editor of the influential magazine *the Review* and, later, of the *New Review*. He was also an exceptionally influential (and acute) poetry reviewer in the 1960s; his *A Poetry Chronicle: Essays and Reviews* was published in 1973. His full-length collections are *The Visit* (1970) and *Fifty Poems* (1988). His editorial work includes the *Selected Poetry and Prose* of Alun Lewis (1966); and his other publications include *The Little Magazines: A Study of Six Editors* (1976) and *Robert Lowell: A Biography* (1983).

HARRISON, Tony (1937–) Born in Leeds, Yorkshire, and educated at Leeds University, where he read Classics. After a period of schoolteaching he lectured at Ahmadu Bello University, Nigeria, and at Charles University, Prague. He subsequently took up the first of a number of creative writing fellowships, at the Universities of Newcastle upon Tyne and Durham. He was resident dramatist at the National Theatre from 1977–9. As a freelance writer since then, he is exceptionally well-travelled and now divides his time between England (where he still lives in Newcastle) and the US. He is married to the opera singer Theresa Stratas. His books include *The Loiners* (1970), *From the School of Eloquence and Other Poems* (1978), *Continuous: Fifty Sonnets from the School of Eloquence* (1981) and *v.* (Newcastle upon Tyne, 1985), which caused a furore when it was read on BBC television: the new edition of 1989 contains the ensuing press articles. His *Selected Poems* was published in 1984. He is a prolific translator of poems and plays, including work by Martial, Palladas, Molière, Racine and Aeschylus; and he is also an opera librettist. His *Theatre Works 1973–1985* was published in 1986.

See: Astley, Neil (ed.), *Tony Harrison* (Newcastle upon Tyne, 1991) (a compendious anthology of critical articles, reviews and interviews).

HARSENT, David (1942–) Born in Devonshire. He has worked as a literary journalist for the *Times Literary Supplement* and the *Spectator*. His books are *A Violent Country* (1969), *After Dark* (1973), *Dreams of the Dead* (1977) and *Mister Punch* (1984). His *Selected Poems* was published in 1989. A novel, *From an Inland Sea*, was published in 1985 and he wrote the libretto for Harrison Birtwhistle's opera *Gawain* (a version of the medieval poem *Sir Gawain and the Green Knight*) in 1991.

HEANEY, Seamus (1939–) Born in Co. Derry, Northern Ireland, and educated at Queen's University, Belfast. After a period of teaching and lecturing at a teachers' training college, he taught at Queen's University, with a year in the University of California at Berkeley in 1970–71. He subsequently moved to Co. Wicklow, in the Republic of Ireland, where he worked as a freelance writer before returning to teaching, at Carysfort College, Dublin, and, since 1982, at Harvard University, where he became Boylston Professor of Rhetoric and Oratory in 1984. He is a director of the Field Day Theatre Company. In 1989 he was elected Professor of Poetry at Oxford. Since his first full-length volume, *Death of a Naturalist* (1966), he has published *Door into the Dark* (1969), *Wintering Out* (1972), *North* (1975), *Field Work* (1979), *Station Island* (1984), *The Haw Lantern* (1987) and *Seeing Things* (1991). His critical essays have been collected in *Preoccupations: Selected Prose 1968–1978* (1980) and *The Government of the Tongue: The 1986 T.S. Eliot Memorial Lectures and Other Critical Writings* (1988). Has also published a version of Sophocles's *Philoctetes, The Cure at Troy* (1990).

See: Andrews, Elmer, *The Poetry of Seamus Heaney: All the Realms of Whisper* (1988).
Corcoran, Neil, *Seamus Heaney* (1986).

Morrison, Blake, *Seamus Heaney* (1982).
Smith, Stan, 'Seamus Heaney: The Distance Between', in Neil
    Corcoran (ed.), *The Chosen Ground: Essays on the Contemporary
    Poetry of Northern Ireland* (Bridgend, 1992), pp. 35–61.
Tamplin, Ronald, *Seamus Heaney* (Milton Keynes, 1991).

HILL, Geoffrey (1932–) Born in Bromsgrove, Worcestershire, and educated at
Oxford. He has taught at the Universities of Leeds, Cambridge and, currently,
Boston. His first full collection was *For the Unfallen* (1959); it has been
followed by *King Log* (1968), *Mercian Hymns* (1971), *Tenebrae* (1978) and *The
Mystery of the Charity of Charles Péguy* (1983). His *Collected Poems* was
published in 1985. He has also published an adaptation of Ibsen's *Brand* (1978)
and two collections of literary essays, *The Lords of Limit: Essays on Literature
and Ideas* (1984) and *The Enemy's Country: words, contexture and other
circumstances of language* (1991).

See: Interview, in John Haffenden, *Viewpoints: Poets in Conversation* (1981),
        pp. 76–99.
    Hart, Henry, *The Poetry of Geoffrey Hill* (Carbondale, 1986).
    Robinson, Peter (ed.), *Geoffrey Hill: Essays on His Work* (Milton
        Keynes, 1985).
    Sherry, Vincent, *The Uncommon Tongue: The Poetry and Criticism of
        Geoffrey Hill* (Ann Arbor, 1987).

HUGHES, Ted (1930–) Born in Mytholmroyd, Yorkshire, and educated at
Cambridge, where he read Archaeology and Anthropology. He married
Sylvia Plath in 1956 (she died in 1963). He spent some time in America in
the 1950s, including a spell of teaching at the University of Massachusetts at
Amherst; during this period he met the painter Leonard Baskin who was to
become a collaborator on a number of his books. He was founding editor,
with Daniel Weissbort, of the influential magazine *Modern Poetry in Translation*
in the 1960s. He has subsequently spent time as a farmer in Devon and has
initiated the Arvon Foundation and its creative writing courses. He was
appointed Poet Laureate in 1984. His first book, *The Hawk in the Rain* (1957),
has been followed, in a very prolific career, by numerous others, including
Lupercal (1960), *Wodwo* (1967), *Crow* (1970), *Gaudete* (1977), *Cave Birds*
(1978), *Remains of Elmet* (1979), *Moortown* (1979), *Flowers and Insects* (1986)
and *Wolfwatching* (1989). His *Selected Poems 1957–1981* was published in 1982.
He has also published a large amount of work for children, including *The Iron
Man* (1968) and *Under the North Star* (1981). His collection of radio talks on
poetry was published as *Poetry in the Making* (1967); his selection of
Shakespeare (with lengthy introduction) was published as *A Choice of
Shakespeare's Verse* in 1971; and his critical/ anthropological study *Shakespeare
and the Goddess of Complete Being* in 1992. He has also edited the work of
Sylvia Plath and has collaborated in translations of the work of Janos
Pilinszky and Yehuda Amichai. His adaptation of Seneca's *Oedipus* was
published in 1969. *Rain-Charm for the Duchy and other Laureate Poems* appeared
in 1992.

See: Faas, Ekbert, *Ted Hughes: The Unaccommodated Universe* (Santa Barbara,
        1980) (contains an important interview with Hughes).
    Gifford, Terry and Neil Roberts, *Ted Hughes: A Critical Study* (1981).
    Robinson, Craig, *Ted Hughes, Shepherd of Being* (1989).

Sagar, Keith, *The Art of Ted Hughes* (Cambridge, 1975; revised edn, 1978).
Sagar, Keith (ed.), *The Achievement of Ted Hughes* (Manchester, 1983).
Walder, Denis, *Ted Hughes* (Milton Keynes, 1987).
West, Thomas, *Ted Hughes* (1985).

JENNINGS, Elizabeth (1926–) Born in Boston, Lincolnshire, and educated at Oxford. She worked as a librarian and publisher's reader until 1961, when she became a freelance writer. She was the only woman poet and the only religious poet (she is a Roman Catholic) associated with the Movement in the 1950s. She is a poet of remarkable consistency, producing (apart from some poems of mental breakdown) formally crafted and intricate lyric poems. Her numerous books include *A Way of Looking* (1956), *A Sense of the World* (1959), *Recoveries* (1964), *Growing-Points* (Manchester, 1975) and *Tributes* (Manchester, 1989). The most recent edition of her *Collected Poems* was published in 1986. She has also published criticism and a number of anthologies. Her translation of *The Sonnets of Michelangelo* appeared in 1961.

JOHNSON, Linton Kwesi (1952–) Born in Chapeltown, Jamaica, and emigrated to England in 1963. He was educated at the University of London, where he took a degree in Sociology. He is arts editor of *Race Today* magazine and has worked as an education officer and a writer-in-residence. He has also produced programmes about Jamaican music for the BBC. His work combines standard English with black street language and Rastafarian apocalypticism to produce a vehemently anti-racist poetry, lent more venom by his own incantatory performances. His books are *Voices of the Living and the Dead* (1974), *Dread, Beat and Blood* (1975) and *Inglan Is a Bitch* (1980). He has also produced various recordings of his work, including *Making History* (1984).

JONES, David (1895–1974) Born in Brockley, Kent, and educated at Camberwell School of Art and Westminster School of Art. He served with the Royal Welch Fusiliers in the First World War and was wounded on the Somme. After the war he converted to Roman Catholicism and lived with the group of artists led by Eric Gill in Sussex and Wales, producing work as an engraver, book illustrator, painter and water colourist. In subsequent years he became increasingly reclusive but maintained his output as an artist and, in his later years, as a maker of inscriptions. He was made a Companion of Honour in 1974. *In Parenthesis*, his long poem about the First World War, was published in 1937. It was followed by *The Anathemata* in 1952 and *The Sleeping Lord and Other Fragments* in 1974. A posthumous collection of *residua* was published as *The Roman Quarry and other sequences* (ed. Harman Grisewood and René Hague) in 1981. His literary, aesthetic and cultural essays are collected as *Epoch and Artist: Selected Writings* (1959) and *The Dying Gaul and Other Writings* (1978). *Dai Greatcoat: A self-portrait of David Jones in his letters* was edited by René Hague in 1980.

See: Corcoran, Neil, *The Song of Deeds: A Study of 'The Anathemata'* of *David Jones* (Cardiff, 1982).
Dilworth, Thomas, *The Shape of Meaning in the Poetry of David Jones* (Toronto, 1988).
Hague, René, *A Commentary on 'The Anathemata' of David Jones* (Wellingborough, 1977).
Hooker, Jeremy, *David Jones: An Exploratory Study of the Writings* (1975).

Matthias, John (ed.), *David Jones: Man and Poet* (Orno, 1989).
Pagnoulle, Christine, *David Jones: A Commentary on Some Poetic Fragments* (Cardiff, 1987).
Ward, Elizabeth, *David Jones, Mythmaker* (Manchester, 1983).

LARKIN, Philip (1922–85) Born in Coventry and educated at Oxford, where his circle included Kingsley Amis. He worked in various libraries, including a spell in Belfast, before becoming librarian of the Brynmor Jones Library in the University of Hull in 1955. He wrote regular jazz reviews for the *Daily Telegraph*, collected in 1970 as *All What Jazz: A Record Diary* (revised edn 1985). His books include *The North Ship* (1945; revised edn 1966); *The Less Deceived* (1955), *The Whitsun Weddings* (1964) and *High Windows* (1974). The *Collected Poems* (ed. Anthony Thwaite) was published in 1988. He also published two novels, *Jill* (1946) and *A Girl in Winter* (1947), and his critical writings are collected as *Required Writing: Miscellaneous Pieces 1955–1982* (1983). He also edited *The Oxford Book of Twentieth-Century Verse* (1973).

See: Interview, in John Haffenden, *Viewpoints: Poets in Conversation* (1981), pp. 114–29.
Everett, Barbara, two essays in her *Poets in Their Time* (1986).
Hartley, George (ed.), *Philip Larkin 1922–1985: A Tribute* (1988).
Motion, Andrew, *Philip Larkin* (1982).
Regan, Stephen, *Philip Larkin: The Critics Debate* (1992).
Rossen, Janice, *Philip Larkin: His Life's Work* (1990).
Thwaite, Anthony (ed.), *Larkin at Sixty* (1982).

LEWIS, Alun (1915–44) Born in Aberdare, a mining village in South Wales, and educated at the University College of Wales, Aberystwyth (where he took a degree in History), and the University of Manchester. After a period of teaching he served in the Army during the Second World War and was killed under mysterious circumstances on active service in Burma. *Raiders' Dawn and Other Poems* was published in 1942 and *Ha! Ha! among the Trumpets*, posthumously, in 1945. He also wrote a number of short stories, some of which were published in *The Last Inspection* (1942). *Letters from India* was published in 1946 and *In the Green Tree*, a volume of letters and short stories, in 1948. *The Selected Poetry and Prose* (ed. Ian Hamilton) was published in 1966; *A Miscellany of His Writings* (Bridgend, ed. John Pikoulis) in 1982; and the *Selected Poems* (ed. Jeremy Hooker and Gweno Lewis) in 1981.

See: Pikoulis, John, *Alun Lewis: A Life* (Bridgend, 1984).
John, Alun, *Alun Lewis* (Cardiff, 1970).
Poetry Wales, Alun Lewis Special Number, vol.10 no.3 (1975)

LONGLEY, Michael (1939–) Born in Belfast and educated at Trinity College Dublin, where he read Classics. After a period of schoolteaching he took up a post as Director for Literature and the Traditional Arts with the Arts Council of Northern Ireland, retiring in 1991. He is married to the critic Edna Longley. His first full-length collection, *No Continuing City* (1969), was followed by *An Exploded View* (1973), *Man Lying on a Wall* (1976), *The Echo Gate* (1979) and *Gorse Fires* (1991). His *Poems 1963–1983* was published in 1985. He edited the *Selected Poems* of Louis MacNeice in 1988.

See: Dawe, Gerald, '"Icon and Lares": Derek Mahon and Michael Longley', in Gerald Dawe and Edna Longley (eds), *Across a Roaring*

Hill: The Protestant Imagination in Modern Ireland (Belfast, 1985), pp. 218–35.

McDonald, Peter, 'Michael Longley's Homes', in Neil Corcoran (ed.), *The Chosen Ground: Essays on the Contemporary Poetry of Northern Ireland* (Bridgend, 1992), pp. 65–83.

McGUCKIAN, Medbh (1950–) Born in Belfast, where she was educated at Queen's University. She has been a schoolteacher and a writer-in-residence at Queen's University. Her first full-length collection, *The Flower Master* (1982), has been followed by *Venus and the Rain* (1984), *On Ballycastle Beach* (1988) and *Marconi's Cottage* (1992). She has also published five brief but illuminating autobiographical essays in Susan Sollers (ed.), *Delighting the Heart: A Notebook by Women Writers* (1989).

See: Docherty, Thomas, 'Initiations, Tempers, Seductions: Postmodern McGuckian', in Neil Corcoran (ed.), *The Chosen Ground: Essays on the Contemporary Poetry of Northern Ireland* (Bridgend, 1992), pp. 191–210.

Wills, Clair, 'The Perfect Mother: Authority in the Poetry of Medbh McGuckian', *Text and Context*, no.3 (1988), pp. 91–111.

MacNEICE, Louis (1907–63) Born in Belfast, Northern Ireland, the son of a bishop in the Church of Ireland, and educated at Oxford. He taught Classics at the Universities of Birmingham and London before becoming a notable feature-writer and producer for BBC radio. During the 1930s he visited Iceland with W.H. Auden, resulting in their jointly written *Letters from Iceland* (1937). His *Blind Fireworks* (1929) was followed by numerous other collections, including *Poems* (1935), *The Earth Compels* (1938), *Autumn Journal* (1939), *Springboard* (1944), *Solstices* (1961) and *The Burning Perch* (1963). His *Collected Poems* (ed. E.R. Dodds) was published in 1966; and a new *Selected Poems* (ed. Michael Longley) was published in 1988. He also wrote a number of radio plays, including *Christopher Columbus* (1942) and *The Dark Tower* (1946). His critical writings include *Modern Poetry: A Personal Essay* (1938), *The Poetry of W.B. Yeats* (1941) and *Varieties of Parable* (1965). His shorter writings have been edited by Alan Heuser as *Selected Literary Criticism of Louis MacNeice* (Oxford, 1987) and *Selected Prose of Louis MacNeice* (Oxford, 1990). *The Strings Are False: An Unfinished Autobiography* was published in 1965.

See: Brown, Terence, *Louis MacNeice: Sceptical Vision* (Dublin, 1975).

Longley, Edna, *Louis MacNeice: A Study* (1988).

McDonald, Peter, *Louis MacNeice: The Poet in His Contexts* (Oxford, 1991).

Marsack, Robyn, *The Cave of Making* (Oxford, 1982).

MAHON, Derek (1941–) Born in Belfast and educated at Trinity College Dublin, where he read Classics. After teaching in England, France, Canada, Ireland and the United States he worked as writer-in-residence at various institutions, including the University of East Anglia and the New University of Ulster. He has also worked in literary journalism and for the Features Department of the BBC. He currently lives in the US. His first full-length volume, *Night-Crossing* (1968), has been followed by *Lives* (1972), *The Snow Party* (1975), *The Hunt by Night* (1982) and *Antarctica* (Dublin, 1985). Much given to revising his work after publication, the current 'established' text is the *Selected Poems* of 1991. He has also published two adaptations of Molière, *High Time* (1985) and *The School for Wives* (1986), and several translations of poetry, including the *Selected Poems* of Philippe Jacottet (1987). He is editor (with Peter Fallon) of *The Penguin Book of Contemporary Irish Poetry* (1990).

> See: Dawe, Gerald, '"Icon and Lares": Derek Mahon and Michael Longley', in Gerald Dawe and Edna Longley (eds), *Across a Roaring Hill: The Protestant Imagination in Modern Ireland* (Belfast, 1985).
>
> Haughton, Hugh, '"Even now there are places where a thought might grow": Place and Displacement in the Poetry of Derek Mahon', in Neil Corcoran (ed.), *The Chosen Ground: Essays on the Contemporary Poetry of Northern Ireland* (Bridgend, 1992), pp. 87–120.
>
> Longley, Edna, 'The Singing Line: Form in Derek Mahon's Poetry', in her *Poetry in the Wars* (Newcastle upon Tyne, 1986), pp. 170–84.
>
> Riordan, Maurice, 'An Urbane Perspective: The Poetry of Derek Mahon', in Maurice Harmon (ed.), *The Irish Writer and the City* (Gerrard's Cross, 1984), pp. 167–79.

MARKHAM, E(dward) A(rchibald) (1939–) Born in Montserrat, West Indies, and emigrated to England in 1956. Educated at Kilburn Polytechnic and the University of Wales at Lampeter. He has worked as a lecturer, theatre director and creative writing fellow and has edited the magazine *Artrage*. His work is written in standard English, but frequently adopts personae usable to shape some subversive black attitudes and postures of defiance. His books include *Lambchops* (1976), *Human Rites: Selected Poems 1970–1982* (1984) and *Living in Disguise* (1986). He has also had a number of plays staged and has published a volume of short stories. He is the editor of *Hinterland: Caribbean Poetry from the West Indies and Britain* (1990).

MIDDLETON, Christopher (1926–) Born in Truro, Cornwall, and educated at Oxford. After a spell in the RAF he taught at the Universities of Zurich and London before taking up the Chair of Germanic Languages and Literature at the University of Texas at Austin in 1966. After an early volume in 1944 his first subsequent full-length collection was *Torse 3: Poems 1949–1961* (1962). Other volumes include *Our Flowers and Nice Bones* (1969), *The Lonely Suppers of W.V. Balloon* (Cheadle,1975), *Carminalenia* (Manchester, 1980) and *Two Horse Wagon Going By* (Manchester, 1986). His *Selected Writings* was published in 1989 and his literary essays have been collected in *Bolshevism in Art and Other Essays* (Manchester, 1978) and *The Pursuit of the Kingfisher* (Manchester, 1983). He has also published a large number of translations from the German.

> See: Honig, Edwin, 'A Conversation with Christopher Middleton', *Modern Language Notes*, vol.91 no.6 (1976), pp. 1588–602.
>
> Schmidt, Michael, 'Christopher Middleton', in his *A Reader's Guide to Fifty Modern British Poets* (1979), pp. 353–9.

MORRISON, Blake (1950–) Born in Burnley, Lancashire but brought up in Yorkshire. He was educated at the Universities of Nottingham, McMaster (Ontario) and London. He is an influential literary journalist and, since 1990, has been literary editor of the *Independent on Sunday*. He has published *Dark Glasses* (1984; revised and enlarged edn 1989) and *The Ballad of the Yorkshire Ripper and Other Poems* (1987). His critical books are *The Movement: English Poetry and Fiction of the 1950s* (1980) and *Seamus Heaney* (1982); and he has also edited (with Andrew Motion) the anthology *The Penguin Book of Contemporary British Poetry* (1982).

MOTION, Andrew (1952–) Born in London, brought up in East Anglia, and educated at Oxford. After lecturing at the University of Hull he briefly edited *Poetry Review* and has since worked in publishing. His first full-length collection was *The Pleasure Steamers* (Manchester, 1978), followed by *Independence* (1981), *Secret Narratives* (1983), *Dangerous Play: Poems 1974–1984* (1984), *Natural Causes* (1987) and *Love in a Life* (1991). He is also the author of two critical books, *The Poetry of Edward Thomas* (1980) and *Philip Larkin* (1982); novels, including *The Pale Companion* (1989); and a biography, *The Lamberts: George, Constant and Kit* (1986). He is the editor (with Blake Morrison) of *The Penguin Book of Contemporary British Poetry* (1982). He is writing the biography of Philip Larkin.

> See: Hulse, Michael, '"I could have outlived myself there": the poetry of Andrew Motion', *Critical Quarterly*, vol.28 no.3 (1986), pp. 71–81.

MUIR, Edwin (1887–1959) Born in Deerness, Orkney, but his family moved to a depressed area of Glasgow when he was a child. He worked there in commercial and shipbuilding offices before becoming a journalist and translator, including a period on the staff of A.R. Orage's journal *New Age*. He lived in Prague for a period after 1920. During the Second World War he worked for the British Council in Edinburgh and, after the war, in Prague and Rome, witnessing the post-war havoc of Europe at first hand. In the 1950s he was warden of Newbattle Abbey College, Dalkeith (the Workers Educational Association College) and subsequently Charles Eliot Norton Professor at Harvard University. With his wife, Willa Muir, he made the first translations of Kafka into English, as well as numerous other translations from the German. *First Poems* (1925) was followed by various other volumes, including *Variations on a Time Theme* (1934), *The Narrow Place* (1943), *The Voyage and Other Poems* (1946), *The Labyrinth* (1949) and *One Foot in Eden* (1956). His critical work includes *Scott and Scotland: The Predicament of the Scottish Writer* (1936) and *Essays on Literature and Society* (1949). *The Story and the Fable: An Autobiography* (1940) was revised as *An Autobiography* (1954). The *Collected Poems* (ed. Willa Muir and J.C. Hall) was published in 1960. *Selected Letters* (ed. Peter Butter) appeared in 1974.

> See: Aitchison, James, *The Golden Harvester: The Vision of Edwin Muir* (Aberdeen, 1988).
> Butter, Peter, *Edwin Muir: Man and Poet* (Edinburgh, 1966). ·
> Huberman, Elizabeth L., *The Poetry of Edwin Muir: The Field of Good and Ill* (New York, 1971).
> Hoffman, Daniel, *Barbarous Knowledge: Myth in the Poetry of Yeats, Graves and Muir* (New York, 1967).

MULDOON, Paul (1951–) Born in Co. Armagh, Northern Ireland, and educated at Queen's University, Belfast. He worked as a radio and television producer for BBC Northern Ireland and has subsequently been a writer-in-residence at various English and American universities, including Cambridge, Columbia and Princeton, and is now resident in America. His first full-length book, *New Weather* (1973), has been followed by *Mules* (1977), *Why Brownlee Left* (1980), *Quoof* (1983), *Meeting the British* (1987) and *Madoc: A Mystery* (1990). His *Selected Poems 1968–1983* was published in 1986. He has also written a television play, *Monkeys* (shown in 1989), about the John Delorean affair, and is editor of *The Faber Book of Contemporary Irish Poetry* (1986).

See: Interview, in John Haffenden, *Viewpoints: Poets in Conversation* (Aberdeen, 1981), pp. 130–42.

Longley, Edna, '"Varieties of Parable": Louis MacNeice and Paul Muldoon', in her *Poetry in the Wars* (Newcastle upon Tyne, 1986), pp. 211–43.

Wills, Clair, 'The Lie of the Land: Language, Imperialism and Trade in Paul Muldoon's *Meeting the British*', in Neil Corcoran (ed.), *The Chosen Ground: Essays on the Contemporary Poetry of Northern Ireland* (Bridgend, 1992), pp. 123–49.

Wilson, William A., 'Paul Muldoon and the Politics of Sexual Difference', *Contemporary Literature* vol.28 no.3 (1987), pp. 317–31.

NICHOLS, Grace (1950–) Born in Guyana, where she was educated at the University of Georgetown, and moved to England in 1977. She has worked as a teacher and a journalist. Her publications include *I Is a Long-Memoried Woman* (1983), an ambitious long poem confronting women's experience of slavery, *The Fat Black Woman's Poems* (1984) and *Lazy Thoughts of a Lazy Woman* (1989). She has also published a novel, *Whole of a Morning Sky* (1989), and several books for children.

PAULIN, Tom (1949–) Born in Leeds but brought up in Belfast. He was educated at the Universities of Hull and Oxford. Since 1972 he has taught at the University of Nottingham. He is also a director of the Field Day Theatre Company. His first full-length collection, *A State of Justice* (1977), was followed by *The Strange Museum* (1980), *Liberty Tree* (1983) and *Fivemiletown* (1987). He has also published plays, including *The Riot Act: A Version of Sophocles' 'Antigone'* (1985). His critical essays have been collected in *Ireland and the English Crisis* (1984) and *Minotaur: Poetry and the Nation State* (1992); and he is also author of *Thomas Hardy: The Poetry of Perception* (1975). He has edited *The Faber Book of Political Verse* (1986) and *The Faber Book of Vernacular Verse* (1990).

See: Interview, in John Haffenden, *Viewpoints: Poets in Conversation* (1981), pp. 157–73.

O'Donoghue, Bernard, 'Involved Imaginings: Tom Paulin', in Neil Corcoran (ed.), *The Chosen Ground: Essays on the Contemporary Poetry of Northern Ireland* (Bridgend, 1992), pp. 171–88.

Robinson, Alan, 'The Civil Art: Tom Paulin's Representations of Ulster', in his *Instabilities in Contemporary British Poetry* (1988), pp. 100–22.

PORTER, Peter (1929–) Born in Brisbane, Australia, where he worked as a journalist before emigrating to England in 1951. He worked as an advertising writer in London for many years. Since 1968 he has been a freelance writer, with various posts as writer-in-residence at universities in England and Australia, including the University of Melbourne in 1983. His first book, *Once Bitten, Twice Bitten* (1961) has been followed by numerous others, including *The Last of England* (1970), *After Martial* (1972) (his versions of the Latin epigrammatist), *Living in a Calm Country* (1975), *The Cost of Seriousness* (1978) (whose title sequence elegises his wife, who died in 1974), *Possible Worlds* (1989) and *The Chair of Babel* (1992). His *Collected Poems* was published in 1983 and *A Porter Selected* in 1989.

See: 'The Poet in the Sixties: Vices and Virtues' ('a recorded conversation

with Peter Porter'), in Michael Schmidt and Grevel Lindop (eds),
British Poetry Since 1960 (South Hinksey, 1972), pp. 202–12.
Bennett, Bruce, *Spirit in Exile: Peter Porter and His Poetry* (Oxford, 1991)
Garfitt, Roger, 'The Group', in *British Poetry Since 1960*, pp. 13–69.
Poetry Review, Peter Porter Special Issue, vol.73 no.1 (1983).
Williams, David, ' "A map of loss": the recent poetry of Peter Porter',
Critical Quarterly, vol. 25 no. 4 (1983), pp. 55–62.

PRYNNE, J.H. (1936–) Born in England and educated at Cambridge. After a
period at Harvard he was appointed to a fellowship in English at Cambridge,
where he has remained since. Apart from his first volume, *Force of Circumstance
and Other Poems* (1962), he has published exclusively with small and private
presses, his books including *Kitchen Poems* (1968), *The White Stones* (1969),
Brass (1971) and *Down where changed* (1979). He collected his work as *Poems*
(Edinburgh, 1982).

See: Davie, Donald, *Thomas Hardy and British Poetry* (1973), *seriatim*.
Forrest-Thomson, Veronica, *Poetic Artifice: A Theory of
Twentieth-Century Poetry* (Manchester, 1978), pp. 47–51, 139–46.
Trotter, David, *The Making of the Reader: Language and Subjectivity in
Modern American, English and Irish Poetry* (1984), pp. 218–30.
Ward, Geoffrey, 'Nothing but Mortality: Prynne and Celan', in
Anthony Easthope and John O. Thompson (eds), *Contemporary
Poetry Meets Modern Theory* (1991), pp. 139–52.

RAINE, Craig (1944–) Born in Shildon, Co. Durham, and educated at Oxford,
where he taught for a number of years before becoming poetry editor for
Faber and Faber in 1981. He returned to Oxford, to take up a teaching
fellowship, in 1990. He is well-known as a literary journalist and for a time
edited the magazine *Quarto*; his literary essays are collected as *Haydn and the
Valve Trumpet* (1990). His first book, *The Onion, Memory* (1978), was followed
by *A Martian Sends a Postcard Home* (1979), whose title gave its name to the
'Martian school' of poets in the 1980s, and *Rich* (1984). He has also published
an opera libretto, *The Electrification of the Soviet Union* (1986) (an adaptation of
a novella by Boris Pasternak) and *'1953'* (1990) (a version of Racine's
Andromaque).

See: Interview, in John Haffenden, *Viewpoints: Poets in Conversation* (1981),
pp. 174–85.
Hulse, Michael, 'Alms for Every Beggared Sense: Craig Raine's
aesthetic in context', *Critical Quarterly*, vol. 23 no.4 (1981), pp.
13–21.
Robinson, Alan, 'Theatre of Trope: Craig Raine and Christopher
Reid', in his *Instabilities in Contemporary British Poetry* (1988), pp.
16–48.

READING, Peter (1946–) Born in Liverpool and educated at Liverpool College of
Art. He worked as a schoolteacher and art lecturer before becoming an
agricultural labourer for ten years. After a period as writer-in-residence at
Sunderland Polytechnic he became a weighbridge operator in an agricultural
feed mill in Shropshire, where he continued until he was sacked in 1992 for a
refusal to wear correct uniform: an affair given much media coverage, like
other episodes in his career, some of which subsequently feature in his work.
A prolific poet, his first full-length collection, *For the Municipality's Elderly*

(1974), has been followed by numerous others, including *Fiction* (1979), *C.* (1984), *Ukulele Music* (1985) and *Perduta Gente* (1989). A selection edited by Alan Jenkins, *Essential Reading*, was published in 1986.

> See: Interview, 'Making Nothing Matter: Peter Reading talking to Alan Jenkins', *Poetry Review*, vol.75 no.1 (1985), pp. 5–12.
> Paulin, Tom, 'Junk Britain: Peter Reading', in his *Minotaur: Poetry and the Nation State* (1992), pp. 285–94.

REDGROVE, Peter (1932–) Born in Kingston, Surrey, and educated at Cambridge, where he read Natural Sciences. His second marriage is to the poet Penelope Shuttle, with whom he has co-authored a number of books. He worked in scientific journalism for many years and then taught at Falmouth School of Art, Cornwall, until 1983. He has also held several creative writing fellowships. He was associated with Ted Hughes in Cambridge and subsequently, in London in the late 1950s and early 1960s, with the 'Group'. His first book was *The Collector and Other Poems* (1960). An exceptionally prolific writer, his other volumes include *Dr Faust's Sea-Spiral Spirit and Other Poems* (1972), *The Weddings at Nether Powers and Other New Poems* (1979), *In the Hall of the Saurians* (1987) and *The First Earthquake* (1989). *The Moon Disposes: Poems 1954–1987* was published in 1987 and in an enlarged edition, as *Poems 1954–1987*, in 1989. He has also written radio and television plays and several novels, including *In the Country of the Skin* (1972) and, with Penelope Shuttle, *The Terrors of Dr Treviles* (1974). *The Wise Wound: Menstruation and Everywoman*, co-authored with Penelope Shuttle, was published in 1978 and *The Black Goddess and the Sixth Sense* in 1987: both are discursive accounts of ideas significant in all his work.

> See: Interview, 'Peter Redgrove: The Science of the Subjective' (with Neil Roberts), *Poetry Review*, vol.77 no.2 (1987), pp. 4–10.
> Garfitt, Roger, 'The Group', in Michael Schmidt and Grevel Lindop (eds), *British Poetry Since 1960* (South Hinksey, 1972), pp. 13–69.
> *Poetry Review*, Peter Redgrove special issue, vol. 71 nos. 2–3 (1981).

REID, Christopher (1949–) Born in Hong Kong and educated at Oxford. He did a succession of jobs (actor, filing clerk, tutor), before moving into literary journalism and publishing. Since 1990 he has been poetry editor for Faber and Faber. His books are: *Arcadia* (1979), *Pea Soup* (1982), *Katerina Brac* (1985) and *In the Echoey Tunnel* (1991).

> See: Interview (with John Haffenden), *Poetry Review*, vol. 72 no. 3, pp. 16–24.
> Robinson, Alan, 'Theatre of Trope: Craig Raine and Christopher Reid', in his *Instabilities in Contemporary British Poetry* (1988), pp. 16–48.

RILEY, Denise (1948–) Born in Carlisle, Cumbria. She has published *Marxism for Infants* (1977), *No Fee* (1978) (with Wendy Mulford) and *Living a Life*. A selection of her work, *Dry Air*, which includes her versions of Holderlin, was published in 1985. She has also written *War in the Nursery: Theories of the Child and Mother* (1983) and *'Am I that name?': Feminism and the category of 'woman' in history* (1988).

RUMENS, Carol (1944–) Born in London and educated at London University. She worked in publicity and advertising before becoming poetry editor for *Quarto* and, subsequently, for the *Literary Review*. She has also held a creative writing fellowship at the University of Kent. Her first collection, *A Strange Girl in Bright Colours* (1973) has been followed by *Unplayed Music* (1981), *Star Whisper* (1983), *Direct Dialling* (1985) and *From Berlin to Heaven* (1989). Her *Selected Poems* was published in 1987. She is also the author of a novel, *Plato Park* (1987), and is editor of the anthology *Making for the Open: The Chatto Book of Post-Feminist Poetry* (1985).

SILKIN, Jon (1930–) Educated at Leeds University as a mature student, after a period as Gregory Fellow there. He has worked as a journalist and lecturer and held many writing fellowships. In 1952 he founded the influential journal *Stand*, which he continues to edit from Newcastle upon Tyne. He writes a poetry attempting a combination of 'image' and 'discourse' in order to seek a space in writing for social responsibility or 'commitment', with a particular emphasis on Jewish themes. His many books include *The Peaceable Kingdom* (1954), *The Re-ordering of the Stones* (1961), *Flower Poems* (Leeds, 1964), *The Psalms with Their Spoils* (1980) and *The Ship's Pasture* (1986); a revised edition of his *Selected Poems* was published in 1988. He has also published a lengthy critical study, *Out of Battle: The Poetry of the Great War* (1972), and has edited a number of anthologies, including *Poetry of the Committed Individual* (1973) and *The Penguin Book of First World War Poetry* (1979).

See: Brown, Merle E., 'Stress in Silkin's Poetry and the Healing Emptiness of America', in his *Double Lyric* (1980), pp. 93–125.
Cluysenaar, Anne, 'Alone in a Mine of Reality: A Matrix in the Poetry of Jon Silkin', in Michael Schmidt and Grevel Lindop (eds), *British Poetry Since 1960* (South Hinksey, 1972), pp. 165–71.
Poetry Review, Jon Silkin special issue, vol. 69 no. 4 (1980).

SISSON, C(harles) H(ubert) (1914–) Born in Bristol and educated at the University of Bristol. He subsequently studied in Berlin, Freiburg and Paris. He served in the British Army Intelligence Corps in India during the Second World War and afterwards spent his working life as a senior civil servant in Whitehall. From 1976 to 1983 he co-edited the journal *PN Review*. A British post-Poundian poet who combines some of the lessons of Modernism with an English Anglican sensibility, his numerous books include *Metamorphoses* (1968), *In The Trojan Ditch* (Manchester, 1974), *Anchises* (Manchester, 1976) and *Exactions* (Manchester, 1980). His *Collected Poems 1943–1983* was published in 1984. He is also the author of two novels, including *Christopher Homm* (1965), and a large volume of literary, political and cultural criticism, some of which was collected as *The Avoidance of Literature* (Manchester, 1978). His many translations include *The Divine Comedy* (Manchester, 1980) and *The Aeneid* (Manchester, 1986). *On the Look-Out: A Partial Autobiography* was published in 1989.

See: Pilling, John, 'The Strict Temperature of Classicism: C.H. Sisson', *Critical Quarterly*, vol.21 no.4 (1979), pp. 73–81.
PN Review, 'C.H. Sisson at Seventy', special issue, vol. 11 no.1 (1984).

SMITH, Ken (1938–) Born in Rudston, Yorkshire, and educated at the University of Leeds. He has taught in England and America and held various writing fellowships, including one at Wormwood Scrubs Prison. He co-edited the magazine *Stand* between 1963 and 1969. He writes a social poetry, sometimes using narrative modes, which combines certain literary resources (such as the figure of the 'wanderer' derived from an Anglo-Saxon poem) with venomous contemporary satire. His many books include *The Pity* (1967), *Tristan Crazy*

(Newcastle upon Tyne, 1978), *Fox Running* (1980) and *Wormwood* (Newcastle upon Tyne, 1987). *The Poet Reclining: Selected Poems 1962–1980* was published in 1982. He has also published short stories and *Inside Time* (1989), about his experiences in Wormwood Scrubs.

SMITH, Stevie (1902–71) Born in Hull, Yorkshire, but brought up in Palmers Green, London, in the house in which she spent her entire life. She worked in a publishing firm in London for thirty years and also broadcast regularly for a time for the BBC. She drew vivid line drawings to accompany some of her poems and also read and sang (or chanted) her work at popular readings later in her life. She became a figure of some 'legendary' status after her death with the West End run (and subsequent film) of the play about her by Hugh Whitemore, *Stevie*. Her first volume, *A Good Time Was Had By All*, appeared in 1937 and was followed by many others, including *Mother, What Is Man?* (1942), *Not Waving But Drowning* (1957), *The Frog Prince and Other Poems* (1966) and *Scorpion and Other Poems* (1972). The *Collected Poems* (ed. James MacGibbon) was published in 1975, and *Stevie Smith: A Selection* (ed. Hermione Lee) in 1983. She also published three novels, the best-known of which is *Novel on Yellow Paper* (1936). *Me Again: Uncollected Writings* (ed. Jack Barbera and William McBrien) was published in 1981.

> See: Spalding, Frances, *Stevie Smith: A Critical Biography* (1988).
> Montefiore, Janet, 'Stevie Smith and other storytellers', in her *Feminism and Poetry* (1987), pp. 43–56.
> Sternlicht, Sanford (ed.), *In Search of Stevie Smith* (1991) (a collection of essays including pieces by Seamus Heaney, Philip Larkin and Christopher Ricks).

STEVENSON, Anne (1933–) Born in Cambridge, England, but brought up in the United States and educated at the University of Michigan. In the 1950s and 1960s she taught in various schools in England and America and subsequently in the University of Glasgow. She has been writer-in-residence at several institutions, including the Universities of Dundee, Oxford and Edinburgh. She was a co-founder of the Poetry Bookshop in Hay-on-Wye in 1979. Her first books, *Living in America* and *Reversals*, were published only in the United States. *Correspondences: A Family History in Letters* and *Travelling Behind Glass: Selected Poems 1963–1973* were both published in Britain in 1974. Volumes since then include *Enough of Green* (1977), *Minute By Glass Minute* (1982), *The Fiction-Makers* (1985) and *The Other House* (1990). Her *Selected Poems 1956–1986* was published in 1987. She is also the author of a critical study, *Elizabeth Bishop* (Boston, 1966) and *Bitter Fame: A Life of Sylvia Plath* (1989).

> See: Montefiore, Jan, ' "Transcending gender": Anne Stevenson', in her *Feminism and Poetry* (1987), pp. 33–8.

THOMAS, Dylan (1914–53) Born in Swansea, South Wales. He worked briefly as a journalist and then as a documentary film maker during the Second World War, and subsequently lived as a freelance writer. He made enormously popular reading tours of the United States in the early 1950s, during one of which he died, in New York. A notorious drinker and riotous liver, the official cause of his death was given as 'an insult to the brain'. *Eighteen Poems* (1934) was followed by *Twenty-Five Poems* (1936), *New Poems* (1943), *Deaths and Entrances* (1946) and *Twenty-Six Poems* (1950). The *Collected Poems 1934–1953* (ed. Walford Davies and Ralph Maud) was published in 1988 and is supplemented by *The Notebook Poems 1930–1934* (ed. Ralph Maud) published in 1989. He also wrote a number of radio plays, the best-known of which is *Under Milk Wood* (1954). His prose includes *A Portrait of the Artist as a Young Dog* (1940). The *Collected Letters* (ed. Paul Ferris) was published in 1985.

See: Ferris, Paul, *Dylan Thomas: A Biography* (1977).
    Ackerman, John, *A Dylan Thomas Companion* (1991).
    Bold, Alan (ed.), *Dylan Thomas: Craft or Sullen Art* (1990).
    Cox, C.B., *Dylan Thomas: A Collection of Critical Essays* (1966).
    Davies, Walford, *Dylan Thomas: New Critical Essays* (1972).
    Davies, Walford, *Dylan Thomas* (Milton Keynes, 1986).

THOMAS, R.S. (1913–) Born in Cardiff and educated at University College Bangor and the University of Wales, Cardiff. He was ordained a priest in the Church in Wales in 1940 and spent his working life in various rural Welsh parishes. His first volume, *The Stones of the Field* (Carmarthen, 1946), has been followed by numerous others, including *Song at the Year's Turning* (1955), *Tares* (1961), *Not That He Brought Flowers* (1968), *H'm* (1972), *Laboratories of the Spirit* (1975) and *The Echoes Return Slow* (1988). His *Selected Poems 1946–68* was published in 1973 and his *Later Poems: A Selection* in 1983. His *Selected Prose* appeared in 1983 and his editorial work includes *The Penguin Book of Religious Verse* (1963).

See: Anstey, Sandra (ed.), *Critical Writings on R.S. Thomas* (Bridgend, 1982).
    Dyson, A.E., *Yeats, Eliot and R.S. Thomas: Riding the Echo* (1981).
    Dyson, A.E. (ed.), *Three Contemporary Poets: Thom Gunn, Ted Hughes and R.S. Thomas* (1990) (a 'casebook' of critical essays).
    Merchant, W. Moelwyn, *R.S. Thomas* (Cardiff, 1979).
    Phillips, D.Z., *R.S. Thomas: Poet of the Hidden God* (1986).

TOMLINSON, Charles (1927–) Born in Stoke-on-Trent, Staffordshire, and educated at Cambridge. He has taught since 1957 at the University of Bristol, with various visiting fellowships at American universities, particularly the University of New Mexico at Albuquerque. He is a graphic artist as well as a poet and has had various exhibitions in England and America; his *Eden: Graphics and Poetry* was published in Bristol in 1985. Since his first full-length collection, *Seeing Is Believing*, published in America in 1958 and in England in 1960, he has published a large number of books, including *A Peopled Landscape* (1963), *American Scenes and Other Poems* (1966), *The Way In and Other Poems* (1974), *The Flood* (1981) and *Annunciations* (1989). His *Collected Poems* was published in 1985 (revised edn 1987). His critical work includes his Clark lectures at Cambridge in 1982, *Poetry and Metamorphosis* (Cambridge, 1983). A volume of reminiscence, *Some Americans: A Personal Record*, appeared in Berkeley in 1981. He is also a notable translator: his versions of the *Selected Poems* of Octavio Paz was published in 1979; his *Translations* in 1983; and his *Oxford Book of Verse in English Translation* in 1980.

See: Ross, Alan, 'Words and Water: an interview with Charles Tomlinson', *London Magazine*, vol.20 no.10 (January 1981), pp. 22–39.
    Davie, Donald, *Under Briggflatts: A History of Poetry in Great Britain 1960–1988* (1989), seriatim.
    John, Brian, *The World as Event: The Poetry of Charles Tomlinson* (Montreal, 1989).
    O'Gorman, Kathleen, *Charles Tomlinson: Man and Artist* (Columbia, 1988).

WILLIAMS, Hugo (1942–) Born in Windsor, Berkshire, son of the well-known actor and playwright Hugh Williams, and educated at Eton but not at a university. He worked on the editorial staff of the *London Magazine* and has subsequently been a literary journalist. In 1981 he was creative writing fellow at the University of East Anglia. His first book, *Symptoms of Loss* (1965), has been followed by *Sugar Daddy* (1970), *Some Sweet Day* (1975), *Love-Life* (1979), *Writing Home* (1985) and *Self-Portrait with a Slide* (1990). His *Selected Poems* was published in 1989. He has also published travel books, including *No Particular Place to Go* (1981).

Index

Whitman, Walt, 145
Williams, Charles, 4
Williams, C.K., 216
Williams, Hugh, 150, 151
Williams, Hugo, 146, 148–52 (302)
Williams, Raymond, 197
Williams, William Carlos, 96, 102, 104,
    105, 106, 135, 164, 170, 171, 200
Wilmer, Clive, 134, 196
Wilson, Harold, 135, 148
Wilson, John, 157

Winter, Bryan, 50
Wordsworth, William, 33, 75, 180
Wright, James, 146, 147

Yeats, W.B., 7, 9, 11, 16, 21, 47, 82, 83,
    93, 106, 107, 118, 181, 183, 184, 211,
    245, 251
Young, Alan, 164

Zephaniah, Benjamin, 198
Zukofsky, Louis, 96